**One of the most revealing books
ever written about big business—**

MONOPOLY takes as its subject the American
Telephone and Telegraph Company and investi-
gates the difference between the public image of
the company and the facts. What emerges is a far
cry from the benign protector of widows and
orphans or the investment haven for small stockholders that AT&T is so commonly thought of as
being. Instead, there is the picture of a gigantic,
government-sanctioned monopoly whose influence
on the daily life of the average citizen is greater
than that of any other corporation, yet whose pre-
vailing attitude is one of "the public be damned."
So great is its power that it can ignore the wishes
and the needs of its customers as easily as it can
avoid the control of its stockholders.

In the tradition of the great muckraking books of
the past *Monopoly* takes a dynamic, trust-busting
stand that should affect the very fabric of American
life.

This is a revised, updated edition of *Monopoly*,
originally published by G. P. Putnam's Sons.

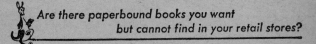

Joseph C. Goulden

MONOPOLY

REVISED EDITION

PUBLISHED BY POCKET BOOKS NEW YORK

MONOPOLY

Putnam edition published June, 1968

Revised *Pocket Book* edition published November, 1970

This is an updated, enlarged and revised edition. It is printed
from brand-new plates made from completely reset, clear, easy-to-read
type. *Pocket Book* editions are published by Pocket Books, a division
of Simon & Schuster, Inc., 630 Fifth Avenue, New York, N.Y. 10020.
Trademarks registered in the United States and other countries.

L

For Dad, who through the eloquence of scornful si-lence dissuaded me from joining the Southwestern Bell Telephone Company as a $125-a-week press agent in Little Rock, Arkansas, at a time when frustration else-where made both the salary and the work appear attractive

Author's Note

This edition of *Monopoly* is an amplified and expanded version of a book which first appeared in July, 1968. Many reviewers of the original book insisted that (a) AT&T provides the best phone service in the world, and therefore should not be criticized; or (b) even if AT&T makes an occasional mistake, it did not deserve such harsh prose. That the United States has a more efficient phone company than Greece or Burma or Poland is a truth that I cheerfully accept, but reject as irrelevant. Americans also enjoy better plumbing, highways and elevator service than do the Greeks, Burmese and Poles. My indictment is brought on different grounds altogether—stated simply, that American Telephone & Telegraph Company, during more than three decades of monopoly, has gotten out of hand, and the time is appropriate for corrective action ere the entire empire crashes down upon our heads.

Portions of Chapter One appeared, in slightly different form, in *The Nation* in November 1969.

Joseph C. Goulden
Arlington, Virginia
December 1, 1969

MONOPOLY

1

mo-nop'o-ly   fr. Greek *monos* alone (plus) *prolein* to sell. Exclusive control of the supply of any commodity or service in a given market; hence, in popular use, any such control in a given market as enables the one having this control to raise the price of a commodity or service materially above the price fixed by free competition.

—*Webster's New International Dictionary*

In mid 1969 the American Telephone & Telegraph Company began a nationwide campaign to brighten its corporate image through lavish spreading of paint. When this effort is finished, some two years hence, no longer will phone company trucks wear the drab green that makes them look like strays from an army convoy or prison farm. Blue and yellow stripes are accentuating the new two-tone vehicle motif (white on top, gray-green on bottom). Also, a new, crisper "logotype" will replace the bell symbol that has adorned company property since the Bell Telephone monopoly was assembled in the 1890's. AT&T internal publications suggest that workers stop calling their employer "Ma Bell"—that the term "Miss Bell" sounds friendlier, and encourages the public to think of the phone company as a mini-skirted young swinger instead of a frumpy old dame in a taffeta dress and sensible shoes.

The Fundamentalist preachers who beviled my southern youth often shouted (in trying to terrorize girls who had succumbed to the evils of lipstick and rouge) that " a little paint covers a lot of dirt, both in a house and in a woman." So be it for Ma Bell—but much more than two-tone trucks and a jazzy

1

emblem are needed to conceal the fact that AT&T is suffering a massive collapse of service and customer relations.

This is truly the era when three-quarters of a century of telephone monopoly has caught up with AT&T. Angry consumer groups and citizens are mad both about the quality of telephone service, which is decreasing, and the size of their telephone bills, which are increasing. Telephone horror stories are sweeping the land; one hears them even in such dignified places as the columns of the *Wall Street Journal*, which isn't exactly anti-capitalist. The *Journal* does, however, have a keenly personal interest in phone service: its offices are on Wall Street, the very eye of telephony's disaster area, where as many as 10 percent of long distance calls don't go through on the first dialing, according to New York Public Service Commission figures; and where staid law firms are suing the New York Telephone Company on grounds that service is "inadequate, uncertain, irresponsible and untimely."

Unable to gain relief from the utility commissions—whorish bodies, on the main, bent upon satisfying corporations, not consumers—discontented Bell customers are turning to that ultimate weapon of citizen protest, the full-page advertisement in *The New York Times*. When hit by such heavy artillery, the phone company occasionally listens. In August 1969 Avery, Hand & Company, an advertising firm with offices in Manhattan and Westport, Connecticut, offered a prize "of no particular value, but of great interest and memorability," to whoever came closest to guessing when New York Telephone would restore a service that ceased a month previously, and remained so despite daily appeals to AT&T. Avery, Hand's phone came alive again at 10:55 o'clock the morning *The Times* ad appeared.

But the rest of us—we who can't afford $1,400 for a full-page ad in *The Times*—reap only frustration. A teacher in a District of Columbia school runs to the corner drugstore phone to notify a parent that a child is ill; she can't get a line through the school switchboard. Dial for the operator, and wait . . . and wait . . . and wait. (My personal records: fifty-seven rings to place a long-distance call from Arlington, Virginia; 109 rings to reach an information operator from a New York booth.)

Nor does contact with the operator mean an end to the citizen's troubles. Miss Bell or Ma Bell—by either name AT&T can be a snappish bitch quick to spew billingsgate at a customer, or abruptly disconnect his call rather than check whether Stewart's name could possibly be spelled Stuart. Their behavior is the more infuriating because it is so sharply divergent from what we were taught to expect from Ma Bell's girls who had that famed "voice with a smile." (To AT&T's credit, the slogan is no longer used.) As a Texas newspaperman I once sought to locate by phone, a man who had been bitten by a rabid dog, who lived in a rural area, and whose comments were deemed of sociological importance by a city editor. The Bell operator in the town knew the man, but said he didn't have a phone. "But if he's being treated," she said, "Doc Smith is the one, and I know he's out on Forney Road tending to Miss Sally. Let me ring him there and I'll tell him to give you what you need." She did, and he did. Call information in the same town today and you are connected with a Southwestern Bell operator who sits in Dallas, with responsibility for all of north central Texas, and with no interest whatsoever in the whereabouts of anyone so insignificant that he isn't listed in a Bell directory.

All this is happening at a time when the Bell companies are trying to gain increases for home telephone service totalling almost half a billion dollars*—a figure that appears to be a fugitive from the Federal budget, rather than a bonus deserved by a monopoly whose earnings and dividends increase annually under existing rates. There is no credible evidence that higher rates would improve phone service. Simon Lazarus, of New York City's Department of Consumer Affairs, a young lawyer who learned quite a bit of Ma Bell's true character while serving as a special assistant to Nicholas Johnson of the Federal Communications Commission, notes that New York Telephone Company has exceeded its authorized 6.5 percent rate of return every year since that rate was established by the Public Service Commission in 1957. In 1968, when the return dropped to 6.9 percent, New York Telephone asked the PSC for $175,000,000 in new revenues and a return of 8.5 to 9 percent. Meanwhile, New Yorkers wait three weeks for phone installations—and almost as long to complete long-distance calls.

Home phone rates are increasing because AT&T is concentrating its technology and cost-cutting on long-distance service. AT&T's favoritism, in the words of Francis Pearson,

* $468 million as of June 1, 1969.

President of the National Association of Regulatory Utility
Commissioners, benefits "a limited class of affluent telephone
users who make approximately 2.5 billion interstate phone calls
a year," but plunges "an economic dagger into the backs of
the users of local telephone service who make approximately
147 billion telephone calls a year." AT&T's motive is greed—
the desire to protect its monopoly against independent communications companies which are devising sophisticated techniques of permitting computers to "talk" to one another
through microwave and other wireless relays. If the Marshall
McLuhans and John Diebolds are to be believed, the interchange of information is to be the deity of our imminent
computerized society, and AT&T wants to be prominent among
the priesthood. The new data transmission systems will service
everything from brokerage houses to libraries, banks and
department stores. Medical researchers even now can "examine" a heart patient in a distant city by studying cardiograms
transmitted over an AT&T line. Computers permit a central
administrative office in New York or New Jersey to oversee
production and shipping schedules for an industry with scores
of manufacturing and warehousing facilities. As William O.
Baker, Vice President of Bell Telephone Laboratories, AT&T's
research adjunct, told the FCC in 1967, Bell is preparing for
"the transmission of new magnitudes of communications, including intermixed batches of data, words and graphics beyond
anything hitherto conceived. These forthcoming requirements
will result from a growth in the accumulation and utilization
of cataloged information, an increasing development in our
society."

The American citizen is providing the money with which
AT&T is preparing to seize control of computerized communications, just as it seized control of voice telephone three-
quarters of a century ago. In 1964, to cite a not untypical year,
AT&T earned 7.5 percent on its overall interstate long-distance
operations, a figure tolerably close to the limits set by the
Federal Communications Commission. Yet a breakdown of this
return into its component parts illustrates how the consumer is
(a) paying for the expansion of Bell's long-distance system so
that AT&T can accommodate the imminent deluge of data-
transmittal business and (b) subsidizing cheap rates for present
business users to freeze out potential competitors. FCC records
show these returns:

Voice telephone—i.e., your call to grandmother, or a daughter at school	10 percent
Teletypewriter exchange service (business)	2.9 percent
Wide-area telephone service (unlimited long-distance for businesses)	10.1 percent
Private line telephone service (business long distance	4.7 percent
Telegraph private line (business)	1.4 percent
TELPAK (private line for voice, data and video transmissions)	0.3 percent

Computer communications is the stuff of which Bell expects its big profits of the future to be made. And so preoccupied is Bell with conquest of this new market that it gives less and less attention to its captive home and business customers. During 1968 the Western Electric plants at Indianapolis and Shreveport, Louisiana, together produced 8,100,000 telephone sets. Only 2,500,000 of them were "general purpose dial phones." The remainder were what Western calls "speciality instruments or new models introduced in the past decade." Again, a full 15 percent of Western Electric's business during 1968 was defense contracts—including the coveted role as prime contractor for the anti-ballistic missile system (ABM), the military-industrial complex's boondoggle of the century.

Sassy and stupid operators, while less complicated technologically, are of more personal concern to the phone customer than data transmission devices and other unseen apparatus. Bell's excuse for its rudeness to customers is "turnover"—that operators and other personnel zip in and out of the system so fast that they are ineffective. According to AT&T figures, the turnover of women operators was 31 percent in 1967; 35 percent in 1968; and even higher the first nine months of 1969. In Manhattan, the figure was 41 percent in 1968, up 34 percent in 1967. This means more than four of each ten operators quit during the year, to be replaced at the switchboard by a raw novice.

The meaning of these figures is that AT&T is not a very good place to work. Save perhaps dishwashers in skid row cafes, or itinerant magazine sales crews, no other United States service industry has such a high rate of turnover. Bell operators deal with the same broad spectrum of the American citizenry as do waitresses, sales girls and receptionists. The fact that the operators don't like their work, and abandon it as swiftly as they can, despite liberal if not lavish pay scales, puts the blame for their discontent upon Bell, not the public.

AT&T operators are at a tactical disadvantage in dealing with the public. They are Bell's equivalent of the point man in an infantry squad—the person chosen to walk ahead of everyone else and make first contact with the enemy. A citizen who waits ten minutes in a sweaty, urine-soaked phone booth for a long-distance operator to take his call thinks not of AT&T board chairman H. I. Romnes nor AT&T director G. Douglas Dillon, the former Eisenhower-Kennedy cabinet member, nor AT&T director Monroe J. Rathbone, former board chairman of New Jersey Standard. To him the operator is Ma Bell incarnate, and it is this hapless creature who endures the public's raw animal hatred for the Bell System and its wretched service. And those of us who yell at her should pay attention to the following paragraphs.

She is absolutely defenseless. She is programmed to be impersonal, even when the customer is in a happy mood and willing to josh with her as he places his call. Says an officer of the Communications Workers of America, the largest Bell union: "Whoever the hell does time studies for AT&T figured out that an operator who smiles or jokes with a customer is wasting a second or two, and that won't do. So she has her little pat phrases she is required to chant at him, mechanically, even when human nature demands that she act human. So the caller thinks, 'My God, what a cold fish this woman is.' His mood changes because no one likes a cold shoulder, even from a phone operator. When he calls the operator again he is brusque or even rude. The girls listen to this all day, and what happens? They, too, become brusque and rude; it's a self-perpetuating process."

Company rules consistently flout common sense—and it's the operator who takes the blame, and the customer's invective. In 1969 a Philadelphia drama critic moved into a new home and requested an unlisted number for his phone, which was then connected in his absence. He called the Pennsylvania Bell business office to ask what his number was to be. "I'm sorry, we can't give you the number of your unlisted phone over the telephone, you must come to the office," the girl told him. "But it's my *own phone*," the critic protested. "I'm talking from it right now; call me back and tell me the number." She replied: "I'm sorry, that's against company rules."

According to management textbooks, efficiency in a large organization depends upon standardization—of machines and of humans. For a Bell operator, however, "standardization" makes life a daily hell. "The pressures are many, varied, subtle and extreme," Lee White, CWA's national public relations director, once told me. "We are finding an unusual number of cases of—well—I guess you would call them cases of nervous troubles—developing in traffic departments.

"The girls are required to sit on a stool of a certain height, always keeping a prescribed distance from the switchboard, looking neither to left nor right, not talking to the girls beside them." According to White, it isn't uncommon for a supervisor to come up quietly behind an operator and hold a pencil alongside her head. "If the girl turns her head far enough to see the pencil, that means she's looking around too much, and she can be reprimanded. . . . Think of that—to sit at a board all day long, and endure something like that . . . And to know that a supervisor is sitting in the back at a console, monitoring every call you handle, making sure you repeat the standard phrases exactly as written in the book, and that you answer all your calls within two seconds."

The Bell System maintains elaborate indexes of "performance norms" for its employees—how many calls operators handle per hour; how many repairs a serviceman makes during a day; how many new phones an installer handles. Fulfilling (or surpassing) these norms determines how fast AT&T managers are promoted through the system, for they are constantly being compared with men doing the same job elsewhere. To AT&T workers, these norms constitute an even faster treadmill which has led, in the words of a resolution passed at CWA's 1967 convention, to "nervous sickness or nervous breakdown, widespread use of tranquilizers, and a large turnover in the traffic force." CWA decries constant prodding of workers "to meet . . . computerized indexes which will only be raised once you meet the objective."

A special CWA committee which surveyed 12,500 union officers and members reported findings in June, 1969, that put a statistical foundation beneath such sweeping charges, to wit:

An alarming four-fifths of the local presidents felt that unfair competition was promoted by the existing index system, and an overwhelming majority felt that the results of such a system were reported inaccurately to top management. . . . One out of every four females was disciplined last year . . . from the index system.

Job observation and monitoring have caused gross irritation among our members. Three out of every five females surveyed responded that such job observation creates an uncomfortable or harassing atmosphere. Existing methods are not only harassing in the extreme, but are degrading to the employee and must be changed if employee morale is to be improved from its present low state.

The adequacy of company training programs was severely criticized by both the local presidents and the individual members. Over three-fourths of the locals gave poor ratings to such training programs. Also, more than a majority reported that management expects too much too soon from newly trained employees.

There is sufficient evidence that the number of employees is insufficient in most cases to provide adequate service to the customer. This naturally throws a greater work load on the employees and a heavier burden on first-line management.

On and on ran the CWA indictment, but the last count constituted the most damning bit of evidence on life with Ma Bell's family: "When asked how they would recommend a company job similar to theirs to a friend outside the company, two-thirds of the employees that responded failed to rate their job as a good one."

Monopoly is the story of American Telephone & Telegraph Company, the world's largest,* most powerful corporation—how its primacy was achieved, and is perpetuated and the things it is able to do because of its dominant position in the United States economy.

This is not a story about a business, or about free enterprise, for AT&T is neither. Rather, it is a unique monopoly whose profits are guaranteed, whose investment is risk-free, and whose conduct is largely outside the control of government, the

* In terms of assets, which as of December 31, 1968, were $40,150,-717,000.

customers it serves, even the 3,142,075 persons and institutions that share its ownership.

AT&T is a corporate state unto itself, a "Super Government" whose presence in the United States is felt more keenly on a daily basis than even that of the federal government.

AT&T now exercises control of varying degree over every form of American communications transmission—from the telephone instrument in your home or office to the press association dispatches in your newspaper and the network television programs in your living room; veritably, the nerve system of our society.

The advent of the computerized society—and the imminent quantum jump in AT&T's importance as a communicator— makes the time appropriate for an examination of America's only officially-sanctioned national monopoly: how well it performs its present mission; what use it makes of its immunity from the natural and government-made laws that control other enterprises; whether AT&T, in fact as well as in theory, attempts to provide the "best possible telephone service at the lowest cost consistent with financial safety," the company's stated goal since 1927. Finally, just how much control over communications can the United States safely surrender to any single entity, governmental or private, without risking an institutionalization akin to dictatorship?

For many decades the existence of AT&T's Super Government was in many respects a blessing for the American citizen. Because of it, he enjoyed better telephone service than residents of any other nation (with the possible exception of the Scandinavian countries). When an American picked up a Bell telephone he was reasonably sure he could establish immediate contact with the party he desired (in France, a full one-third of all calls go astray). When he called a Bell office and asked for a phone, he was reasonably sure he would have one within twenty-four hours (in Mexico, telephone stock ownership is a requisite for service, and installation takes up to seven years).

But there have also been ominous and frustrating features of the Super Government—ones which are increasingly being felt by the lay citizen who is paying more for less. Why and how this has come to pass is the primary concern of this book.

Monopoly isn't always a nice book, for AT&T isn't always a nice company. Indeed, its rapacious attitude toward potential competitors, its frequent contempt for government at all levels, the press and other institutions of a free society, are as disgusting, as brutal, as anything found in the robber baron era of American capitalism. *Monopoly* documents, among other things:

—The way AT&T gained control of the American telephone industry, first through the monopoly given it by a controversial, much-litigated patent, then through refusal to connect competing companies into regional or national systems, and through blocking their access to capital. AT&T eventually tolerated the survivors among the independent (that is, non-Bell) companies to appease public opinion.

—The to-the-death tactics through which AT&T has protected the existence of its captive, very profitable manufacturing subsidiary, the Western Electric Company, and the effect the relationship has upon American phone bills.

—The intricate campaign through which AT&T took over the tax-financed communications satellite program and, by doing so, denied American phone users access to the satellites for domestic long-distance calls.

—The demolition campaigns AT&T wages against companies bold enough to challenge its equipment market, thus foisting higher charges and outdated telephones on the American public.

—The inner workings of the Super Government's super lobby, and the techniques it uses against the Congress, the state, and federal regulatory agencies, public opinion, and the press.

—The inability or unwillingness of the regulatory agencies, state and federal, to make meaningful examinations of the rates charged by AT&T and its subsidiary operating companies and the resultant overpricing of American telephone service. One bookkeeping fillip alone caused the public to pay $4 billion more in phone charges in a recent twelve-year period than was necessary, and similar rate abuses are easily detectable, yet uncorrected, throughout AT&T's Super Government. Conservatively, the overpricing costs the American public an excessive $1 billion per year.

—AT&T's subordination of consumer preference to operational efficiency, and the lack of channels through which a protesting citizen can make his voice heard when Ma Bell is standing on his toes.

—The widespread eavesdropping on telephone conversations,

both by AT&T (in the name of operational efficiency) and by persons assisted or condoned by AT&T, both officially and unofficially.

—AT&T's membership in the military-industrial complex that so alarmed former President Eisenhower, and its quiet role in the decision to proceed with construction of the multi-billion dollar ABM.

The complexity of many of these subjects makes them unknown to the average citizen. His complaints about the Super Government are on a more personal level: his angry mutterings about a Princess telephone that flops around the nightstand as he tries to dial it; his bewilderment with a company that can relay phone messages by bouncing them off a satellite 22,300 miles in the sky, yet simultaneously permit a citizen to swelter in an airless booth for ten minutes before an operator will condescend to place a long-distance call for him (and then cut him off in mid-conversation as chastisement for his ill temper).

Yet, as shall be amply documented, such gripes are trivial when weighed against the total AT&T operation—the issues which mean billions of dollars to the collective American public, rather than a lost dime to the individual American citizen; those which entail a perversion of government and the American economic system, rather than rudeness which annoys a single phone subscriber.

There is no intrinsic evil in bigness in American business, for our economists and political philosophers are sophisticated enough to recognize that national commerce requires enterprises national in scope, especially in communications. The United States, in one respect, is fortunate in having a company with the financial and technological capacity to make use of the magic of the computers and to bring their economic advantages to the general public. Yet bigness also demands added responsibility from an American enterprise, an accountability commensurate with its potential for good or for mischief.

The issue of AT&T bigness is pertinent to *Monopoly* only because the company's economic weight is sufficient to disturb the checks and balances scales both of government and of the marketplace. AT&T's assets of $47.2 billion are more than possessed by any other company in the world. Its gross revenues ($14.4 billion in 1968) are greater than those of the five largest state governments combined—California, New York, Texas,

Pennsylvania, and Michigan—as well as of Great Britain or France.

Discounting the Department of Defense and the Post Office, AT&T has more employees (956,000) than does the federal government. Western Electric alone had enough sales in 1969 ($4.8 billion) to make it 11th on Fortune Magazine's compilation of the 500 largest U.S. manufacturers. In 1965 just under 2 percent of the U.S. gross national product originated within AT&T. Its capital (construction) budget of $6.5 billion in 1969 was 7.5 percent of the nation's total expenditures on plant and equipment. AT&T's capital assets represent about 4 percent of the total productive facilities employed by U.S. business today.

The statistics go on and on: the largest motor vehicle fleet in the U.S.; the most bank deposits; the most retired employees. So elephantine is AT&T that the slightest activity affecting it affects the entire nation. In the spring of 1961, Lee Loevinger, then a Deputy U.S. Attorney General, later a member of the Federal Communications Commission, suggested that the Justice Department might seek divestiture of AT&T's overseas service because of antitrust violations.

The market value of AT&T stock dropped $1,069,975,250 in one day.

A few months later Loevinger commented adversely on AT&T's link with Western Electric, and the stock dropped a further $1.7 billion. Finally, the announcement by the FCC in late 1965 of an inquiry into AT&T's rates and earnings contributed to a stock drop from $65 per share to just under $50—a paper loss to investors of some $8 billion.* When the hearings began, Paul McCracken of the University of Michigan described AT&T as an "economic complex whose strength and vigor are directly of vital and significant importance to the whole economy" and cautioned that any adverse ruling on its earnings "would have substantial effects on the economy . . . [and] would certainly erode this economy's capability for expansion."

McCracken spoke as an AT&T witness, and there is con-

---

* This decline came during the general market slump of 1965–1966, and not all of it is attributable to the FCC, critics of the commission to the contrary. The actions of investors in the three cited instances prove again the turkey-flock rationale of amateurs in the stock market, for AT&T's income and dividends continued to increase despite Loevinger's announcements, the FCC investigation, and the excitement in Wall Street.

siderable contradictory evidence about what effect lower phone rates would have on AT&T, as we shall see in due course. The important point illustrated by these events, however, is that the United States has produced a corporation so vast, so far-flung, so rich, that the chance remark of a middle-echelon government official, *or even the announcement that a regulatory agency intends to carry out its statutory duty,* can cause a twenty-four hour stock decline of more than a billion dollars—and, further, that the nation risks disrupting the economy when it meddles with AT&T. . . .

Monopoly is not an objective book about the American Telephone & Telegraph Company, or a definitive history or (as should be apparent by now) an "authorized" book. Rather, it is an examination of certain AT&T practices and policies that should be of concern to those of us who use the telephone; to those of us who are interested in the institutions which dominate American political, social and economic life; and to the officials charged with regulating a public utility that is unique in size, power and function.

Ben S. Gilmer, now the AT&T president, told the Federal Communications Commission during the 1965–1967 rate inquiry: ". . . the ultimate criterion of all we do is service to the public. This is our responsibility and our license to exist. . . . In our business, service means being ready, willing and able to respond to the existing and emerging communications needs of our nation." Gilmer's definition of AT&T's mission is cruelly short-sighted: Men expect more of their government than trains that run on time—and the American citizen should expect more from AT&T's Super Government than inhumanistic efficiency and a devotion to profit.

2

<hr />

In the office we call it "The System," and use of
the word "the" means dogmatic finality. The wall
comes up pretty fast when you start tampering with
the way things are done within The System, and
you either slow down and do things Bell's way or
knock your brains out.

—AT&T junior executive, spring of 1967

<hr />

THE American Telephone & Telegraph Company, despite its
domination of the United States telephone industry, owns outright very few telephones. What it does own is a controlling interest in twenty subsidiary telephone companies, known within
The System as operating companies, and a lesser interest in two
other companies which collectively own 88,007,000 telephones
(of 110,000,000 in the nation).

These operating companies (Bell's interest ranges from 69.5
percent to 100 percent) and the Bell Telephone Company of
Canada (2.1 percent) provide telephone services and facilities
within their respective territories with the aid of services
furnished by AT&T.

AT&T is 100 percent owner of the Western Electric Company, which engineers, manufactures, and installs central office
and other communications apparatus for the operating companies. Western acts as warehouse and repair center for telephone equipment. Finally, Western and AT&T are 50-50
owners of the Bell Telephone Laboratories, Inc., a research
and development adjunct.

The four together—AT&T, the operating companies, Western, and Bell Labs—constitute the Bell Telephone System, a name used interchangeably with AT&T (often in the abbreviated forms Bell, Bell System, or simply The System).

AT&T is to the Bell System what a general staff is to an army, and AT&T seems somewhat proud of the parallel. A company writer calls the military-modeled general staff "the greatest contribution to the art of management" of the first half of the twentieth century; pridefully he notes that AT&T adapted for its own use many of the staff concepts developed by Frederick the Great, Von Steuben, and Napoleon.

AT&T's Pentagon is a nondescript building, at 195 Broadway in lower Manhattan, which serves as the company's general offices.* It is here that the chains of command are held, and it is here that Bell System fiscal and operating policies are dictated —from the mechanics of a multimillion-dollar bond issue to the type of screwdriver carried by a telephone installation man.

Channels are well defined in The System. At any level of the company the division of work is threefold: commercial, which "sells" phone service and accessories to the public and handles billing and other business functions; plant, which keeps the telephone equipment in good order; and traffic, which is responsible for getting calls from one phone to another.

A traffic manager in the smallest of Bell offices reports to the traffic manager directly above him in the next largest office— area to district to regional to operating company and ultimately to 195 Broadway—just as an Army G-1 officer has a counterpart from battalion level all the way up to the Defense Department.

AT&T sits atop The System and acts as codifier of all information and experience gained in the operating companies. Its general department has staffs of specialists for every area of the telephone business: engineering, plant, commercial, accounting, public relations, finance. The entire process is based on the assumption that if a local plant manager can't find the answer to a problem by himself, it is passed through the chain of command until it reaches a point where someone else can do so—either by previous experience or by virtue of the authority to make a policy decision.

Supervision is tight (one supervisor per five operators, to

---

* Fear of adverse public reaction keeps Bell from putting up something more fancy.

give one example), and standard operating procedures are standard in the strictest sense of the word, from the phrases used by an information operator to the wording of applications to regulatory agencies for rate changes. Bell relies heavily on conferences and intracompany committees to maintain uniformity: Twice a year all the operating company presidents come to New York for week-long conferences with the AT&T president and staff. Their vice-presidents concurrently meet with their counterparts on the AT&T staffs. Similar meetings are held within each of the operating companies. Policy changes are easily detectable as they are instituted within The System. A Newark resident who reads that the New York Telephone Company is cutting its price for Princess telephone rentals can expect his own New Jersey Bell to follow suit in short order.

Every unit within The System is subjected to continuing efficiency ratings: the number of equipment malfunctions; the handling and frequency of customer complaints; average installation costs for new phones; delinquent accounts. The ratings derived are used as scores in the internal competition through which AT&T executives are promoted. A traffic operating manager (TOM) in Omaha is constantly compared with men doing similar work in Baltimore, Spokane, and Tampa.

AT&T doesn't consider red tape to be dirty words. "Routines are the embodiment of previous experience. Red tape is the rules that grow out of previous practice," Arthur Page, longtime AT&T vice-president, wrote in an analysis of the company. Page considered initiative useful but cautioned that it be used with discretion. "The bull in the china shop was full of initiative." *

AT&T is banker and financial consultant for the operating companies, advising on day-to-day money problems and arranging for the issuance of securities. As lender, it maintains a pool of funds which it advances to the operating companies

---

* AT&T's respect for chains of command slows the execution of orders which 195 Broadway issues to lower levels. In 1966 AT&T promised full cooperation with a U.S. Senate subcommittee in an investigation that touched certain of its operations and assigned a Washington representative to act as liaison with the operating companies. Despite the blanket authorization of cooperation, the Senate panel's counsel says, "The liaison man couldn't just pick up the phone and tell Southwestern Bell to make a witness available to us. Everything he did was through channels. Based on this experience I'd say that AT&T's control is not as authoritative, as immediate, as it might appear at first blush—although there's no doubt as to who is the boss."

both for operating capital and for permanent new capital. The amounts involved are substantial: In 1968 the operating companies held advances totaling $1,267,025,000; four companies had more than $100,000,000 each.

AT&T, of course, earns interest on these advances ($59,-587,390 in 1968). Another source of revenue is a 1 percent levy which the operating companies pay AT&T on their local and long-distance revenues, in return for AT&T's administrative services and for the right to use telephone equipment on which AT&T owns patents ($131,150,982 in 1968). And, as Chart A shows, AT&T receives considerable dividends on the stock it holds in the operating companies and in Western Electric—$1,433,496,527 in 1968.

AT&T's other major function, performed by its long lines department, is to provide long-distance service for the operating companies and the 2,300 independent (i.e., non-Bell) telephone companies in the United States. Long lines interconnects the various operating companies and the phone systems of some 190 foreign countries and territories, the latter via submarine cables, satellites, and radiotelephones.

The long-distance revenues go into a common pool from which each operating company is reimbursed for its expenses and taxes chargeable to its participation in the service. The balance is split among the companies in proportion to the value of the equipment they use for long-distance calls—giving each the same percentage rate of return. Interstate long-distance revenues make up about 25 percent of the Bell System's income in any given year.

Chart A

Components, Revenues and Earnings of the Bell Telephone System

Company	AT&T share (percent)	Revenues (1967) (in thousands)	Dividends to AT&T (1968) (in thousands)	Return on Equity (1967)
New England Tel & Tel	69.5	$ 617,899	$ 50,242	9.3
New York Tel	100.0	1,612,815	163,704	9.7
New Jersey Bell	100.0	539,249	77,250	9.4

Company	AT&T share (percent)	Revenues (1967) (in thousands)	Dividends to AT&T (1968) (in thousands)	Return on Equity (1967)
Bell Telephone of Pa.	100.0	$601,949	$72,000	9.4
Diamond State Tel	100	39,573	5,040	8.6
Chesapeake & Potomac Tel of D. C.	100	123,834	11,200	7.8
Chesapeake & Potomac Tel of Md.	100	267,671	26,600	8.5
Chesapeake & Potomac Tel of Va.	100	240,651	24,850	8.9
Chesapeake & Potomac Tel of W. Va.	100	89,597	11,200	8.5
Southern Bell	100	1,504,243	124,880	9.2
Ohio Bell	100	438,430	53,375	8.6
Michigan Bell	100	487,637	56,166	9.6
Indiana Bell	100	180,300	21,945	8.7
Wisconsin Bell	100	194,207	23,010	8.3
Illinois Bell	99.3	819,259	113,314	10.0
Northwestern Bell	100	470,852	65,100	9.6
Southwestern Bell	100	1,277,053	147,839	9.8
Mountain States Tel & Tel	86.8	537,546	53,079	8.9
Pacific Northwest Bell	89.1	341,377	33,992	8.8
Pacific Tel & Tel (and subsidiaries)	89.7	1,551,591	139,853	6.89
Southern New England Telephone	17.9	216,542	4,438	—
Cincinnati & Suburban Telephone	26.7	84,860	2,164	—
Western Electric	100	4,050,700	86,200	9.7

In sum, AT&T is a holding company with managerial authority over a host of operating units. It is the ultimate recipient of their profits, the undisputed arbiter of their policies and their operations. Its long lines department makes the Bell System truly national in scope.

Thus, why the charade of separate operating companies and the duplication of effort inherent in the existence of more than a score of corporate entities when one would suffice for practical purposes?

The Federal Communications Commission, after a study of the telephone industry in the late 1930's, said that describing the AT&T subsidiaries as autonomous corporations "is only justified in the strictest legal sense, for they function simply as parts of an integrated corporate system completely and directly controlled by the holding company [AT&T] officers."

In some states separate operating companies are required because of bans on ownership of utilities by "foreign" (out-of-state) corporations. But even in areas where consolidation is permissible, Bell chooses to maintain its present setup for two very good reasons: political and public relations.

Citizens are less cognizant of the Super Government's bigness when they see trucks and office buildings marked OHIO BELL or NORTHWESTERN BELL than if all bore the name of the true owner, the American Telephone & Telegraph Company. Most literate American adults realize that Bell is a national company; yet the multiplicity of seemingly local Bell companies contributes to a vagueness about who actually controls what. The elusiveness continues when one studies the annual reports issued by the operating companies: lavishly printed booklets with good prose and striking photography, chockful of information about advances in the art of telephony. Yet a reader could search in vain in the Michigan Bell 1967 report (to cite only one example) for the fact that the company is 100 percent owned by AT&T.

Existence of the subsidiaries as separate corporate entities enables AT&T to fill their boards with local men whose reputations merit public endorsement—a political asset of inestimable value. Legally, AT&T could elect these subsidiary company directors as it saw fit, for the AT&T president is entitled to vote AT&T's controlling blocks of stock. What happens in practice is that the operating company president talks with incumbent board members (all "local" men) and strikes a consensus on who they think should be picked to fill vacancies. The AT&T president screens the nominees, but no instance has come to public attention when he rejected anyone.

Once seated, the operating company directors have the legal authority to elect their own president. In this instance, however, AT&T management takes command and decides who receives this job and other top-rung positions in the subsidiaries. AT&T transfers men as freely among the operating companies as the U.S. Army does among its divisions. Ben S. Gilmer, prior to becoming AT&T president, was president of Southern Bell for nine years and before that had been vice-president, in succession, of Northwestern Bell, Pacific Telephone & Telegraph, and Southern Bell. John D. deButts, vice-chairman and director of AT&T, during a five-year period was vice-president of the Chesapeake & Potomac Telephone Companies, president of Illinois Bell, and executive vice-president of AT&T. In the same years he was a director of both New York Telephone and Southwestern Bell. (Every AT&T president since the company's earliest days has come up through the ranks; the current board chairman, H. I. Romnes, began as a lineman for Northwestern Bell in Minnesota.)

Directors of the Bell operating companies form a solid cross section of the business community of the state or region which their company serves, buttressed always by at least one AT&T vice-president, sometimes by as many as three. The weight is in the financial and investment fields, but a majority of the boards include a college president or other educator for leavening.

As is the case with most American corporations, the directors have little to say about telephone company operations, for even long-range planning is done at the AT&T corporate offices. In essence, they are figureheads, handpicked on the assumption they are and will remain nonindependent and amenable to endorsement of policies set by AT&T management. Their lack of meaningful authority is further enhanced by the fact that directors of fifteen of the twenty operating companies cannot hold directly a single share of stock in them—because they are 100 percent AT&T owned.

An internal FCC study has noted the existence of a "vast system of interlocking directorates tying AT&T to the major manufacturing, banking, and insurance interests of the nation." The common denominator found in the professional backgrounds of the current AT&T directorate is banking and finance. Because of AT&T's staggering capital requirements— during 1968 Bell companies obtained more than $1.5 billion in new capital through bond issues, bank borrowings and sale of commercial paper, and through its immense long-term debt ($12.8 billion as of December 31, 1968)—the phone monopoly is extraordinarily attractive to bankers.

Twelve of the nineteen AT&T directors are also on the boards of the nine largest banks in the United States: First National Bank of Boston, State Street Bank and Trust Company, National Bank, Chase Manhattan Bank, First National City Bank, Manufacturers Hanover Trust Company, Morgan Guaranty Company, Chemical Bank New York Trust, and Union Commerce Banks.*

The subsidiary Bell companies interlock with the banks at other levels. Bell Telephone Company of Pennsylvania has three directors who also are on the board of Girard Trust Company of Philadelphia; two who are interlocked with the First Pennsylvania Banking and Trust Company of Philadelphia; three with Philadelphia National Bank; and one who is interlocked both with New Jersey Bell and Provident National Bank of Philadelphia. Three Michigan Bell directors are on the board of Manufacturers National Bank of Detroit; four on the board of the National Bank of Detroit. The pattern permeates the entire Bell System.

The FCC looked into these relationships during a 1965 inquiry into competitive problems of Western Union Company *viz. a viz.* AT&T, but not in depth. As Commissioner Kenneth Cox has said, "Without staffing, and our lack of investigators, we have never been able, really, to find out that this 'interlocking of directors' was of sufficient priority to justify use of our people." But he did concede that it was a "matter of concern" that if the question is ever put to a board as to whether the company should continue using Bell services, turn to Western Union, or build its own private microwave system, "that the Bell System is going to get very friendly consideration under the circumstances. . . ."

---

* See Appendix A for directorships of the AT&T board members.

The lack of authority over telephone company operations extends to the people who own it. No individual, person, corporation, or institution holds anywhere near as much as 1 percent of AT&T's stock, and the diffusion ensures that AT&T is a management-dominated corporation.

At the end of 1964, to cite a typical situation, the largest single holder of AT&T stock was Massachusetts Investors Trust, a mutual fund, with 462,000 shares, less than one-tenth of 1 percent of those outstanding at the time. Billy Rose, the late showman, then enjoyed public identification as the largest individual shareholder—but lagged a 100,000 shares behind Massachusetts Investors Trust.

Four years later the mutual funds turned away from Ma Bell to seek speculative stocks with greater growth possibilities. The largest holder at the end of 1968 was Merrill Lynch, Pierce, Fenner and Smith, the brokerage house, with 7,320,593 shares. Other brokers and banks and insurance firms rounded out the other largest thirty shareholders (including the Societé de Banque Suisse of Basele, Switzerland, with 1,698,379 shares; Credit Suisse of Zurich with 1,553, 440; and the Societé Interprofessionnelle Pour La Compensation Des Valeurs Mobilieres of Paris, 981,379).* Of Merrill Lynch's seven-odd million shares, 4,486,438 are held in the name of Cede & Co., which is a stock certificate holding service for Wall Street. Holdings through other brokers run Cede & Company's grand total to 12,956,244 shares.

With 549,263,904 shares outstanding (as of December 31, 1968) no individual institution or group of a workable size is ever likely to buy enough stock to seize AT&T from the incumbent management. Therefore, management's job is to keep the [3,142,075] shareholders happy enough to resist the piper's tune of any dissidents who might wish to start a proxy fight.

Who are these stockholders?

"The widow's stock," as lay investors call AT&T, is an image the company happily fosters because of its connotation of respectability and stability. Also, what regulatory agency or politician would want to disturb the earnings of a company that hints it is a free-enterprise counterpart of social security. During one period the *Saturday Evening Post, Harper's,* and other

---

* See Appendix B for a listing of the thirty largest AT&T shareholders.

national magazines regularly carried an AT&T advertisement showing a sweet little old grandmother peeling potatoes in her kitchen, her untroubled face above the caption "One of the Owners of the Bell System."

AT&T is now somewhat more subtle, but those 3,142,075 stockholders make a good statistic to bandy about when stressing "broad ownership." Indeed, AT&T states that based on the number of shares held by brokers and investment trustees and in the names of two persons, "more than 4,250,000 people have savings invested in AT&T."

After that one firm statistic, however, we encounter much fuzziness about who owns how much stock. Figures on the subject are carefully compiled—and zealously guarded—by AT&T. The AT&T treasury department each year prepares a booklet entitled *Ownership of AT&T* and labels it "For use within the Bell System."

The booklet, unfortunately for curious researchers fortunate enough to obtain a copy, presents the bulk of its material in the form of charts and bar graphs, rather than in specific figures. The emphasis throughout is on the small stockholder. The 1960 report states that "17 percent of the shareholders held 10 shares or less; 26 held from 11–30 shares, and that more than half the owners held 40 shares or less."

The only hint of the extent of upper-bracket holdings is in a chart that indicates that some 25,000,000 of the 223,000,000 shares then outstanding were in the hands of persons who owned 3,000 shares or more each—in other words, about one-tenth of the AT&T shares are owned by persons whose holdings are valued at more than $156,000, based upon the late-1967 market price of $52 per share. Just how many persons are in this category is not stated, although another chart shows that about 200,000 persons had 300 or more shares each, worth $15,600. The *average* holding of all shareowners was 119 shares, valued at a modest $6,188.

According to the 1960 breakdown, 42 percent of the shares were held by women; 21 percent by men; 31 percent in joint accounts; and 6 percent in fiduciary accounts and by institutions. No substantiation is found for the "widow's stock" theory. In fact, the probability is greater that many of these women are wives of men who play the stock market. For instance, wives of five of the nineteen AT&T directors are shareholders. No discourtesy intended, but these are not women one would expect to find out in the kitchen peeling potatoes.*

Only once has AT&T been forced to reveal a detailed breakdown of its ownership, and holdings were found to be both diverse and uneven. The Federal Communications Commission, during its study of the telephone industry in the 1930's, discovered that 5.1 percent of the stockholders had 50.5 percent of the shares; that slightly more than one-tenth of 1 percent of them owned 16.6 percent.

At the other extreme, 36.8 percent of the shareholders had only 3.8 percent of the stock, an average of 2.87 shares each. AT&T at that time had 644,095 stockholders. Forty-three of them held 5.2 percent of the stock, an average of 22,688.2 stocks each.

Widow's stock? AT&T got its reputation for protecting the interest of stockholders during the Depression by maintaining the $9 per year dividend which had begun in 1921. Other U.S. corporations suspended dividends, even went into bankruptcy, but AT&T owners received their $9 per share regularly, even though income was not sufficient to support this level. The difference was taken from accumulated surplus, $141,000,000 worth, that had been built up during the 1920's. A greater portion of the price for the "security" of AT&T stock was paid by its labor force. AT&T reduced its payroll by nearly 185,000 workers, or 40 percent from the level of December 31, 1929.

"I think that labor is much better off because we maintained the dividend than it would have been if we had not maintained a dividend," AT&T president Walter S. Gifford maintained later in defending the payroll cuts. "We tried for a long time to keep people on, we were as slow as possible in laying them off, and we did everything we could think of [sic] to ease that situation, but that is the tragedy of a depression."

N. R. Danielian, economist for the FCC during its phone study, estimated that a $1 cut in the dividend would have saved the jobs of 18,000 workers. AT&T chose to protect the

---

* A further tip-off to the character of AT&T ownership is revealed in a special study the New York Stock Exchange did of the institutional trading activity during the week October 24–28, 1966. Of the 842,000 shares of AT&T stock that changed hands, 47.9 percent represented sales and purchases by institutions and intermediaries, rather than individuals.

dividend, exposing its workers, but not its shareholders, to "the tragedy of a depression." The largest shareholder in this period drew annual dividends of $317,097. Danielian maintained this person wouldn't have missed the $35,233 per year which a $1 dividend cut would have cost him, nor would the reduction have made an appreciable difference in the lives of the 382,000 stockholders who owned 57.5 percent of the stock and received $9 to $90 per year in dividends. AT&T opted for the stockholders and created a reservoir of goodwill, upon which the incumbent management is still drawing.

3

We have nothing to say depreciatory of Mr. Bell at all, for he has real merits; but we think that this obscure mechanic [Daniel Drawbaugh] did do the thing, and that he is entitled to the merit of being the first inventor.

—U.S. Supreme Court Justice Joseph P. Bradley, in dissenting opinion in the telephone patent cases

THE American Telephone & Telegraph Company exists today because of a 4 to 3 ruling of the U.S. Supreme Court that Alexander Graham Bell invented the telephone and that persons to whom he assigned his patent rights were entitled to develop them commercially.

The split verdict was easily the most valuable in the Court's history. Because of it, AT&T used the Bell patents to jerk down the wires of competing companies; for twelve crucial years during the infancy of American telephony the only telephone bells that jingled in the nation belonged to AT&T. Had the Court ruled differently, the telephone market would have been an open range for dozens of inventors who produced devices capable of transmitting the human voice over wire. Additionally, the Court assured Alexander Graham Bell a private pedestal in the nation's history books—one he was not compelled to share with other inventors who did work parallel to his in developing the telephone.

Not that the other inventors didn't try. Some 600 separate challenges tested the Bell patent. But it was the "obscure mechanic" of whom Justice Bradley wrote who came the closest to yanking the telephone from Bell's hands. Daniel Drawbaugh, a backwoods Pennsylvania inventor with no formal education ("just common schools, and when I went they were *very* common"), was either an imitative charlatan or an unaware genius, depending on whether his backers or AT&T attorneys were making the assessment. Drawbaugh's workshop occupied the basement of an old barn; his scientific equipment included a teacup, a glass tumbler, a tin cup, and a mustard can—each of which in turn was used as a transmitter for his primitive telephone instrument. Perpetually penniless, Drawbaugh borrowed $5 to attend his father's funeral. He had a proved penchant for "adapting" inventions, such as electric clocks, he saw in catalogues, obtaining patents on minor innovations he made, and then marketing the revised gadget as his own.

Despite this spotty background, Drawbaugh survives as the only patent litigant among hundreds who persuaded any Supreme Court Justice—three out of seven, the other two didn't participate—that he and not Alexander Graham Bell invented the telephone.

Neither Bell, Drawbaugh, nor any other litigant claimed to have originated the idea that an instrument enabling persons to talk with one another over a distance could be built and that it could be profitable. A student in eighteenth-century Germany envisioned a network of "speaking tube" stations along roadways, to be manned by stout-lunged functionaries who would shout messages on their way by megaphones. The French Army tried to transmit signals by forcing compressed air through trumpets, producing an earsplitting version of the Morse code audible for 6 miles.

But these rudimentary schemes were only slightly more advanced than the trumpets Hannibal used when routing the Romans in the Battle of Cannae (216 B.C.). A German, Professor Phillip Reis of Friedrichsdorf, is generally recognized as the first scientist who realized that electricity could be more effective than whoops and horn toots in transmitting sound. In 1861 he borrowed a barrel bung from a beer garden, hollowed it, and covered the cavity with the skin of a German sausage. This was the first telephone transmitter. As a receiver Reis used a knitting needle surrounded by a coil of wire and placed on a violin that acted as a sounding board. The sausage skin vibrated in resonance to a particular pitch or note, and Reis was able to reproduce the sound, after a fashion, on the sounding board.

The reproduction, however, was faint. Any tune Reis played, Brahms or polka, squeaked like a child's tin trumpet. As a scientific curiosity, the Reis device attracted considerable attention on the Continent and was demonstrated to learned societies. Copies of it appeared in the 1860's and 1870's in college physics laboratories in the United States, where a generation of inventive youngsters and professors sought the secret of sending the sound of the human voice over a wire.

Which brings us to Alexander Graham Bell—"Aleck" during his boyhood in England, "Graham" the remainder of his life, the Alexander reduced to a solitary *A* in his signature. Son of a frustrated English Shakespearean actor and elocution instructor (who was the inspiration for Henry Higgins in George Bernard Shaw's *Pygmalion*), Bell was an early student of the human voice and how it produces sound. Accident and an ignorance of German started him toward the telephone. A German philologist, one Helmholtz, had experimented with the re-creation of vowel and consonant sounds with a tuning fork. Borrowing a copy of his report, written in German, young Bell somehow got the idea from the unfamiliar language that Helmholtz had sent spoken words via telegraph. So he tried to reconstruct what he thought Helmholtz had already invented. Not until he came across a French translation of the report did he realize that he was in fresh territory. Bell said in later years that had he read German fluently, he might never have begun the research which ultimately resulted in his gaining credit for the invention of the telephone.

Bell worked first in England, as part of his speech studies, then in America, to which he came in 1871 seeking to cure his tuberculosis. Settling in Boston, Bell gave speech lessons to deaf-mutes—and here again was a circumstance that helped his telephone work. One of the students was the son of Thomas Sanders, wealthy leather merchant in Haverhill, a Boston suburb. Another was Mabel Hubbard, comely daughter of Gardiner Greene Hubbard, a Boston lawyer who later was elected to Congress.* Bell lived in the Sanders home, and when his experiments began to look like more than an idle attic pastime, Sanders and Hubbard underwrote him financially in return for

---

* Bell eventually married Mabel Hubbard, after months of courtship so intense that he almost lost interest in the telephone.

a one-third share in any inventions that resulted. This agreement, made orally, was the gestation of what was to become the American Telephone & Telegraph Company.

From his speech experiments Bell concluded that sound is a "mere motion of air." His problem was to transmit the waves of sound through a wire. He tried to do so first by making a so-called harmonic telegraph which would send up to six messages simultaneously over the same wire by using a different pitch for each signal. Bell thought that varied combinations of the six pitches could reproduce human speech. The idea didn't work, but Bell did succeed in making a harmonic telegraph. So did another inventor, Elisha Gray, of Chicago—later to become an important name to Bell.

Bell's imagination raced onward, unwilling to settle for the transmission of mere dots and dashes and musical notes. The harmonic telegraph depended on an electrical current that was alternately opened and broken to produce sounds, with a resultant lack of fidelity range. Bell decided this system would never re-create true speech. As he said later:

> I had gradually come to the conclusion that it would be possible to transmit sounds of any sort if we could only occasion a variation in the intensity of the current exactly like that occurring in the intensity of the air while a given sound is made. . . . I had obtained the idea that theoretically you might, by magneto electricity, create such a current. If you could only take a . . . good chunk of magnetized steel, and vibrate it from the pole of an electromagnet, you would get the kind of current we wanted.

Bell reached this conclusion in the summer of 1874, when he was twenty-seven years old. But he lacked the mechanical skill to construct the instrument he wanted. To do the benchwork, he recruited a young machinist, Thomas A. Watson, from a Boston electrical shop.

Watson and Bell rented a workroom in a boardinghouse and filled it with reeds, tuning forks, and wires, futilely trying combination after combination. At one point Bell tried to use the human ear as a model for his receiver. A physician friend supplied a medical school cadaver, from which he extracted the inner ear bones and drum. Bell and Watson made a scale model; it didn't work. Next, they put together a monster ear with a diaphragm of boiler iron 3 feet in diameter and ½ inch thick. This didn't work either, although one roomer in the house was so shaken by the noise he sought other quarters.

Ultimately Bell and Watson returned to the harmonic telegraph, evoking increasingly encouraging sounds from it with modifications. Convinced this device was workable, Bell in October or November, 1875, began writing a patent specification. Out of national pride he insisted that the patent be filed first in his native England. A friend agreed to take the papers to London and left at the end of the year. Bell then made another draft of the papers—lucky that he did, as it proved later—for the U.S. filing. When the London agent didn't report back promptly Sanders became nervous; he knew other inventors were busy on similar gadgets and didn't want Bell to lose by tardiness. He persuaded Bell to file his application for the U.S. patent in Washington on February 14, 1876.

The Patent Office granted Bell the telephone patent on March 3, his twenty-ninth birthday—No. 174,465, which has earned more money than any other piece of paper ever issued by the office.

A week later, on March 10, 1876, Bell and Watson finally coaxed audible conversation from the telephone, the first sentence being Bell's "Mr. Watson, come here, I want you." Bell didn't plan his words; he had spilled acid on his pants and indeed *needed* Watson. Perhaps that's why he added a second, less quoted sentence: "God save the Queen."

Development of the laboratory telephone into something of commercial utility proceeded briskly. Bell created a minor sensation at the 1876 Philadelphia Centennial Exposition with a demonstration ("My God, it works!" exclaimed a visiting English nobleman) and gradually increased the phone's power until by autumn it carried a conversation 26 miles between Boston and Salem, Massachusetts.

By this time Hubbard and Sanders had invested $100,000 in Bell. To recoup some of the sum, they arranged a lecture tour. Railroad telegraph wires connected halls in adjacent cities. Bell, Watson, and their newly hired business manager, Fred Gower, went to separate locations and carried on three-cornered conversations to demonstrate the invention. The newness caused occasional complications. When Bell told a Hartford audience it would hear Watson play a trombone solo from

Middletown, Gower instead chimed in from New Haven with a solo baritone, "Oh Do Not Trust Him, Fair Lady."

Such mishaps aside, the phone was a success. Hundreds of persons paid 50 cents each to hear the talking machine and begged for telephones of their own. The lecture revenues were important, for they gave Bell's backers enough capital to be able to rent, rather than sell, the telephones which they put into subscribers' homes. Retention of ownership of the telephone instruments was a foundation of the entire Bell System.

Modifications were necessary. For instance, customers couldn't remember to push down the button on their phones after completing a call, a necessary step for putting them back into the town circuit. So Watson designed an automatic switch operated by the weight of the receiver. "This straightened out the switch matter for it now merely required that the user should hang up his telephone when he finished using it. This the public learned to do quite well after a year or two," Watson said laconically in his autobiography.

Too, Bell's transmitter required a vigorous shout if the caller expected to be heard at the other end. Quipped Watson: "This was the time when they used to say that all the farmers in a country store would rush out and hold their horse's head when they saw anyone preparing to use our telephones."

In April, 1877, Bell had 6 demonstration phones; by fall there were 3,000 (and the first switchboard, in New Haven, Connecticut). Hubbard and Sanders set up a formal organization to run the business, the New England Telephone Company, first incorporated ancestor of AT&T.

Then came trouble—challenges to Alexander Graham Bell's patent.

The same day that Bell filed his telephone patent, another inventor, Elisha Gray, of Chicago, with whom Bell had competed on the harmonic telegraph, came into the Patent Office a few hours later with his own telephone specifications. There was one significant difference in what they requested. Bell, even though he had not succeeded in making his telephone work, asked for a patent on his model. Gray sought only a caveat, by simplest definition the registration of a statement by an inventor that he is working on something which he has not perfected. (The Patent Office has since abandoned the caveat.)

The Boston inventor and the Chicago inventor gave markedly similar descriptions of their work. Bell entitled his application "Improvement in Telegraphy" and began it with the words "Be it known that I, Alexander Graham Bell, have invented certain new and useful improvements in telegraphy." Farther down he defined his improvement as follows: "The method of and apparatus for transmitting vocal or other sounds telegraphically or by causing electrical undulations similar in form to the vibrations of the air accompanying the said vocal or other sounds."

In his caveat application, Gray said his intention was "to transmit the tones of the human voice through a telegraphic circuit and reproduce them at the receiving end of the line so that actual conversations can be carried on by persons at long distances apart. I claim as my invention the art of transmitting vocal sounds telegraphically through an electric circuit."

Because Bell filed his document first, the Patent Office disregarded Gray's request for a caveat. Gray at first accepted his apparent defeat in good grace and continued his own telephone demonstrations in and around Chicago, as Bell was doing in the East. A clash was inevitable, and an article in the Chicago *Tribune* became the precipitant:

Many of the Eastern newspapers are favoring their readers with sketches of Professor A. M. [*sic*] Bell, the "inventor" of the telephone. Meanwhile, the real inventor of the telephone— Mr. Elisha Gray, of Chicago—minds his own business, and apparently concerns himself not at all with the spurious claims of Professor Bell. Persons acquainted with the subject need not be informed that Mr. Gray's claims are incontrovertible. Science long since recognized them. They were established in the columns of the *Tribune* years ago, before Professor Bell was so much as heard of. They are officially approved in the Patent Office in Washington [*sic*] and they have already brought in large returns in money as well as in reputation to the inventor. . . .

The article made claims which Gray was not making, for it mistook his harmonic telegraph—which indeed was workable—with Bell's telephone. Shortly afterward, however, the hapless Gray wrote Bell and asked for permission to demonstrate the Bell telephone in conjunction with his own devices. He made clear he intended to give Bell credit, then noted that he had filed a description of a "talking telegraph" with the Patent Office on the same day as did the Boston professor. "The description is substantially the same as yours," Gray wrote. "I was unfortunate in being an hour or two behind you. There is no evidence that either knew that the other was working in this direction."

Bell responded with a stern telegraph: "If you refute in your lecture, and in the Chicago *Tribune*, the libel upon me published in that paper February 16th, I shall have no objection. Please answer."

Gray refused. He also wrote, "So far as I knew, the 'libels' are mostly on the other side, if assertions of *originality* etc. may be so considered. The papers here have been full of articles of late, copied from the Boston papers, claiming the whole development of the telephone for you." Gray denied responsibility for any Chicago articles unfavorable to Bell, claiming he frequently defended the Bostonian against disparaging remarks. "Now, if we are going into the refutation business," he said, "I suggest that it be mutual. . . . If we undertake to follow up the newspapers, we will have our hands full."

Bell cooled considerably by his next letter. He said that he always credited Gray, in his lectures, with the harmonic telegraph, but not for the telephone because he felt them to be two different inventions—the one for musical tones, the other for voice—and that he knew of no work by Gray in the voice field.

"It certainly was a most striking coincidence that our applications should have been filed on the same day," he said, recounting his delays owing to the English patent quest.

In reply, Gray used three sentences that Bell's defenders, both in court and in official biographies, cited as evidence that the Chicago inventor conceded his rival invented the telephone:

I give you full credit for the talking features of the telephone as you may have seen in the Associated Press dispatch that was sent to all the papers. Of course you have had no means of knowing what I had done in the matter of transmitting musical sounds. When, however, you see the specification you will see that the fundamental principles are contained therein. I do not, however, claim even the credit of inventing it, as I do not believe a mere description that has never been *re-*

duced to *practice* in the *strictest sense* of the phrase should be dignified by the name "invention."

In actuality, *was* Gray's letter a concession? The italicization of the words in the phrase *"reduced* to *practice* in the *strictest sense"* called Bell's attention to what Bell had not achieved when he "dignified" his telephone, in the patent application, with the word "invention."

So far as Bell was concerned, the matter ended. Gray, however, plodded on, and soon with a powerful backer: the Western Union Telegraph Company, at the time one of the richest and strongest corporations in the United States, with $41,000,000 in capital and the pocketbooks of the financial world behind it. To Western Union, Bell's telephone at first was a joke: In August, 1877, company officials laughed at Hubbard's offer to sell the phone patents for a meager $100,000. The humor soured as the phones became a public fad. Western Union's immediate concern was a profitable subsidiary, the Gold & Stock Telegraph Company, which reported prices on the gold and stock exchanges with a telegraph that was a granddaddy of the present broker's ticker. Gold & Stock customers found the two-way conversations on the telephone quicker and more confidential than the ticker and switched to Bell en masse.

Western Union turned on the Bell group with the studied, contemptuous ruthlessness typical of American business' robber baron era. First, it purchased the patents of Gray and another inventor, Amos E. Dolbear, a Tufts University physics professor, for their harmonic telegraphs. Then it recruited Thomas A. Edison, the electric light inventor, to outtelephone Bell. This Edison did, inventing a transmitter employing carbon, which was vastly more powerful than the Bell instrument. ("I found it startlingly loud and clear in its articulation," Watson remarked.)

At another level Western Union barred Bell from the right-of-way monopolies it owned for its wires along highways and railroads. Western Union had its instruments in every major hotel, railway station, and newspaper office in the nation, under terms which forbade installations of telephones. A Bell manager in Philadelphia was forbidden to erect lines anywhere in the city; his workers frequently were jailed on complaints sworn by Western Union. The telegraph company's political influence in Washington kept Bell phones from federal offices (an ironic contrast with the power AT&T now brandishes in the capital).

An early telephone historian, Herbert N. Casson, wrote that "no matter what direction the Bell company turned the live wire of Western Union lay across its path." (The direct competitor was actually a subsidiary of Western Union, the American Speaking Telephone Company.)

Edison's better transmitter posed another competitive problem. Bell agents reported Western Union methodically beat them each time the two systems were in direct competition. In attempting to better Edison's carbon transmitter, the Bell people ran the same patent-infringement risks which they accused Western Union of committing. Emile Berliner, a young German who had emigrated to the United States only eight years previously and who clerked in a Washington dry goods store, wrote Bell about a transmitter he had made. Watson visited Berliner to see the invention—fashioned from a child's drum, a needle, a guitar string, and a steel dress button. Watson was dubious, for the device was dangerously similar in principle to the Edison instrument. But Berliner claimed to have invented the transmitter "many months before" Edison—which, if true, would have given him the basis for a patent. Watson hired Berliner. A few months later he bought another carbon transmitter even more similar to that of Edison, this one made by Francis Blake, a government clerk.

The improved instruments revived Bell's spirits, and in four months the company added 22,000 subscribers.* The American Speaking Telephone Company, happy to escalate, scornfully moved into Bell's home country, Massachusetts. Whereupon Bell filed suit against American Speaking's representative in the state for patent infringement. Bell also warned persons using the rival telephones that they risked having to pay second rentals.

Western Union offered three main defenses: (1) Gray, Edison, Dolbear, and others had priority of invention; (2) Bell's instrument as described in Patent No. 174,465 could not trans-

---

* Edison's telephone was also promoted in England, and the company offering it employed it for a while George Bernard Shaw in what he called "my last attempt to earn an honest living." Shaw was dubious about the telephone, which he described as having "such stentorian efficiency that it bellowed your most private communications all over the house, instead of whispering them with discretion." Shaw said the American promoters in England spent much time adoring Edison and denouncing his "Satanic adversary," Alexander Graham Bell.

mit articulate speech; and (3) Bell's invention had been "anticipated" in a long list of prior publications, including descriptions of Phillip Reis' barrel-bung and sausage-skin "telephone" of 1861. (The theory of anticipation prevents the patenting of items in general longtime use, such as the wheel.)

In addition to the financial resources necessary for prolonged court battle, Western Union had a strong case since it owned an undisputed patent on an induction coil developed by Gray that was essential to effective long-distance telephony. But according to official AT&T historians, George Gifford, Western Union general counsel, decided after an exhaustive study that Bell's basic patent was impregnable and told his client to make the best settlement possible. Western Union stipulated in court that Bell was the inventor, that it would abandon the phone business, and that it would sell its system (56,000 phones in fifty-five cities) to Bell.

Bell, however, agreed to pay Western Union 20 percent of its receipts from telephone rentals or royalties for seventeen years—a sizable override for a company still in the red. For this reason the settlement left glaring doubts that the litigants were candid in their public announcements about the reasons for ending the suit. Western Union had just concluded a bitter struggle with financier Jay Gould, who lured away one of its top officers, built a telegraph system of his own, and then sold it to Western Union at a heavy "nuisance" price. Gould then began buying Bell franchises and let word leak to Western Union that he was thinking of acquiring the entire Bell System as a prelude to another fight.

Put simply, Western Union had a profitable telegraph monopoly. A fight with Bell would be costly and drawn out, with Gould the potential winner. All risks considered, Western Union would have to pay too high a price to extend its monopoly to include telephones. So it settled. Bell did agree to keep out of the telegraph business; thus, Gould was prevented from starting another struggle with Western Union even if he did secure control of Bell. Bell's major gain was the opportunity to create a monopoly of its own without "competition"—one of the dirtiest words in the American businessman's vocabulary during this capitalist-eat-capitalist period.

Although still suspicious, Gray at this time agreed Bell invented the telephone. But he soon thereafter stumbled onto what he considered evidence that Bell was privy to confidential information from Gray's caveat application and for that reason alone had been able to make his version of the telephone work.

Gray reopened his claim to the patent on grounds summarized in a U.S. Supreme Court brief: "Mr. Bell's attorneys had an underground railroad in operation between their office and Examiner Wilbur's room in the patent-office, by which they were enabled to have unlawful and guilty knowledge of Gray's papers as soon as they were filed in the patent-office."

Gray's lawyers stated in the same brief "that an important invention, and a claim therefore, were bodily interpolated into Bell's specification, between Feb. 14, 1876, and Feb. 19, 1876, by Pollok [Bell's attorney], in consequence of the guilty knowledge which the latter already had of the contents of Gray's caveat. . . ."

Circumstantial evidence partially supported Gray's accusations. The transmitter which Bell described and illustrated in his patent application was not the same creature over which he and Watson exchanged the first telephone conversation. Gray's lawyers emphasized the fact that the certified copy of Bell's specifications, as found in a file in the Patent Office, differed materially from the patent which he later received. Zenas Fisk Wilbur, patent examiner who handled the filing, admitted that contrary to law, he had notified Bell's attorneys when he discovered the clash between Gray's caveat and the patent application. Upon hearing of this, Bell visited Wilbur but said he was unable to see the caveat "as it was a confidential document."

Bell continued: "But he [Wilbur] indicated to me the particular claim in my application with which it conflicted. I therefore knew it had something to do with the vibration of a wire in a liquid. I do not remember what it was that led me to suppose that that liquid was water." Differences were found between Bell's U.S. and English applications. The latter, for instance, omitted any mention of the variable resistance phase of the Bell telephone, the key to the entire invention.

For his part, Gray told a Congressional committee which investigated the Patent Office in 1885 that it was long after issuance of Bell's patent that he discovered the Bostonian used a liquid transmitter "substantially the same as that described in my caveat but wholly unlike anything" mentioned in Bell's application. Gray said bluntly that he thought Bell had obtained a copy of his caveat and "that he made use of that knowledge and constructed the instrument with which he first successfully transmitted articulate speech . . . and by this means got credit for my invention."

The Congressional committee took no sides, saying it "expressly refrains from attempting to find out whether the Bell patent was obtained fraudulently or whether Bell was the inventor. . . ." But the U.S. Supreme Court, which heard Gray's claim in connection with a patent suit involving other self-professed telephone inventors, found for Bell. It said the evidence was "not sufficient to brand Mr. Bell, and his attorneys, and the officers of the Patent Office, with the infamy which the charge made against them implies." The Court said the differences in Bell's English and U.S. patent applications indicated painstaking care, not the chicanery charged by Gray.

Gray died believing he was cheated of fame and telephone fortune. A scrap of paper found in his belongings after his death in 1901 said, "The history of the telephone will never be fully written. It is partly hidden away in 20 or 30 thousand pages of testimony and partly in the hearts and consciences of a few whose lips are sealed—some in death and others by a golden clasp whose grip is even tighter."

The Bell group counted on the Western Union settlement to resolve the patent issue once and for all. Such, however, was not to be the case. Hordes of inventors trooped forward, claiming a share of the telephone's riches. Some of the more pathetic cranks received a pat on the back, a few dollars, and a hearty farewell at the door.

Others, however, were more serious. They found financial backers and actually set up little telephone companies, claiming that their discoveries antedated that of Bell. The Bell people brought more than 600 patent-infringement suits between the Western Union case and the last diehard in 1898. The AT&T library in New York contains more than 300 volumes of testimony, briefs, arguments, and decisions from district courts, intermediate appellate courts, the U.S. Supreme Court, and the Patent Office, a mass of wordage that one judge called "the most important, the most protracted litigation that has arisen under the patent system in this country." Representatives of rival inventors scoured the literature and scientific archives of Europe for evidence that someone produced a workable instrument before Bell. Any person who felt he had a prior claim was encouraged to enter the lists.

And that brings us back to Daniel Drawbaugh, whose lushly engraved business card announced him as "inventor, designer and solicitor of patents (also models neatly made to order)." Drawbaugh lived in Eberly's Mills, a community about 3 miles west of Harrisburg, the capital of Pennsylvania. The village consisted of a grist mill and companion properties, from which its name was derived. The villagers didn't match the prosperity of the surrounding Pennsylvania Dutch farmers, nor was there much of note in their town. Abner Wilson's general store provided the social life during most of Drawbaugh's productive years. But Wilson came to grief. As a witness stated in one of the scores of sparkling, but totally irrelevant, sidelights which mark the Drawbaugh trial record, Wilson "had a keg of powder too near the fire, blowed him up, or the goods. . . . It so completely busted the shell of the house . . . that he left and never returned."

For his shop Drawbaugh used part of an old grist mill on a little peninsula formed by the junction of Cedar Run, which had turned the mill, and Yellow Breeches Creek. Born in 1827, Drawbaugh inherited a strong mechanical bent from his blacksmith father; while still a schoolboy, he made clock parts, a rifle, and a small steam engine. His first patents were for devices used to make barrel staves, which were marketed by a salesman in the South who disappeared into the Confederate Army with $5,000 belonging to Drawbaugh. Farm implements, a machine for making nails (which flopped when put into commercial use), a syrup pump—all came from Drawbaugh's crude workshop on the banks of Yellow Breeches Creek.

Drawbaugh was an unprofitable mechanical prophet, however, and thus without honor in his own household. Mrs. Drawbaugh, imbued with just a bit of the shrew, emphatically disapproved of her husband's work. A villager told of a conversation: "I heard her say that Daniel was at that —— old shop, fooling his time away, while they, the family, hardly knew how to get anything to eat. She also told me . . . that she smashed up a lot of photography and other things about the house, in order to stop Daniel from fooling with them."

Brother John "Squire" Drawbaugh testified, "When I first discovered that he was working on this talking machine, as it was then called, I accused Dan'l quite severely of wasting his time on foolish inventions." Despite his familial and professional troubles, neighbor Ephraim Holsinger said Drawbaugh was temperate: "I don't think I ever seen him drink a glass of whiskey; chance times he would take a glass of beer, but not unless somebody bought it for him."

The exact date that Drawbaugh began tinkering with telephones was a point bitterly debated but never resolved in court. He fixed the time at around 1863, working with a "variable resistance transmitter" consisting of a powdered substance in the bottom of a teacup through which feeble, incoherent speech allegedly could be heard. When his son was born in 1870, Drawbaugh said, he was so advanced in his experiments that Mrs. Drawbaugh, confined to bed, used the instrument to hear what happened in the rest of the house. Drawbaugh conceded that "whispered" words could not be heard audibly—but maintained normal speech could be. If this claim was true, of course, it meant Drawbaugh beat Alexander Graham Bell to the phone by some six years.

At any rate, Drawbaugh definitely had his workshop cluttered with telephone paraphernalia in 1878, to the dismay of a Harrisburg investor who had given him money to finance other inventions. The investor, variety-store owner Edgar Chellis, pestered Drawbaugh to forget the telephone "as he could not antedate Bell."

"I don't know about that; I have been working at it a good while," replied Drawbaugh. A visitor in the shop chimed in that sure enough he had talked over the phone as far back as 1870.

The astute Chellis knew the implications of this claim. He hurried to a Harrisburg attorney, who in turn contacted Lysander Hill, former judge and prominent patent lawyer in Washington. The three men talked with Drawbaugh, who readily agreed to form a syndicate with them. Lacking funds, Hill allied with a New York group which had everything needed to operate a telephone company save a telephone. Drawbaugh signed over his right to the invention for $20,000 cash and a block of stock. This was on July 21, 1880. Five days later Drawbaugh's promoter friends filed for a patent, and publicity drums boomed across the country. A story from the Cincinnati *Commercial* (hometown of one of the promoters) retains a suspicious odor even after eighty-eight years:

An application for a patent was filed today that, in consequence of its vastness of interest, as well as wealth of prospect, renders it a subject of national interest. A company of leading businessmen had been formed that has bought up all the telephone patents antedating those now in use and known as the Bell, Gray and Edison patents. . . . The cash capital of the company is $5,000,000, with headquarters in New York, and in about sixty days they will open up the telephone, which will certainly result in the driving out of all telephones in the market, or else the compelling [of] the Gray, Bell and Edison lines to pay the new company a munificent royalty. . . .

The Cincinnati *Commercial* claimed poverty prevented Drawbaugh from offering his telephone earlier. The *Journal of Commerce* in New York gave a somewhat different appraisal of Drawbaugh, saying that "his neighbors who knew of his experiments looked upon him as a harmless lunatic."

On August 30, 1880, the promoters incorporated the People's Telephone Company in New York and began offering telephones. The Bell interests brought suit on October 20 in U.S. District Court there, and the show was on.

Drawbaugh's task was twofold: to find persons who could testify that he made a working telephone prior to 1876, when Bell had filed for his patent, and to explain satisfactorily why he had dallied for more than a decade before going to the Patent Office.

In proving the first point, Drawbaugh's lawyers, led by Judge Hill, brought in a high percentage of the residents of Eberly's Mills and Lower Allen Township, in which the hamlet is situated. Neighbors, friends, fishermen who had come into the shop, even bill collectors, testified about the talking machine. Some of the "memories" went back to 1867: Forty-nine persons avowed they talked on or heard speech from Drawbaugh's phone before Bell's patent; seventy had seen others using the telephone. They recollected magnets and wires on the wall; one mentioned "something like a horseshoe" among the apparatus. The memory stuck with a merchant from Dover, Delaware, who, when he saw the Bell phone at the Philadelphia Centennial Exposition, supposed that Drawbaugh "had got a man named Bell to go with him."

Typical of the witnesses was tailor George Freese, who testified he sold Drawbaugh a coat for $2.50 and tried three times

to obtain payment during 1869: "Dan tried to draw my attention to this machine and my attention was after the $2.50. This
instrument that he had I thought was so insignificant in my
estimation—I thought it was hardly anything. Says he, 'George,
if I have this thing accomplished. . . .'" But Freese cut him
short. "I still had in my mind that he was drawing my attention
to this kind of foolery, I was after the two dollars and a half,
didn't care about this infernal machine."

Another visitor swore that Daniel's six-year-old son sang
"Don't You Want to Be a Christian While You're Young?"
into a jelly glass in the basement and that he heard the sound
perfectly through a mustard can attached to the other end of
the line upstairs. An old farmer, hearing Daniel's claim that he
could "talk across the Atlantic Ocean," counseled, "Try it first
across Yellow Breeches Creek."

The suit went into tedious tangents as the lawyers tried to
prove or disprove the dates cited by witnesses. One man was
certain of the time he heard human voices on Drawbaugh's
phone because it was the same date he was in Eberly's Mills
to buy a hydraulic ram (a water pump) and was never there
again. Lawyers and investigators talked to practically every
mentally competent resident of the township, minor and adult
alike, in trying to fix the date of the ram. "The ram and telephone is about all that is talked of up there now," one man
testified. Seventy-five witnesses were summoned on this totally
collateral issue alone. A man who came in all the way from
the Dakotas remembered seeing the ram in operation in 1876.
How could he be certain? Well, he and his friend talked that
day about washing clothes, something in which he lost interest
a year later, when he married.

Bell explained away the eyewitnesses by claiming that they
(1) had either heard speech after 1876 on a *copy* of his telephone or (2) were misled by a string phone. Telling witnesses
against Drawbaugh were two railway telegraph superintendents
and a patent specialist, all his friends, who testified he never
mentioned the phone to them—although of all the persons
involved, they were the most likely to assist him in making
practical use of it.

In defense Drawbaugh pleaded poverty, and he easily proved
that much of his adult life had been spent within uneasy range
of constables and bill collectors. Many small judgments were
recorded against him in Lower Allen Township courts, and his

taxes were in perpetual arrears. A cobbler said Drawbaugh had to "pay out" a shoe repair bill of 50 cents. A nephew testified, "He buried two children, I think, in one day, or near; and for a long time he had a daughter living, a living skeleton. . . . She told me that they had been getting her a great deal of medicine from New York, and it was doing her a great deal of good, and it was very expensive, and she wanted some more, but they had not the money to get it."

Bell lawyers attacked Drawbaugh's claimed poverty by reconstructing his personal finances to where they could account for virtually every cent he received and spent from 1867 through 1879. Even after spending $2,000 for a house, losing $400 in an "apple speculation," and paying a $1,200 assessment in a development company in which he had an interest, Drawbaugh made $2,325 from his inventions in ten years; additionally, he earned about $110 per year as a mechanic— amounts which Bell said gave him ample funds to pay the $35 to $50 necessary to obtain a patent, had his phone in fact existed.

It was on the final issue—Drawbaugh's competence to construct a telephone—that the Bell attorneys were able to depict the backwoods inventor as such a humbug that the trial judge referred to him as "vain, ignorant and fantastic." Drawbaugh helped Bell make its case. It was certainly not inconceivable that a mechanic of Drawbaugh's skill, working with Reis' apparatus for the reproduction of pitch, could have staggered blindly into the telephone. After all, only slight modifications were needed to make Reis' instrument capable of transmitting speech.

Drawbaugh wasn't sharing the credit with Reis or anyone else. Stroking his flowing beard and gazing unblinkingly at the courtroom, he denied ever hearing of the Reis telephone until after 1876 and claimed that the telephone emerged, full-grown, from his own inventive brain without the slightest assistance from an outsider. Nor would Drawbaugh halt there: He also asserted credit for the microphone and carbon transmitter, thereby encompassing not only the Bell invention, but also those of Thomas Edison and other scientists.

Whereupon Bell attorneys made Drawbaugh look downright silly. They coaxed from him an admission that he had not the slightest idea of how he went about inventing the telephone. "I don't remember how I came to it," he testified. "I don't remember of getting it by accident, either. I don't suppose anyone told me."

Nor could Drawbaugh remember the various combinations of equipment which he used during his experiments. "I had a number of crude apparatuses, but can't remember exactly the shape of any of them. I had membranes stretched over hoops . . . and I had electromagnets, and the arrangement was varied. I don't remember exactly the arrangement."

The trial judge wrote:

> An inventor can hardly forget the processes of thought by which a great intellectual conception germinates and matures into the consummate achievement, but Drawbaugh's memory is a blank. If the untutored Drawbaugh educated himself into an accomplished electrician by his own experiments and observations, the incidents and phenomena which revealed new discoveries, and illumined the way for new advances, would be indelibly impressed on his mind.

Much of Drawbaugh's "inventiveness" was shown to be in fact mechanical mimicry. An electric clock he patented as a "new article of manufacture" proved to have been described in an encyclopedia which he had before him when he made his "alleged invention," as the trial judge called it. The Reis telephone, which Drawbaugh's device resembled, was detailed in the *Scientific American* in 1876, and Drawbaugh admitted to being a sometime reader of the magazine. He also said he spent "four or five days" at the Philadelphia Centennial at which Bell's phone was shown. And finally, when Bell telephones were installed in Harrisburg in 1877 or early in 1878, Drawbaugh visited an office which had one, examined its insides, and borrowed it for inspection in his workshop. The court agreed with Bell attorneys that the borrowed instrument bore a "close resemblance" to what Drawbaugh claimed to have made three to five years previously.

All this took four years to elicit in the courtroom. On December 2, 1884, Judge William J. Wallace found for Bell, saying that Drawbaugh was not an inventor, but an unsuccessful "experimenter" until he learned enough from a study of Bell's instruments to make his version of the telephone operable.

The Drawbaugh syndicate went to the U.S. Supreme Court,

their cause ultimately being lumped with five other telephone patent cases. Bell, meanwhile, contested a host of other claimants. One colorful character, Antonio Meucci, who had fought with Garibaldi, claimed he transmitted words over wire while working in a Havana, Cuba, movie house in 1849; unfortunately, his wife sold the phone as junk while he was sick. Meucci didn't get far in court. Such out-and-out frauds helped AT&T, for in the public mind all the patent challengers were lumped together in one laughable group.

The Supreme Court majority opinion, written by Chief Justice Morrison R. Waite, paralleled the trial court decision and said that to give credit to Drawbaugh would "construe testimony without regard to the ordinary laws that govern human conduct." Justice Waite noted particularly that Drawbaugh was brought into the phone business by "the instrumentality of his associates," an implicit rejection of the entire case as a promotional scheme.

The part of the decision that AT&T still prefers to overlook in its authorized histories of the telephone was written by Justice Joseph P. Bradley and joined in by Justices John M. Harlan and Stephen J. Field. The key points of their dissent:

> We think that Drawbaugh anticipated the invention of Mr. Bell. . . . We think that the evidence on this point is so overwhelming, with regard both to the number and character of the witnesses, that it cannot be overcome.
>
> We are satisfied, from a very great preponderance of the evidence, that Drawbaugh produced, and exhibited in his shop, as early as 1869, an electrical instrument through which he transmitted speech. . . .
>
> [The witnesses, although many of them were semi-literate country folk], heard the words through the instrument, and that is a matter about which they cannot be mistaken. It does not require science or learning to understand that.
>
> Drawbaugh certainly had the principle, and accomplished the result. Perhaps without the aid of Mr. Bell, the speaking telephone might not have been brought into public use to this day, but that Drawbaugh produced it there can hardly be a reasonable doubt.
>
> It is perfectly natural for the world to take the part of the man who has already achieved eminence. . . . So it was with Bell and Drawbaugh. The latter invented the telephone without appreciating the importance and completeness of his inven-

tion. Bell subsequently projected it on the basis of scientific inference, and took out a patent for it. But, as our laws do not award a patent to one who was not the first to make an invention, we think that Bell's patent is void by the anticipations of Drawbaugh.

Bitterly disappointed, Drawbaugh spent the remainder of his life squabbling with the Patent Office about other minor telephone inventions he sought to protect—one a wireless telephone, in which signals traveled between iron rods driven into the ground. Still muttering about how his "telephone was stolen," Drawbaugh died in 1911, leaving an estate after payment of debts of less than $350.

Another telephone patent case deserves mention if only to show the odiousness of some of the pretenders and the general climate in which the Bell protective fights were waged. Public disgust was generated after the organization, in 1883, of the Pan-Electric Telephone Company, which promoted the "inventions" of a man named Rogers. General Joseph E. Johnston, the old Confederate hero, was made president, and two United States Senators, Isham G. Harris of Tennessee and Augustus H. Garland, who was also a former governor of Arkansas, served as directors.

Garland accepted stock valued at $500,000 and acted as attorney for Pan-Electric, his official position notwithstanding. The company had nothing to offer save bald infringements of Bell's patents, yet subcompanies were formed which paid cash fees to the promoters for the right to sell Rogers' "invention" in various cities.

Pan-Electric tried to have Congress void the Bell patents and actually lobbied a bill through the House (it died in a Senate subcommittee). In 1884, when Grover Cleveland was elected President, he unwittingly brought Garland—Pan-Electric stock and all—into his Cabinet. Garland's business friends clamored for "their attorney" to have the Justice Department challenge the Bell patents in court. Garland would not do so himself and went on vacation to Hominy Hall, his Arkansas farm, telling his office he wanted no messages forwarded to disturb his rest.

As soon as Garland departed, the U.S. Solicitor General (Acting Attorney General while Garland was away) brought suit against Bell. A U.S. attorney went into court in Baltimore and asked cessation of a patent-infringement action Bell had there against a Pan-Electric affiliate, stating that the government action had precedent. If this request had been granted, Pan-Electric would have gained carte blanche to continue its operations indefinitely.

The odor attracted the New York *Tribune,* which exposed Garland's connection with Pan-Electric. Angered, Cleveland ordered the suit withdrawn. Garland was hauled before a Congressional committee, which heard him deny use of his official position to help Pan-Electric. The majority report exonerated him, although Republicans called for his firing.

Although Garland kept his office the rest of the Cleveland Administration, his career was tainted and he lost a chance to become the first Southern appointee to the U.S. Supreme Court since the Civil War. A Thomas Nast cartoon depicted him saying mournfully, "Nobody will take the [Pan-Electric] stock off my hands," with Columbia answering, "Can't I get somebody to take *you* off my hands?"

At the outset of the patent suits Bell withdrew in melancholy distrust to Canada, saying he was through with telephones and intended to teach again "as soon as he could find a position." Only the cajoling of his company's attorneys persuaded him to testify in the patent trials; he eventually did so in fairly good humor and at length, spending nine weeks on the stand during one case alone. Except for these appearances, he took no active part in the phone business after 1878.

Bell's interest turned to flying machines, among other things, and Thomas A. Watson tells of his solemn inspection of a dead gull found on the beach near his retreat in Nova Scotia. And when Bell died on August 2, 1922, he was still mad at Drawbaugh and other persons who challenged his title of Father of the Telephone.

4

In fully 90 percent of the locations where independent companies have sprung up . . . there has been an oppression on the part of the Bell interests that has become unbearable . . . in rates and in the class of service and in the treatment of the subscribers.

—*Independent phone official's testimony to New York legislative committee, 1910*

THEODORE N. VAIL, the onetime Post Office superintendent who built Alexander Graham Bell's invention into the world's most powerful communications system, called the telephone a "natural monopoly." Scornful of outsiders who attempted to enter the industry and of the citizens who welcomed them as an alternative to Bell's abuses, Vail used such adjectives as "aggressive" and "destructive" when referring to competition. "The reason for the public's encouragement of such competition lies in the belief that from it they will derive some benefit," Vail wrote in 1913, the exasperation dripping from his pen. "In the long run, however, the public as a whole has never benefited by destructive competition."

And the United States' one experiment in true telephone competition proved Vail right, as well as confirmed three corollaries that at first blush might appear mutually contradictory:

1. Competition in the telephone field over a sustained period, with two companies attempting to serve the same customers, would be an unutterable nuisance for the American

citizen, with so many practical and financial disadvantages as to be unworkable.

2. Competition in the telephone field, during the brief time that it existed, was an invaluable blessing for the American citizen, for it shook Bell from a deliberately adopted lethargy that retarded for decades the development of telephone service.

3. Competition in the telephone field, as a prospective ultimate weapon of regulation, could be a damnably effective means of resolving the problems the American citizen continues to encounter with the major telephone company.

The number and prospective seriousness of the patent suits notwithstanding, they actually had little direct effect on Bell's operations. Most of the 600-odd companies sued promptly went out of business once court papers were served. Even Daniel Drawbaugh had more potentiality than phones, for his backers were enjoined from using the disputed instruments while his suit was heard.

The result was an era of total telephone monopoly for the Bell interests, beginning with settlement of the Western Union case in 1879 and continuing through the expiration of the basic Bell patents in 1894–95. The Bell owners, conservative New Englanders, considered the telephone industry a private gold mine to be worked at their leisure, with profits having priority over public convenience and service. Stockholders received annual dividends ranging up to 18 percent of their investment. By 1893, seventeen years after the beginning of commercial telephony, Bell had installed only 266,431 phones, most of them in urban areas, requiring a minimal investment in lines and transmitting equipment.

It will be recalled that Alexander Graham Bell shared ownership of the patent with his father-in-law and financial backer, Congressman Gardiner G. Hubbard. When commercial exploitation of the telephone began in 1878, the Boston banking community supplied the money—in return for control of the company. Within a year Hubbard was but one of many directors, and inventor Bell's title was simply "electrician."

The operational genius which multiplied the financiers' dollars came from Theodore N. Vail, whose family earlier in the century had aided Samuel Morse in the invention of the telegraph. As a boy in Morristown, New Jersey, Vail worked in a drugstore that housed the local telegraph office and in two years learned more about telegraphy than pharmacy—to the distress of his parents, who wanted him to study medicine. The bickering ultimately caused Vail to leave home. An uncle found him a job with Western Union in New York, and in three years there he compiled the sort of record that would blackball a modern youth from AT&T's executive staff. Vail's diary mixes shamed moralizing about his sporting life with wide-eyed accounts of the fun a country boy can have in the city. "Staying up late of nights playing billiards and drinking lager is not what young men should be doing and for one I am determined to stop it," Vail wrote. Elsewhere he lamented of "getting into difficulties and out again, only to get into fresh ones. When will I become so sober and settled that I shall not continuously involve myself?" Vail managed to become assistant to Western Union's city superintendent, who watched him awhile and decided, "I think you'd better look up another job."

Reconciled with his parents, Vail moved with them to sobering Waterloo, Iowa. He gained local acclamation as the star of a baseball team that thrashed Cedar Rapids, 84 to 30, joined the Union Pacific Railroad as a woodcutter to work in Utah (where the fortuitous arrival of a cavalry troop saved him and another youth from a scalping by Indians), and eventually was appointed a rail postal clerk.

To say that Vail made the postal system what it is today is not meant as an insult. He devised the mail-handling procedures that enabled the U.S. Post Office to be one of the world's most efficient—a near century ago. The trouble is that no one has done much to improve it since Vail.

The Post Office which Vail joined in 1868, if the historians are to be believed, was even worse than today's. Consider the mail trains. Mail destined for stations along a Union Pacific line was dumped in bags into boxcars. The bags would be thrown off at a stop, where the postmaster sorted through them to pick out letters for his town. He would then cram the remainder into the bags and start them on their travels again— in the right direction if he knew it and was in a good mood that day. The bags could ricochet around the country for days —even weeks—while letters became tattered and outdated.

Vail had the idea of sorting the bags and bundling mail for each Union Pacific station into a separate package, which he marked with an identifying slip. The postmasters liked the service, so he extended it to outlying towns, which connected to the train via stagecoach, and drew up charts for other clerks showing which stations served as distribution centers for other points.

All this soon attracted Washington's attention, and Vail went there to work out a nationwide distribution system. State by state he studied the rail network, reducing to chart form the when and where of mail sorting and routing. At his urging the Post Office hired mail trains and cut the New York–Chicago time to twenty-four hours. Competitive exams removed the worst political hacks from the department.

But Vail had troubles. A spendthrift who savored good food and wine, he was chronically at the mercy of loan sharks. Congressmen didn't like Vail's arrogance and scorn of the patronage system. Nonetheless Vail was aware of the political realities of Washington during the Grant Administration: He admitted to helping arrange for a political fixer to receive a 10 percent kickback from railroads on government mail subsidies in return for continued appropriations. But Vail generally found Congress frustrating, especially so when it threatened to end the $5 per day "expense allowance" he received in addition to his $1,600 a year salary.

Vail thus was restless in 1877, when he left Washington as escort for a prolonged inspection tour by the House Postal Committee, of which Congressman Gardiner Hubbard was a member. Hubbard apparently was more interested in demonstrating the new telephone—two of which he brought along—than looking at post offices. Fascinated by the gadgetry, Vail helped him and had a pair installed in his house when he returned to Washington. Although dead broke, he pestered friends and colleagues for money so he could buy stock in the Bell company. Vail's enthusiasm impressed Hubbard. So did Vail's proved organizational genius. After a spate of negotiations Vail left the government and joined Bell for $3,500 a year.

Vail's colleagues good-naturedly told him he was a fool to abandon an organization as modern, progressive, and efficient as the Post Office to join the telephone company. One official thought that Vail should have "a telephone tube fastened to your ear and another connecting at the top of your head . . . and while in this condition be compelled to listen to the sweet by-and-bye's [sic] of every whelping canine and the solos of all the tom cats in the State of N. Y. Telephone! Well, it may be useful as well as ornamental, but listen to the prophecy of an old fool to a friend. One or two years hence there will be more telephone companies in existence than there are sewing machine companies today."

And, truthfully, the telephone company consisted of little more than a name and an idea, its headquarters a one-desk office with a crate of instruments in the corner. Nor was there much money: One gloomy day early in AT&T's history a New York hardware company refused to deliver an order until it received payment in advance—less than $10. (The massive New York Telephone Company building now occupies this store's old site.) Yet Vail never envisioned the telephone as anything other than a national, interlocking communications system, with Bell as the dominant partner.

Because of the unpredictable outcome of the court suits, Vail could not rely on the patent to give Bell the monopoly he desired. "What we wanted to do was to get possession of the field in such a way that, patent or no patent, we could control it," Vail said. Also, even a patent monopoly would not be immortal, for patents eventually run out. So he went about building a monopoly from three routes:

1. Bell sought out small local promoters who were willing to organize phone companies in their towns, enlist subscribers, and sell stock, substituting "their energy and their ambition and their prospects for profit" for money, as Vail put it. The bulk of these contracts were for five years; in addition to selling the telephone instruments, Bell got a share of the stock. The local companies had to agree to have no dealings with independent phone companies or other competitors. After the contract period lapsed, Bell reserved the right to purchase the equipment at a price not exceeding its cost. Dependence of the companies upon Bell for telephone instruments, technical advice, and maintenance "placed them completely at the mercy of the licensor," the Federal Communications Commission was to state half a century later after an exhaustive study of how Bell built its telephone monopoly.

In a handful of larger towns Bell gave permanent contracts but took in return a stock interest of 30 to 50 percent. Vail himself received the New York franchise as an extra inducement to leave the Post Office. The New York Telephone Company arrangement was typical of the permanent contracts: Bell took 40 percent of all stock and a $10 annual rental fee for telephones in return for the "exclusive right to use and rent telephones at and between all places within the district of 33 miles of the City of New York (not including any part of the State of Connecticut), and the whole of Monmouth County, New Jersey, and the whole of Long Island." In addition to stock ownership, Bell demanded the right to representation on boards and executive committees of these licensee companies, restricted them from borrowing money without Bell's consent, and directed that expansion be paid for by capital stock issues —not from profits. Bell also required the licensees to "make such reports, giving such information regarding the operations of their exchanges and the prices charged as the licensor [Bell] may from time to time request." The license contracts thus enabled Bell to fulfill its two basic objectives: control and profits, the latter from both phone rentals and the general business of the licensed companies.

2. Bell absolutely forbade its licensee companies to interconnect with non-Bell franchises for long-distance calls. "No exchange could exist without being tied up with every other exchange," Vail said, and this meant outsiders ultimately could be isolated and starved out of business. Commercial long-distance telephony was introduced in 1885, first between Boston and New York, and became increasingly important on the Eastern Seaboard in the next few years—but only between Bell cities.

3. Bell vigorously pursued patents on the myriad devices necessary for telephone service. Vail said that as Bell got into the exchange systems, "we found out that it would develop a thousand and one little patents and inventions with which to do the business . . . and that is what we wanted to control and get possession of." Vail set up a Bell engineering department to "examine all patents that came out with a view to acquiring them, because . . . we recognized that if we did not control these devices, somebody else would, and we would be more or less hampered in the development of the business."

Vail had completed the basic framework for the Bell System as it exists today by 1885—and then quit the business in disgust. The Boston financiers, he discovered, had no real interest in providing telephone service, only in fast profits. In 1885, for instance, the Bell company had a return of less than $3,000,000 and paid dividends of more than $1,500,000. Vail thought more of the profits should be plowed back into the company for new lines and new exchanges. Too, there was considerable clatter in the press and legislative bodies about putting telephone cables underground to remove their ugly presence from the urban landscape. Vail wanted to spend money for this operation lest public opinion became so unfavorable that legislatures decided to do something about Bell's monopoly position. The financiers, however, wanted to get everything they could from Bell before the patents expired. In his resignation Vail said, "My present position in the company is not such as I had hoped to attain, and is also in some ways embarrassing and unpleasant." For the next fifteen years he tried assorted enterprises: Latin American traction companies, an ice plant, a scheme to heat New York homes and businesses with a public steam system. Bell, however, had not heard the last of him.

After Vail left, Bell adopted a policy which, if not "the public be damned," certainly was "the public be ignored" and before the turn of the century had severely damaged its position. Vail's job passed to John E. Hudson, a lawyer and one-time Greek scholar at Harvard, who thought telephone use was a privilege, rather than a service. For seven years Bell remained at a standstill, adding few exchanges, permitting its equipment to deteriorate, the incessant clang of the cash register the only sound emitting from the monopoly. Bell installed telephones at its leisure and at the customer's expense, levied whatever fees it thought the market would bear, and made maintenance a sometime thing.

All this came to an abrupt halt in 1894, when the Bell patents expired. The ill will Bell had so arrogantly accumulated in the last decade was hurled in its owners' faces. Populists made Bell-baiting a national sport, and "dollar a month service" their rallying cry. The richness of the Bell profits was common knowledge, which made it easy for promoters to huckster stock in independent companies. Small-town blacksmiths fashioned crude, but operable, facsimiles of Alexander Graham Bell's telephones and ones which worked just as well —more an indictment of the run-down condition of the Bell system than an endorsement of the independents' skill.

Bell's post-Vail niggardliness toward its engineers helped the independents. After Vail left, if a Bell researcher made a device that improved phone operations, he had the choice of taking $100 or $200 from Bell in return for the patent or retaining rights to it himself and selling them on the open market. Independent equipment manufacturers bought these secondary patents in wholesale lots. D. Elbert Reynolds, a Michigan Democratic politician and businessman prominent in the independent movement, asserted without contradictory evidence that the independents, in their first years, had a "very much better system than the Bell employed at the time." Some Bell subsidiary companies had the further burden of paying the parent company 27.5 percent of their net receipts in royalties on the phone gear they used. "We bought our instruments for less money than they paid annually in royalties on their patents," said Reynolds.

The independents' aggressiveness in acquiring new equipment enabled them to be the first to offer automatic connections between subscribers. The Bell companies used what was called the magneto system, in which electrical batteries were located at both the customer's house and the central phone office. The caller took the phone off the hook, flashing the operator, who plugged into the circuit, obtained the number, and rang the other subscriber. Privacy was negligible, for the operator could hear whatever was said as long as she remained on the circuit. The independents in the early 1900's introduced the dial system, with the power supply in the central office.

Bell fought back on several fronts, including a revival of the old patent-infringement issue. Emile Berliner's microphone invention had been purchased by Bell in 1877, but remained cubbyholed in Washington until November 18, 1891, when the Patent Office finally granted it. No discernible reason could be found for the delay, and Bell consequently had the opportunity to extend its monopoly through 1908. But antimonopolists remembered the description of the Patent Office as Bell's "personal underground railroad" only a decade previously and howled in protest. The Rochester *Herald* said Bell sought to keep alive its monopoly by "the dishonorable trick of keeping up a sham contest in the Patent Office the last 14 years." Even Bell's friends warned that the issue took the monopoly onto shaky ground. Boston attorney James J. Storrow, a close adviser to Bell management, wrote the day Berliner's patent was granted:

The Bell company has had a monopoly more profitable and more controlling—and more generally hated—than any ever given by any patent. The attempt to prolong it 16 years more [*sic*] by the Berliner patent will bring a great strain on that patent and a great pressure on the courts. This has nothing to do with the validity of the patents, or the duty of the courts to sustain it. . . . Patents which would stand ordinary litigation have been known to give way under great strain, if they turn on questions where it is humanly possible to take an adverse view.

The federal government sued Bell to void the patent, alleging that Bell failed to expedite its application and that the Berliner microphone wouldn't work anyway. The Supreme Court threw out the government case, stating, "There is seldom presented a case in which there is such an absolute and total failure of proof of wrong." Yet the patent was subsequently interpreted so narrowly that it was easily circumvented by independent equipment manufacturers. The courts limited the patent's coverage to microphones with metallic contacts. But other inventors now used carbon electrode contacts, whose more efficient performance destroyed the usefulness of the Berliner patent.

Bell's willingness to make competitors prove in court the legitimacy of their equipment was an effective psychological weapon. In Bell's 1892 annual report its patent attorney noted that independent phone companies, especially those in the West, "seem to be rather frightened at the idea of infringing patents, and the great number of the projected and organized rival concerns alter their construction in order that they may not infringe the patents of the Western Electric Company [Bell's equipment subsidiary]. . . ."

The lawyer said Bell's policy of suing for infringements "is an excellent one because it keeps the concerns which attempt opposition in a nervous and excited condition since they never know where the next attack will be made, and since it keeps them all the time changing their machines and causes them ultimately in order that they may not be sued, to adopt inefficient forms of apparatus."

The startling feature of the independent movement, all things considered, is the drubbing it gave Bell even when its equipment and service were grossly inferior. Farmer companies had a brief, but spectacular, vogue, with subscribers connected by barbed-wire fences or iron wire nailed to trees. Static was so bad that a conversation sounded more like a Fourth of July fireworks shoot than civilized intercourse, but the farmers didn't mind. They didn't even try to match the service standards which Theodore Vail had sought to bring to American telephony, because "they feel satisfied with what they are getting," as Elbert Reynolds put it.

In one New York hamlet, Bell offered far better equipment than the farmer company—and had 5 subscribers to its rival's 100. Reynolds explained, "The Bell [is] giving excellent service, and the independent or farmer company gives service from about 7 or 8 o'clock in the morning until 8 or 9 at night, provided the lines are in order, and a great deal of time the lines are out of order and the service entirely unsatisfactory. But inasmuch as one service costs $24 and the other less than $4 a year, they [the farmers] seem to be satisfied with what they are getting."

The independents also proved Bell overpriced in the cities from which came the bulk of its profits. In Lansing, Michigan, for instance, Reynolds found his exchange operated at a cost of $4.83 per phone per year. "We were charging $24 a year for business and $18 a year for residences, as against the Bell former price of $48 for business and $36 or $40 for residences, I forget which. . . ."

That Bell grossly overcharged subscribers during its total monopoly period was decisively proved during the era of competition. Bell revenue per telephone station dropped from $88 in 1885 to $63 in 1890 and $43 in 1907; the decrease continued for the next decade, but at a lower rate.

Any measuring rod employed credits the independents with an impressive showing during the period. Bell began competition with 266,431 phones in service (in 1894) and a decade later had 1,317,178. The independents, which had no stations, during the same period went to 1,053,866.

For the subscribers, the competition meant better chances of obtaining a telephone. The frightened Bell rapidly expanded its exchanges. From 1885 to 1894 it had increased phones by an average of 6.2 percent annually; from 1895 to 1906 growth was 21.5 percent a year.

But the independent movement had ingrown problems, and overeagerness for new business was foremost among them. In the Middle West particularly, the independents wooed franchises from city councils by pledging low rates—only to find they had so underpriced themselves they could not stay in business. Companies which could not wheedle increases went broke (or ignored their authorized tariffs and charged what they felt they could). Nor did Bell show any mercy when an independent got into trouble. Many times a Bell subsidiary bought up foundering independents and ceremoniously heaped their instruments in the town square for a public burning—as both a purge for the past and a warning for the future. The onetime president of the Bell Telephone Company of Missouri and Kansas, Charles S. Gleed, said these demonstrations so angered many independent stockholders that they forbade company officers to negotiate with Bell upon pain of civic disgrace or worse. Gleed went to one small Kansas town to discuss the purchase of an ailing independent company and was told to wait anonymously in his hotel room until midnight. Sharp upon the hour there was a knock on the door, and in slunk a man with a false beard and turned-up coat collar. It was the independent phone president, fearful his stockholders would learn he had talked with the demon Bell.

An idea of how Bell treated customers in this period comes from an angry declaration New York State Senator D. F. Davis made to a legislative committee investigating phone competition in 1909:

> The individual is treated as though he were under obligation [to the phone company] that could never be fulfilled . . . for the reason that they put an instrument in his house and run a wire to it. The fact is that . . . conditions should be established where the citizens' rights are clearly established, or else there ought to be the widest open door for business competition to come in against them.

Bell's practice of stringing its wires on fences or over housetops rather than on poles—whether the homeowner was a phone subscriber or not—saved the company money but also made citizens devilishly unhappy. The New York legislative committee heard Bronx resident Henry P. Schmidt declare, "The wires will be chopped down by the property owners if you put them on the fence, so please take due notice."

Bell squeezed minority stockholders from its subsidiary companies to increase its control—and profits. In some instances this was done through consolidations: The assets of a company which Bell controlled would be distributed pro rata as a liquidating dividend, thus paying off the minority stockholders. Bell would then reinvest its proceeds from the sale in stock of the buying company. Bell also used dummy buyers to conceal the purchases it made from minority holders if they were unwilling to sell to Bell directly.

Under these circumstances the prices received by the minority holders were liberal. Yet Bell could also be ruthless. Investigators for the Federal Communications Commission later ticked off some of the methods used to drive stock prices down:

—Forcing subsidiary companies to suspend dividend payments.

—Directing subsidiaries to divert all earnings (after provisions for interest deductions) into depreciation and maintenance reserves, rather than permitting their distribution as profits. The Bell comptroller actually wired the subsidiary Central Union Telephone Company in 1909: "Advise such depreciation as will leave no net earnings after paying interest."

—Use of propaganda to discourage minority stockholders and depress the market price of their stock.

—Giving minority stockholders discouraging advice and recommending that they accept prices offered by Bell.

All this could be done without financial loss to Bell. After 1900 Bell adopted the practice of supplying its subsidiaries with operating funds for expansion through short-term loans, which grew until they became three to four times the value of the outstanding stock. Interest on these loans would be paid even though, for tactical reasons, the subsidiaries would not declare any dividends. Reduced to chronic discouragement, the minority holders were prone to (1) sell at whatever price they could receive and (2) decline to buy new offerings of stock, the latter enabling Bell to increase its voting controls from a bare majority to 80 or 90 percent. Bell took a high profit from these loans. L. G. Richardson, president of the Central Union Telephone Company (Illinois, Indiana, Ohio, and Iowa), wrote the parent company in 1909 that he could have placed a $15,000,000 bond issue outside Bell at a cost of $10,000 less per month in interest.

All this time the parent Bell company maintained its base in

Massachusetts. But corporate laws there proved overly restrictive. Any increase in capitalization had to be approved by the legislature. Stockholdings in subsidiary companies were limited. New stock could not be issued for less than the market price.

So the American Bell Telephone Company in 1900 went to New York and reorganized and reincorporated under the name of what had been its long-distance division, the American Telephone & Telegraph Company.

Wall Street participated in the reorganization, and the New York investment bankers opened their purses to supply the funds AT&T needed to counter its competition. Previously, the Bell company drew upon the financial resources of Boston bankers; now, however, Boston could not meet the demands. From 1900 to 1904, a period of severe inflation, AT&T borrowed money, $150,000,000 at a clip, for a rapid multiplication of its exchanges. In 1906, when the economic boom showed signs of cresting, the New York bankers worried about their investments and persuaded Theodore Vail to leave retirement and resume the presidency. This period is significant in company history because it marks a passage of control of AT&T from New England to New York and the birth of hereditary management, with each president in turn choosing his successor, subject to the as yet unexercised veto of New York investment houses.

The return of Vail opened a span of Bell's life which company historians gingerly refer to as an "era of great expansion." Stated more keenly, Bell used the cities in which it was entrenched as unassailable redoubts from which its financial shock troops marched forth to annihilate the independents.

The long-distance division gave Bell a means of interlocking its scattered operating companies with an efficiency the disorganized independents could not match. Each time the independents tried to put together their own system, Bell toppled it like jackstraws, by either purchasing a key company from it or using financial connections to deny it money.

Philadelphia transit magnates Peter A. B. Widener and W. I. Elkins led the most ambitious independent effort to build a long-distance system. The core of this attempt was a group of Western companies operating outside the Bell System, but with Bell patent rights, and comprising 15 percent of Bell's licensed stations.

This group, the Erie Telephone & Telegraph Company, virtually controlled the phone business in seven states. Widener and Elkins, together with second-rung New York promoters, incorporated the Telephone, Telegraph & Cable Company for $30,000,000 and announced plans to buy Erie and mount nationwide, coordinated competition with Bell.

Within a month one frown by J. P. Morgan doomed the venture.

Morgan didn't want an outside company to threaten the millions of dollars of bonds his house had invested in Bell. He pointedly reminded several New York members of the new telephone syndicate of the help he had given them in a just finished fight with John D. Rockefeller for control of New York's gas distribution system and hinted that he could reopen the matter if he so desired. The bankers understood Morgan perfectly. They persuaded Elkins and Widener to abandon the plan. Members of AT&T's corporate hierarchy took over a $7,500,000 loan which the Erie company had made from a Boston bank and could not repay—and the long-distance venture died.

The larger the independents, the harder it was for them to obtain the large amounts of capital required to attempt meaningful competition with AT&T. A local phone company could meet its meager needs from the local bank—but could not amass enough capital to expand. The FCC later was to call this a "slow financial strangulation" through which Bell System regained the monopoly position it had held prior to expiration of the patents.

Political muscle protected Bell elsewhere. The New York legislature in 1901 passed a law designed to promote telephone competition by directing cities to grant franchises to all applicants. The Frontier Telephone Company, run by Daniel J. Kefenick, went into the Bell monopoly city of Buffalo and found municipal officials aligned with Bell. True, they granted Frontier a franchise, but "with every possible exaction that could be made," as Kefenick described the experience. "In the first place, they required the Frontier Telephone Company to pay $50,000 in cash, which had never been exacted of the Bell, not a penny. They required the Frontier Telephone Company to give them [100] free phones for the city. . . . No such imposition was put on the Bell." Also, the city levied a 3 percent gross receipts tax on Frontier—but not on Bell. Bell was permitted to charge 3 cents per call, while Frontier was restricted to a flat $48 per year. Had it been permitted to match Bell's rates, Frontier would have taken in $1,500,000 a year; as it was, it received less than $500,000. Kefenick got a New York legislative committee to agree with him that these conditions were "onerous" and "awful," but he nonetheless went broke.

Why were politicians so friendly to Bell?

Bribery was the answer in at least one city, San Francisco, where Bell had an experience that serves as an object lesson of the intricacies—and dangers—involved in ensuring that bought politicians remain bought.

Bell went into California in 1880 with the Pacific Bell Telephone Company, which by January, 1906, had become the Pacific States Telephone & Telegraph Company. Abe Ruef, San Francisco's roguish little political boss, took a $1,200 monthly "retainer" from Pacific States (more than was paid the company's general counsel). But this didn't prevent Ruef from making a deal with the Home Telephone Company, run by an Ohio syndicate, under which San Francisco's docile board of supervisors would grant a rival telephone franchise. Ruef's price was $125,000, of which $25,000 would be paid in advance and the remainder after the franchise ordinance passed.

Whether Pacific States' political fixsters knew of the Ruef deal was never established, but they tried to block Home Telephone by going around Ruef and buying the supervisors directly. Pacific States' Theodore V. Halsey treated a cloddish supervisor to dinner and, as the Sauterne flowed, lectured him on the virtues of telephone monopoly. Halsey found the man receptive, whereupon, according to testimony later, he summoned eleven supervisors to a discreet Montgomery Street office and gave them envelopes containing $4,000 or $5,000 each. "I want you to be friendly with the company," Halsey told one of the supervisors, a hack driver. "I'd like you to have that for your friendship."

Ruef exploded into froth-spitting rage when he learned of the payoffs—because the supervisors dared make deals on their own, violating the "rules of conduct" he had established for the efficient exaction of graft, and because Bell lobbyists had worked behind his back. (That Ruef was simultaneously double-crossing Pacific States by working with Home Telephone apparently was secondary.) One slap on the table, and the cowering supervisors passed the Home Telephone Company franchise, Ruef storming, "Halsey tried to steal my supervisors away from me, but I taught him a lesson." When Ruef calmed, he pacified Halsey by pressuring the supervisors to return half the bribe money they took from Pacific States (few actually did so).

When the Ruef graft gang collapsed the next year, a grand jury put the blame for the telephone bribes on Louis Glass, executive vice-president of the Bell subsidiary. Pacific States by this time had become the present-day Pacific Telephone & Telegraph Company, with AT&T continuing the majority ownership it had held since the company's founding. The indictments were based on evidence that Glass had drawn the funds from the company treasury and authorized Halsey, his brother-in-law, to pay the bribes.

Special prosecutor Frank Heney, who spent three years trying to purge San Francisco of Ruef's corruption, was contemptuous of the AT&T subsidiary's morals:

> The moment the Home Telephone Company endeavored to get in here these people—these respectable broadcloth wearers, these highest members of society—deliberately went into the field and commenced to debauch your supervisors, undermine your government, corrupt your officials so that this city will have disgrace upon it for all time as the worst-governed city in the United States. At whose door should you lay that? Not at the door of the poor devils who accepted their filthy money, but at the door of those men who went out and invited those poor fellows [the supervisors] to lunch—with a little sauterne afterward. . . . Oh, if it were not that I love my country, these conditions would fill me with disgust, and I would vomit in reply.

At the first trial the Pacific States auditor refused to repeat grand jury testimony about checks he had drawn to Glass, and the jury deadlocked. The second jury took only twenty-five minutes to find Glass guilty. He went behind bars to start a five-year prison term, retaining, nonetheless, his listing as first vice-president of Pacific Telephone.

The Ruef prosecutions, meanwhile, slipped deep into the bottomless muck of California politics and appellate court wranglings. Witnesses disappeared, the reformers found themselves criticized for "blackening San Francisco's name" through their exposures of corruption, and Balkanish plots and subplots diverted the citizenry's attention. Ill health kept Halsey out of court until 1910, when postreform prosecutors had taken charge of the Ruef cases, and he was acquitted. A couple of months later Glass' conviction was set aside on somewhat abstruse technicalities. Home Telephone Company could do little with its franchise and went broke.

Bell devoted considerable time to defending its New York City monopoly, the nation's richest telephone territory. The Hudson River Telephone Company, situated in New Jersey, formed part of the defensive perimeter. In the words of a New York Telephone Company officer, Hudson River Telephone was no more than a "buffer" against competition that might sneak toward Manhattan from the West.

William Proctor bought 100 shares of Hudson River Telephone stock in 1897, when it was still an independent company. After ten years his dividends abruptly halted. Proctor found Bell had taken over Hudson River and was using it to cut rates in New Jersey to fight the independents. "The Bell," he complained, "was more interested in driving out the independents than they were in having dividends on the stock." Bell repeated this same stratagem in city after city—sacrificing immediate profits in the knowledge that it would prosper once the independents were dashed.

Beginning in 1904, various state legislatures passed laws providing for compulsory physical connections between phone companies, even if they were separately owned, so as to enable the independents to break out of the confines of their limited territories. The legislature saw no reason for residents of non-Bell cities to be denied long-distance service because of AT&T's monopolistic aspirations. The federal government put its weight behind this movement in 1912 with a court agreement in which Bell said it would connect with independents with which it was not in direct competition in a territory. Yet D. Elbert Reynolds of the independent movement avowed that Bell found ways to evade the requirement.

"They might manipulate the operating coil in which the line terminated in such a way as not to throw the signal," he said. "In that case the connecting company might continue to call as long as they wished; the company transmitting [Bell] would not know that they were calling, and their excuse would be that it was out of commission or out of order. These tricks have been resorted to and continued until they wore the people out, and finally [the industry] went on in the old way."

AT&T's position on interconnection had business logic—but was an indefensible one for a public utility to take, for it effectively denied long-distance service to hundreds of thousands of American families. "It would give a competing exchange advantage of our big system without any corresponding advantage to us," Theodore Vail said of interconnection. Vail ignored the fact that a Bell subscriber living in one city might want to talk with a friend living in a non-Bell city and that AT&T and the independent company could find a way to share the revenue produced by the call. Destruction of competition, rather than the best service possible to the phone user, was Vail's obsession as he built AT&T into a monopoly.

The threat of loss of interconnection rights dissuaded licensee companies from leaving the Bell System. Even if they "had the power or the right . . . or the apparatus or the patents to go ahead, they could not connect with any of our exchanges," Vail said.

With the interconnection bludgeon AT&T worried little about the independents. "[N]o matter how well supported they may be by home conditions, or home influences, or anything, they don't do away with our telephone business," Vail boasted. "A man of course could do all his business within the limits of the city without coming to us, *but to get outside he has got to come to us.*" Vail told of an instance when Bell was opposed by the "strongest financial and political influences" in a city which he left unnamed. "We burned down completely. We were out of existence for I don't know how long." But AT&T had the surrounding territory so blanketed "that they had to come to us, and we bought it . . . for about half what it cost."

Vail had acumen enough not to decimate totally the independents, leaving a fringe of safe small companies intact in deference to public opinion and the antitrust laws. In 1919 he wrote Senator W. Murray Crane, of Massachusetts, an AT&T investor: "The independents in Ohio are whipped and badly whipped, and it will only require the continuance of our present program to eliminate them as a factor. . . ." But Vail said it was "probably undesirable from our standpoint to ever consider any arrangement which would eliminate the *so-called competition*." He said the Ohio independents and others in Pennsylvania mentioned in the same letter "do not affect our business and satisfy the small number of people [*sic*] who desire competition."

Bell's rapacious appetite for competing companies eventually frightened the survivors into asking the U.S. Justice Department for antitrust protection. The Attorney General, George W. Wickersham, worked out an agreement with J. E. Kingsbury, an AT&T vice-president, on Bell's future policies on the acquisition of independents. In substance the agreement (called the Kingsbury Commitment, dated December 19, 1913) was that Bell would not acquire, directly or indirectly, control over any competing company and that Bell would connect its system with independents, provided the companies' equipment met Bell's operating standards. Bell agreed to vacate the telegraph business by selling the controlling interest it had acquired several years previously in Western Union and to confine itself thereafter to the telephone business. The Kingsbury Commitment, however, did leave Bell free to purchase noncompeting companies, and this it did with enthusiasm, concentrating on urban areas, ignoring the less profitable countryside.

Despite the good intentions of the Justice Department, the Kingsbury Commitment did not make possible the creation of a national independent network capable of competing with the Bell System. Indeed, many independents thought the commitment unfair, for Bell was the best potential buyer for owners who tired of unworkable competitive situations and desired to sell. In 1921 the Justice Department, at AT&T's request and with no objections from the independents, declared that the Kingsbury Commitment was no longer binding.

Whereupon Bell intensified its acquisitions until the independents were isolated in the country and a handful of smaller cities, surviving (in the phraseology of the FCC) "largely at the sufferance of the Bell System."

The decline of the independents and Bell's purchases of companies in the major revenue-producing centers had a drastic impact on American farm families. Smaller companies were left with antiquated equipment and little opportunity for growth, dependent oftentimes upon Bell even for "long-distance" connections to the county seat.

During 1920 and 1940 the number of rural phones dropped from 2,498,493 to 1,526,959; many of those remaining were so outdated as to be useless, with wires sagging until they touched the ground, the supporting poles rotting and swaying in the slightest breeze.

Much of this decline, of course, was directly attributable to the Depression. But many telephone critics, including Representative W. R. Poage, the Texas Democrat-Populist, believed Bell's greed for high rates had to bear much of the blame.

AT&T vice-president E. K. Hall summarized Bell's rate philosophy for the period in a 1922 speech: "There is only one mistake that the public service commissions can make about rates, only one—and that is by keeping these rates too low. They can never make a mistake by making them too high."

Congressman Poage said this principle "forced a million farm homes in these United States to disconnect their telephones when money became scarce in the 1930's." Bell not only sought to keep its rates high but pressured independents to do the same. Bell helped independents in rate cases without charge, and Poage asserted it was not difficult to convince most of the companies to raise their tariffs to a par with Bell fees.

Mutual and cooperative companies which didn't increase rates found they could no longer afford to pay the interconnection charges assessed by Bell and the larger independents for long-distance calls. Said Poage: "Most of the farmers' mutual-owned lines and exchanges tried to hold their subscribers by holding down rates, but they could not give the needed exchange or long-distance service. They lost the more profitable business. They were left with only the least lucrative areas. Naturally their service, which was never too good, suffered."

In the mid-1940's Poage and other Congressmen sympathetic to the farmers' phone plight began working for a federal program to bring service to areas that Bell and the independents wouldn't help. Poage and Senator Lister Hill, the Alabama Democrat, proposed to do so by extending the benefits of the Rural Electrification Administration (REA) to rural telephony. Loans at 2 percent over thirty-five years, they felt, would enable cooperative and mutual companies to buy needed equipment and extend their coverage by stringing wires over the electrical poles already erected by REA subscribers. REA had brought electricity to 4,000,000 American farm homes during the first decade after its creation in 1935.

Bell, however, fought to keep the federal government from entering even this phase of the phone business. Hill and Poage introduced their first bill in 1945, and Bell lobbied it to death. They tried again in 1949 and this time produced graphic evidence that many farmers knew of the telephone only by hearsay.

According to the 1940 census, only 3.6 percent (8,254) of Alabama's farms had phones; by 1945 this had increased to 5 percent (11,000)—"progress by inches where we had miles to crawl," Hill said. On the other hand, thanks to the REA, 7 of 10 Alabama farms had electricity. Nationally, the Department of Agriculture said in a survey reported on July 1, 1948, only 37 percent of U.S. farms had phones.

Hill said farm people "are still isolated in large measure from each other and from their business and social centers." Senator Milton R. Young, the North Dakota Republican, agreed. "I find it impossible to call almost any farm regarding business or anything else. Either he [the farmer] has no phone at all, or the system is so obsolete you cannot even hear him on a call to Washington."

Billy Bryan, of the Cattle Electric Cooperative of Binger, Oklahoma, bore Bell no grudge for not putting phones on farms in his area. "I do not think Bell would ever reach them because they are too thin." F. V. Heinkel, of the Missouri Farmers Association, said, "Thousands of farmers who have implored the telephone companies from time to time to give them service have just about given up hope." Claude R. Wickard, the REA administrator, said his Indiana farm home still used the same phone "that was installed there when I was a small boy, almost half a century ago." The community of Paisley, Florida, complained its nearest phone was 10 miles distant. The agricultural agent for Pulaski County, Tennessee— one of the state's largest, with 5,000 farmers—said phone service there "is practically nothing." A dairyman in Appomattox, Virginia, said he had "tried in every way to get a telephone" for twelve years. In areas that did have service, 20 to 25 subscribers shared a line; a farmer who wished to place an important long-distance call drove into town, rather than attempt using a system whose wires were nailed onto trees and shielded by "insulators" fashioned from soft-drink bottles.

Because of such conditions, one might expect Bell to view charitably an attempt by the federal government to open up areas which it failed to help. Bell didn't. At hearings on the Hill-Poage bill, Bell spokesmen devoted their time to bragging about the rural phone program they had begun since the Second World War and complaining about federal intervention. "The job should be left to the telephone companies for completion without federal subsidies and without adding to the taxpayers' burden," said V. E. Cooley, president of the Southwestern Bell Telephone Company. The Southern Bell president, H. S. Dumas, claimed his company had installed 1,000,000 rural phones since 1945 (these hearings were in 1949), then was asked by Senator George D. Aiken what percentage went to homes "where the people living there depended on the farm for a living."

Dumas hemmed and hawed and replied, "I am sorry, I do not know that." Aiken pointed out that many of the so-called farm phones installed by Bell actually were in country stores, garages, sawmills, and packinghouses. The insistent Dumas said that they "are available to the rural population for use."

Harold V. Bozell, president of the General Telephone Company and a vice-president of the United States Independent Telephone Association, the non-Bell trade group, offered a unique explanation for the lack of farm phones. Many farmers, he said, "will not take service even though the telephone lines go right in front of their houses," with a 50 cent a month rate. Bozell said these people "constitute a considerable part" of phoneless farm homes.

This was immediately debunked by Gordon Persons, president of the Alabama Public Service Commission, who was not impressed by businessmen "who throw up their hands in holy horror" at the sight of the federal government. As of January 1, 1949, Southern Bell had 45,750 applications for farm phones in Alabama alone. "More than you can say grace over," Persons put it. Southern Bell's back orders in its eight-state territory totaled more than 300,000. Persons concluded that if Bell and the independents in more than forty years' operations, "put telephones in less than seven percent of our [Alabama] farm homes, I think they must realize something else must be done."

Bell finally agreed to "support" an amendment that would have prevented the REA from going into an area covered by a phone franchise, regardless of whether the residents had phones or prospects of obtaining them. Of Bell and the independents supporting this amendment, Hill said: "Their interest lies in preserving a monopoly in all the rural areas of the United States. This is the same dog-in-the-manger attitude taken by the commercial power companies when the rural electrification program was first established. These companies regarded rural America as their own green pastures to be electrified when and how they saw fit."

Hill won. Congress put the Rural Electrification Administration into the phone business, and as a result more than 80 percent of U.S. farm homes now have telephones. Bell survived the competition.

Now that the independents are not a competitive threat, they find most of the fire gone from Bell's breath. Bell's attitude toward these companies—and they shall not be called "competitors" for the same reason I wouldn't call Paraguay a "competitor" of the United States in hemispheric politics—is officially and genuinely cooperative.

One reason is that the independents, because of the strikingly grass-roots nature of minute business operations, are effective lobbying partners in the state legislatures. In Texas, for instance, the Southwestern Bell Telephone Company generally permits one of the small independents to do the talking when there is dangerous legislation to be butchered, on the assumption that lawmakers look more kindly on the interests of the Dripping Springs Telephone Company than they do on those of AT&T.

The 2,050-odd independents, as of 1968, have 10,760 exchanges covering a shade more than half of the United States' geographic area, and their 17,100,000 phones are almost the total of those in Britain and France combined. (Bell, with the remaining half of the country, has more than five times as many phones.) The independents range in size from General Telephone of California, which has 1,750,000 phones, mostly in Los Angeles suburbs, down to the Myrtle Telephone Company of Thayer, Missouri, whose 160 phones produced a net income of $1,773 in 1965, the last year reported.

As delightful contrast with the era when little more than the game and fish laws protected the independents from the

American Telephone & Telegraph Company, the keynote speaker at the 1965 convention of the United States Independent Telephone Association was H. I. Romnes, then AT&T president.

5

———•◆•———

He thought that we could readily find practices
that we might agree to have enjoined with no real
injury to our business. . . . He said if we tried we
could certainly find things of that sort that could
be used as a basis for a consent decree.

*—AT&T vice-president reporting Attorney General
Herbert Brownell's suggestion on how Bell could
find a gentleman's solution to the federal antitrust suit against its tie with Western Electric*

———•◆•———

THE American Telephone & Telegraph Company views the
inauguration of a Democratic Administration in Washington
with the trepidation of a farmer watching small boys walk
toward his field of ripe watermelons.

And with good reason, for the scant regulatory troubles
AT&T has experienced with the federal government have come
when the Democrats have been in power: Justice Department
challenges to the Bell patents during the Cleveland Administration; the temporary federalization of the Bell properties
during the last months of the First World War; establishment
of the Federal Communications Commission in 1934, under
President Franklin Roosevelt; and, finally, the only significant
probe of AT&T during the FCC's first thirty years of existence,
from 1935 to 1938.

But the worst AT&T scare—one which was never realized—
was provoked by the Truman Administration in an antitrust
suit initiated in 1949. The suit asked that the Bell System be
forced to yield ownership of the Western Electric Company, its
wholly owned combination of a personal manufacturing empire and quartermaster corps.

Western Electric is an operation unique in American industry. It has one master, AT&T, and one principal customer, AT&T. Western Electric manufactures every telephone used by Bell subscribers. Western Electric wire is strung over poles provided by Western Electric and connects telephones through switchboards made by Western Electric. The relationship is cradle to grave: When outdated phone equipment is scrapped, it goes to the Nassau Smelting and Refining Company, Inc., on Staten Island, AT&T's private junkyard, where the metal is reclaimed and sold at a profit.

Because of these myriad activities and its possession of the most lucrative captive market in the history of business, Western Electric is predictably and lushly profitable. During 1968 Western Electric had sales of $4,050,757,000, of which $3,374,871,000 were to the Bell System. (Military and other government contracts accounted for $539,674,000 of the non-Bell sales.)

The methods AT&T used to fend off the antitrust action during the years 1949–52, when the Democrats controlled Washington and how AT&T ultimately was handed an acceptable settlement by a friendly Republican Administration constitute a casebook on the application of corporate power.*

Here is the type of cooperation which the GOP gave AT&T: AT&T officials wrote letters that a Secretary of Defense signed, begging the Justice Department to soft-pedal the suit. Attorney General Herbert Brownell, within six months after he took office, listened to entreaties of AT&T officials in the comfortable privacy of White Sulphur Springs, Virginia, the spa of American big business, and in the Washington hotel suite of a powerful New York banker. Brownell put "prosecution" of the suit in the hands of a lawyer with negligible antitrust experience, who told colleagues he thought the entire thing was "silly, unwise, even evil." (At hearings Celler accused him of acting as an "advocate" for AT&T.) The Justice Department accepted at face value AT&T submissions on key issues in the suit without doing an hour's legwork of its own, despite the

---

* Details of the AT&T campaign were painstakingly amassed by Representative Emanuel Celler, the New York Democrat, during a two-year study of the Justice Department's antitrust activities by his Antitrust Subcommittee of the House Judiciary Committee. The subcommittee's report was given to Congress on January 30, 1959. References hereafter shall be to the Celler committee or the Celler hearings.

pleas of key antitrust division staff members that the Bell System's information should be verified. The Federal Communications Commission contributed a letter which an FCC representative later conceded to Celler was a "misrepresentation" and a "one-sided" view of the effectiveness of the regulatory agencies which have jurisdiction over AT&T. And, finally, AT&T lawyers wrote seven of the nine points in a consent decree which the Justice Department had a federal judge approve to conclude the case.

The Republicans' out-of-court settlement of the suit—which Celler called a "blot on the enforcement history of the antitrust laws"—left intact AT&T's parenthood of Western Electric. More important, AT&T avoided having to give in court the answers to such possibly embarrassing questions as:

—Whether AT&T, through its controlled supplier mechanism, retards the development of telephony by keeping innovations from the market until a Bell System bookkeeper says all possible dollars have been squeezed from existing equipment.

—Whether Western Electric uses fiscal sleight of hand in determining the prices it should charge AT&T for equipment. The higher the price, the higher the value of the plant upon which AT&T can demand a fixed percentage of return from regulatory agencies. Excessive profits for Western Electric are immaterial, since the money stays in the family.

—Whether operational efficiency, a contribution to the U.S. defense effort, and general professions of virtue entitle AT&T to exemption from the antitrust laws under which all other U.S. businesses must operate.

Western Electric dates to 1856, when the Western Union Telegraph Company purchased and consolidated several small firms which manufactured its telegraphic equipment. Elisha Gray, Alexander Graham Bell's old patent rival, had an interest at one time, and he was one of five principals when Western Electric was incorporated under that name in Chicago in 1872. During the period when Western Union competed with Bell in the telephone field, Western Electric developed and obtained patents for several key pieces of telephone equipment; it originated, for example, the first switchboard which utilized inner wiring rather than the manual connections made by a human operator. Because of its combined telephone and telegraph activities, Western Electric by 1879 was the largest electrical equipment manufacturer in the United States, with the most skilled inventors and workmen, the biggest physical plant, and a superior internal organization.

The Bell-Western Union patent fight settlement of 1879 reduced drastically Western Electric's telephone business; simultaneously, the peace made possible the marriage of Bell and Western Electric.

In 1880, when Theodore N. Vail became president of the American Bell Telephone Company, predecessor to AT&T, he set about creating a three-legged monopoly. One leg was American Bell's financial control of its operating companies in various regions; another was its long lines department, which melded the individual companies into a nationwide system by providing long-distance service. The third leg was somewhat more involved. Vail wanted a private supplier of telephones to ensure uniformity of equipment throughout the system and to give the parent company the manufacturing profits that then went to outsiders. American Bell at first had used as its supplier the little Boston machine shop where Alexander Graham Bell recruited Thomas A. Watson, later adding other manufacturers under licensing agreements when the demand for telephones increased. Vail disliked this arrangement. He wanted a manufacturer answerable solely to Bell, not to the entire telephone industry. That Western Electric was best in the field was enough to alert his attention; its ownership of basic patents on the multiple switchboard, essential to the development of large telephone exchanges, also made Western attractive.

Vail began buying Western Electric stock at about the same time financier Jay Gould started his fight for control of Western Union. Mindful of Western Union's holdings in Western Electric and fearful of any financial deal involving Gould, small Western Electric shareholders snapped up every dollar Vail offered for their stock, until he gained a controlling interest for American Bell.

Soon thereafter, on February 26, 1882, Western Electric and American Bell signed a manufacturing contract unique in American business, one that is still at the core of AT&T's monopoly of the telephone industry. The contract gave Western Electric the exclusive right to manufacture telephones under patents owned and controlled by American Bell. It restricted Western Electric from selling any telephone gear—whether covered by its own patents or those of Bell—to anyone but American Bell. Also, American Bell received the right to dictate both design and prices.

American Bell's subsidiary operating companies were not obligated—in so many words—to buy everything from Western Electric, but American Bell required them to use equipment built according to American Bell specifications—and the specifications, because of the patents, could be met only by Western Electric. In return, American Bell was required to cancel the contracts it had maintained since the 1870's with the other small telephone equipment manufacturers.

Predictably, the combination proved a success—so much so that AT&T feared the size of the profits would attract the unfavorable attention of the trust-wary federal government. When Western Electric issued profit and annual sales figures to the public in 1906, AT&T quickly warned it not to be so talkative. "The Western Electric Company is making too much money," AT&T president F. P. Fish wrote the Western head, E. M. Barton, "and at the present time it would be enormously harmful to that company and to our general interests if it were known what its profits were. I trust that there will be no information given until matters are in better [sic] shape. . . . I think it well for you to destroy this letter."

This antitrust nervousness caused AT&T to revise its contract with Western Electric in 1908 to permit Western to sell equipment to companies not a part of the Bell System. The decision wasn't altogether altruistic. Bell wanted the independent companies to achieve uniformity of equipment so that their take-over by Bell would be simplified. Technology had expanded the long-distance market by permitting conversations to be transmitted with clarity for hundreds of miles. By connecting with the independents and giving them standardized equipment, Bell increased its long-distance income. Finally, by going into direct competition with small manufacturers, Western Electric began squeezing them out of the market.

With its guaranteed market—one that became more firm as Bell gradually eliminated the independents—Western grew rapidly. Between 1896 and 1906 alone its sales went up 1,000 percent, from $6,000,000 to more than $630,000,000. Its assets, $1,114,000 when incorporated in 1882, by 1936 had soared to $203,099,000.

Western spawned litters of subsidiary special-function companies for its nontelephone activities—Teletype machines, movie sound equipment, and vacuum tubes essential to the fledgling radio industry, to name a few.

Time and again Western followed the acquisitive nature of the parent AT&T when an outside supplier manufactured an item needed by The System. During the 1920's Bell was forced to buy its telephone booths from the Turner Armour Company of Chicago, which owned a key patent on a folding door. Bell told Turner Armour in 1929 to begin a multifold expansion of production but refused to guarantee that it would buy an increased number of booths. Turner Armour was unwilling to run the financial risk (not many people other than Bell have any use for telephone booths) and thus was amenable to selling when Bell came around again. It is now a branch of Western Electric.

Attempts at competition by other manufacturers were parried with subtle methods. In 1910 General Electric and Westinghouse Electric Corporation purchased Western Electric's sizable power equipment branch. The sales contract said nothing about GE and Westinghouse's abandoning the telephone equipment field, which both had recently entered. But an FCC study stated later that "it is significant that neither ever has manufactured telephones or telephonic equipment" since 1910.

The propriety of the AT&T-Western relationship was prominent among the questions studied during the FCC's investigation of the 1930's. Bell officials obligingly supplied carloads of documents about Western—the bulk of which proved surprisingly uninformative. The FCC staff found that not only did Western Electric not know its actual manufacturing costs on equipment, but it seemed to go out of its way to avoid ascertaining them even for internal accounting purposes.

Commissioner Paul A. Walker, chief of the FCC's telephone division, who headed the probe, wrote of the problem:

All efforts to obtain manufacturing costs of Western materials constituting the plant of a telephone company have been thwarted. . . . It is significant of [AT&T's] policy that the Western Electric Company is perhaps the only large manufacturer which keeps no records of the cost of sales, and maintains such a voluminous, intricate and unreliable mass of records and estimates as a substitute for a cost accounting system that the determination of true and actual costs is an impossibility.

Unable to find what it wanted from Western, Walker and the staff used another investigative technique.

The staff members—302 of them at the peak of the probe—studied the costs of independent telephone equipment companies making similar apparatus and then drew comparisons. They found some significant price differentials.

Western had a piece part price (the price of an individual component of telephone equipment) for most items that was considerably lower than that of independent manufacturers. Yet when the parts were assembled into a complete unit, the independents' price was 13 to 19 percent lower, depending on the type of equipment involved. The disparity resulted from diametrically dissimilar pricing policies: Western simply added up the piece part prices, tacked on an engineering charge, and made the total its selling price to the Bell operating companies. The independents, as is typical with most manufacturers, would sell a complete unit at a lower price. (A person who buys a 1968 Chevrolet part by part from a supply house is certainly going to pay more than the man who drives a complete car away from a dealer.)

On a few piece parts, Western Electric's prices were markedly higher than the independents: 17 percent on hand telephone sets; 25 percent on pay stations; 35 percent on fuses and cable terminals.

The overall Western Electric price structure had suspicious nooks and crannies. Between 1930 and 1933 many of the state regulatory agencies took the position that reproduction costs of telephone equipment, rather than the original cost, would be used as the basis for evaluating a telephone plant for rate-making purposes. Western chose this period to increase its prices an average 30 percent, although concurrently the Depression caused other U.S. manufacturers to cut their prices.

Why would an increase be useful to AT&T? Suppose a switchboard's original cost was $1,000, and the Bell company was permitted a 6 percent return on its plant. The switchboard, under original cost regulation, would return $60 per year. But under reproduction cost regulation, Bell could increase the switchboard's value on its books to what it would have to pay for a new one—say $1,300, to use the average—

and the annual return would become $78 (6 percent of $1,300). Projected throughout the entire Bell System, this price juggling made possible astronomical increases in AT&T revenues.

Walker concluded the various overcharging techniques enabled AT&T to inflate the "value" of its operating companies by more than $300,000,000, resulting in unwarranted extra costs to phone subscribers of about $51,000,000 a year. He estimated that Western could cut its prices on sales to Bell by approximately 37 percent and still earn a yield of 6 percent on its investment.

Finally, he said there was no doubt that Western Electric enjoyed a "monopolistic position" in the telephone manufacturing field and found significant a statement by an AT&T vice-president in the 1930's that Western was "in a position to undersell any independent telephone manufacturing company in the country. . . . [And] it could put them out of business if that was the ethical thing to do." The only reason Western permitted the independents to survive, Walker said, was to dampen antitrust sentiment and to use selected prices of the independents as comparisons to justify its own costs. (Because of its captive consumers, Western had no sales overhead; thus, on some items it was able to show that it sold for less than the independents.) The overall result, Walker said, was that the American telephone users suffered financially because of the monopoly.

As solutions Walker suggested (1) regulating Western Electric as a public utility, with realistic limitations on its prices and profits, or (2) requiring AT&T to permit the operating companies to buy equipment through competitive bidding in which the independent manufacturers could participate.

AT&T attacked the report bitterly, calling it biased, inaccurate, and too flimsy to justify the degree of regulation advocated by Walker. AT&T lobbyists in Washington succeeded in removing much of Walker's acerbic language before the report was officially adopted and published with the imprimatur of the entire FCC. However, AT&T could not rebut Walker's factual data, which remained in the report.

Unfortunately for Walker and the FCC, the report was published at a politically inopportune time—June 14, 1939, when official Washington's attention was jerked away from domestic matters by the oncoming Second World War. The report was consigned to governmental limbo, and Walker's investigatory staff disbanded, many of the persons shifting to other federal agencies.

One of these men was Holmes Baldridge, who served as Walker's principal attorney, directing the gathering of information from AT&T, questioning witnesses during public hearings, drafting sections of the final report. Because of this insider's position, Baldridge quite possibly learned more about the inner workings of AT&T than did any single member of the staff.

Baldridge's interest in telephone matters continued after he joined the Justice Department's antitrust division as chief of the general litigation section. On separate occasions in late 1947 and early 1948, Baldridge received visitors with similar complaints—one the general counsel for the Tennessee Public Utilities Commission; the other a lawyer from the Minnesota Public Service Commission. Each attorney said, Baldridge reported, that his commission "had been unable to effectively determine the reasonableness of Western Electric's charges" on sales to Bell and thus could make only semieducated guesses at whether phone subscribers in their states paid fair prices.

The state officials asked Baldridge if something couldn't be done to open Bell equipment purchases to competitive bidding. The tenor of their conversations, as related by Baldridge, indicated clearly the state regulatory agencies had ascertained from the Bell operating companies that such bidding would in fact lower their equipment costs.

Baldridge agreed. He talked with his superior, Attorney General Tom C. Clark (later the U.S. Supreme Court Justice) who approved the drafting of an antitrust suit. Baldridge had one of his investigators, Elmo D. Flynt, also a Walker probe veteran, update the findings made in the 1930's and compile figures on Western's current control of the Bell System market.

On January 14, 1949, Baldridge went to court, choosing as the jurisdiction the U.S. District Court in Newark (because Western's chief manufacturing plant is in Kearny, close by). The seventy-three-page complaint charged Western and AT&T with "unreasonably restraining and virtually monopolizing" the production, sale, and installation of telephone equipment, in violation of the Sherman Antitrust Act. By doing so, the government said, the defendants fixed the types, quantities, and prices of equipment purchased and controlled Bell System plant investments and operating expenses which are the basis on which federal and state regulatory agencies must fix charges for local and long-distance service. The meat of the government's complaint was contained in these paragraphs:

> The absence of effective competition has tended to defeat effective public regulation of rates charged subscribers for telephone service since the higher the price charged by Western for telephone apparatus and equipment the higher the plant investment on which the operating companies are entitled to earn a reasonable return. The non-competitive prices of Western's manufactured products have the dual effect of increasing manufacturing profits and of raising telephone operating profits by inflating the rate bases of the Bell operating companies. Both increases accrue to the benefit of AT&T. The difference between the apparent and the real costs of telephone service represents hidden profits which are beyond the reach of public regulation.
>
> The defendants' triple monopoly of development, manufacture and sales markets of telephones, telephone apparatus and equipment has been so used as to delay and retard the introduction of improvements in the art of telephony, which would have made telephone service more efficient and less costly to the subscriber.

The suit asked twenty items of relief, but its major intentions can be summarized in three only: (1) that Western be divorced from AT&T and split into three competing manufacturing concerns; (2) that AT&T and its operating companies be compelled to buy equipment on a competitive basis, with every manufacturer entitled to submit bids; and (3) that the defendants be obliged to license their patents to all applicants on a nondiscriminatory and reasonable royalty basis and furnish the applicants with necessary technical assistance and know-how so that the patents might be put to use. (By opening up the Bell patents, the Justice Department sought to preclude AT&T from refusing to buy equipment from outsiders on the ground that it would not be compatible with that already in use in its system.)

In a statement after the filing, Attorney General Clark said:

> The chief purpose of this action is to restore competition in the manufacture and sale of telephone equipment now pro-

duced and sold almost exclusively by Western Electric at non-competitive prices. This, in turn, will lower the costs of such equipment and create a situation under which State and Federal regulatory commissions will be afforded an opportunity to reduce telephone rates to subscribers. The suit does not seek to interfere with the American Telephone & Telegraph Company except to separate it from Western Electric, and will not disturb the operating efficiency of telephone service in this country.

AT&T filed an answer on April 27, 1949, admitting it was in the telephone business but little else. There was no further contact between the parties until August 24, 1951, when the government asked AT&T to produce documents on some 100 subjects covered by allegations in the suit. And AT&T at this point made a basic policy decision: to fight the case out of court, rather than in a trial on the merits.

AT&T's first defensive ploy was to recruit the Defense Department—by girth and pocketbook the most powerful agency in Washington—as an ally against the rest of the U.S. government.

Dr. M. J. Kelly, president of the Bell Telephone Laboratories, Western and AT&T's jointly owned research arm, appealed directly to the then Secretary of Defense, Robert A. Lovett. Dr. Kelly maintained that a proper defense of the case would require key AT&T and Western officials to be taken off military projects essential to conduct of the Korean War. Without making any independent investigation of the validity of AT&T's claims, Lovett had his staff draft a letter to the Justice Department adopting the AT&T position and asking a postponement. Lovett let AT&T lawyers "review" the letter before sending it to the Acting Attorney General, Philip Perlman.

Perlman refused, saying that to halt the case "would seem to mean a rather premature abandonment of the government's efforts to terminate acts by the defendants it believes are in violation of the antitrust laws and detrimental to the people of the country. . . ." The suit, Perlman added, "could very well be handled satisfactorily by the attorneys on both sides of the litigation."

AT&T, still working through the agreeable Lovett, kept trying. It reduced its request for an "indefinite" suspension to two years, then to eighteen months. Then came the election of

Dwight D. Eisenhower, and action stopped in the case, pending the change of administrations. Baldridge resigned and went into private law practice in Chicago.

Not wanting to waste its groundwork, AT&T lobbyists wrote a memorandum for the departing Lovett to leave for his successor. The paper told why it would be good for the Defense Department to continue supporting AT&T in the case. Lovett signed it in "substantially the same form" as it was submitted (in the words of a Bell lawyer).

During the 1952 campaign Republican orators complained loudly about the "persecution of business" under preceding Democratic administrations and promised a different attitude in Washington if General Eisenhower was elected. Shortly after the inauguration, Attorney General Herbert Brownell, in several speeches and interviews, expressed displeasure with the antitrust cases his office inherited from the Democrats and promised a thorough review of them.

H. S. Dumas, AT&T vice-president and the attorney responsible for the antitrust defense, heard Brownell's views with interest. He decided to present AT&T's case to Brownell personally, and in doing so, he didn't waste his time with appointment secretaries or administrative assistants or even the Justice Department lawyers assigned to the case. He called Bayard Pope, board chairman of the Marine Midland Corporation, a major New York bank, and also a director of the New York Telephone Company, one of the larger AT&T operating companies. Dumas knew that Pope was personally acquainted with the Attorney General.

Asked by Representative Celler why he chose this route, rather than a direct approach to Brownell, Dumas replied, "I thought it would be very preferable if someone Mr. Brownell knew introduced him to me."

Rep. Celler: Why?

Mr. Dumas: It seemed natural to me to want someone to sort of let one know you are who you say you are and that you are a decent, reasonable sort of fellow.

Pope arranged a meeting for Dumas and Brownell in mid-April, 1953. The setting befit "decent, reasonable" fellows—lunch in Pope's suite in the Statler Hotel in Washington.

Dumas made a strong plea for dismissal. He asserted the suit was unwarranted, would disrupt the Bell System's effectiveness, and would hamper the Korean War effort. To the Celler committee Dumas denied that Pope showed any signs of "having any heavy personal influence with Brownell" and also maintained the Attorney General made no commitments at the meeting.

"You know," Dumas told Representative Celler, "Mr. Brownell is one of the most uncommunicative men I ever had any dealings with."

Dumas did admit he told Brownell that "if any suits were dismissed, certainly this was one that should be because . . . the prosecution of it would hurt very badly the telephone and communications using public of this country, and also would be very damaging to the defense of our country."

That AT&T, through Dumas, at this stage wanted *dismissal* of the suit outright, rather than an out-of-court *settlement* which would cause changes in its operations, was very significant, as later developments shall reveal.

AT&T's next overture to Brownell came at the Greenbrier Hotel in White Sulphur Springs, West Virginia, where it isn't uncommon for golf foursomes to have combined assets of a billion dollars and where the seclusion is ideal for businessman-to-businessman conversation. (Some key meetings in the electrical manufacturers' price-fixing cases took place at the Greenbrier.) AT&T's approach this time was by T. Brooke Price, AT&T vice-president and general counsel. The occasion was a judicial conference, which Price attended as the guest of a judge. Brownell was also there to give a talk on antitrust laws and to reveal his intention to appoint a commission to revise them. After Brownell finished the speech, Price went over to shake hands with him. Price give a lucid account of what followed in a memorandum Celler's investigators obtained from AT&T files:

> He [Brownell] remembered me and chatted for a moment, and I asked him if I might have a talk with him before he left. On the following day, June 27, I called his cottage and he invited me to come up to see him. He was occupying alone the manager's cottage on the hill above the hotel. He came out on the porch to meet me and we sat on the porch and talked for 25 minutes. Nobody else was present or near.

...d seen Brownell, "and I don't consider myself a very im-
...ressive looking man, and I thought maybe the Attorney
...eneral might have forgotten me by this time." Brownell,
...cording to Dumas, refused to consider outright dismissal, but
...d Justice and AT&T should begin talks toward a "possible
...osition."

...At first blush Brownell's stance on nondismissal might be
...sidered a disfavor to AT&T. It wasn't. The Justice Depart-
...t's willingness—even insistence—that AT&T take a consent
...ee by giving up the "harmless items" as suggested by
...nell was the most valuable possible outcome of the suit,
... Bell's viewpoint. The consent decree would give legal
...ion to the AT&T-Western Electric relationship—an um-
... to shield their marriage from court action by a latter-
...ttorney General who might be more interested in trust-
...g than was Brownell.

...expedite the settlement, Brownell took the case away
...Barnes, Kramer, and other experienced antitrust lawyers
...t it in charge of his "confidential assistant," Edward A.
...who had held a number of government legal jobs since

...assignment puzzled the antitrust division. Foote had
...ied an antitrust case, and he admitted to Celler's com-
...hat his experience in this highly specialized field was
...y much." AT&T attorneys soon realized the abilities
...ian the Justice Department put in charge of one
...ggest antitrust suits ever brought under the Sherman
...ote came into this thing cold from the outside," said
... Price. "He did not know anything about our case
...d not know anything much about the antitrust divi-
...." At large meetings Foote was lost, and Price re-
...e indicated to us he would like to get a more in-
...wn-to-earth contact with this case and generally an
...y to talk it out in an informal way." So Foote
...ce to his Washington home for dinner one cold
...ening in 1956.

...ing was an extraordinary one. Foote told Price that
...confidence in the government's case and that he
...as "silly" to consider going to trial. Foote volun-
...he government had the "wild idea" of submitting
... judge on a set of agreed facts. Foote told Price
...arnes, the antitrust division chief, had never ruled

I had brought with me the memorandum we had recently filed with Judge Barns [head of the antitrust division] presenting our arguments for dismissal of the case; and at this time the policy of the company was to insist on dismissal and not to discuss settlement. I asked Mr. Brownell whether he had seen the memorandum and offered to leave a copy with him to read. He told me that he had read it, was quite familiar with it, and considered it an excellent piece of work.

I then made a number of statements about the injury the case threatened to our efficiency and progress as a communications company and to our contribution to the national defense, told him that under the previous administration we had temporized by asking for postponement only, but that we were hopeful that he would see his way clear to have the case dropped. He hesitated over this a bit and then asked me to give him the particular items sought in the prayer for relief. I did this in general terms, not having a copy of the complaint.

He reflected a moment and said in substance that a way ought to be found to get rid of the case. He asked me whether, if we reviewed our practices, we would be able to find things we are doing which were once considered entirely legal, but might now be in violation of the antitrust laws or questionable in that respect. He went on to say that he would be surprised if in a business such as ours things of this sort did not exist. The interpretation of the antitrust laws had changed and the courts had very different views today about many business practices from the earlier opinions. Consequently, he thought that we could readily find practices that we might agree to have enjoined with no real injury to our business.

I told him we had thought about the matter but I was not prepared at the moment to say that we could proceed in that fashion. He said if we tried we could certainly find things of that sort that could be used as a basis for a consent decree. (I noted carefully that here for the first time he was specific in using the term "consent decree.") He was now so specific that I felt I had to go one way or the other and I did not feel at liberty to weaken on what I understood to be our position at the time. I said that our management had not been willing to so admit that any injunction ought to be entered against the company, but they felt that the case ought to be dropped. He said, "I don't think that's a very sensible attitude for them to take." I said, "They are sensible people, and they will give this matter further consideration. . . ."

As I got up to go he walked down the steps with me and repeated his statement that it was important to get this case disposed of. He said the President would understand this also and that if a settlement was worked out he could get the President's approval in five minutes.

As I was leaving, I reminded him that we had applied to Judge Barnes to have the case dismissed, and I said that I assumed it would be all right if we did not hear from Judge Barnes in the near future to get in touch with him to find out what was to be done. He said that was right.

Price confessed later that Brownell didn't seem to know much about the case and the issues and evidence involved. "I doubt if he ever made a detailed study of it during my time because I got the impression that he was leaving the thing pretty well to the antitrust division and was doing no more than giving us a *little friendly tip* as to how we might approach them to get something started in the way of negotiation."

Brownell, then, was proposing that AT&T consent to a decree that would save a bit of face for the government and that also would preclude obtaining the basic relief sought originally by the government—AT&T divestiture of Western Electric.

The Celler committee said Brownell's actions denoted:

partiality towards the defendants incompatible with the duties of his public office. It may be added that it hardly is in keeping with the ethics of the legal profession for an Attorney General—who is entrusted with the responsibility for all litigation brought by the United States—to give his adversary a "friendly little tip" to approach the Justice Department with a proposal whose acceptance would prove harmless to his clients.

Understandably, AT&T wasted little time in responding to the Attorney General's "friendly little tip." As soon as Price reported home, Dr. Kelly of Bell Labs met with Secretary of Defense Charles Wilson and his deputy, Roger M. Kyes, and asked them to lobby the Justice Department on Bell's behalf for a settlement which would not involve divestiture of Western Electric. Kyes asked Dr. Kelly to write a memorandum saying why Defense should be interested in the case. Whereupon Dr. Kelly produced the paper "with the thought in mind

that it could be used" as a statement of the Department.

That is exactly what Defense Secretary Wilson letter to Brownell on July 10. Wilson made only changes—the word "would" was changed to "it ap at one point, and a redundant phrase about pr Bell System was deleted in favor of a clause abo potential hazard to national security [*i.e.,* the can be removed or alleviated."

The letter in no place identified the actual unaware, the Secretary of Defense had mad study of a situation and offered his opinion committee noted, the Pentagon "uncriticall championed the view of the public interest urged upon the government by self-intereste defendant [in the action]." As Celler brough

REP. CELLER: So that in a certain sense, yo ghostwriter for the Department of Defense that?
DR. KELLY: To the extent that they use that Mr. Kyes asked me to prepare, that

AT&T's maneuver, however, was so t trust division staff that it gave scant co tagon letter. Insofar as these lawyers we remained that of either trying the case sought in the original petition. "The a ing Judge Barnes, was rather cyn Defense Secretaries seeking postpo cases," said Victor H. Kramer, attorneys.

Kramer at this time didn't know tween Brownell and AT&T—con working staff most intimately invo direct orders from Brownell, Bar antitrust attorneys didn't move t rapidly as AT&T desired.

Thus, again AT&T went to th more arranging a luncheon in t mas and the Attorney General set up this second meeting bec

out dismissal, but that Victor Kramer, an assistant, was insisting that he would rather dismiss the case than "take a weak decree." Foote admitted telling Price these things because "I thought he would be interested" (and indeed Price was) and asserted, "I saw no reason for not telling him."

Representative Celler disagreed. "If any man in my office would take that attitude—and I have a pretty busy law office in New York, Mr. Foote—and I would ask him to confer with the attorney for the defendant in the case, and right off the bat he said it was silly to try this case, I wouldn't keep that counsel . . . five minutes."

In its formal report the Celler committee said that Foote's disclosures:

> had the effect of seriously undermining the government's bargaining position at the negotiating table. It stands to reason that when the chief government negotiator tells the other side that he has no sympathy with the case, and that from his standpoint it is silly to consider trial, most unusual would be the counsel who, so forewarned, did not hold out for a more favorable settlement than he might otherwise be willing to accept.

Even the GOP minority on the committee said it felt Foote to be "guilty of an indiscretion."

The pace now began to quicken. Bayard Pope once again took Dumas to Brownell—this time at the Justice Department—and the Attorney General promised a disposition of the case "as quickly as possible." Foote served as expediter. At his request AT&T wrote a memorandum outlining the pros and cons of the various settlement possibilities and hand-carried it to him. In a staff memo an AT&T lawyer wrote, without identifying the source of his information, "We have reason to believe, but have no official knowledge," that Foote urged Brownell and Judge Barnes to settle "along the lines set forth" in the AT&T paper. Such a decree began taking place in the fall of 1955.

First, however, came a display of AT&T's friendship with the Federal Communications Commission. For the record, Brownell directed his staff to solicit FCC views on the effect of divestiture on rates. Kramer, for one, thought this a waste of time. FCC professional staff members displayed uneasiness

at even discussing the subject when approached by Justice
Department lawyers.

Kramer testified:

> In addition to that, I was aware that the chairman of the
> commission, Mr. [George C.] McConnaughey, had been asso-
> ciated as counsel for the Ohio Bell Telephone Company, and
> I was afraid that his experience with that company, coupled
> with this vague apprehension that the [FCC] staff showed to
> me when I visited them, would result in an answer which
> would perhaps not fully reflect the views that the staff had, and
> might reflect the views of the telephone company. . . . Stating
> it most briefly, I thought that the answer was a foregone con-
> clusion, and that not too much weight should be given to it.

AT&T's Washington lobbyist, Horace P. Moulton, got to
work on the FCC. "I discussed with them [the commissioners]
the effect that divorcement of Western Electric would have on
telephone service," he said. "The primary matter discussed
with them was the effect that the divorcement of Western from
The System would have on their authority and on all regulatory bodies with respect to the control of Western's prices and
profits." (Moulton's statement is puzzling as it stands, for *no
agency,* federal or state, has effectively controlled Western's
prices and profits.)

Celler was unable to fathom to his satisfaction the depth of
Moulton's influence with the FCC. The FCC referred the Justice Department's query to its Common Carrier Bureau, which
has jurisdiction over AT&T matters. The bureau, after study,
concluded that the issue of divestiture was a legal question, not
a regulatory matter, and made a justifiable plea of ignorance.

The bureau said that the "principal matter, namely, the
effect of divestiture on prices for telephone . . . equipment was
just something we had not sufficient information on to enable
us to address ourselves to the question at all." In this letter the
bureau confined itself to divestiture and did not go into another area in which it did possess considerable information—
the reasonableness of the profits which Western Electric earned
as part of the Bell System. In a draft letter written for the
commission the bureau said only that if what AT&T had told
the Justice Department about the consequences of a breakup

were true, divestiture would have a "significant effect" on rate-making agencies.

The FCC rejected this draft as giving "too short shrift to the Attorney General" and directed Bernard Strassburg, bureau telephone expert since 1943, to prepare a more detailed reply.

Strassburg was ready, for his bureau in past years had voiced frequent concern about the Western-AT&T link. Because of his close and continuing study of AT&T finances, Strassburg perhaps knew more about Bell than any other man in official Washington. Only two months previously, for example, the Common Carrier Bureau had alerted the commission that Western's returns in 1950–54 raised a "regulatory question as to whether Western's prices to its sister companies of the Bell System may be unreasonable, and to the extent that they are or have been, whether the claimed investment and operating expenses of the operating companies for ratemaking purposes should be adjusted to eliminate any excessive Western profits."

Strassburg had this in mind when he wrote the new draft letter. He also had in mind the grossly inadequate staff the FCC then had assigned to regulation of AT&T—thirty-two persons, professional and clerical. But three members of the seven-man commission, including former Bell System attorney McConnaughey, bridled when these observations appeared in the draft letter. The interlineations show some of the editing done by the commission to distort completely the thrust of Strassburg's letter:

[It] would appear that adequate powers reside in the regulatory authorities to deal with the matter of Western's prices and profits, insofar as they may affect the investment and expenses of affiliated companies. It must be recognized, however, that the degree of effective regulation of these powers is largely dependent upon the resources of the respective regulatory agencies to examine and evaluate all of the matters necessary to an informed determination of the reasonableness of Western's prices and profits.

It will be recalled that the government initiated the antitrust action because two state regulatory agencies *could not* find out anything about Western's pricing policies. By removing Strassburg's qualifying sentence, the FCC misled the Justice Department. Strassburg said that the revised letter was a "misrepresentation" of the situation, that it lacked objectivity and omitted material facts "that ought to be there for the Attorney General to have before him." The editing helped Brownell and Foote build a formal record which would justify their acceptance of a weak settlement. The Celler committee said the FCC's deletions "reflect a singular receptivity to the AT&T point of view and a potent indifference to the public interest."

The FCC exchange marked the last mention of the word "divestiture" by Brownell, an abandonment that cut the heart from the suit. The decision staggered certain of the staff members. The three men most intimately involved in preparation of the case (excluding Foote, whose sole role was that of settlement) filed written memoranda of dissent—Kramer, Walter D. Murphy, head of the trial staff, and W. D. Kilgore, Jr., chief of the division's judgment and judgment enforcement section.

The Justice Department refused to let the Celler committee examine these documents, claiming executive privilege. Testifying from memory, Kramer said he objected to the Brownell-Foote settlement for these reasons:

—The Sherman Act condemns every scheme for interstate monopolization and does not distinguish between "good" and "bad" monopolies.

—Congress made no exception from the Sherman Act for manufacturers of telephone equipment.

—A decree failing to divorce Western from AT&T and otherwise limiting its role as exclusive supplier for the Bell System would not accomplish the objectives of the Sherman Act.

—No field examination had been made to test the AT&T contention that divestiture would result in higher phone costs.

—The major premise of the Sherman Act is that monopoly is contrary to the public interest and that competition ultimately produces more goods and lower prices. If this premise is erroneous for the manufacture of telephone equipment, Congress alone has the power to enact an exception, and it has not seen fit to do so.

—In the absence of a directive from the President that national defense considerations made trial of the case impossible, the Department of Justice was in no position to refuse to press the case in court.

—Should all these arguments fail to convince, dismissal of

the complaint without prejudice was preferable to a consent decree that would recognize Western Electric as a "chosen instrument of monopoly" and tie the hands of future Attorneys General by putting a cloak of legal sanctity over AT&T's shoulders.

If Brownell insisted on a consent decree, Kramer argued, it at least should have a time limit and provide for a reexamination of the facts after perhaps twenty years to determine whether the case should be reopened. Consent decrees without a time limit are subject to reopening only when there is evidence of gross or criminal violation of their provisions. AT&T, however, wasn't interested in anything with a time limit; it wanted protection in perpetuity, and that is what Brownell surrendered on behalf of the United States government.

Subsequently, Kramer refused to sign the consent decree, "because after a great deal of soul searching I did not see how I could sign it and remain consistent with the oath which every attorney takes when he joins the Department of Justice to support and defend and protect the Constitution and the laws of the United States adopted thereunder. . . ."

Brownell insisted to a Celler committee investigator during an interview that "everybody" who worked on the case recommended the consent decree and that he never heard a suggestion that any staff members opposed it. This claim is in direct contradiction to testimony by Foote, who stated that he and Barnes told Brownell "that the staff didn't agree" with the decree. Foote said, "This I am clear about." Since the Justice Department refused to give Representative Celler its files on the case, the discrepancy remains unresolved. (Brownell did not testify.)

Defending Brownell later, Judge Barnes argued that courts would not have upheld divorcement of AT&T and Western Electric. Staff members, however, were not so pessimistic. Both Kramer and Murphy expressed reasonable certainty they could win a favorable verdict in the U.S. Supreme Court, if not at the trial court level. But Brownell, by his decision to accept the consent decree, effectively removed the question from the jurisdiction of a court, choosing to substitute his own judgment for that of a court's determination of the actual facts and the application, if any, of the Sherman Act.

And so, on January 12, 1956, the AT&T and surviving government lawyers trooped into the U.S. District Court in Newark and presented the consent decree—the bulk of which was written by Bell lawyers—to Judge Thomas F. Meany for approval. In a situation where the lawyers on both sides have agreed on a settlement, a judge for practical reasons accepts it, and Judge Meany followed the rules. After a short discussion in chambers he mounted the bench and approved the consent decree.

The only section of the decree approaching antitrust significance was a requirement that Bell license existing and future patents to all applicants at reasonable royalties. Divestiture was not mentioned, nor was the government's original demand for competitive bidding on equipment by Bell System companies. Western Electric was also required to sell the Westrex Corporation, a subsidiary which manufactured sound-recording equipment for the movie industry and which contributed a minute portion of Western's annual income.

Brownell and other Justice Department spokesmen called the decree a "major victory" and "miraculous" for the government. Then more discerning observers examined the decree. *Business Week*, which by no means can be called anticapitalist, said in an analysis that what the government called a victory "turned out on second look to be hardly more than a slap on the wrist for the biggest corporation in the world."

AT&T was so pleased that executives had to strain to contain their delight. Frederick R. Kappel, then president of Western Electric and later to become head of AT&T, told a company meeting the decree "generally makes legal an integrated Bell System—and to that extent, it is my opinion we preserved the really important thing. In fact, we have good legal proof and a court order says it is OK—a long-posed question settled." On his copy of the decree Kappel scrawled the notation that the captive supplier system is "harmless from Sherman Antitrust Act because it is regulated legal monopoly."

The AT&T general staff, in explanations of the decree prepared for circulation among Bell System executives, gave assurances that revenues wouldn't be significantly reduced, that independent equipment manufacturers could not increase their share of the Bell market, that Western Electric would not change its policies on sales to independent phone companies, that the "operations that must be eliminated are not substantial."

All in all, Bell treated the decree as something of an insider's joke. Moulton, the Washington lobbyist, went through his copy of the order, scribbling in the margin such comments as "general prohibition against sin"; "nothing to undo, no intention and no need to do—boilerplate!" Another AT&T executive's marginal note included the telling summary: "It is only window dressing."

The only restraint on AT&T's jubilation was that of having to avoid acting like a victor, for that might cause American citizens to think a more vigorous government effort might have reduced their phone bills. As Kappel put it in an outline for a talk for Western Electric officials: "Use discretion in passing along. Don't brag about having won victory or getting everything we wanted. . . . Antitrust suit disposed of, but still have politicians, etc., to think of."

6

I don't think the President understands the bill. The damned Republicans and some Democrats are trying to give away public property. The public spent $25 or $30 billion developing satellites and the communications system ought to be publicly owned. The Republicans will give away everything if you don't watch them.

> —*Harry S. Truman, commenting on the Communications Satellite Act of 1962, which extended AT&T's monopoly into outer space*

IN 1961 an official of the Hughes Aircraft Company proposed giving the American public tangible benefits from the space program financed by its tax dollars. If Hughes were permitted to build a communications satellite system then on its drawing board, he said, station-to-station telephone calls could be placed to any spot on the globe for a dime. Hughes asked the federal government for permission to build such a system.

Whatever happened to the predicted dime phone calls?

The American Telephone & Telegraph Company persuaded Congress to bequeath it working control of America's communications satellites. AT&T did so by outpoliticking the astute political warriors who lobby for the aerospace industry and by pitting government agency against government agency in a refinement of the techniques learned in the smashing of the Western Electric antitrust suit of the 1950's. In accomplishing this, AT&T exhibited an astounding facility for strategic retreat and immediate counteradvance to even stronger new positions, its moves so swift and subtle that onlookers mistook tightly coordinated close-order drill for the innocence of a waltz. When the gyrations ended in Congress, AT&T's monopoly of the telephone industry had been strengthened with dollars furnished by the American taxpayer. As a smokescreen, AT&T used one part virtue and nine parts hokum—a mixture aromatic enough to beguile leading New Frontiersmen of the Kennedy Administration.

Consider the following statement to Congress by an AT&T official in explaining Bell's motives for wanting a share of the satellites:

> AT&T has no desire or intention of seeking to control the communications satellite system to its competitive advantage either in the provision of international communications or in the furnishing of equipment. Hard as it may be for some to understand, our sole interest is in the earliest practicable establishment of a worldwide commercial satellite system useful to all international communications carriers and agencies both here and abroad.

The carefully chosen words of AT&T display a misstatement —or a most unlikely misunderstanding—of a key issue in the dispute. Any number of communications and fiscal experts, both in and out of the government, argued that the tax-created satellites should be put to use in *domestic* service, as well as *international*, so that the American citizen who paid for them would enjoy reduced phone rates. The use of satellites to relay telephone, television, and radio signals thousands of miles in an instant was a milestone in the history of communications approximating Alexander Graham Bell's invention. Satellite capacity is relatively boundless. Its per unit cost of relaying messages is far below that of the submarine cables and radio-relay systems previously used in domestic and international long-distance telephony, even when the cost of putting a satellite into orbit is considered.

The question of who was to own, operate, and benefit from the satellites was resolved in a savage politico-economic conflict between strained, amorphous alliances of government agencies, communications companies, and the space industry. In a battle in which all sides stake an early claim to virtue, the participants must be judged by their actions, not by self-serving statements. And in this particular battle there is an immeasurable gulf between the actions and the words of AT&T's Super Government.

The idea of using satellites to carry man's messages around the world is almost as old as the idea of satellites themselves. In 1945, twelve years before the launching of the first Sputnik by the Soviets and at a time when few people could envision anything in space other than stars, AT&T scientist Arthur C. Clarke discussed a satellite communications system in a British technical publication. The Bell Telephone Laboratories, the research arm of AT&T and the Western Electric Company, began experimentation in the 1950's, recognizing even then: (1) the potential profits to be reaped from space-borne telephone and communications services and (2) the threat to its monopoly position, were another company to be first to plant an ensign in space.

From the beginning, the overwhelming percentage of the research and development was done by the government as an adjunct to its space program. AT&T, despite its proficiency with communications gear on the ground, lacked the essential first step in satellite communications: putting a satellite into orbit.

The Army Signal Corps has credit for the first crude space talk. In 1946 it bounced radio signals against the moon and received them on earth, proving that relatively low power could transmit signals over a great distance. In 1958 the Air Force transmitted the first actual "voice" from space. Its SCORE satellite carried aloft a taped recording containing President Eisenhower's Christmas message and, on signal, played it to the nation.

The third "first," however, belongs neither to the government nor to the multibillion-dollar space and communications corporations. In February, 1960, two teen-age radio enthusiasts bounced code signals between New York City and Bethesda, Maryland, by reflecting them off either Explorer VII or Sputnik III, both soaring over the Atlantic Seaboard—the first point-to-point reflective two-way communication via an artificial satellite.

The same accomplishment, on a much more scientific and elaborate scale, was carried out later that year using Echo I, an artificial moon consisting of a balloon 100 feet in diameter, with a plastic skin one-quarter the thickness of a human hair. AT&T participated in experiments in which Echo I reflected messages across the United States (including more "Ike" remarks) and to England and France. In October, 1960, the Army put up Courier, a delayed repeater satellite, which stored on tape messages transmitted from the ground and repeated them on signal when it reached the listening party on the other side of the globe. To scientists, Echo and Courier were significant because they showed the feasibility of both active and passive communications satellites. These milestones also show that many agencies other than AT&T shared the development of the satellites.

From a commercial viewpoint, a satellite system was important because of the rapid rise in transoceanic communications. Overseas calls quadrupled in the decade preceding the advent of satellites, from 1,000,000 in 1950 to almost 4,000,000 in 1960. Communications experts estimated the volume at 20,000,000 annually by 1970, far beyond the capacity of existing systems. The presatellite traffic traveled over two systems: (1) radiotelephone circuits, scratchy and unreliable because the signals must be bounced off the ionosphere (an ionized section of the upper atmosphere) and (2) underwater coaxial cables, which cost $15,000 a mile and which are sorely limited in capacity.

In the early 1960's AT&T had fewer than 100 connections for the North Atlantic sector, busiest of all international routes and all the more congested because the six-hour London-New York time differential jammed the bulk of business calls into the 9 to 11 A.M. (U.S. time) period. Limited as was this capacity, however, it enabled the American telephone subscriber to talk with 98 percent of the world's telephones and 90 percent of those in Asia and Africa. AT&T international long-distance revenues soared from $6,606,000 in 1947 to $41,884,000 in 1960, the eve of the satellite debate in Congress. Telegraph carriers increased their international income at a lesser, but still healthy, rate, from $42,592,000 in 1947 to $84,212,000 in 1960.

Another reason for developing satellite communications rested in the capricious nature of the ionosphere, which at times bounced back radiotelephone signals with the crispness of a Ping-Pong service return and at other times soaked them up like a sponge, leaving international phones dead. Since the ionosphere owes its existence to radiation from the sun, its consistency varies from day to night, from season to season, and over an eleven-year cycle. Sunspots created by magnetic storms on the solar surface cause frequent disruptions of the ionosphere, limiting the amount of the radio spectrum that can be used for effective transmission. In addition, nuclear explosions foul up the ionosphere; the Atomic Energy Commission found that its 1958 test series adversely affected high-frequency radio traffic throughout the Pacific and completely blanked out the area around Johnston Island, the detonation point. AT&T and the telegraph carriers sought to avoid these atmosphere handicaps with the underwater cables but saw the impossibility of laying them fast enough to match the increase in traffic.

Yet satellites alone were of no value in overcoming these transmission difficulties. Receiving reflected or retransmitted telephone messages or television programs in the home was impossible because of the high-powered sophisticated equipment required; to be of commercial value, satellite signals would have to connect into existing or new communications systems.

No company recognized this fact more keenly than did AT&T. And AT&T also recognized the threat to its monopoly position by the many aerospace firms conducting research in the field for the National Aeronautics and Space Administration (NASA). Drawing on lucrative government contracts, the aerospace industry had the financial resources to invest heavily in such research; further, because of their newness, these firms hadn't learned that it is not polite to compete with AT&T in any area involving communications.

Both AT&T and the aerospace industry had their collective eyes on the rich stakes. Dr. Elmer W. Engstrom, then a senior vice-president of the Radio Corporation of America, estimated satellite income at $1 billion per year by 1970. This figure represented a sevenfold increase over the 1960 revenues from international telephone and telegraph services, yet it was unrealistically low because it did not consider such things as transoceanic television and data transmission or adaptation of the satellite for domestic long-distance telephone calls.

At any rate, by the end of the 1950's the contestants knew the implications of control of a satellite system, and thus began the jockeying.

I had brought with me the memorandum we had recently filed with Judge Barns [head of the antitrust division] presenting our arguments for dismissal of the case; and at this time the policy of the company was to insist on dismissal and not to discuss settlement. I asked Mr. Brownell whether he had seen the memorandum and offered to leave a copy with him to read. He told me that he had read it, was quite familiar with it, and considered it an excellent piece of work.

I then made a number of statements about the injury the case threatened to our efficiency and progress as a communications company and to our contribution to the national defense, told him that under the previous administration we had temporized by asking for postponement only, but that we were hopeful that he would see his way clear to have the case dropped. He hesitated over this a bit and then asked me to give him the particular items sought in the prayer for relief. I did this in general terms, not having a copy of the complaint.

He reflected a moment and said in substance that a way ought to be found to get rid of the case. He asked me whether, if we reviewed our practices, we would be able to find things we are doing which were once considered entirely legal, but might now be in violation of the antitrust laws or questionable in that respect. He went on to say that he would be surprised if in a business such as ours things of this sort did not exist. The interpretation of the antitrust laws had changed and the courts had very different views today about many business practices from the earlier opinions. Consequently, he thought that we could readily find practices that we might agree to have enjoined with no real injury to our business.

I told him we had thought about the matter but I was not prepared at the moment to say that we could proceed in that fashion. He said if we tried we could certainly find things of that sort that could be used as a basis for a consent decree. (I noted carefully that here for the first time he was specific in using the term "consent decree.") He was now so specific that I felt I had to go one way or the other and I did not feel at liberty to weaken on what I understood to be our position at the time. I said that our management had not been willing to so admit that any injunction ought to be entered against the company, but they felt that the case ought to be dropped. He said, "I don't think that's a very sensible attitude for them to take." I said, "They are sensible people, and they will give this matter further consideration. . . ."

As I got up to go he walked down the steps with me and repeated his statement that it was important to get this case disposed of. He said the President would understand this also and that if a settlement was worked out he could get the President's approval in five minutes.

As I was leaving, I reminded him that we had applied to Judge Barnes to have the case dismissed, and I said that I assumed it would be all right if we did not hear from Judge Barnes in the near future to get in touch with him to find out what was to be done. He said that was right.

Price confessed later that Brownell didn't seem to know much about the case and the issues and evidence involved. "I doubt if he ever made a detailed study of it during my time because I got the impression that he was leaving the thing pretty well to the antitrust division and was doing no more than giving us a *little friendly tip* as to how we might approach them to get something started in the way of negotiation."

Brownell, then, was proposing that AT&T consent to a decree that would save a bit of face for the government and that also would preclude obtaining the basic relief sought originally by the government—AT&T divestiture of Western Electric.

The Celler committee said Brownell's actions denoted:

partiality towards the defendants incompatible with the duties of his public office. It may be added that it hardly is in keeping with the ethics of the legal profession for an Attorney General—who is entrusted with the responsibility for all litigation brought by the United States—to give his adversary a "friendly little tip" to approach the Justice Department with a proposal whose acceptance would prove harmless to his clients.

Understandably, AT&T wasted little time in responding to the Attorney General's "friendly little tip." As soon as Price reported home, Dr. Kelly of Bell Labs met with Secretary of Defense Charles Wilson and his deputy, Roger M. Kyes, and asked them to lobby the Justice Department on Bell's behalf for a settlement which would not involve divestiture of Western Electric. Kyes asked Dr. Kelly to write a memorandum saying why Defense should be interested in the case. Whereupon Dr. Kelly produced the paper "with the thought in mind that it could be used" as a statement of the Defense Department.

That is exactly what Defense Secretary Wilson did, in a letter to Brownell on July 10. Wilson made only two minor changes—the word "would" was changed to "it appears could" at one point, and a redundant phrase about preserving the Bell System was deleted in favor of a clause about how "this potential hazard to national security [*i.e.*, the antitrust suit] can be removed or alleviated."

The letter in no place identified the actual author. To the unaware, the Secretary of Defense had made an objective study of a situation and offered his opinion. As the Celler committee noted, the Pentagon "uncritically adopted and championed the view of the public interest that was being urged upon the government by self-interested, private parties defendant [in the action]." As Celler brought out:

> REP. CELLER: So that in a certain sense, you became a sort of ghostwriter for the Department of Defense? Would you say that?
>
> DR. KELLY: To the extent that they used the memorandum that Mr. Kyes asked me to prepare, that is correct.

AT&T's maneuver, however, was so transparent to the antitrust division staff that it gave scant consideration to the Pentagon letter. Insofar as these lawyers were concerned, their job remained that of either trying the case or achieving the relief sought in the original petition. "The antitrust division, including Judge Barnes, was rather cynical about letters from Defense Secretaries seeking postponement or settlement of cases," said Victor H. Kramer, one of the government attorneys.

Kramer at this time didn't know of the direct contacts between Brownell and AT&T—contacts which bypassed the working staff most intimately involved in the case. So lacking direct orders from Brownell, Barnes, Kramer, and the other antitrust attorneys didn't move the case toward settlement as rapidly as AT&T desired.

Thus, again AT&T went to the top, with Bayard Pope once more arranging a luncheon in the Washington Statler for Dumas and the Attorney General. Dumas said he asked Pope to set up this second meeting because it had been a year since he had seen Brownell, "and I don't consider myself a very impressive looking man, and I thought maybe the Attorney General might have forgotten me by this time." Brownell, according to Dumas, refused to consider outright dismissal, but said Justice and AT&T should begin talks toward a "possible disposition."

At first blush Brownell's stance on nondismissal might be considered a disfavor to AT&T. It wasn't. The Justice Department's willingness—even insistence—that AT&T take a consent decree by giving up the "harmless items" as suggested by Brownell was the most valuable possible outcome of the suit, from Bell's viewpoint. The consent decree would give legal sanction to the AT&T-Western Electric relationship—an umbrella to shield their marriage from court action by a latter-day Attorney General who might be more interested in trust-busting than was Brownell.

To expedite the settlement, Brownell took the case away from Barnes, Kramer, and other experienced antitrust lawyers and put it in charge of his "confidential assistant," Edward A. Foote, who had held a number of government legal jobs since 1939.

The assignment puzzled the antitrust division. Foote had never tried an antitrust case, and he admitted to Celler's committee that his experience in this highly specialized field was "not very much." AT&T attorneys soon realized the abilities of the man the Justice Department put in charge of one of the biggest antitrust suits ever brought under the Sherman Act. "Foote came into this thing cold from the outside," said T. Brooke Price. "He did not know anything about our case and he did not know anything much about the antitrust division either." At large meetings Foote was lost, and Price reported, "He indicated to us he would like to get a more informal down-to-earth contact with this case and generally an opportunity to talk it out in an informal way." So Foote invited Price to his Washington home for dinner one cold January evening in 1956.

The meeting was an extraordinary one. Foote told Price that he lacked confidence in the government's case and that he regarded it as "silly" to consider going to trial. Foote volunteered that the government had the "wild idea" of submitting the case to a judge on a set of agreed facts. Foote told Price that Judge Barnes, the antitrust division chief, had never ruled

In December, 1959, even before the success of the Echo experiment in which it participated, AT&T asked that NASA give it title to the entire satellite communications field.

James E. Webb, NASA administrator at the time, says AT&T told NASA in essence, "If we can sit down and agree as to the specifications for a communications satellite, we will build it and launch it, and become the instrument of the government if the government will provide us with all the franchises and other things necessary. So we will do the whole job with our own money."

AT&T estimated the cost at around $170,000,000. Webb, however, put the figure even higher: "Between $400 and $600 million is my guess or estimate as to about what somebody is going to have to spend in the way of capital investment and funds to do the interim operational job until you actually get going and begin to get the revenue in substantial amounts." (This sum did not include the billions spent by the federal government to develop the launchers that would put the satellites into space.) Since AT&T has only one source of revenue—the phone bills paid by its subscribers—somewhere around half a billion dollars would be posted by the telephone-using public. And because AT&T is permitted to include such expenditures in its rate base, regulatory agencies would have little choice but to permit its income to increase by commensurate amounts.

Two years later when AT&T tried to discourage other satellite aspirants, it belittled the value of such a system. "It shows a promise, but by no means an unqualified guarantee of success," an AT&T spokesman told Congress. One might legitimately ask if AT&T habitually risks $170,000,000 or more of its stockholders' money on uncertain ventures. The obvious answer is ample affirmation of the value everyone in the field placed on the satellites. And as Senators Russell Long and Estes Kefauver frequently asked: If the satellite system was useless, why did the AT&T lobby so strenuously struggle to obtain control of it?

NASA and the Eisenhower Administration gave long and hard scrutiny to the AT&T proposal. So did the aerospace firms, which howled lustily. NASA didn't think much of the idea. For one thing, the success of the U.S. space program in large part stemmed from the fact that NASA could draw on the best scientific minds of the nation; when companies must compete to win contracts, they work harder, and NASA benefits from the multitude of ideas produced by fresh and energetic minds. AT&T's Bell Labs possessed unquestioned scientific competence—but so did other companies.

Another factor was AT&T's contention that the satellites were a "communications," rather than a "space," program and thus in the legitimate province of a "communications" company. NASA disagreed. It also wanted to continue its policy of requiring competitive bidding on projects, to cut costs. So on behalf of the government it declined the AT&T proposal.

The seriousness of the NASA decision became immediately apparent to AT&T. On the first major satellite project after the ruling (for an active satellite that repeats, rather than reflects, signals) the Radio Corporation of America submitted the best proposal and received a $50,000,000 contract.

The rebuffed AT&T then attempted to bypass NASA. It went to the Federal Communications Commission, historically a friendly forum for Bell, and reiterated the same "communications program, not space program" argument already rejected by NASA. Again Bell's plan was audacious, for it proposed nothing less than exclusive occupation of outer space.

AT&T wanted to put 50 satellites into polar orbit at a 3,000-mile altitude. Bell estimated the cost at $170,000,000 for a system providing 600 telephone circuits, plus television, to about 13 world terminals. Because of the necessity of plugging into telephone systems abroad, AT&T offered to share ownership with foreign communications companies—but not with any in the United States. This proposal was markedly similar to the plan already turned down by NASA.

Privately, AT&T worked to change NASA's mind, arguing basically that the satellites were only a "new kind of telephone pole" and that they necessitated no changes in the basic structure of the existing communications industry. The Eisenhower Administration slowly came to heel—and with it came NASA.

In October, 1960, T. Keith Glennan, then NASA administrator, said, "Traditionally, communications services in this country have been provided by privately financed carriers competing with one another [an interesting, if factually questionable, interpretation of communications history] to serve the public interest under Federal controls and regulation. *There seems to be no reason* [emphasis added] to change that policy with the advent of communications satellites." Further, Glennan said, NASA should continue space communications research and development "only so long as necessary to assure that timely development of a commercially feasible communications system will be completed by private industry."

And "Ike," in his farewell address, gave his blessing to a policy favoring private development of a satellite system: "The government should aggressively encourage private enterprise in the establishment and operation of satellite relays for revenue-producing purposes."

The change of administrations, however, brought uneasiness to AT&T, for the company could not predict with certainty the type of ownership that the incoming Democrats might favor. It was at this point that Bell decided on a full-speed-ahead course that would make its space domination a *fait accompli* by the time the question of ownership came up for discussion. Here we encounter a suspicious coincidence of dates: On January 19, 1961, the same day President Kennedy took office, the FCC gave its first license for a privately owned communications satellite. The recipient was AT&T, which obtained permission to conduct communications across the Atlantic on an experimental basis with a 175-pound satellite at a 2,200-mile altitude. Bell would construct the satellite; NASA would launch it. This was Telstar, which was to attract so much favorable attention for Bell in the summer of 1962 during a critical stage of the debate over satellite control.

The continuing space communications work of the aerospace industry, meanwhile, irritated AT&T. The change of administrations definitely encouraged the space firms which had built satellite hardware and didn't share Bell's views that anything remotely connected with telephones was AT&T's private province.

The Lockheed Aircraft Corporation, for instance, began its space work in 1954 and by 1961 had emplaced more than 85 percent of the U.S. satellite payloads successfully orbited—twice the combined total of all other countries. Lockheed felt that ownership of a satellite chain should be shared among communications carriers and the space firms, arguing that the latter had made an essential contribution to the system and were as deserving of a share of the profits as was AT&T.

The General Electric Company, another major space supplier, set up a subsidiary, Communications Satellites, Inc., as a framework for a satellite operating company and suggested open ownership, with no firm permitted more than a 10 percent share, so as to preclude monopoly. In an FCC application GE's subsidiary asked permission to start regular satellite communications service, rather than the experimental service authorized for AT&T. The Hughes Aircraft Company, armed with a military contract, concentrated on a high-altitude satellite, Syncom, which would hover 22,300 miles over the earth in fixed position and handle twenty-two times the existing volume of long-distance telephone service in the United States. RCA worked on a similar satellite for NASA.

An observer unfamiliar with AT&T political capabilities might have mistaken all these churnings as symptoms of trouble for Bell's satellite aspirations. But the FCC, in three months of brisk, but brutal, hatchet work, cleaved away the competitive hopes of the aerospace firms.

The first step was to remove NASA from the communications field. NASA, needing work done on the communications problems astronauts would encounter in space, granted dozens of research contracts. Each time it did so, however, the aerospace firms put their feet deeper inside AT&T's territory, to the distress of AT&T. FCC member T. A. M. Craven, in Congressional testimony, described the problem as a "little misunderstanding." Some people within NASA disagreed with the FCC view that the entire field of space communications should be turned over to private industry. Dr. Werner von Braun suggested that space communications revenues be used to underwrite the astronaut flights and relieve citizens of a tax burden.

The dispute was solved by a "memorandum of understanding" between NASA and the FCC, signed on February 28, 1961, which restricted NASA to the technological phase of space communications development and put "implementation and utilization" policy in the hands of the FCC. In other words, NASA would supervise building of the system, but the FCC would make the key decision of who would use it and under what rules.

The FCC next issued a notice of inquiry into the administrative and regulatory problems that might arise in the operation of the system.* This action was significant in that it espoused

---

* The FCC issues a notice of inquiry to initiate a fact-finding proceeding aimed at setting policy in a particular area of communications.

the AT&T view that the satellites were "another variety of telephone pole" that should be integrated into existing communications. The FCC avoided the question of whether the satellites were in fact a new technology of such importance to the nation that they warranted a restructuring of the system and made clear that it intended to decide by itself who should own the government-developed resource. FCC chairman Newton Minow, questioned by Congress on the legal basis for the decision, replied that "our present statutory authority" gave the commission this prerogative.

The notice also adopted the AT&T position that satellites should be used for *international* communications only; not once did the word "domestic" appear in the order. The FCC invited response from any interested parties, including the Justice Department because of the antitrust problems that might arise by virtue of ownership of the system by more than one common communication carrier.

Justice responded with four conditions for the FCC's guidance: (1) that *"all interested communications common carriers"* be given a chance to share in ownership of the system; (2) that they be given unrestricted and nondiscriminatory access to the facilities, whether or not they chose to buy a share; (3) that "all interested parties engaged in the production and sale of communications and *related* equipment" be permitted to buy into the system; and (4) that they be given the opportunity to act as suppliers on a competitive basis.

The Justice Department said, "The satellite system can well revolutionize the communication industry by providing vastly expanded facilities for the transmission of telephone and telegraph service at substantially lower costs than exist today and may provide the means of disseminating [domestic] television programs." Thus, Justice felt the promotion of competition and the discouragement of monopoly vital in a new industry "so closely concerned with the national interest." Any plan failing to meet its conditions, particularly those on unrestricted ownership, "may be subject to abuse by the dominant party," Justice said. The department's antitrust chief, Lee Loevinger, said that "dominant party" meant AT&T and that the conditions were necessary if the systems were to be "consistent with the antitrust laws."

In its answer to the FCC notice of inquiry, AT&T displayed its desire to monopolize the system. Acting in concert with the

International Telephone & Telegraph Company, the largest U.S. international telegraph carrier (and no relative of AT&T, despite the similarity of name), AT&T insisted to the FCC that ownership be limited to international communications carriers, "such entities participating to a degree consistent with the relative use of the system."

Translated, this criterion meant that AT&T would own "maybe 80 percent" of the satellite firm, in the estimate of James E. Dingman, Bell System vice-president, who was the chief company spokesman before Congress during the Comsat (communications satellite) debates.

The General Telephone & Electronics Company, the largest non-Bell phone company (4,200,000 subscribers, 1,000,000 in the Los Angeles area alone), saw no reason it shouldn't share in the ownership, along with the other 3,000-odd independent phone companies in the United States. And Lockheed, General Electric, and Western Union proposed ownership by the carriers, manufacturers, and "possibly" the public.

The FCC, however, unflinchingly adopted the AT&T-IT&T position, ruling out both domestic carriers and the equipment manufacturers as prospective owners. In language paralleling AT&T views, the FCC said that satellite communications would be a "supplement to, rather than a substitute for," existing international service; that the international carriers "express a willingness and indicate a capability to marshal their respective resources" for developing the facility; and that because of their experience the international carriers knew what they needed. By formal order the FCC established an *ad hoc* committee of international carriers to frame a corporation to operate the satellites. As a criterion for membership in this select group the FCC included only the companies it had licensed to transmit international communications.

Just who were these "international" carriers, and what role did each intend to play in the satellite field under the FCC guidelines?

Foremost, of course, was AT&T, which handles all international phone calls from the United States. There were six subsidiaries of IT&T, the major telegraph carrier. There were Western Union and RCA Communications, Inc., an RCA subsidiary. Then the list drops off in a hurry.

The United States-Liberia Radio Corporation has $15,765 worth of equipment, and its sole mission is to send messages between the office of its owner, Firestone Rubber Company, and African rubber plantations.

There was the South Puerto Rico Sugar Corporation. When Senator Russell Long invited the company to send a witness to his 1961 Comsat hearings, its Washington attorney asked what the dickens Long had in mind: "My client is in the sugar business."

"Forget it," Long said. "There must be some mistake."

The attorney called apologetically a few days later to say, indeed, South Puerto Rico Sugar had some communications activities and an international carriers license—but only to connect its cane-growing operations with offices.

Said Long: "The thought occurs to me that the standards they [the FCC] are using might have made eligible some diplomat who might have a little telephone in the back of his automobile."

The other two "international" carriers—Press Wireless, Inc., run by news media, and the Hawaiian Telephone Company—RSVPed the FCC their regrets and said they wanted nothing to do with the satellites.

The FCC didn't notify the Justice Department in advance of its decision that it was ignoring the antitrust directives on diversity of ownership. Justice, to understate, was miffed and urged the FCC to reconsider, to "lessen the likelihood that the system will be controlled by a single company." The lower consumer costs possible through satellites "can best be realized if there is competition in the furnishing of communications services of all types," Justice said.

Bell's survival as the only "voice" carrier in the ownership group upset General Telephone. The company's general counsel, Theodore F. Brophy, complained to the Long committee about the anomalies. GT&E has phone service between the U.S. mainland, Alaska, and Canada, but was not considered an international carrier by FCC definition. Yet Hawaiian Telephone was given membership on the *ad hoc* committee by virtue of its service to the mainland.

GT&E petitioned the FCC for reconsideration and was told its appeal would have to be heard by the *ad hoc* committee. With AT&T leading the opposition, the committee blackballed GT&E, provoking this colloquy later before the Long committee:

LONG: Your competitors are going to decide whether or not you will be permitted to compete?

BROPHY: We somehow have the feeling somewhat like a lawsuit where the judge says, "I have not made up my mind, but I would like the plaintiff to draft an order here and we will see how it looks."

Long complained he could not understand the FCC's exclusion of domestic carriers and its repeated comments that the satellites were suitable only for international service. Even Dingman, the AT&T spokesman, admitted that "if we get started on a satellite system and we find out, after we get experience with it, that the cost factors and other factors make economic sense for use between the east coast and the west coast of the United States or from Bangor to Louisiana, I am sure they are going to be used for that." Craven of the FCC could see only a "remote possibility" of satellite use for domestic service—and that during hours when international traffic is off-peak.

The decision excluding domestic carriers meant that the independent domestic telephone companies—General Telephone and 3,000 others—did not have an insider's view into the Comsat operating company and the opportunity to ascertain for themselves whether use of the satellites would be more economical for their customers than continued reliance on AT&T's long lines department.

The FCC justified its exclusion of the domestic carriers and the non-Bell equipment manufacturers on the grounds that the *ad hoc* committee was to furnish only "information" and that its plan would not necessarily be binding upon the commission. Minow conceded that the insider companies would have an advantage but maintained this would be offset by an FCC mandate that they seek advice from everyone in the field and that any organizational plan include competitive bidding for equipment. Questioned closely by Representative John E. Moss at a House hearing, Minow agreed, however, that the insider group was unlikely to recommend an ownership plan that included people other than international common carriers—an accurate prediction.

The great fear that AT&T was careful never to express openly was that its domestic and international long-distance facilities could suddenly be made obsolete by a satellite system owned by other companies.

Minow, for one, professed to see no reason why AT&T should be protected. "As science and technology develop, this is a part of the business of being alive. I do not think the government would have to reimburse anybody as technology develops new systems. . . . I would not conceive it to be our duty to bail anybody out as the result of a technological advance."

At the same time Minow made this statement, he and fellow FCC members were in fact bailing out AT&T by protecting it from financial and technological competition.

Before the Long committee, Dingman seemed pleased that the aerospace manufacturers were isolated from the satellites. "The common carrier industry has pioneered in the research and development of *all phases* of communications . . . ," Dingman said. The launching of satellites, he added, would be an "essential prologue but nevertheless ancillary to the operation of one portion of the communications system." Besides, he noted, if AT&T wanted anything from the aerospace people, it was always there for sale.

By taking such a position, AT&T skirted close to the violation of common business decency. Firms of the size of GE, Lockheed, and Hughes Aircraft were well able to defend themselves, and one certainly cannot weep because such a prosperous trio lost a political fight. But the space industry is composed of far more than the giants.

Echo I, "AT&T's satellite," was constructed on a subcontract by a Minnesota outfit called the G. T. Schjeldahl Company, which was formed in late 1955 with capital of only $100,000 and which is unknown outside the industry. More than 10,000 firms have contributed to the U.S. space program, as manufacturers and suppliers, and most of them are Schjeldahl-sized.

Antitrust chief Loevinger said flatly that the FCC caught itself in a "violation of logic" by accepting the AT&T demand that manufacturers be denied a share of ownership. A modicum of hypocrisy is also involved.

"This arises out of the fact that the largest equipment manufacturer in terms of assets in the field is Western Electric, which is a wholly-owned subsidiary of AT&T," Loevinger testified to Congress. "Therefore, by including AT&T and excluding the equipment manufacturers, they [the FCC] are not, in fact, excluding equipment manufacturers, but, rather, allowing one equipment manufacturer to have an ownership interest, whereas the others are denied an ownership interest. . . ."

Another FCC line of reasoning which attracted Long's attention was its stand against permitting individual citizens to buy a share of the satellite system. The commission spokesman, member T. A. M. Craven, urged that the satellite setup "take its place within the framework of our private-enterprise system" and then wandered off into puzzling explanations of his definition of private enterprise. Long said 40,000,000 families in the United States each had an average of $600 invested in satellites by virtue of their tax payments. "Assuming that you have got something that is really futuristic, that is going to be terrific for the future, and it sounds to me as though it is, why should not everybody be entitled to buy his share in this venture rather than just one company taking it over?"

Craven replied lamely that he wasn't sure that all those estimates on satellite wealth were accurate and started to quote something that somebody had said before some House committee. But Long wouldn't let him continue:

"Well, that is the fine thing about free enterprise. You can take a chance on it. You can invest your money and lose it. I have lost it many times, have you not?"

Craven kept on disputing the potential value of the satellites, and Long droned in again: "Let us look at it this way. It is good enough that AT&T wants it. They ought to know, should they not? It is good enough that GE and General Telephone want it. They ought to know something about it. If you want to make an investment, it is good to talk to somebody in the field, and everybody who knows anything about it [the satellite communication system] wants to have some of it."

In related testimony later before the Senate Aeronautical and Space Sciences Committee, headed by Senator Robert Kerr of Oklahoma, which was studying the actual bill which established the Comsat operating company, Dingman of AT&T said he had "difficulty in seeing the advantage of extending the ownership in just a piece of the total communications system."

Senator Stephen M. Young, the Ohio Democrat, proceeded to test Dingman with one of the few unfriendly series of questions which AT&T witnesses heard from the Kerr committee:

YOUNG: Wouldn't it be a great advantage to have ordinary men and women all over the country to be able to say "Our satellite system," just because they own ten or 100 shares in that system? I am curious about that.

DINGMAN: Well, that would be one advantage. On the other hand, there are stocks of communictaions carriers that are available to anyone that wants to buy them, and there they not only would have a chance to spread their risks, and get the same return on their investment, but they can also say that they owned a piece of a satellite communications system if the carriers owned it.

YOUNG: In other words, they could buy more AT&T stock?

DINGMAN: Well, not just ours alone. They might buy some stock in the other carriers.

AT&T also opposed setting of the stock price in the satellite company at $100, rather than the $1,000 recommended by the FCC's *ad hoc* committee. A lower stock price, Dingman said, would bring in the "so-called marginal investors" who might become discouraged if the satellites were not an immediate success, sell their stock, and "depress the market." Dingman said, "You could have quite a few disappointed people." The $1,000 price, of course, meant the stock was tailor-made for AT&T and institutional investors, rather than the small citizen.

The rejection of the Justice Department's carefully drafted guidelines on competition made the Kennedy Administration suddenly and painfully conscious of the inevitable tenor of any FCC-sponsored plan for satellite ownership. Loevinger made his objections forcibly known at the White House and to his superior, Attorney General Robert F. Kennedy. Both Kennedys gave him a receptive ear. On July 24, 1961, the President issued a policy statement which put the ownership decision on a higher level and into a forum where AT&T would be less persuasive and powerful. Although the statement did not halt outright the work of the AT&T-oriented *ad hoc* committee, it did not once mention the FCC, and it gave the National Aeronautics and Space Council, a Presidential advisory group headed by Vice-President Lyndon Johnson, the responsibility for "recommending to me any actions needed to achieve full and prompt compliance with the policy." The statement said that "private ownership and operation of the U.S. portion of the [satellite] system is favored," provided that eight policy requirements could be met:

1. New and expanded international communications services be made available at the earliest practicable date.

2. The system be made global in coverage to provide efficient communication service throughout the whole world as soon as technically feasible, including service where individual portions of the coverage are not profitable.

3. Opportunities for foreign participation through ownership or otherwise be provided in the communications satellite system.

4. Nondiscriminatory use and equitable access to the system by present and future authorized communications carriers.

5. Effective competition, such as competitive bidding, in the acquisition of equipment used in the system.

6. Structure of ownership or control which will assure maximum possible competition.

7. Full compliance with antitrust legislation and with the regulatory controls of the government.

8. Development of an economical system whose benefits will be reflected in overseas communications rates.

With this statement Mr. Kennedy made the satellite ownership question a matter for national policy determination by Congress. His decision was a setback for AT&T, for it meant the FCC lost the power to allocate ownership of the system.

Nonetheless, the FCC *ad hoc* committee continued at work, and the AT&T lobbyists that summer applied pressure for prompt creation of a satellite operating corporation, the President's contrary wishes notwithstanding. In his statement Mr. Kennedy had stressed prompt action but made plain that "public interest objectives be given the highest priority." AT&T, however, wanted Satellites Now. Its hurry-up tactics, its insistence that the FCC go ahead with whatever plan the *ad hoc* committee produced, ultimately aroused Congressional curiosity. On August 24 a group of three Senators and thirty Representatives asked Mr. Kennedy for a moratorium on communications satellite development work being done by the government.

The letter charged that information was lacking on satellites, about both the type of system that should be used and the corporate framework through which it should be operated. Limitation of ownership to international carriers, as proposed by the FCC, violated both the Presidential policy directive and the antitrust laws, the Congressmen argued. They urged that the government retain control of the field pending development of a working system and only then decide whether it should be publicly or privately owned. They said:

> We have seen from past experience how the American Telephone & Telegraph Company has been able to expand its monopoly position and strengthen its hold on the American economy by combining, under the aegis of one holding company, its equipment manufacturing concern, the Western Electric Company, and the operating divisions of the Bell Telephone System. Only by insisting upon the widest participation by all interested communications and aerospace manufacturers and operators can there be any hope that such a monopoly can be forestalled in this new and vital field.

One of the signers, Senator Hubert Humphrey, was later to argue vociferously on the Senate floor for a bill that did not allow participation by "all interested parties," a philosophical change of horses that angered his liberal friends. Lawrence F. O'Brien, JFK's assistant for Congressional relations, replied to the Congressmen it was impossible to delay ownership and control questions until the system was operational "if we are to move swiftly." O'Brien did say that Mr. Kennedy agreed there should be no monopoly and that the system should be open to use by all carriers.

The Administration delayed the actual drafting of a satellite bill until the report of the FCC's *ad hoc* committee. Since the Kennedy policy statement, this group had been a lame duck, for no one in Washington (not even AT&T) expected its recommendations to meet the Administration's guidelines. Sure enough, they didn't—and are cited only as further documentation of the type of total monopoly sought by AT&T.

The committee recommended that ownership be limited to international carriers and that each carrier be permitted to construct its own ground stations. The corporation would be a nonprofit cooperative venture with the sole purpose of servicing its common carrier owners. Each participating company that invested more than $500,000 would be entitled to two directors, and no more; a single investor would be chosen by those investing less. The President would name three "public" directors.

So far, so good. But cost estimates for the various systems discussed in the report ranged from $45,000,000 to $150,000,-000, and it was here that AT&T could exert its influence. Because of the organizational uncertainties and lack of firm estimates on costs, only five of the nine international carriers were willing to estimate their investments. RCA, for example, viewed the incorporation as "somewhat premature" and said selection of the type of satellite system to be employed was much more important. Of the total $77,800,000 pledged by five companies, AT&T offered to put up $65,000,000—a financial presence that would smother other part owners.

The *ad hoc* committee's report was issued on October 12, 1961, and rejected before sundown by the Administration and Congressional leaders. President Kennedy asked Lyndon Johnson to put his space council to work on a bill incorporating the Administration's guidelines.

The AT&T lobbyists also went to work, and their target was Senator Robert Kerr, the Oklahoma Democrat who was the wealthiest man in the Senate. Just what transpired between Kerr and the AT&T people during those late autumn months isn't known, for Kerr is now dead and people watching from the outside had no idea what AT&T said to him in the privacy of his office. The important thing, however, is that when Kerr's Committee on Aeronautical and Space Sciences finally wrote a satellite bill, it wasn't quite what the Administration had expected.

Kerr's bill (sponsored in the House by Representative Oren Harris of Arkansas) called for creation of a Communications Satellite Corporation as the "chosen instrument" of the U.S. government, to act in concert with NASA in development of a space communications program, under regulation by the FCC, and subject to State Department direction on providing links to parts of the world where commercial service might not be profitable.

The only antimonopoly feature of the bill was a provision for two classes of stock: A, which would be purchased by any individual or group, including communications carriers, and B, which would be restricted to international carriers approved as owners by the FCC and on which no dividends would be paid (although the amount of the holdings could be included in the carriers' rate base for earnings purposes. That is, if the FCC permitted the carrier a 6 percent return on its investment, the stockholdings would be counted as an asset on which this profit was permitted. Since the Comsat Company was not expected to earn a profit for the first years of its existence, the carriers with Class B stock in this respect had an advantage over the Class A shareholders). Six directors each would be selected by A and B shareholders, and three more would be appointed by the President as "public" representatives.

The stock ownership was mere window dressing. The bill made no provision for participation by domestic telephone companies (other than AT&T) who might try to make Comsat a competitor with Bell in the domestic long-distance field. And AT&T received authority to buy as much of the so-called "public stock" as it could afford.

"This was a Bob Kerr deal all the way," another Senator mused while tracing the history of the satellite dispute. "Bob ran some important committees, and Jack Kennedy couldn't afford to offend him if he expected to get any New Frontier legislation through a Senate that was wobbly in the first place. The feeling at the time was that the President made a list of priorities and decided that satellites weren't as important as some other things, such as Medicare. So when Bob Kerr came up with this bill, and got Lyndon to endorse it, the President just got out of the way."

AT&T made some ritual public moans about the great loss it was suffering—then fought for the Kerr bill with all the vigor that can be mustered by the world's most powerful corporation.

Simultaneously, another issue occupied the attention of Congressmen and scientists: the selection of the type of satellite system on which the United States would stake its international reputation and on which citizens would stake their investment dollars.

It will be recalled that in 1960 AT&T proposed to fill the skies with some fifty satellites at the low (for space) altitude of 3,000 miles. By early 1962 few scientists doubted that such a system could be put into operation or that it would work. From the standpoint of availability of a system that could be put to use immediately, therefore, AT&T had a lead on would-be competitors. But knowledgeable people in both the space and communications industries argued that the rush wasn't all that important, that the United States should take its time and erect the best possible system. And the best possible system, they maintained, was by no means the Bell low-altitude balloon litter.

The most serious drawback to the Bell satellite system was that low-altitude satellites outrace the earth and are in view from any given point for only a matter of minutes. Once the satellite drifts out of range, the ground transmitter must immediately pick up another one to relay the message, or the signal is lost. The receiving apparatus, similarly, must flick to the other end of the horizon and sight in on a new satellite. To avoid interruptions during all this switching, dual transmitters and receivers are needed, so that one pair can communicate with Satellite A while the second pair hones in on Satellite B.

The process is somewhat more difficult than aiming a rifle or a telescope: AT&T's ground installation at Andover, Maine, which was used in the Telstar experiments, weighed 250 tons and was enclosed by a plastic bubble twice the size of the seating area of Radio City Music Hall.

The high-altitude synchronous satellite, conversely, would be put into position 22,300 miles above the earth. At this altitude the speed of the satellite equals the speed of the earth's rotation, so that it remains fixed in relation to the earth's surface. Once the ground equipment locks on it, the connection would be permanent, with none of the continuous frantic sighting and aiming inherent in Bell's low-altitude system. Because of its altitude, the synchronous communications satellite system (Syncom by common abbreviation) would cover vastly more territory than the Bell version. Only three Syncoms would be needed to service the entire world (with the exception of small patches at both poles): one generally over the Atlantic for transatlantic and Latin American calls; another over the Pacific for transpacific service; a third over the Indian Ocean to handle that segment of the globe.

The only serious difficulty in the Syncom was the amount of time required for a signal to make the 22,300-mile trip from earth to satellite and back to earth. Although less than half a second, the interval created an echo that tests showed would annoy some users. However, Syncom developers said the problem could be solved as readily as Bell had taken the echo out of its first long-distance lines more than half a century previously.

Any schoolboy who has watched astronaut launchings on television knows that it costs more money to put fifty satellites into orbit than it does to send three aloft. And satellites cannot be hurled into space as if they were bird shot. Multiple launchings, three to a booster, were and remain an unreliable art. Cost per booster at the time of the Comsat debate was $9,500,000 to $10,500,000 for the carrying vehicle itself, plus about $1,000,000 for use of the launching pad, tracking once the thing was skyborne, and miscellaneous costs. The U.S. Senate, which contains a firm bedrock of common sense beneath its occasional forays into folderol, heard these figures and began to ask out loud just what AT&T was attempting to prove with its advocacy of the low-altitude system.

Based on what the Senators found at a series of committee hearings, three reasons may be cited for AT&T's advocacy of low-altitude satellites:

1. Another company, Hughes Aircraft, had the ground floor on the Syncom by virtue of its military contracts, and its engineers said the satellite was readily and rapidly adaptable for civilian commercial use. In the fall of 1961 Hughes told the FCC it could "have a commercial intercontinental communications satellite system in operation within one year of the time we are permitted to proceed." Hughes said that the Syncom would have a capacity of 1,200 voice channels and, with only 40 channels in use, could make a profit *even if it were to charge half the then AT&T rate for the sixty-five channels Bell had to Europe*. Further, Hughes maintained, "This system will have capacity in excess of the expected demand, and it can be expanded as needed." Thus, AT&T, to protect its existing monopoly, was forced to propagandize the low-altitude system and to do its utmost to downgrade any other.

2. Few Congressmen, sadly, had the time or tenacity to acquaint themselves with the technical questions at issue. The percentage of informed citizens was even lower, especially because of a virtual press blackout on intelligent discussion of the question. By proceeding pell-mell with the medium-altitude Telstar, AT&T was able to flash a gaudy but commercially worthless trinket across the skies at an opportune moment, while its pitchmen on the ground trumpeted, "See? What did we tell you? AT&T is first, and AT&T, therefore, shows its system is best."

3. Since Bell had done the work on Telstar, its manufacturing subsidiary, Western Electric, would have an advantage over other firms if the medium-altitude satellite were selected as the basic communications vehicle. As noted earlier, Bell makes money in carload quantities on anything manufactured by Western Electric. Therefore, AT&T would have a two-level profit.

Senator Russell Long, who says he spent a full year educating himself on satellite communications, immediately spotted "the bug under the rug." He charged that AT&T was attempting to "fill the sky with a bunch of junk that will quickly become outdated" in order to drive other firms out of the satellite corporation. In this instance, Long said, use of the least efficient and more costly system would actually be to Bell's advantage. How?

"For one thing," Long said, "the low-altitude system would be so expensive that there would be no prospect for profit [for the operating corporation] at any time in the near future. Why would it be of great advantage to [AT&T] to sponsor, promote and push a project that would be unprofitable? The reason is that that great corporation would be able to get back its losses by charges on telephone users, because that corporation is entitled, after taking care of all its losses and paying all taxes, to a fair return on its investment.*

"Another reason why AT&T might want to adopt the low orbit system is that while it would be unprofitable for a great number of years, corporations which are not regulated utilities would find it a poor investment, and therefore AT&T would find it easier to chase other companies out of competition in this field, because such companies would not be able to make the money back at the expense of the public. AT&T would," Long asserted.

An added factor was the great expense involved in construction of ground stations for the medium-altitude system. Long

---

* The Federal Communications Commission, which has jurisdiction over interstate and international long-distance phone rates, and the state public utilities commissions permit AT&T and its operating companies to earn a fixed percentage annually on their investment (the amount varies from jurisdiction to jurisdiction). If there is a loss on one segment of the service, rates are adjusted elsewhere to compensate for it.

estimated this at $15,000,000 (based on AT&T's cost for the Andover, Maine, tracking station for Telstar), compared with about $750,000 for the less complex tracking apparatus for the Syncom. AT&T had to purchase "practically an entire valley in the State of Maine," Long said; otherwise, the radio "of the local sheriff" could have put the whole system out of kilter. AT&T, Long said, is the only U.S. carrier with the funds to invest in such a receiver and is thus able to freeze out other carriers who might be able to have their own ground stations were the less expensive high-altitude system to be employed.

Long debunked Telstar as an expensive practical joke on the American public. "They are in no hurry to make money on it," he said. "If they lose money now they will run the shoe clerks out [of the Comsat corporation], if I may use a poker player's expression." He derided Telstar's technical defects:

"Suppose the Senator wanted to call somebody in Europe. He would have to wait until next week, when the satellite was between Andover and Germany. It would not be in position until then, and then only for ten minutes. If it came over at 7:30 in the morning, and the Senator was a late sleeper, he would not be able to get up in time to make the telephone call. He would do better by relying on the pony express, or he might get the message there quicker if he used an ocean-going turtle."

While AT&T lobbyists and propagandists pushed Telstar on the political front, the competitive Syncom faced serious internal opposition within the U.S. military and space establishment.

One obstacle was Dr. Brockway McMillan, who was with Bell Laboratories from 1946 to 1961, when he went to the Pentagon as Assistant Secretary of the Air Force for Research and Development. Senator Estes Kefauver stumbled across interesting intelligence concerning Dr. McMillan during a survey of former Bell people working on space communications for the government. To ascertain just what Dr. McMillan did in his Defense Department job, Kefauver obtained from the Air Force a stack of documents written by him.

"What did I find?" Kefauver asked the Senate. "Much to my amazement, I found that Dr. McMillan not only did not disqualify himself from decisions bearing on AT&T, he has also deliberately and gratuitously gone out of his way to help AT&T with the low-orbit Telstar system and disparage the efforts of AT&T's competitors who want to develop a synchronous system.

"Before that, when he was still with Bell Laboratories, he had testified and filed a statement with the FCC, in which he, with other AT&T employees, discussed the space problems in which AT&T is interested.

"I do not know to what extent Dr. McMillan has acted out of pure motives or bad motives. I do not know if he consciously intended to help AT&T. . . . I do know, however, that with his background it is shocking to find him taking on an active role in furthering the fortunes of AT&T and spiking those of its competitors, and in disparaging the Advent program, the synchronous satellite proposal."

The documents Kefauver obtained were classified secret, but he gave the gist of them to the Senate. In one paper, Kefauver said, Dr. McMillan downgraded the Syncom, "the obvious purpose of which was to . . . get us committed to the low-orbit system, Telstar, or something like it."

In another document, Kefauver said, Dr. McMillan recommended that the Air Force juggle its budget to put $1,350,000 into Telstar. He spoke indignantly of the "Society of the Friends of AT&T in Government":

"I think it is obvious that the primary purpose for AT&T's honeycombing the government is to protect its monopoly and, further, to protect its huge investment in such things as underseas cables from being obsoleted by such revolutionary things as space satellites."

Dr. John R. Pierce, known in the Bell System as the Grandfather of Telstar, also took a critical view of the Syncom system while working as a space communications consultant to the government. Dr. Pierce criticized Syncom in an article in *Electronic News,* a communications trade publication, and remarked on a television program that legislative and legal difficulties were a bigger problem for Bell's Telstar than technical ones. Kefauver expressed concern about the "propriety as well as the accuracy" of Dr. Pierce's implied criticism of Congress.

Senator Wayne Morse, the Oregon Democrat, summed up the fight over merits of high- and medium-altitude satellites as "part of the great battle which is going on behind the scenes.

"AT&T wants these vested legal rights now, through this [Kerr] bill. Then Howard Hughes can develop his high-altitude satellite, but he will have to deal with the corporation by way of the legal instrument which is to be created by the bill." And the corporation of which Morse spoke would have been dominated by AT&T.

The provision of Kerr's Administration-supported bill calling for public access to ownership of the voting, dividend-bearing stock convinced most Congressmen the measure was not a giveaway. Other people in Washington, however, were more skilled at sorting through the plethora of technological and political issues involved.

One of these men was Bernard J. Fensterwald, Jr., a no-nonsense lawyer who worked for Senator Kefauver. Fensterwald spent quite a bit of time in 1961 digging into Comsat material and then on August 14 wrote a "Dear Boss" memorandum stating he was "convinced (1) that the question of ownership should be put over for awhile and (2) eventually we may want to have public ownership."

"Keep working, inclined to agree," Kefauver scrawled in answer.

Later that fall Kefauver posed the public ownership idea to President Kennedy, saying that the satellites were a great natural resource and should be run by a public agency patterned after the Tennessee Valley Administration. Mr. Kennedy was noncommittal, and the Administration's later acceptance of the Kerr bill signaled Kefauver's rejection.

Russell Long, Kefauver, and Senators Wayne Morse and Albert Gore during committee hearings in the spring of 1962 elicited enough information to convince themselves that the Kerr bill was premature and ill conceived. Their objections:

—The Federal Communications Commission, which would be responsible for ensuring that savings made possible by the satellite would be passed on to the public, cannot be trusted to do the job. Senators cited time and again the FCC's own admission that it had never conducted an in-depth study of Bell's long-distance rate structure.

—The Administration was making wasteful haste by pushing the Comsat measure because even its own witnesses testified that creation of the satellite operating corporation was not essential to the development of a working system.

—Despite the limitations on the amount of Comsat stock that could be held by one firm or individual, Senators asserted that AT&T, by sheer financial weight, would dominate any activity it entered. In one antitrust case the U.S. Supreme

Court held that a 23 percent holding by General Motors in the DuPont Corporation constituted control; federal statutes for various types of holding, investment, and utility companies say "control" begins when they own as little as 10 percent of the stock in another company.

—The federal government, despite its development expenditures in space, would pay exactly the same rates to use the system as would anyone else, although President Kennedy and his Administration had said a desired function of the satellite was to give the United States a cheaper access to underdeveloped nations via radio and television programs prepared by the United States Information Agency.

—The Comsat Act violated long-standing public policy that one type of carrier cannot own another—*i.e.*, barge lines and railroads are prohibited from holding an interest in trucking firms and airlines. Opposing Senators questioned how vigorously railroads would have pushed development of the trucking industry had they controlled it in the early 1920's.

But few people were in a mood to listen to dissension. Only nine dissenting votes were cast in the House of Representatives, which acted first on a bill identical with that sponsored by Kerr.

One reason is that other communications carriers which earlier argued against AT&T domination suddenly changed their positions and supported the Kerr bill. AT&T was responsible for the shifts. The International Telephone & Telegraph Company, for example, was dependent on AT&T for leased cables. Comsat didn't threaten its *existing* operations; an angered AT&T could, so IT&T publicly stated support for a bill it really didn't like.

Hughes Aircraft, at the same time, began encountering trouble with NASA over its synchronous satellite; rightly or wrongly, it suspected AT&T to be responsible, and its spokesmen made peace by testifying for the Kerr Bill. (The duality of Hughes' position was demonstrated when its Washington lobbyist supplied Senator Russell Long with three large charts to use when he filibustered against the bill.)

The previous year, when there was a chance that the FCC *ad hoc* committee recommendations might prevail, AT&T had flown in a battalion of its local managers to call on Congressmen with whom they were friendly. When the Comsat issue got to the voting stage in 1962, members found themselves deluged with telephone calls, telegrams, and letters from their hometown bankers and financial supporters, all urging support of AT&T.

Press comment on the bill indicates the division lines. The *Wall Street Journal,* in an editorial entitled "Socialism in the Sky," opposed public ownership and supported Mr. Kennedy's "very wise decision" in favor of private development.

The New York *Post* lamented, "On days such as this it is hard to believe that Mr. Eisenhower is no longer president." The Chicago *Sun-Times,* confusing AT&T's payments for Telstar with the American taxpayers' payments for the rest of the space program, said, "American free enterprise developed global communications for public use. Let's be the first nation to put free enterprise in space." The *New Republic* was unhappy about "fingers in the space pie."

The *Bell Telephone Magazine* denounced public ownership in an article entitled "The Space Domination Myth," whose thrust was revealed in the patent silliness of the opening sentence: "Who can conceive of a monopoly in space? There is so much of it." In the next breath after denunciation of public ownership, it moved to the horrors of the Iron Curtain: "Press, radio and television are strictly censored. Telephone and other private communications, including mail, of course, are rigidly inspected. Here is government monopoly, indeed, unregulated and unrestricted by any consideration, either political or economic, other than the edicts of the central dictatorship." Just how public ownership of the satellites would give the U.S. government the right to open mail wasn't made clear—and a citizen who uses the U.S. mails for his communications has more privacy than a citizen who talks over a telephone owned by AT&T.

The Senatorial opponents held a meeting after the House passage and decided they didn't stand much of a chance of killing the bill outright. Kerr had replaced Lyndon Johnson as the Senate's most powerful man, and a quick nose count showed that he had a majority ready to vote in his favor. By this time the dissidents were ten in number: Morse, Kefauver, Russell Long, Gore, Mrs. Maurine Neuberger, Joseph S. Clark, Ernest Gruening, Ralph Yarborough, E. L. Bartlett, and Quentin N. Burdick.

So the opponents decided to try to delay the bill until autumn by filibustering in the hope that public opinion could be mobilized against it. Kefauver clung to the hope that it might then be possible to retain public ownership.

Having decided on a filibuster, the opponents promptly committed tactical blunders which made it impossible for their filibuster to succeed. Wayne Morse wanted to begin immediately (this was in mid-June), for the Senate was then considering an increase in the government debt limit. If the limit was not raised before June 30, the end of the fiscal year, the government would run out of money. Morse wanted to seize the floor on a parliamentary pretext and keep talking until Kerr and the Senate leadership promised to table the Comsat bill until the fall.

But Long, Gore, and Kefauver were unwilling to take so drastic a step when it would put them at public odds with the Kennedy Administration. Too, they had an interest in some of the legislation that was piled up behind the debt limit bill and did not want to see it delayed. And, finally, the White House did some flag-waving that convinced Kefauver a filibuster at this particular time could be injurious to the defense effort. So on June 21 the opponents postponed their filibuster.

The Senate leadership quickly disposed of the debt limit, some important New Frontier legislation (including the brutal burying of the President's Medicare plan), bowed politely to Morse and the others, and invited them to filibuster as long as they wished.

The situation was hopeless. Only two of the Senators—Long and Morse—had ever participated in a filibuster before; the group lacked the physical stamina and discipline necessary for success. Bernard J. Fensterwald, Kefauver's staff man, gamely took the job of filibuster coordinator. Three Senators a day had floor duty; one to make the main speech, the other two to "engage in colloquy, ask questions and help out generally." Other Senate staff men collected material on AT&T and satellites so that their bosses would have something to say during the debate. Benjamin Gordon, economist for Long's Small Business Committee, alone wrote enough speeches to fill more than fifty closely printed pages of the *Congressional Record*.

Not all members of the Kennedy Administration were happy with the bill, although Democratic floor leaders constantly referred to it as "the President's bill." The State Department didn't like a provision that gave the operating corporation the authority to conduct negotiations with foreign governments that owned national telephone and telegraph companies. The Justice Department didn't like AT&T's prospective domination of the new corporation.

But President Kennedy didn't attempt to override Kerr, nor would he give his blessing to any attempts at significant amendments. Doubts on the merits of the bill nonetheless persisted. Persons waching the President handle his first big public interest legislation wondered why the qualms were not brought into the open. Columnist Doris Fleeson opined, "The President obviously does not consider [the doubts] of sufficient importance to inject them as still another factor in his war with the Congressional standing committees."

The filibuster droned on for fourteen days, and a surprising portion of the dissidents' floor arguments was devoted to sober analysis of the bill and its defects. But as the futility of their cause became apparent the dissidents lapsed into traditional filibustering techniques: the 3,000-word question to which a Senator would yield to rest his throat; laborious reading of the Senate rule book; verbose acknowledgment of letters from constituents; even poetry duets, as witness this exchange between Long and the friendly, but nonparticipating, Senator Paul Douglas:

LONG: The law locks up. . . .
DOUGLAS: Both man and woman. . . .
LONG: Who steals the goose. . . .
DOUGLAS: From off the common. . . .
LONG: But lets the greater felon loose. . . .
DOUGLAS: Who steals the common from the goose.

But a majority of the Senators had already closed their minds, and the filibustering clique could not raise their voices loud enough to arouse any public indignation. A TV network asked Senator Albert Gore to appear with another opponent for an hour debate with two supporters. After two and a half days the program idea died: The producer, after talking to eighty Senators who said they favored the bill, told Gore he could not find a single one who desired to defend it publicly.

Republicans for the most part remained silent and enjoyed the intra-Democratic fight (Barry Goldwater breaking in once to mutter that the delay was "aiding Communism").

And at the peak of the debate AT&T administered the *coup de grâce*. It launched Telstar on July 10—a masterstroke of public relations timing that: (1) excited the public about satellite communications by giving them a nibble at interoceanic television and (2) led the public to believe that AT&T was responsible for the entire technology.

The first satellite show consisted mainly of pictures of the satellite ground stations, beamed into homes in the United States, Great Britain and France. Frederick R. Kappel, head of AT&T, spoke the first words to Vice-President Johnson in Washington: "This is Fred Kappel talking, calling from the earth station, Andover, Maine. . . ."

AT&T's concurrent advertising broadside on Telstar drowned out the space conversations. Full-page advertisements in newspapers and national magazines chortled: "Bell System micro-wave-in-sky satellite is latest American triumph in communications arising from *telephone research*" (author's italics). The overall theme was that AT&T developed and launched Telstar without any help from the taxpayer. Noticeably absent from the advertisements was any acknowledgment that government-financed research and government-built rocket boosters actually put Telstar into orbit. The ads said flatly that Telstar "was launched from Cape Canaveral at Bell System expense."

The claim is truthful as stated—but nonetheless grossly misleading. During hearings leading up to the summer of 1962 floor debate in the Senate, Congressmen talked themselves into circles in attempting to elicit from NASA director James E. Webb just how much of the actual cost was met by AT&T. Webb's answers to the House Commerce Committee were a blend of guileful hedging and lofty praise for AT&T. Representative Peter F. Mack, Jr. (Democrat, Illinois), finally pinned him to the mat and squeezed out a semblance of an answer:

> MACK: . . . It seems to me that it would be very difficult for you to actually divide the cost or charge AT&T for the appropriate cost of developing the booster or for any research that has been done. You are talking about charging them only for—
> WEBB: The out-of-pocket costs for the launching is what we expect to charge them under the contract.

At another point Webb conceded, "The expenditures which

the government will make and which will be refunded to the government by AT&T relate to the launching of the satellite, the tracking of the satellite, and the reporting in of the data from our tracking stations." Webb said this included "all of the extra cost that the government incurs by this but . . . we do not try to go back and accumulate all of the research cost that might have gone into the tracking, the worldwide tracking network, for instance."

Webb was also less than candid when the House Commerce Committee asked him to supply figures on NASA expenditures for satellite communications research and development. His answer was restricted to research and development for active satellites for fiscal 1961 and 1962—a relatively modest $91,350,000.

But figures compiled by the staff of the Senate Aeronautical and Space Sciences Committee are more inclusive and thus closer to the truth. According to the staff report, $312,000,000 of a total NASA budget of $6.8 billion from 1960 through 1963 was for communications satellites. The Defense Department, from the beginning of its Comsat research in the 1950's through 1963, spent $250,000,000, making the NASA-Defense total $571,600,000. Even this figure is misleadingly low, for no computation has ever been made, nor is one possible, of the number of space dollars spent in other areas—from booster motors to Cape Canaveral real estate—that made Telstar's flight possible. But no one seriously disputed the use of the sums $20 billion and $25 billion by Senators Kefauver, Long, Morse, and Gore during floor debate.

The AT&T claim that it financed Telstar, however, made a lasting indentation in impressionable Congressional heads, particularly those with Pavlovian reactions whenever Bell used the words "free enterprise." Lee Loevinger, the Justice Department's antitrust man, lectured Representative Peter H. Dominick on this point when the Colorado Republican said AT&T was "spending all its own money" on Telstar.

"There are more *billions* of public money invested in the development of that missile [the vehicle that carried Telstar into orbit] that AT&T will be paying *millions* for the specific costs," Loevinger declared. "A second factor that I think must be considered also is that AT&T is not an ordinary private company. It is a regulated public utility which, in effect, levies through governmental action a charge on the people which, in many respects, is something in the character of a tax.

"Included in its rate base are its costs, including, presumably, experimental and developmental costs. So when AT&T says it is going to spend money, what it is saying, in effect, is that, 'We will collect from our users to cover this cost,' and it is not taking money out of an accumulated capital such as a more limited private company would when it increases its costs. It goes to the regulatory agency and increases its rates, if necessary, if there is not enough in there to absorb it."

What AT&T was attempting to do, Loevinger said, was to use one monopoly position to gain another which it had never been granted "by intentional governmental action, by legislative action, or by any considered determination of fact." He concluded: "It would be sort of rolling dice with the public to see whether AT&T could develop patents out of this particular project that would enable it to control the new system."

Representative Dominick was unconvinced. "They [AT&T] could presumably sit back and let the general taxpayers spend the money and get the same degree of benefit out of it."

Loevinger retorted: "I assume that they believe they would *not* get the same degree of benefit out of it, sir." *

After the Telstar launching the rout of the filibuster was a matter of time. The opponents made blunder after blunder. In a parliamentary wrangle one day Senator Morse momentarily lost his temper and stopped just shy of calling the Majority Leader, Senator Mike Mansfield, a liar. "We were dead after that," one of Morse's supporters recalls. "The Senate *had* to pass the bill to rebut Wayne's charge. The leadership bowed its back and after that point was not about to accept any amendment. I really think that we were beginning to wake up the Senate when this happened, which makes it truly unfortunate."

Senate Majority Leader Joseph T. Robinson once said that "nobody but Almighty God" can interrupt a Senator on the floor. After fourteen days, however, the Senate leadership

---

* Loevinger's testimony, mostly unfriendly to AT&T, came during the summer of 1961, when the Kennedy Administration was still talking publicly about finding a way to put the satellites under control of a corporation that would not be dominated by a single carrier. After acceptance of the Kerr bill by the Administration, Loevinger and other government witnesses ceased their criticisms of AT&T.

moved for cloture to shut off the debate. Only three months earlier the Senate had refused to stop a filibuster on an Administration civil rights bill aimed at ending discriminatory literacy tests for voter registration. This time the Senate imposed cloture by 63 to 27—the first time a filibuster had been voted to an end since 1927. Five embarrassed Southern Senators who supported the Administration took fishing trips to avoid having to vote against a filibuster; others voted "no" only after success of cloture was assured. One avowed non-hypocrite was Senator Richard Russell of Georgia, who boomed, "I'll vote to gag the Senate when shrimps learn to whistle 'Dixie.' "

After that the rout was swift, and AT&T lobbyists sitting in the gallery began to relax and smile expansively. The liberals, now limited to one hour per man, trotted out tested and well-worn old horses, but none got anywhere. Morse and Joe Clark tried to tag on an antidiscrimination rider, noting that AT&T and four Bell System companies were the subject of complaints to Vice-President Johnson's Equal Job Opportunities Council.

Russell Long gave up in midafternoon on August 17, the twentieth full day of debate. He sent twenty-eight amendments to the clerk's desk for simultaneous debate—and defeat —rather than dole them out one at a time. Kefauver, Morse, and Gore followed with mass (and also futile) submission of their amendments. Vice-President Johnson, presiding, complained of the noise in the chamber, then gaveled the bill to a vote. It passed 66 to 11.

Did the American public and American press realize what Congress did with the Communications Satellite Act? Apparently not, and a good example of the confusion is found in *Time*, which is edited by intelligent men who should know better. *Time* thought the filibuster good sport and poked fun at the opponents in a piece captioned "Head Winds." After its laugh *Time* declared that the bill would give 50 percent of the stock "to the public" and 50 percent "to companies" and that the "public would be safeguarded against excessive rates by the Federal Communications Commission"—cheerful optimism at best. What the media and the general citizenry never seemed to realize was that the "public" stock was also available for purchase by AT&T and other international common carriers and that non-Bell domestic telephone companies were being excluded from the system.

When the stock went on the market, AT&T promptly bought up 29 percent of it.

The Communications Satellite Act must be adjudged a failure, for it created more problems than it solved—most notably the issue of use of the system for domestic commercial television and telephone service. At AT&T's bidding Congress put these services outside the jurisdiction of the satellites, and the gravity of this decision began coming home to the communications industry and public in short order.

The three major television networks pay about $60,000,000 annually to AT&T for use of its system to transmit programs from coast to coast. In 1966 they decided they could cut this tariff considerably by using their own domestic satellites, rather than AT&T's system, and asked the FCC for permission to do so. The Ford Foundation and the Carnegie Commission on Educational Television, asserting that space and its use are a natural resource, suggested that part of the network savings be used to support educational television and radio broadcasts.

AT&T, of course, opposed any such system, as did the Communications Satellite Corporation. The AT&T position is that any domestic satellites should be run by Comsat. "It is AT&T's view that there are no benefits, certainly not to the public as a whole, to be achieved through authorizing private systems," the company said in a brief filed with the FCC. "To the contrary, the most efficient way to exploit the new satellite technology is by *incorporating the use of the satellites into the systems of the common carriers.*" Use of private systems (*i.e.,* non-Bell or non-Comsat) would "result in substantial economic injury to the common carriers," by taking away its heavy-volume traffic while leaving it responsible for carrying low-volume traffic.

In rebuttal the Ford Foundation said that to permit Comsat control of the domestic satellites would "give the corporation a monopoly . . . unprecedented even for public utilities." It also pointedly asserted that since six of the fifteen directors represent common carriers (three of the six being AT&T officers), they "are not free to concentrate on the development of communications satellites—they [the six] must also be aware of, and sensitive to, the large common carrier investment in microwave and other land facilities." (This could have been a sentence, syllable for syllable. from one of Senator Russell Long's 1962 filibuster speeches.)

A host of peripheral disputes has also plagued the ill-conceived Comsat Corporation. The Defense Communications Agency, the Pentagon's communications service, tried to contract directly with Comsat in leasing military channels, only to have the carriers with whom it had dealt previously complain to the White House. So it still must work through the carriers, and the U.S. government's investment in the space program doesn't entitle the U.S. government to reduced rates when it uses the satellites its dollars developed.

Indeed, a Government Operations Committee report issued in 1965 said that had not the Comsat Act passed, NASA "conceivably" would have carried its development and flight-testing program to the point where the government could have had a working satellite communications system years earlier than it ultimately acquired one. "After all," said the committee, "it only takes a few satellites of the synchronous type to create such capacity, and whether they are called experimental or operational depends on their design and intended use."

So the muddle continues. AT&T and IT&T announce plans to install new transoceanic cables, despite Comsat's protests that satellites should supply the new required capacity. AT&T's influence in the Comsat Corporation isn't enough to control outright the corporation's policies, as the filibusters feared in 1962, but any assessment of legislation must start with the question: "Has the legislation accomplished what it was supposed to accomplish?"

The Communications Satellite Act has accomplished only chaos, but in another sense, the chaos has enabled AT&T to fend off the potential competition inherent in the new communications medium.

7

A handsome wall or desk phone extension will save you time and steps in your home, and they are modestly priced at just 90 cents per month. The Princess phone is a beautiful addition to any room. Its light-up dial gives you calling ease and comfort at night. Costs just 65 cents a month, plus the normal extension charge.

—New Jersey Bell advertising brochure

Why spend a lot for an extra phone? Standard Dial Phones—Only $9.95. Saves extra steps and costly rental charges.

—Advertisement of the Madison Telephone Supply Company, New York

---

THE American Telephone & Telegraph Company's ownership of the Western Electric Company and reliance on it for the instruments used throughout the Bell System constitute what one independent manufacturer has called "an almost impregnable wall" around the telephone equipment industry.

Western Electric has exclusive sales rights to 85 percent of the multibillion-dollar telephone market, the portion that is controlled by Bell. An analogy? By population, assign General Motors every auto manufacturing plant, dealership, repair shop, and service station in the United States except for New England. Everyone else in the auto industry could "compete" there—Ford, Chrysler, American Motors, the foreign car importers, the dozens of oil companies.

The Western Electric equipment monopoly has many implications for the people who make telephones and the people who use telephones.

For the subscriber, the monopoly means the compulsory use of whatever gear is supplied by the Bell operating company. His only alternative is to pay a hefty conversion charge if he desires non-Bell equipment—a fee that Bell collects regardless of whether any actual work is done on the instrument. A citizen who needs specialized equipment not offered by Bell or who wants to avoid AT&T's perpetual rentals is subjected to harassment and threats of loss of service—despite the fact that regulatory commission rulings of the past have left a rather broad gray area in regard to what nonstandard phone attachments are legal.

For the communications equipment industry, the monopoly means that AT&T is able to develop and make available telephone innovations at its own pace, generally a leisurely one. Time and again independent manufacturers have perfected telephone attachments before Bell, only to be excluded from the Bell market.

M. A. Odom, president of Marcom, Inc., an Oakland, California, electronics firm, complained, "New companies established as a result of producing new concepts first realize the existence and strength of Bell's impregnable wall when highly profitable new innovations must be presented for evaluation to requirement standards set largely at the discretion of the [AT&T] monopoly."

Odom's experience with the "impregnable wall" came when he invented a call diverter, a device which a person could attach to his home or office telephone to shunt his incoming calls to other locations where he planned to be. Bell did not offer any such service when Marcom began marketing its call diverter, although its engineers were testing a similar instrument.

Bell Telephone Laboratories, Inc., which screens any independently produced equipment which is likely to be offered to Bell subscribers, obtained one of Marcom's diverters. After tests, the AT&T home office sent bulletins to each of its operating companies derogating the equipment and stating "such a device could have a serious degrading effect on the quality of service." Odom disagreed. Standards of Bell Labs, he stated, are "so rigid they are not closely approached in the Bell System—standards they are unable to meet themselves, but which are demanded of the outsider."

Independent companies which used the Marcom diverter found nothing wrong with its performance, but Odom was soon effectively excluded even from this limited market. AT&T refused to connect the diverter to its telephone lines so that it could be demonstrated at state conventions of independent telephone conventions. It is at such gatherings that independent manufacturers make many of their sales—and such gatherings are normally held in cities served by Bell companies.

Marcom eventually went into federal court with an antitrust suit, asking $150,000,000 damages from AT&T and the Bell operating companies. The suit quickly died. The judge ruled that the issue of permissible equipment should be decided by the regulatory agencies, not by the courts, and that the approved tariffs under which the utilities operate give them authority to control what is used in their systems.

The Federal Communications Commission, which has jurisdiction over AT&T's interstate and foreign operations, is undergoing a slow evolution of attitude toward nonstandard equipment; twice in the last decade it has directed the Bell System to permit the use of previously barred devices—the Hush-a-Phone, a muffling device which permits a person to carry on a conversation without others in the room hearing what he is saying, and the Carterfone, an instrument which enables telephone conversations to be relayed over a two-way radio system to remote areas lacking conventional service. Yet each lowering of the barriers has come in response to a challenge posed by the maker of a particular item; there is no blanket authority for the use of non-Bell equipment, and the FCC declined to issue one the last time it had a chance to do so.

AT&T's authority for outlawing most independently manufactured equipment produced in the United States is contained in two paragraphs of its regulations that are included in the FCC-approved tariff under which it conducts its interstate long-distance business.*

---

* Tariffs governing intrastate operations and approved by the state regulatory agencies contain similar wording.

Unauthorized Attachments or Connections

No equipment, apparatus, circuit or device not furnished by the telephone company shall be attached to or connected with the facilities furnished by the telephone company, whether physically, by induction or otherwise except as provided in this tariff. In case any such unathorized attachment or connection is made, the telephone company shall have the right to remove or disconnect the same; or to suspend the service during the continuance of said attachment or connection; or to terminate the service.

Miscellaneous Devices Provided by the Customer

The provisions of [the preceding] paragraph shall not be construed or applied to bar a customer from using devices which serve his convenience in his use of the facilities of the telephone company in the service for which they are furnished under this tariff, provided any such device so used would not endanger the safety of telephone company employees or the public; damage, require change in or alteration of, or involve direct electrical connection to, the equipment or other facilities of the telephone company; or interfere with the proper functioning of such equipment or facilities, or impair the operation of the telephone system or otherwise injure the public in its use of the telephone company's services. Except as otherwise provided in this tariff, nothing herein shall be construed to permit the use of a recording device or of a device to interconnect any line or channel of the telephone company with any other communications line or channel of the company or of any other person.

AT&T's official defense of the monopoly is that each of its 85,000,000 telephones must be compatible, lest the entire interconnected system collapse. The Bell companies assert that they are now solely responsible for the quality of telephone service and that if interconnection with others' equipment were to place a portion of the system beyond their control, they could no longer accept responsibility for the quality of communication. They contend further that such divided control would hamper innovation and increase the cost to the public of basic telephone service. Finally, Bell claims not to be unreasonable—

that it will permit the use of almost anything if a subscriber is convincing in his arguments that his particular situation requires it. However, Bell reserves the right to be the judge of such situations.

The manufacturers and distributors of non-Bell equipment and, to a lesser extent, subscribers to Bell service sense less altruistic motives: protection of a market and the maximization of profits through prolonged use of equipment that, although outmoded, continues to return revenues. In its noncompetitive situation Bell can leave telephone instruments in service for upwards of three decades; were customers able to pick and choose in the freedom of a competitive market, AT&T's replacement schedule would likely accelerate appreciably.

The rental of telephone attachments adds a substantial increment to Bell's revenues. There is no discernible relationship of these fees to the value of the service provided. A trivial example: An office I once occupied in the National Press Building in Washington was equipped with a telephone buzzer that was used to notify the telegrapher, who worked in another room, when he had a call. This buzzer could be purchased in any hardware store in the District of Columbia for $3 and installed in minutes. The Chesapeake & Potomac Telephone Company, however, rented it for 50 cents per month and has done so, at varying fees, since before the Second World War. There were five desk telephones in the office, each with six buttons, which brought a $3.50 monthly rental charge each. The hold mechanism on each of the instruments cost another $1.50. These rentals, multiplied by every business office in the nation and by every home that has any other than the basic telephone instrument, produce quite a pile of money for the Bell System, and therefore, AT&T protects its equipment monopoly with commensurate vigor.

AT&T's insistence on restricting the equipment used in its system and the deliberate pace at which it makes new instruments available to the public are policies that are deeply rooted in company history. The telephone handset is what you pick up when making a call—the unit that houses both receiver (earpiece) and transmitter (mouthpiece). This instrument dates to the beginning of telephony; indeed, Alexander Graham Bell's original telephone of 1876 was used alternately as mouthpiece or earpiece. The first set was soon followed by one in which two phones were mounted on a common handle—in function little different from the present handset.

Soon thereafter, however, Bell switched to a transmitter too bulky for handset use. The two-piece set became standard in American homes and offices—the mouthpiece in a permanent wall mount or in a desk stand, the earpiece separate and attached by a cord.

Not so on the Continent. A refugee from Western Union's abortive telephone subsidiary, which was put out of business by Bell in the 1879 patent agreement, took with him to France a handset and introduced it into exchanges he helped establish there. Frenchmen found it light, attractive, and easy to use, and by 1885 the handset was standard throughout Europe.

In the United States, meanwhile, Bell's monopoly position permitted a different pace. The head of the AT&T engineering department actually recommended in 1892 the complete abandonment of research into methods of telephony. "I think the theoretical work can be accomplished quite as well and more economically by collaboration with the students of the [Massachusetts] Institute of Technology and probably of Harvard College," he said.

AT&T's interest in the handset was forcibly revived during the Spanish-American War by Army and Navy complaints about the difficulties encountered in trying to keep the two-piece instrument operative in the field. Added impetus came from the independents, who by 1903 offered subscribers several varieties of one-piece handsets. Bell worked up some samples and sent them to twenty-four subsidiary companies for comment. Twenty of them replied the equipment should be used—several insistently so. One dissident was John J. Carty of New York Telephone, an opinionated engineer who simply did not like handsets.

Western Electric began mass production and by mid-1907 supplied 3,020 handsets to the subsidiaries. Then AT&T's internal reorganization following Theodore N. Vail's return to the presidency put Carty at the head of the engineering department. Within twenty-four hours he halted handset production and recalled those that had been shipped. AT&T executives with desk handsets lost them.

Not until 1917 did development work begin again; not until 1926 were handsets offered to the general public (as "French" telephones, commentary of sorts); not until 1934 was a truly workable unit available. Conversely, the Kellogg Switchboard & Supply Company, a major independent supplier, had inundated non-Bell areas with handsets two decades previously.

Bell's two-piece set, which customers were obliged to use until 1934, was markedly inferior, and the major defect was one which Bell could have easily corrected. "Sidetone" is the term telephone people use to describe the echo of a person's voice in the receiver of his own phone when he speaks into the transmitter. The speaker hears sidetone, assumes he is talking at an earsplitting level, and drops his voice below ordinary conversation volume, thereby reducing the energy transmitted to the telephone line and making it difficult for him to be heard on the other end.

The fundamental patent on a method of preventing sidetone was acquired by Bell in 1890 and was strengthened at intervals thereafter by the company's purchases of various refinements. An AT&T engineer, in studies between 1904 and 1906, proved the antisidetone gear could be installed without affecting the efficiency of Bell phones then in use.

Not until 1918 did Bell begin installing sidetone controls and then only on the phones of its own operators. No customers need apply. Independent companies, meanwhile, made sidetone controls standard. In 1934, forty-four years after acquisition of the sidetone patent, Bell finally removed the cave-shouting effect from its customers' phones—and charged an extra fee for the "new, improved telephone."

Why the delay?

The Federal Communications Commission, in its study of Bell during the 1930's, attributed much of the sluggishness to AT&T's noncompetitive position. The manufacturers who competed among themselves for the independent market had to scramble for new ideas to survive, and thus, they produced new ideas.

There was another reason for AT&T's "suppression," to use the FCC's word, of new telephone inventions. Giving subscribers better equipment would mean junking the existing apparatus and expensive retooling by Western Electric. Sure, it might cost more to operate a national telephone system with obsolete switchboards, but that problem could be solved with higher rates. And if the Bell customer struggled with a cumbersome two-piece handset long after customers of independent companies had the modern one-piece handset, so what?

By the 1950's Bell's standard telephone, its Model 500, was a very efficient piece of machinery—no sidetone, a relatively foolproof dial, a bell of variable loudness, stout enough to remain moored to the table when dialed and to survive most falls to the floor. In short, an efficient piece of machinery in which Western Electric could take pride.

The problem was that it also looked like a piece of machinery—squat and black, with a metallic or plastic housing, a coil of tightly curled wire protruding from one side, the gleaming chrome hook which controlled the dial finger, the neatly printed letters and numbers on the face. Customers called it the "black beauty"—but with derision, rather than affection.

Antique dealer Ben Jamil was a man who used the term. An intense, restless New Yorker, Jamil spent much of his time in out-of-the-way shops looking for out-of-the-way things. Old telephones fascinated him: the ornate cabinets from New York town houses of the mauve decade just before the turn of the century; the garish, jewel-inset instrument owned by a silent-screen star; the solid mahogany cases custom-built to hold the phones of the New York rich during the 1920's.

Jamil sensed a market for these phones and bought all he could find. "Bell had done very little pertaining to decor," he recollected. "Their instrument was a monstrosity, garbage from a decorator's point of view. The taste-conscious housewife who spends $35,000 to $40,000 for a home was forced to mar its character with a telephone that was functional but completely out of character."

Jamil also found that the phones worked well after cleaning and minor refurbishing (the replacement of a worn screw or a frayed wire). "There's no great mystery about the telephone. All of those used in the world are completely compatible—whether they are in Moscow or Bangkok or Paris or Buenos Aires. They have to be; otherwise how could you have international long-distance service?" He gestured toward an 1890's Bell-made instrument on the wall of his Manhattan office. "This still has the original mechanism, and you could use it to call anywhere in the world. The volume might be a bit less than that of a new phone, but not so much that it would be noticed by the layman."

Word of Jamil's limited sales got back to AT&T. For a while there was no response whatsoever. Jamil thinks AT&T considered the antique phone thing to be an innocuous little fad that would soon go the way of all fads. Too, the initial antique prices of $175 to $200 per instrument kept him out of the mass market. He chuckles. "My first customers included some rather high-ranking executives of the American Telephone & Telegraph Company."

The antiques proved so popular even on this limited scale that Jamil tested the public appeal for phones that were new but different. From Denmark he purchased a batch of gracefully designed, one-piece instruments with lightweight soft-colored plastic housings. "They hit like a bombshell. The housewife wants to add to the beauty of her room. Offering her a pretty phone was like offering a chance to wear a pretty new blouse." First-year sales were 30,000 to 40,000 phones—some to Bell subscribers in over-the-counter sales; others to persons living in independent-company areas; many directly to independents, who in turn made them available to customers.

Bell's ears perked. But still no overt response.

Then Jamil escalated. He found a supplier in Japan who produced top-quality antique reproductions and any number of way-out designs. Jamil's sales jumped to 8,000 to 10,000 a month; gift shops and retailers all over the country sent in orders. The impact on Bell was oblique. "A person who lived in a Bell area would visit a friend who had obtained an antique phone from an independent company. He'd like it, call Bell to ask about obtaining one for his own home, and be told that he couldn't do so, that it was 'illegal.' When this happened several thousand times, people began to recognize Bell's intransigence for what it was: protection of a market.

"Now here they made a bad mistake. Bell is not the government or the police, automatically entitled to respect and obedience. People didn't like being told by somebody in *business* what they could or could not buy."

Bell also hurried its own color telephones onto the market—the standard Model 500, in multihued plastic cases. However, Bell wanted a $10 initial fee and then a rental ranging from $1 to $1.25 monthly—a price that recouped the cost of the instrument within a year, but that continued in perpetuity. The Bell color phones caused barely a ripple in Jamil's business, for he offered style as well.

By 1962 Bell was alarmed enough that the operating companies sent mailers to subscribers warning against the use of "unauthorized" equipment, citing the proviso in company regulations that only Bell phones were legal, and very gently threatening the cessation of service for violators. New Jersey Bell, for instance, stated that the rules on nonstandard equipment were so important they "include provision for suspension or termination of service of people who do not comply. These regulations are binding on us and our customers."

People ignored the warnings. So Bell went after Jamil, reasoning it would be easier to deal with one supplier than scores of thousands of buyers.

An AT&T representative visited Jamil in 1962 and told him he would be an ideal person to work on "styles and innovations" for Bell. The agent said AT&T was prepared to give Jamil an $800,000 development grant and pay the salaries of his entire staff for twenty-five years while they did research.

The offer interested Jamil, for he had worked at a killing pace for three years, was not a rich man, and wasn't sure that he would ever be one. The AT&T visit, polite as it was, bore the unmistakable scent of trouble. "Here I was, one very small man up against the giant American Tel & Tel Company and offered a large sum of money."

Then the Bell man said, "Of course, there is a stipulation: You must agree to stop selling nonstandard equipment to the public."

How about the items he developed for Bell if he came into the company as a consultant? Jamil asked. Would they be put on the market?

"Oh, no, not necessarily. Our policy is to introduce new equipment as warranted, and that requires many years of testing, of both technical capability and customer needs and desires."

Jamil refused. AT&T tried once more. It offered to hire Jamil and his staff and assign them to a Western Electric development branch in Pennsylvania—a bonus, full salaries, firm, long-term contracts. As before, however, AT&T wanted the stipulation that would put Jamil out of the phone business. And again it would not agree to market what Jamil developed under Western Electric auspices.

"They wanted us to keep busy doing nothing," Jamil says. "I didn't want any of this. I was in the telephone business."

Jamil next saw Bell in court. AT&T filed suits asking that dealers handling his phones be enjoined from selling them and that they be forced to pay damages for allegedly encouraging customers to violate Bell tariffs by installing unauthorized equipment.

Most of Jamil's outlets capitulated immediately when challenged by Bell—and with economic justification. A gift shop that sold one or two antique phones per month as a sideline could not waste time and money in court. But Bell also hit some larger merchants. In 1964 Southwestern Bell Telephone got a permanent injunction barring Foley's of Houston, the city's largest department store, from selling antiques. A suit against Rothschild's, the big Oklahoma City store, asked both an injunction and a list of people who had purchased antiques so that Southwestern Bell could compute damages.

Sales of the antiques were not illegal so long as retailers didn't try to instruct buyers on how to attach them to Bell lines. "They tried to trap us," Jamil said. "They would send a Bell employee into a store, ostensibly to buy an antique phone. He would go into a long tirade about how unfair it was that the phone company would charge him an extra monthly rental for a Princess phone or a color phone and ask the salesman how to install the phone without calling Bell."

Louis Lefkowitz, the New York state attorney general, troubled the antique dealers. His Office of Consumer Complaints went after Telephone Center, Inc., of Manhattan, which specialized in working models of turn-of-the-century American and European phones. Both Jamil and Telephone Center were dubious of the attorney general's motivations. According to Lefkowitz, citizens complained they had been misled into thinking the telephone company did not object to such equipment, only to be threatened with loss of service. The Telephone Center signed a pledge that it would tell customers of the phone company's rule but branded as an "absolute lie" the accusation that it tried to conceal the rules from customers. But, as Jamil noted, "Who enjoys getting into a fight with the attorney general, even when you are in the right?"

By 1964 the nonstandard equipment manufacturers and suppliers had pretty well decided that Bell must be challenged, lest the war of attrition it was waging wear down all dealers singly. The forum which was chosen was ideal for three reasons: (1) the subscriber who wanted non-Bell equipment was motivated by more than a casual whim; (2) the manufacturer involved had the resources required to contest AT&T in a protracted conflict before a state regulatory agency; and (3) the California Public Utilities Commission, which heard the case, has the reputation of being open-minded.

The test case began casually enough. James W. McAlvin, administrator of Doctors General Hospital in San Jose, California, stopped overnight in a motel in Kalama, Washington, in 1962, and was intrigued by the telephone in his room. It was an Ericofon, a one-piece Swedish unit resembling a poised cobra, with the dialing mechanism in the base. The graceful style of the Ericofon won it recognition as one of the twenty best industrial designs of the twentieth century and a permanent display niche in the Museum of Contemporary Art in New York City.

McAlvin liked the Ericofon for other than esthetic reasons. Doctors General Hospital was modernizing, and McAlvin had ideas on what a telephone could contribute to an efficient operation. His requirements were simple: He wanted a telephone that could be put down anywhere after completion of a conversation so that a bedridden patient wouldn't have to strain to return the receiver to a hook. Noise was a factor. "The constant battle is for hospital people to keep noise levels down," he said. "Therefore, it is our desire to have a telephone that will have a signaling device that is of a softer tone, not of a bell, for a bell does create considerable noise." McAlvin found the Ericofon easy to cradle under one arm—or even between the knees—for dialing if the patient had one arm immobilized.

McAlvin played with the Ericofon for several hours, was satisfied with the way it worked, bought a model, and suggested to the hospital architect that it be used in the new portion of the hospital. The architect agreed. His plans included a wall cabinet beside each bed with the telephone and controls for radio, television, the intercom system, and the window louvers. The Ericofon fit nicely into the cabinet. "It was decided that we had a telephone here that would work into our program in an acceptable way," McAlvin said.

On September 19, 1962, Doctors General Hospital routinely notified the Pacific Telephone & Telegraph Company of its intention to use Ericofons.

PT&T's San Jose marketing office, after considerable delay, said the hospital couldn't use Ericofons—that their transmission was poor and unsuitable for use in the Bell System. Besides, Western Electric was working on a similar phone—called the Shmoo because of its resemblance to the Al Capp cartoon creature—which the hospital should use. However, Bell couldn't show any specifications on the Shmoo, which the architect needed for his planning, nor could it guarantee delivery in early 1964, when the hospital was to be completed.

Since Bell didn't have what the hospital wanted, McAlvin renewed his notice of intention to use the Ericofons.

PT&T suddenly realized the dogged hospital administrator was the kind of person that the Bell System calls "a problem," and intraoffice memos began flying. One of them admitted that the Ericofon was "within the agreed acceptable transmission band." However, it continued, "If these telephones were used by him [McAlvin] we would have to provide similar service for all subscribers and . . . in many instances the service would not be acceptable." (It will be recalled that PT&T's original objection was based on the "poor transmission" issue. At this point the *real* reason for its opposition begins to surface: the fear of mass use of non-Western Electric gear.)

PT&T in another memo peeked into the corners to see if it could find a troublemaker behind the Ericofons. Eventually it came up with the intelligence that a physician member of the hospital board was "reputedly active" in the Anti Digit Dialing League, a West Coast organization which was fighting PT&T's inauguration of all-numeral dialing. The only counterlever which PT&T could find—not a very strong one—was the fact that it had donated $1,000 to the hospital's building fund.

The negotiations continued through the first half of 1963, with Bell hurriedly working to put together an alternative phone and with McAlvin worriedly watching architectural and construction deadlines. On May 20, 1963, PT&T said it would not connect with Ericofon and ruled it unsuitable for hospital use. It claimed patients' lack of familiarity and a 90 percent weekly turnover would require constant instruction on the use of Ericofons by hospital personnel. With the switch in the base of the Ericofon, Bell said, patients would make too many accidental hang-ups during calls and overburden the hospital switchboard.*

All AT&T would promise the hospital was to provide the "most up to date instrument available when the hospital was ready" and showed pictures of an instrument, *still under development*, which is called the dial-in-handset, a variation of Western Electric's one-piece Trimline model, the phone shaped like a shoe. Doctors General Hospital tested a model of the dial-in-handset, found it inadequate, could get nowhere in further negotiations with PT&T, and filed a formal complaint with the Public Utilities Commission.

Testimony at the hearings which followed proved several points which non-Bell equipment manufacturers had stated for years: that in a particular situation, phones made by someone other than Western Electric can perform better; that Western Electric has lagged in developing the diversity of phones desired by a modern society; that because of its monopoly position, AT&T can remain dogmatically stubborn and insist on having things its own way even when wrong.

For the independent manufacturers the Doctors General Hospital hearing was a good test case because an issue of substance was involved. Here was no phone subscriber insisting on non-Bell equipment simply because he wanted an oddball phone built by the local inventor. The Doctors General Hospital witnesses ticked off a long list of reasons why, for their purposes, the Ericofon was better than Bell's dial-in-handset:

—The Ericofon, when ringing, emits a pleasant, chirping sound; the dial-in-handset has a harsh gong sound. A PUC examiner asked a PT&T witness whether the bell was designed to be "so irritating that the called party will answer promptly." The PT&T man said, "I don't think we would like to put it that way, but there is a certain amount of that in the design. Mr. Examiner, if I may comment, we usually call it 'urgency.' "

—The Ericofon has its dial in the bottom of the instrument; Bell's dial is smaller in diameter and is centered on one side of the instrument between the transmitter and the receiver. Patients in tests found the Ericofon easier to dial.

---

* AT&T's logic has a self-perpetuating dizziness. The public doesn't know how to use Ericofons properly because it is unfamiliar with them. The public won't have a chance to learn how to use Ericofons because Bell won't permit any practice, *Ergo,* no Ericofons.

—The Ericofon is stable on a slope of 40 degrees; the dial-in-handset slides on a slope.

—The dial-in-handset wasn't suitable for the hospital cabinets, for patients would have to lean out of bed to maneuver the handset back into the mounting; the Ericofon could be set back on the shelf.

—The dial-in-handset has an off-on button in the hand unit, as well as in the cradle in which the unit rests when not in use. Hospital officials feared patients would use the button to answer calls and to hang up and keep the hand unit in bed with them, rather than return it to the cradle—"an undesirable hospital practice." They said patients could become tangled in the cord, roll over on the phone during their sleep, or contaminate it.

PT&T's objections centered on accidental hang-ups because the off-on button was in the bottom of the Ericofon;* alleged transmission difficulties (a revival of the original complaint); and the contention that maintenance problems with the Ericofons are substantially higher than with Bell sets.

All of this was convincingly rebutted by witnesses from the North Electric Company, of Galion, Ohio, the Ericofon's United States manufacturer. North Electric began making the phones in 1958; by 1964, the hearing year, it had some 115,000 in use in independent companies. Another 1,000,000 or so were used in various European and Latin American systems. Forty governmental telephone administrations throughout the world, as well as the Rural Electric Administration for companies under its farm-phone loan programs, approved the Ericofon.

Before the Ericofon was marketed, North Electric field-tested it with 1,000 independent telephone company subscribers, more than 90 percent of whom preferred it to their previous telephone. "In fact, they said they would want to keep the Ericofon even at an increased rate," said North Electric's Robert E. Pickett. Independent companies using Ericofons received no complaints from the Bell companies with which they connected, Pickett said; from an engineering standpoint the instrument performed equally with Bell's standard Model 500 telephone (the plastic black beauty).

---

* While living in Mexico City during 1966, we had an apartment with an Ericofon; I recall one accidental hang-up during seven months, that during the first week. One soon learns to rest the Ericofon on its side.

A typical independent, the Lincoln Telephone & Telegraph Company, of Lincoln, Nebraska, charged a $25 installation fee when it first offered Ericofons. "We thought they might cause us considerable trouble, but we found this was not the case," said one of its executives. The fee was reduced to $5, and $20 was refunded to prior subscribers. "We have not found that these telephones cause us any more trouble than the conventional-type sets and in our opinion they are completely compatible with other telephone equipment." The transmission capability, while "not quite equal" to Western Electric instruments, "would not be noticed by the users," and was "entirely adequate for normal use."

Opinions were mixed on maintenance. One independent California company said it had 9.2 troubles per 100 Ericofons per year and 4.8 per 100 sets of different origin, while another set its figures at 5.2 per 100 Ericofons and 5.8 per 100 for other phones. The PUC staff, after its own study, found that the Ericofon was "suitable for use on Pacific Telephone's system" and that it "will not impair the service to any other subscribers."

The Pacific Telephone & Telegraph Company said it saw no inconsistency between its restrictive equipment practice and its intention (as stated in the 1963 annual report): "We cannot stand still in serving our customers and their changing, varying needs." To James M. Henderson, of PT&T's commercial department, the company's primary responsibility was to provide the most efficient, yet economical and usable, telephone service to subscribers. Yet Henderson said that needs and desires of individuals *"would be subordinate to the requirement for all the large body of telephone users. . . ."* PT&T would gladly consider service ideas offered by subscribers, but to be acceptable they must be "consistent with the good of the whole."

The PUC got some interesting admissions from other Bell witnesses. L. R. Krebs, of the Bell Telephone Laboratories, after a lengthy discourse on the shortcomings of Ericofon, admitted that save for a brief period after the end of the Second World War, Bell *never* approved for use in its system any "common garden variety" telephones other than those made by Western Electric.

Richard C. Frey, a PT&T vice-president, said the company installs 600,000 to 700,000 new phones a year, both as replacements for outmoded models and for newcomers to California. He said it was "obvious" that AT&T profits would be cut if non-Bell equipment were permitted in the system.

(By how much? An unanswerable question. But the California PUC, in a rate proceeding concluded just prior to the Ericofon hearing, accused Western Electric of systematic, long-term profiteering. During the years 1916–61, the PUC said, Western Electric realized earnings of $340,740,000 more than the returns found fair for PT&T, a difference between Western Electric's composite 9.1 percent return for the period and the composite 6.5 percent that the PUC had said was fair for PT&T.)

PT&T lost. The PUC on June 29, 1965, held that the dial-in-handset was "insufficient and inadequate" and no substitute for the Ericofon and that the Ericofon would not impair service on the PT&T system. It ordered PT&T to connect the Ericofons at the regular installation rate.

The PUC also cut the rate Doctors General Hospital would have to pay for service once it had its own equipment. Previously, PT&T charged $1.50 per month for flat rate service and $1 per month for message rate service (this for phones connected to a private switchboard). The PUC held that of these rates, 50 cents a month was a "reasonable allowance for the costs of providing a telephone set" and ordered the hospital's rate reduced by this amount monthly. The price North Electric charged the hospital for each phone was not put into the hearing record. However, the retail price for an Ericofon is $49.50, indicating a wholesale price in the neighborhood of $25 to $30. At a saving of 50 cents a month for rental and $10 per unit for installation the hospital therefore could regain its investment in several months.

AT&T realized the potential calamity of the decision. In the unlikely event each of the 70,000,000-odd phone subscribers in the nation suddenly insisted on owning his own instrument, Bell could lose monthly revenues of $35,000,000, plus the Western Electric manufacturing profits. Rescind the order, Bell begged the PUC, and it would provide Ericofons to the hospital at its own expense—anything to preserve the status quo and to remove a dangerous precedent from the utility casebooks. The PUC declined the offer, and Doctors General got its telephones from North Electric.

The California outcome convinced AT&T that it was bucking an irresistible tide of public opinion, and in October, 1965, it changed its position on the "foreign attachments." Without undue publicity Bell operating companies began giving approval to installations of whatever kind of phone its customers wanted—be it one of Ben Jamil's 1880 Danish cradle jobs covered with red ostrich leather or a chic North Electric Ericofon. AT&T's vice-president for planning, Gordon Thayer, told the *Wall Street Journal* the change "will get us off the hook" with customers who demanded novel phones.

AT&T does make such installations costly, however: it insists that the internal working mechanism of the antiques and foreign phones come from Western Electric or have the approval of Bell. Most state commissions permit the company to charge $10 for this modification when no parts must be replaced and $25 for a complete conversion.

Ben Jamil thinks this charge an outrage. "What Bell has to do to most of these phones is worth no more than $2 or $3," he said. "In many cases the serviceman cleans and checks the contact points, and nothing more, and still the company sends a bill for $10 or even $25."

The availability of non-Bell equipment had an immediate impact on the prices AT&T companies charge for their own decorator instruments (an illustration again of the benefits of occasional telephone competition and also an indication that AT&T was overcharging the public). The nonrecurring initial charge for a color phone at one time was $10; by 1967 this was down to $4. The Princess phone, formerly $1 a month extra, was 50 cents. Bell justifies the charge for a color phone by saying it costs money to keep a full stock of multicolor instruments. The colored plastic housings, according to independent equipment manufacturers, cost well under $1.

Bell's major loss to the nonstandard equipment industry, however, is on the monthly rental it levies for business and residential extension stations. A homeowner who wants an upstairs or workroom extension phone, if he uses Bell equipment, has to pay an extra 90 cents monthly as long as it is used. This can be avoided by (1) having the phone company install a jack where the phone is to be placed, at a onetime fee of $7, and (2) purchasing the second phone on the open market, where reconverted instruments can be found for less than $7.

Legally these phones are subject to the initial Bell installation fee of $10 or $25, depending on the amount of conversion required. In practice, however, there appears to be widespread violation of the phone company's regulations. A New York dealer advertises in a mail brochure, "All phones equipped with cord and plug ready to plug into a jack for instant use." The same brochure states, "These are factory reconditioned phones completely equipped with standard cord and plug. It is absolutely legal to buy your own phones. Thousands are bought every year by prudent buyers. If you have a jack for a portable phone, our phone will plug right in." The brochure says the buyer's "only obligation is to be sure you do not interfere with telephone service." What he does *not* state is that a person caught using one of these instruments that has not been "converted" by Bell faces loss of his phone service.*

Bell's billing system tends to keep phone users ignorant of the charges they pay for extra equipment. A citizen who requests an extra-long cord sees the charge of 35 cents stated separately on his bill only one time. The next month the cord charge is lumped into the monthly bill, along with his Princess phone rental and the extra $1 he pays for an extension downstairs. Were the citizen to see this 35 cents itemized month after month, he might realize that he is paying $4.20 a year for a piece of cord that he could buy from an independent telephone supply house for 35 cents.

Massachusetts State Representative Helen H. Guliano did some investigating in this area in the early 1960's and found a person who had an extra-loud gong signal removed from his phone, but who continued to pay rental on it for six years, simply because he did not compare billings. Had the gong been listed separately, the error would have been caught after one month. Another Massachusetts resident discovered that he paid rental on three extension phones for years, although he had only two in the house. Mrs. Guliano introduced a bill requiring Bell to itemize all charges, but it perished in committee.

Bell doesn't like customers to think that they are paying

* Bell can find illegal "second phones" by determining whether there is extra drainage on the line when the number is dialed. It is said the way to hide a bootleg extension phone is to disconnect its bell: no ring, no drain on the line, no discovery by Bell. Whether this is right, I know not, but as stated earlier, AT&T can stop the service of people who do such things.

"additional" or "more" for extra phone equipment. "None of these [words] are helpful phrases or words for you," a Southwestern Bell Telephone Company merchandising man counseled. "None of them help the customer to want the system particularly. . . ."

His suggestion was to respond: "Mrs. Jones, you have only one telephone now? Two telephones, one in the kitchen and one in the bedroom, would be only $6.25 a month for both of them in color." He continued: "[People] don't like to pay 'additional' for anything. Do you? People don't like to pay 'more' for something. Do you? People are really not interested in the 'rate' and they don't particularly like to hear the word 'charge' associated with something in which they have expressed an interest. The job of the salesman, then, is not just to answer questions to satisfy a customer's needs, but to use words *to help people want things. . . .*"

How is this done? "[Suppose] you were to say, 'Mrs. Jones, may I make a suggestion?' The customer *must* say, 'Yes.' No one is going to turn down a suggestion. And then you go on: 'My suggestion would be telephones in the bedroom in color and a telephone in the kitchen in color; this would save your running back and forth to answer the telephone; also, you would have more privacy. . . .' "

The merchandising man advised that his hucksters avoid using the word "recommendation" because "it's a long, formal, expensive-sounding word. To some customers it suggests work —the effort of making a decision."

Press agentry enables AT&T to blur the fact that many of its "new services" and "innovations" in equipment actually are ancient history in non-Bell telephone areas. For decades London residents have been able to summon a bobby, a firewagon, or ambulance by walking into a pay station and dialing 999, with no coin required. Bell's phones are mute until fed with a dime.

Not until the summer of 1966 did AT&T begin experiments with free emergency calling. The test was run in the relatively peaceful city of Hartford, Connecticut, and the first three days indicated the service was useful. Special operators logged forty-eight dimeless emergency calls in the period—a fire, robbers breaking into a store, a teen-age gang fight, a man leaving a parking lot without paying.

Nonetheless, Bell still was calling the system experimental

the following January, when it inaugurated free emergency service in certain booths in the Greenwich Village area of Manhattan. In all the hoopla (Mayor John Lindsay made the first call) no one ever mentioned that the British had enjoyed similar service for years.

The AT&T companies now are enthusiastic over their "introduction" of the push-button dial system. ("Coming in 1967: the popular Trimline telephone with Touchtone service," boasts the 1966 annual report of the Ohio Bell Telephone Company.) Actually, the minute Chardon, Ohio, Telephone Company, part of Ohio's Mid-Continental Telephone System, put push-button dialing into use on December 18, 1962, while the Bell companies had done no more than test installations.

The home telephone is the keystone of the entire Bell System, for it supplies the bulk of revenues for both the operating companies and Western Electric. AT&T is equally zealous, however, in protecting what could be called the peripheral market—any communications equipment remotely connected with the telephone or which could be replaced by a Bell-owned instrument. AT&T's battle plan is an "aggressive defense," in which Bell invades areas of communications which are almost, but not quite pure telephony and then bargains from conquered territory. An AT&T executive once stated the strategy: "The nearer the trading can be carried to the major field of our competitors, the more advantageous trading position we are in." Bell feels that unless this is done, the competitors will "carry their offensive right up to the wall of our defense. . . ."

One area in which Bell extended its "wall of defense" into previously non-AT&T land involved the municipal fire alarm industry—the manufacturers who produce and install the red fire alarm boxes that are found on street corners in almost every city of America.

The industry has nothing to do with public telephone communications. Although some police call boxes have phones inside them, these are for the use of policemen to call their station houses, not for the general public. Fire alarm boxes normally do not contain phones; instead, they transmit a telegraphlike signal to the nearest fire station.

AT&T went into the fire alarm business in 1953, and right away its presence was noted. The fire alarm industry is brutally competitive. As Senator Ernest Gruening of Alaska stated in a floor speech on August 13, 1962, "It is characterized by a good bit of hard selling and sometimes at least apparently devious practices. . . . Because the products are sold almost exclusively to municipal governments, there are sometimes opportunities for influence peddling."

AT&T felt right at home in the field—indeed so much so that the previous leaders had to call for help. The Gamewell Company of Newton Upper Falls, Massachusetts, in 1953 had been the leader among eight or ten manufacturers. In 1962, however, Gamewell was so hard pressed by AT&T that it appealed to the Justice Department, charging that AT&T should have been kept out of the fire alarm business under the 1956 antitrust case consent decree. Gamewell noted the decree's provision that AT&T could not enter new nontelephonic business. The company put together a massive dossier for the Justice Department. After study, however, Justice decided it could do nothing about the situation.

But a copy of the Gamewell report got to Senator Gruening, who used it in a Senate speech to document what he called the "predatory, anticompetitive conduct" of AT&T. Gruening cited Gamewell charges that AT&T packed town meetings with its employees to pressure local governments and used public officials who formerly worked for Bell to influence city decisions. Gamewell said Bell gave city employees free vacations "thinly disguised as 'educational trips' and offered jobs to relatives of city officials. AT&T argued that its tax payments (sizable in any community) entitled it to consideration over other, smaller firms.

On and on the Gamewell list went: AT&T used advertising to influence local newspapers to favor its fire alarm system over others when reporting contract negotiations. Bell personnel in influential civic groups lobbied with city halls. AT&T's size enabled it to field a sales force thirty times larger than the rest of the industry combined. Its "unmatchable institutional advertising"—financed by telephone subscribers—was used to sell fire alarm systems. Cities that would not buy the Bell alarm system were denied access to Bell poles and ducts needed for installation of non-Bell systems.

Gruening further reported that Gamewell claimed that in New Haven, Connecticut, Bell threatened to cancel plans to construct a new office building unless it received a fire alarm contract. The withdrawal would have disrupted New Haven's valued downtown urban renewal program. While none of Gamewell's reported charges have been proved, in the New Haven instance Bell received the contract.

Gamewell's complaint to the Justice Department and the publicity given the situation by Senator Gruening were to no avail. In 1957, by industry estimate, AT&T controlled 60 percent of the fire alarm market, with Gamewell and the other companies splitting the remaining 40 percent. By 1961 AT&T had installed more than 1,000 fire alarm boxes in more than 100 cities.

AT&T sold the fire alarm systems as part of a communications package for city governments that included direct lines to offices that bypassed switchboards (the Centrex) and inter-communications equipment. AT&T offered business houses and factories much the same package—and here again was able to use its girth to advantage. The American Communications Association, composed of independent manufacturers, wholesalers, and retailers of intercommunication equipment, documented scores of cases where Bell systematically excluded competitors from making sales in this field. The favored persuader was the refusal to put telephone lines into a conduit containing other wiring. The businessman was thus left with three alternatives: give up his telephone service, pay for additional conduits, or throw out the non-Bell intercommunications system and buy the intercom offered by Bell. The Justice Department supported Bell's assertion that this was not a proscribed field under terms of the 1956 consent decree.

In Euclid, Ohio, the school board wanted to eliminate direct lines in its buildings and reduce a $2,000 monthly phone bill. Leonard F. Zaller, president of Electronic Products & Equipment, Inc., offered to install for $3,000 an intercom system that met the school board's specifications. No further expenditure would be required for the intercom equipment. The Ohio Bell Telephone Company offered intercom service as part of a package which included a telephone bill of $1,539 a month for five years. Ohio Bell got the contract. The Cleveland *Plain Dealer,* in reporting the meeting at which this decision was made, stated: "Board President Dale E. Mansperger said the board's decision to contract with Ohio Bell was not based on cost alone, but rather on consideration of service and convenience, *as well as a tax-factor. Ohio Bell pays $105,000 a year* in utility taxes."

Use of the private intercom system would have saved the Euclid school board an estimated $5,000 a year in billings. Leonard Zaller, however, didn't pay $105,000 a year in taxes, so he lost.

Leaders in the private communications industry find solace in what they consider hints that the FCC is beginning to question the fairness of the equipment monopoly. The FCC's attitude is changing slowly—indeed, so slowly that a full decade intervened between its two positive antimonopoly actions—and no person in the industry or at the FCC staff level can yet make an educated estimate of whether a true revolution is beginning.

The first landmark decision, in 1957, permitted the use of a device called the Hush-a-Phone on Bell equipment. The Hush-a-Phone fits onto the mouthpiece and permits a caller to speak at a normal conversational level without his words being overheard by anyone else in the room. There is no direct physical connection between the two instruments. The sound is transmitted by induction, a process in which an electrical field created in the Hush-a-Phone acts as a carrying electromotive force.

The Hush-a-Phone, put on the market in the early 1950's, was popular with people who had to do telephone work in cramped offices and in business operations with a battery of telephones in the same room. Bell fought introduction of the device, and the manufacturer, after considerable legal wrangling, finally obtained a federal court order declaring the ban unfair. The court told the FCC to amend AT&T's tariffs to permit use of the Hush-a-Phone. Whereupon the FCC issued a ruling that AT&T could not outlaw Hush-a-Phone "or any other device which does not injure [Bell's] employees, facilities, or the public in its use of [Bell's] services, or impair the operation of the telephone system."

To private equipment manufacturers the latter part of the order seemed sufficiently broad to throw open the telephone market. So, apparently, did AT&T. There was a flurry of backstage activity, and within thirty days the commission hurried out an explanatory note stating the order did not permit the "interconnection of telephone company lines or channels with any other lines or channels except as presently provided in other tariff provisions." The sum of these notices was to permit AT&T to continue as the judge of what should go on its lines— and to require independent manufacturers to go to the expense of proving in court or before a regulatory agency that their equipment was compatible with the Bell system and thus eligible for use.

Thomas F. Carter, of Dallas, Texas, started working with radio and electronic equipment as a child; after completing military service in 1946, he opened a business that specialized in mobile two-way radio systems.

Many of Carter's sales were to oil companies, whose drilling crews often must work in remote locations where there is no telephone service. Even a two-way radio system has shortcomings: If a field engineer wants to communicate with someone who is not at the radio base station, his message must be repeated into the telephone by the radio operator. The Chevron Oil Company does considerable drilling in very rural southern Louisiana, where telephones are scarce and the French-American populace speaks a patois unlike that heard anywhere else in the world. Frank S. Bird, a Chevron engineer and a communications specialist for the American Petroleum Institute, an industry group, says relaying of even routine queries is difficult. "This gets more complicated when it is a geologist reporting to his superior that he has some particular five-syllable long name fossils at a particular depth and the supervisor comes back and wants to know if they are this type or that type and the man in the middle speaks with a strong French accent." Bird says Chevron frequently has situations develop at "two o'clock Sunday morning where $20,000 or $30,000 decisions have to be made quickly."

Thus, Chevron and other oil companies were happy when Carter developed a device, the Carterfone, that enabled people with a two-way radio to speak directly into a telephone via a base station, eliminating the need for the operator to act as an intermediary.

The person who initiates the call first contacts the base station operator of the private radio system where the Carterfone is located, by either radio or telephone. The operator then contacts the called party, again by either radio or telephone, as the case may be. When both parties are ready, the operator places his telephone handset into a cradle on the Carterfone that has been designed to receive it. A voice control circuit in the

Carterfone switches the radio transmitter on when the party using the telephone is speaking and returns the radio to receiving condition when he is finished. As was the case with the Hush-a-Phone, there is no physical interconnection (wire-to-wire) of the instruments; the sound interchange is via induction.

The Carterfone went on the market in 1959, with Carter promoting it by direct mail and through trade publication advertisements, selling both directly and through dealers. The response was wide, with some 3,600 units being sold in seven years. "In New Mexico and West Texas," says Carter, "I know of several ranchers who are using Carterfones in areas where there is no telephone service available."

The Bell System companies provide mobile two-way radio service that interconnects with phone lines and as of June, 1966, had 30,500 such units in operation. However, the mobile systems cover only about one-third of the country's total land area, and there is a shortage of frequencies in many areas. Bell has a waiting list for mobile service in such cities as Los Angeles, New York, and Chicago; in the remote West, where the need is greatest, the service is nonexistent, and this is where the Carterfone business was best.

Carter (and a lawyer working for him at the time) thought the Hush-a-Phone decision made his phone legal. Bell disagreed and, beginning in 1961, warned persons using and selling Carterfones that their phone service would be discontinued. The dealers began shipping Carterfones back to Dallas. As a firm in Topeka, Kansas, said in a letter: "We are not a large enough company to engage in costly litigation with the Bell System . . . we are indeed sorry that we cannot do business with you inasmuch as we feel there is a definite market for your product." Carter received scores of similar letters as his business came to an abrupt halt, and he went out of business in January of 1966.

Bell's opposition was based on several grounds: that the Carterfone interferes with the quality of telephone transmission; that the longer time required to complete calls and the extension of telephone calls by private radio into distant toll zones would impose an unpredictable burden on the telephone system with a consequent increase in costs; that the phone companies would be blamed for service complaints actually caused by Carterfones. Besides, Bell asserted, it offered equipment that worked as well as Carterfones.

Or did it? Bell's version was the Speakerphone, a desk-top amplifier resembling the squawk box portion of an intercommunications system. Set this down alongside the radio microphone, Bell said, and the telephone caller could talk quite well with the man in the field. Bird of Chevron Oil says that he tried the instrument and that it was so noisy and so susceptible to interference by sounds in the room that he rated it as "very poor."

There is credible circumstantial evidence that Bell's opposition to the Carterfone was motivated by a desire to protect its equipment rental market. The city engineer of Idaho Falls, Idaho, talked with a Carterfone distributor about putting the instruments into municipal cars and trucks. Bell objected. Its local manager insisted on renting its own mobile phones to Idaho Falls at $57 per vehicle per month. Wells L. Brady, the Carterfone distributor, wrote Carter: "It came out that the telephone company would have all the money back in four months and the city would have no radio equipment." (Carterfones sold for around $248 retail.)

Wells Brady gave his opinion on what caused Bell's objections. "The telephone company has just installed a transmitter here for car telephones and I can see their concern. If the word got out the city was using it [Carterfone] everyone would want one."

On November 29, 1965, his business wrecked because he could not market his invention, Thomas Carter brought an antitrust suit in the U.S. District Court in Dallas, claiming damages of $450,000. His lawyers, Ray Besing and Bill Brice, charged in their brief that AT&T and its affiliate "wrongfully used [their tariffs] . . . to accomplish a violation of the antitrust laws of the United States. Such tariff does not and may not authorize or excuse the . . . violation of the antitrust laws. . . ." Bell's rules, they averred, "have substantially lessened . . . competition" in the telephone equipment field "and have tended to create and further maintain the monopoly over said facilities now held by the defendants."

Carter lost the first round. Both the district court and circuit court of appeals held that under the doctrine of primary jurisdiction the FCC was the proper body to determine initially whether the tariff was in fact being applied properly by AT&T.

So attorneys Brice and Besing took the Carterfone case to the FCC, which agreed to review Bell's equipment tariffs.

Hearing examiner Chester F. Naumowicz, Jr., ruled against Bell on virtually every substantive issue raised in the case. He agreed with Carter that there was a substantial unfilled demand for such service and that it was not available in many parts of the country. Noting that Bell had produced evidence of only one instance where a citizen tampered with its equipment in installing a Carterfone, he said misuse of 1 of 97,000,000 telephones "can hardly be said to demonstrate the extended use of the device will uncover a widespread urge toward vandalism of the telephone system." Naumowicz said, "In general, there is no reason to anticipate that the Carterfone will have an adverse effect on the telephone system or any part thereof." Its continued prohibition "would be inequitable and discriminatory in favor of the telephone company."

Yet the prohibition up until the time of the hearing was not necessarily "unjust, unreasonable, discriminatory or otherwise unlawful," Naumowicz found. "Quite possibly some interconnecting devices could have damaged the phone system, and the phone companies had no way of knowing Carterfone was harmless." Lacking this knowledge, he ruled, it was not improper to lump Carterfone with other devices in a general prohibition against interconnection devices, for to do otherwise "would have been to expose the integrity of the telephone system as a whole to risks of undeterminable gravity."

Naumowicz seemed to recognize the contradictory nature of his opinion and the unfairness of a system which forces a small businessman to go to great legal expense to gain access to a market. For this reason, he noted: "Possibly, the time has come to consider the establishment of a process whereby those wishing to market or use attachments to the telephone system might submit them to the telephone company for expeditious approval or disapproval under previously expressed objective standards with a right of simplified appeal to the judgment of regulatory authorities."

The full commission, by a 6 to 0 vote, went even further than did Naumowicz. In the summer of 1968 it declared that "the tariff has been unreasonable, discriminatory, and unlawful in the past, and . . . the provisions prohibiting the use of customer-provided interconnecting devices should accordingly be stricken." It said further, " . . . the present unlawfulness of the tariff also permeates its past. . . . Furthermore, the tariff was the carrier's own. It was not prescribed by the commission." (Nor, for that matter, was it *challenged* by the commission. The 1968 language notwithstanding, the FCC shares the blame with Bell for the foreign equipment ban.)

The language of the Carterfone decision apparently barred the telephone monopoly from prohibiting future use of customer-owned telephone gadgets that didn't impair the working of the phone system. The FCC told Bell and General Telephone, another defendant party, to file a new tariff in compliance with its order. The FCC first set a deadline of November 1, 1968; then, heeding Bell protests and pressures, extended it to January 1, 1969. AT&T put the time to good use—when the tariffs were finally announced, they amounted to arrogant disregard of what the FCC had ordered.

AT&T said it *would not* change its restrictive rules on ownership of equipment by residential phone users. AT&T said it *would* permit use of customer-owned acoustic or inductive devices (such as the Carterfone) to connect private radiotelephone systems to its telephone network; but customer-owned devices to connect communications *other than* radiotelephone systems would still be banned.

Although the new tariffs violated both the spirit and the letter of the Carterfone decision, the FCC adopted them unflinchingly on December 24, 1968—surely the most valuable item Ma Bell found in her Christmas stocking. The formal order said that in permitting the tariffs to become effective "we are not giving any specific approval to the revised tariffs." This sentence is semantical legerdemain. By failing to object to the tariffs, the FCC acquiesced in their applications—and in doing so gave them the force of law. One commissioner refused to join his colleagues in hoodwinking the public. Nicholas Johnson, in a vigorous dissent, noted the Carterfone decision "was heralded as a commendable effort to open up competition in the communications business." Johnson continued:

> As experienced reformers have long since discovered, however, the political victories that are won after long struggles under the light of public scrutiny can be very quickly lost in the dark back rooms of practical implementation. The new legislation or agency decision is praised and then forgotten. And when—if ever—anyone goes back to see how it all

worked out he finds the situation very little changed from before. The swampwaters have returned to their former level.

Further, the FCC closed all further public discussion of foreign attachments by ruling—at Bell's request—that subsequent proceedings be conducted "off the record," with only AT&T officials and commission staff present. By doing so the FCC effectively silenced opponents to the new tariffs—including the Justice Department and International Telephone & Telegraph Company. Utility expert Willis Park Rokes of the University of Nebraska, criticizing this decision in *The Nation* of June, 1969, declared it was "highly questionable practice for the FCC to bar interested parties from the hearings. Whether AT&T is to remain the sole provider of all telephone appliances . . . is a serious matter on which the ordinary person will apparently have no effective voice, and of which, indeed, he is likely to be totally unaware."

After the Carterfone decision Dallas attorneys Brice and Besing returned to Federal court to press their antitrust suit. Brice recognized the implications of the Carterfone ruling. Shortly after it was issued, he wrote me, "I told the Bell lawyers earlier in the case that our situation could be likened to a little man standing in front of the Empire State Building telling the owners. 'You have stolen a penny of mine and it is somewhere in that building. I want my penny and if you don't give it to me, I am going to start at the top and take that building down until I get my money back.' Bell would not give us our penny and we have begun the demolition job."

Bell did not choose to fight. In an out-of-court settlement in the spring of 1969 it paid Tom Carter a six-figure settlement.

Another form of equipment which AT&T tries to keep off the market—and here we move away from the legitimate dealers—comes from the so-called telephone underground. This gear is of diverse origin and function but has a common purpose: to cheat the Bell System out of long-distance revenues. (And because it is illegal, certain portions of the following paragraphs are deliberately vague.)

Consider the black box, a device that is no larger than a matchbox, but that nonetheless fools Bell's equipment into thinking that incoming long-distance calls are not completed.

Bookies like this item because it saves them money on calls from out-of-town bettors and leaves no record of who called them, when or from where.

When a Miami man was sentenced to jail for a year in 1965 for manufacturing—and using—black boxes, an attorney for the Southern Bell Telephone Company asked for an injunction keeping secret details on how it worked. Even a patent application, he said, could put enough information on the record to cause Bell grievous loss of long-distance revenues.

A companion gadget is the blue box, which enables a long-distance caller to bypass AT&T's billing equipment. Bell's long-distance routing equipment is activated by tone signals, two per number. The blue box has a standard telephone dial, a duplication of the operator's key, and a mechanism that reproduces the tone signals. The swindler first calls a long-distance number which he has reason to know will not answer—a pay station in Denver, for illustrative purposes. After a couple of rings he punches a blue box button which produces a tone terminating the Denver call but leaving the long-distance line open. Now he can call anywhere in the country he desires by piping tone signals into the wire with the blue box. All that shows on phone company records is that he made an incomplete long-distance call to Denver.

Varieties of the blue box frequently appear on Eastern college campuses. Indeed, the person who actually invented the thing was reputedly only seventeen years old when he found the tone combinations. The story (perhaps apocryphal) is that AT&T was so impressed that it sent him to the Bell Laboratories rather than to jail.

A group of teen-agers that the New York Telephone Company security chief calls "several young electronic geniuses" put a blue box to profitable use for months during 1963 from a hotel on Long Island. The youths had their own rate structure —one-third what Bell would charge for a call. The scheme lasted for months before the New York Telephone security people found out about it and made arrests.

The third in the box series is the cheese box, which enables bookies to receive, at a remote location, calls made to another point. (The first man to put together one of these devices housed the electronic gear in an empty cream cheese container —hence the name.) The gambler rents an apartment and installs two phones—A, the number of which is given to his customers, and B, his private number. He attaches the cheese box between the two phones.

The gambler goes to a distant pay station and calls Phone B, the private line. The cheese box mechanism answers the call automatically and leaves the line open. Soon customers start calling their bets in to Phone A. The cheese box shunts them over to the open line B, so that the gambler can carry on a conversation from the safety of his pay station.

It's easy enough for police to find the number of Phone A, for they'll go to the drugstore, bar or candy shop where known horseplayers congregate and install a device called a pen register on the phone, which punches onto a tape any number dialed. But when they obtain the bookie's Phone A number and go to the location, all they find are the two phones and the cheese box.

The police next start trying to find the pay station from which the gambler makes the incoming call to Phone B. This process takes twenty minutes, so the gambler, to stay ahead of the cops, must change booths at least every fifteen minutes.

The cheese box has a fringe benefit. When the gambler calls into a cheese box from a pay station, some mechanical quirk returns his dime. Bernard B. Spindel, former wiretap consultant for the New York City Anti-Crime Commission, told a Senate committee once, "This part disturbed the telephone company more than the fact that they [the gamblers] were using the device."

The box racket—blue, black, and cheese—reached serious enough proportions in 1965 for AT&T to ask legislatures to make their manufacture illegal in Maryland and California, two states that were the prime sources of supply. A Hollywood man advertised for sale through a national electronics magazine plans for "toll-free distance dialing—bypasses operators and billing equipment . . . built for $15." He sold 149 sets of blueprints before AT&T and the police put him out of business (and picked up a list of his customers).

Another gyp device that turns up occasionally is a tape recording that duplicates the sound of nickels, dimes, and quarters cascading into the coin box of a pay booth. Less sophisticated procedures cheat as efficiently. In the early 1950's a University of Texas athlete, while placing a call to a girl friend at an Eastern college, suddenly found the booth tilted on its side by prankster friends. He continued to drop coins in the slot—and found that the inverted position made falling nickels sound like falling quarters, to the operator's ears at least. For the rest of the year Texas athletes enjoyed an 80 percent discount on long-distance calls. Bell finally became suspicious over the lack of coins in such a busy booth and moored it with strong bolts.

Students elsewhere are more sophisticated. Ron Kessler, one of the few reporters for daily media in the nation who knows enough about Bell to write about the company intelligently, has documented several of the more advanced schemes for the *Boston Herald* and the *Wall Street Journal*. His prize specimen is a group of five Harvard and Massachusetts Institute of Technology students who found no less than six ways to bypass long distance operators to make free calls—even to Mexico and Peru.

The students' discoveries began by accident. Two of them were experimenting with a tape recorder. Wanting some strange sounds to transcribe, they dialed telephone numbers at random to obtain incorrect numbers which would produce the wail of a "wrong number" signal. The students heard two distinctive clicks preceding one of the numbers, and recognized them as the sounds preceding a long distance call from Marblehead, Massachusetts, to Boston.

They dialed a third number and found that the combination connected them with an "inward operator" in Boston—that is, a woman who helps regular operators complete long distance calls. She thought they were phone company employees (after all, no one else should have the number) and connected them to any local numbers they desired. Thus they avoided the toll for Marblehead-Boston calls.

Excited by this success the students turned upon the entire Bell System. According to Kessler, they enlisted three other students and began dialing possible area codes and exchanges not listed in the directory. They discovered a ten-digit number that connected them with the inward operator in Kleena Kleene, British Columbia, Canada. "The operators in Kleena Kleene, apparently no match for Harvard and MIT students, would connect them to any telephone in the United States free," wrote Kessler. "The students sometimes called telephones in Cambridge via Kleena Kleene. . . . As their expertise increased, they put more and more hours into their wild research, sometimes neglecting to go to sleep at night. They said they were more interested in breaking the puzzle of the phone system, which represented a challenge, than making free calls. They spent most of their time chatting with operators and calling unknown telephone offices in such spots as Snake Rock, Montana."

Over the months the students' scheming became increasingly ingenious. They built both black boxes and blue boxes. They found the three-digit number which, when dialed from East Boston exchanges, would put them in touch with an inward operator in Mexico City. "The inward operator would connect them to any number in the world," wrote Kessler. With woodwind musical instruments they duplicated the tones which enabled them to cut into the Bell long-distance network.

All this happened between October 1962 and the following April. The stunt ended when a company employee who had given them surreptitious aid suspected they were trying to obtain secret defense information (all the students wanted to do was to plug into the Pentagon's phone network and chat with Strategic Air Command bases) and informed the FBI. Bell chose not to prosecute. But the company did force the students to surrender the 121 pages of notes they made during the experiments, and to write a 40-page report on how they did it.

Kessler also found a young engineer in St. Louis who fed into a computer all the listed phone numbers in local exchanges. The computer printed out a compilation of combinations that weren't listed. "The man dialed all those numbers, found out which ones would hook him into open long-distance lines leased by corporations, and then dialed those numbers for toll-free calls to many cities—courtesy of the corporations."

Until recently gamblers had yet another method of sponging off Bell. The phone companies used the numbers 9900 and 9906 in each exchange for transmission test lines. The bookie would call LO 3-9906, for example, and stay on the line as long as he desired. His customers, by prearrangement, would dial the other test number, LO 3-9900, and an electronic quirk enabled them to converse with the bookie. The phone company halted this built-in cheese box by making one of the transmission test lines permanently busy. If a bona fide telephone lineman wants to make a test, he must first call the central office to have the busy signal removed briefly. The transmission test numbers are also changed frequently, so don't waste time dialing 9900 or 9906; it doesn't work anymore.

In addition to manufacturing Princess telephones, Western Electric also makes components for guided missiles, nuclear weapons, anti-submarine systems and assorted other military gear—enough to make the parent AT&T a prominent member of the military-industrial complex. AT&T is the nation's sixth largest defense contractor (as of the end of 1968)—yet Ma Bell maintains an image worlds away from the paraphernalia of war and devastation: what could be more pacific and tame than the phone company? Bell seems no more likely a purveyor of nuclear missiles than does Macy's or the corner A&P. Because of her discretion there was unintended irony in the advertisements it ran during the first part of 1969 in house organs of the military-industrial complex.* The stark white page bore only a small AT&T trademark and two brief lines of miniscule six-point type. The first line, centered in mid-page, whispered "Command/Control Systems use our network." The second, at the very bottom, observed, "We know how to keep a secret."

Indeed Bell does, for these ads appeared at the height of the national debate over the wisdom and necessity of installing the controversial anti-ballistic missile (ABM) system. One fact went virtually unmentioned in the torrent of speeches and articles on the ABM: AT&T, through Western Electric, is prime contractor for the system that has become the very symbol of military-industrial boondoggling. And this despite a demonstrably greedy record: Through adept use of a technique called "profit pyramiding" in the defense industry, Western Electric has run up profits as high as 31.3 percent on ABM's predecessor systems, while helping the Pentagon accumulate military junk that was never used. Here some background is in order to understand how Western Electric arrived at such high status in the military-industrial complex.

Western Electric's involvement in rocketry—the basic in-

---

* The May 1969 issue of *Air Force/Space Digest,* published by the Air Force Association and June 1969 issue of *Army,* published by the Association of the United States Army, were two of the many publications in which the advertisement appeared. In addition to giving these military trade associations financial support through its advertising AT&T is a featured exhibitor at their annual conventions in Washington, which are attended by the shiniest brass the Pentagon can muster.

gredient of the ABM—began with a man named C. N. Hickman, onetime student and longtime associate of Dr. Robert N. Goddard. In June, 1940, Hickman was working for Bell Telephone Laboratories. Bell was casting around for an entrée into defense work, and Hickman wrote Goddard asking permission to present the possibilities of development of his rocket ideas to the government. Goddard replied he had attempted to do so himself, without success, and added, "Go ahead, and God bless you."

According to the official history of the World War II Office of Scientific Research and Development (OSRD), Hickman first obtained approval of the Guggenheim Foundation, which had been financing Goddard's work during the 1930's, then presented the rocket proposal to Dr. F. B. Jewett, who wore an interesting combination of hats. At the same time that Dr. Jewett was president of Bell Labs he was chairman of one of the divisions of the newly formed National Defense Research Committee (NDRC), and therefore in a position to influence the allocation of defense research and spending. Hickman's idea "much impressed" Jewett, and he asked for a report on the "possibilities of developing useful rocket weapons." Hickman's paper convinced the Pentagon where Goddard had failed, and NDRC formed a special section for rocket research and development—a section which drew heavily upon the personnel and scientific talents of the Bell System. The first consultant appointed was one Emory Lakatos, a Bell Labs engineer who wrote a report on the internal ballistics of rockets. Ma Bell had her foot in the door.

By August 1, 1941, work had progressed to the point where Dr. C. C. Lauritsen, an NDRC section chief working closely with Bell people, recommended to Dr. Vannevar Bush, the head of the government science program, that there was an "urgent need" for rockets for armor-piercing bombs; for plane-to-plane use, and for assisted takeoff for aircraft. Six weeks later contracts were awarded for the work that the OSRD history states "then seemed large and now seem small"—$25,000 for General Electric Company; $10,000 for Western Electric; and $200,000 for the California Institute of Technology. The official history states: "Under these [contracts], Western Electric was to furnish engineering services and advice and special material through the Bell Telephone Laboratories. . . ."

In historical perspective, Western Electric's share of World War II military spending seems piddling. Its military research contracts totalled only $17,091,819 (fifth behind Massachusetts Institute of Technology's $116,941,352 and three other "educational institutions"). What was *not* piddling for Western Electric, however, was the fact that it acquired a preeminent position in aircraft defense—one it retains to this date.

Toward the end of the war Western devised a control system that vastly improved the army's antiaircraft gun batteries. Radar detection was joined to a computer which automatically aimed the gun at the incoming target. This system, known as the M-33, was in production at Western plants at the end of the war. When German scientists, with their advanced knowledge of rocketry, fell into U. S. hands, the army decided to replace the antiaircraft shell with a missile that could be guided from the ground. On February 8, 1945, the Army issued Western Electric its Letter Order W-30-069-ORD-3182 for "investigation and research and development work required to produce a suitable guided missile." This contract was for only $181,450— but its actual value is well stated in a Pentagon special study dated June 19, 1962, entitled, "The Changing Pattern of Defense Procurement."

. . . [A]ny company which has conducted or managed the research, design, development and test work on a new weapon system—or a major component—and has assembled the engineering talent and experience for this purpose, is obviously in an exceptionally strong position to compete for the follow-on production contracts and for new developmental contracts as well. It is logical, then, that production contracts for the newer sophisticated items, which will figure in future procurement, may tend to be placed in areas where RDT & E [research, development, testing and evaluation] has been centered. The point is reinforced by the fact that the development and test work represents a much larger share of some types of procurement than others.

AT&T's progress was steady: The Nike-Ajax, first fired in 1949 at a drone B-29 bomber at the White Sands, New Mexico, proving ground; next the Nike-Hercules, equipped with a nuclear warhead to give it the capability of "destroying entire fleets of incoming aircraft" [the Pentagon's words, not mine]; then the Nike-Zeus, designed as "the bullet to stop a bullet" [once again, the Pentagon speaking]; and, currently, but by no means finally, the Sentinel Safeguard ABM system.

All this activity has spanned nearly a quarter-century—and AT&T has insisted piously all the while that it would rather be concerning itself with digit dialing, Yellow Pages and other mundane telephone activities. In language put into a 1964 Senate report AT&T claimed that in 1945 "there was . . . some reluctance on the part of Western Electric to undertake work in what then appeared to be a dying defense industry. It had wanted to concentrate all of its available plant and manpower in catching up and expanding as suppliers of telephones and telephone equipment for its parent company. . . ." AT&T chairman H. I. Romnes claimed in an interview with the *Washington Star*'s Stephen Aug in November 1969 that Bell "has tried several times unsuccessfully to discontinue such research, but has been asked by the Defense Department in each case to continue it. The company has never solicited military research." But Romnes offered no evidence to suggest that Ma Bell has ever attempted to say "no" to the militarists with whom she has been living in profitable cohabitation since 1945.

One reason is that Western Electric makes a higher profit on sales to the U.S. government than it does to Bell System companies. In 1968, sales of Western Electric reached an all-time high of $3,944,576,000 (an increase of $315,000,000 over 1967). Sales to the government were $511,673,000—13 percent of the total. Western's return on its average net investment was 9.5 percent for Bell business, 10.9 percent on government business. On individual contracts, however, Bell's gross return has been much higher, the most glaring example being its performance with the Nike antiaircraft missile, the system that is the immediate predecessor to the controversial ABM. This story begins in 1951, when the Defense Department ordered production of the first series of Nike missiles, and gave Western Electric, as "weapons system manager," the responsibility for delivering ready-to-fire units.

Now despite its expertise, Western Electric could not single-handedly build a Nike, which was composed of four completely separate types of systems:

1. *Electronics.* The radar, the computer, and the guidance section of the missile itself.

2. *Aerodynamics.* The missile body, in the nature of a pilot-

less aircraft, the electronic guidance package replacing the pilot.

3. *Mechanical*. The rails and launcher loader, which position the missile and elevate it into firing position.

4. *Automotive*. A group of trailers and vans to house the personnel, radars, and computers.

Western Electric decided to concentrate its efforts on the electronics phase, the area where it had the most experience. Western selected the Douglas Aircraft Company as the principal subcontractor and assigned it responsibility for research, development, and production of the other subsystems. Douglas, primarily an aircraft manufacturer, in turn gave a third-tier contract to the Consolidated Western Division of United States Steel for the mechanical subsystem and to the Freuhauf Trailer Company for the vans and trailers that constituted the automotive subsystem.

Western Electric's contract was on a cost-reimbursable basis. Because of the newness of the work, exact costs could not be determined beforehand. Western agreed to a 10 percent fee of the estimated costs and 6 percent on the costs of the major subcontractor, Douglas. (Under this type of contract, if the manufacturer does the job for less than the estimated cost, his fee remains the same, although his percentage return increases. For example, if he agreed to a fee of $600,000 on a $10,000,000 job, his fee would be 6 percent. If the estimate proved high and he actually did the work for $5,000,000, he would receive the same $600,000, but his percentage return on actual costs would then be 12 percent.) Douglas Aircraft, in turn, made profit-percentage deals with its subcontractors.

The Army ultimately paid Western Electric $1,545,100,000 for production of the Nike under this contract. (Western Electric got approximately $1,000,000,000 more for research and development.)

Just how much of this money represented profit for the manufacturers? An investigations subcommittee of the Senate Government Operations Committee, headed by Senator John L. McClellan, sought to answer that question in 1964 and made some disturbing discoveries.

Of the $1,545,100,000, Western Electric took $112,500,000 for profit, plus $1,432,600 for "reimbursement of expenses," which on the surface shows a profit of 7.9 percent, certainly not exorbitant for such an involved project.

But McClellan's investigators checked further. Through laborious compilations of invoices they found that Western Electric's in-house work (*i.e.,* the actual work done on Western Electric premises by Western Electric personnel) totaled only $359,300,000 (including a generous $82,400,000 for general and administrative expenses). Relating the $112,500,000 profit to the in-house work showed a return of 31.3 percent on effort. Subcontractors did the remainder of the work.

What the McClellan committee called "the taking of excessive profits on work done by others" was not limited to Western Electric.

Douglas Aircraft received $645,000,000 in Western Electric subcontracts for the aeronautical, mechanical, and automotive subsystems, consisting of "costs" of $599,000,000 and a respectable-appearing $46,000,000 in profits (7.6 percent of the $599,000,000). Yet McClellan's group found that Douglas in turn had sub-subcontracted the mechanical and automotive systems, which totaled $486,000,000, leaving its own in-house work at only $103,000,000. Thus, Douglas' profit on the work it actually performed was 44.3 percent—$46,000,000 on $103,000,000.

The contracting gimmick was used throughout the Nike program to generate unearned profits for Douglas and Western Electric. To wit:

Douglas subcontracted for Nike launcher loaders to Consolidated Western Steel, which produced thousands of them between 1950–61 and delivered them directly to Army bases. Consolidated was paid its full costs of $146,000,000 and was allowed a profit of $9,300,000, also paid by the government. The Consolidated invoices increased Douglas' cost base and were the basis for another profit (by Douglas) of $10,400,000. In turn, Western Electric's cost base was broadened by the pyramided Douglas invoices, and the government was required to pay Western Electric a third profit of $9,800,000.

The three separate profits totaled $29,500,000, or 20 percent over actual production costs, as follows in millions:

To the producer (Consolidated)	$ 9.3
To the nonproducing subcontractor (Douglas)	10.4
To the nonproducing prime contractor (Western)	9.8
	$29.5

McClellan wrote in a report to the Senate:

> The subcommittee finds no justification for paying both non-producing upper tiers in the pyramid more profit than the actual manufacturer. The payment of these profits becomes more difficult to understand when it is found that Western Electric's actual assistance to Consolidated Western Steel amounted to a few inspectors and one technical visitation in all the years the launcher was being produced.

The profit taking was even greedier on another contract, under which Consolidated manufactured and delivered 1,032 launcher loaders directly to the Army at a price of $13,500,-000, including its profit. Douglas made a plastic rain cover for the lot, costing about $3 each, for certified total Douglas costs of $3,361. However, Douglas took a profit, not only on the $3,361 it spent, but also on the $13,500,000 in costs incurred by its subcontractor, Consolidated. Douglas was allowed a profit of $1,211,771 on $3,361 of effort—*a rate of 36,531 percent*.

Thereafter, on this same order, Western Electric had $14 expense each on the launchers in checking them over after their delivery at the Army bases, for a total of $14,293. However, Western Electric based its profit on Douglas' "costs" of $14,-700,000—taking a pyramided profit of $955,396 on an in-house effort of $14,293, a profit of 6,684 percent.

How did Western Electric manage to collect this type of profit for more than a decade?

The McClellan committee noted without comment that the Army had assigned one contracting officer to deal with Western Electric for seven of the ten years studied, during which time he was responsible for more than $2 billion in contracts. At one point a lower-echelon auditor called the contracting officer's attention to the "unreasonable profits" being made on some of the contracts. The officer ignored the comment and paid the full amount. Said McClellan: "The contracting officer taxed the subcommittee's incredulity by his testimony that he took no action regarding the auditor's report because it was not the auditor's responsibility to comment on profit rates."

Western Electric also successfully resisted what in military contracting parlance is known as break-out—the procuring of subsystems directly from the manufacturer, rather than through a middleman, so as to cut down on costs. Western Electric began its chore as Nike manager in 1951; within two years the chief of Army Ordnance reported millions of dollars could be saved if the Army could break out certain parts. Western Electric immediately complained to the Secretary of the Army, Robert T. Stevens, who ordered that Western's concurrence be obtained before any break-out was done. Said the McClellan committee:

> For the next eight years, by one means or another, the Western Electric Company was successful in thwarting any substantial purchases of Nike subsystems directly by the army. *The contractor's motive was obvious. Western Electric was paid $77 million in profits for work done by others.* To have freely permitted breakout and direct purchases of parts or components from the subcontractor or actual producers would have had a serious effect on Western Electric's profitability of the Nike undertaking. They [Western Electric] would have been paid a profit only on the work they did—about 25 percent of the production.

Not until the McClellan committee began its investigation in mid-1961 did Western Electric consent to break-out; indeed, foreseeing the Congressional storm ahead, Western actually suggested it. Even then the break-out was for direct purchase of missiles from Douglas—beginning in 1963. The McClellan committee commented:

> Thus, for 18 years, from 1945 through 1963, the army has been buying tens of thousands of missiles from Western Electric, which has yet to make its first missile. Western Electric merely passed the job on to Douglas, but was allowed a substantial profit, or brokerage, all these years. This middleman markup constitutes an unnecessary burden on the defense appropriation.

The Army did succeed in breaking out production of the spare parts van that was included in each Nike complex. The effect on costs was immediate: When buying the vans through the pyramided-profit contract system, the government paid $20,000 per trailer. Through direct purchase from the Fruehauf Trailer Company the price fell at once to $14,300, a savings of almost 33 percent. (The Army felt that had it been permitted to ask for competitive bids, the Fruehauf price would have dropped even lower.)

The Army bought 520 missile highway transporters through the Western Electric-Douglas Aircraft chain for $12,000 each. When break-out occurred, the price went down to $10,300. A year later competitive bidding reduced it to $5,304—less than half what had been paid under profit pyramiding.

Western Electric *was* willing to bargain when the Army asked for permission to buy spare Nike parts outside the profit-pyramiding system. Knowing that the Army didn't have the capability to manage the system by itself, Western Electric simply said that it would not "maintain responsibility for systems integrity" unless all Nike parts were supplied through it. But it offered a concession: Western Electric said it would not object if the Army wanted to procure its own screwdrivers, pliers, antifreeze, and paper cups to use at the missile sites. An Army colonel quoted a Western official as saying, "We feel that you should buy those items that are compatible with the system from us. Other items, as an example, screwdrivers, pliers, and so forth, why don't you go buy them from a hardware store?"

Western Electric found any number of ways to jack up its Nike profits. For instance, it did much of the Nike production work at two government surplus plants. Under the ordinary method of doing business, the government would have supplied the plants to Western Electric without cost. This would have considerably diminished Western's investment in the Nike operation, and the cost of the plants could have been excluded in computing the overall project costs which formed the profit base for the work.

However, Western Electric chose to rent the plants from the government, and for some unknown reason some unknown bureaucrat let the company do so. At first glance this might seem a good deal for the government, for Western Electric paid more than $3,000,000 in rent for the time it used the buildings.

Yet not only did the government reimburse Western Electric for these rents (as part of the contract costs), but it also paid Western Electric a profit on them—$209,000. Western Electric tried to minimize the amount of this additional cost during the McClellan hearings, but as the committee report stated, "[It] should be kept in mind that this figure is more than the annual salaries of the eight U.S. Senators on the Government Operations Committee at the time of these hearings."

Because of its vested interest in the Nike, Western Electric kept boosting the missile even when its effectiveness came under a cloud. In 1958 the Eisenhower Administration was cool toward the Nike-Zeus, saying there was a question whether it actually could knock down incoming enemy missiles, as it was supposed to do, whereupon lobbyists for the military-industrial complex convinced their friends in Congress to add $137,000,-000 to the defense budget for production of the antimissile missile. But President Eisenhower declined to spend the money, saying, "Funds should not be committed to production until development tests are satisfactorily completed."

The missile advocates then tried to generate additional pressure on the President. One medium was *Army*, the official publication of the Association of the United States Army, which suddenly burgeoned with articles and advertisements about Nike-Zeus. Western Electric and eight of its subcontractors bought a full-page advertisement in *Army* which featured a map showing where the $410,000,000 they wanted for Nike-Zeus would be spent—and what Congressman wants to vote against a project that means money for his district? Army officers on active duty contributed editorial praise for the antimissile missile. "Loose the Zeus through America's magnificent production line," cried Representative John McCormack, the House Majority Leader.

The propaganda campaign worked. Nike-Zeus development funds went into the budget, and anti-missilery survived. Through the end of fiscal 1968, according to Pentagon figures supplied to the Senate Foreign Relations Committee, AT&T received "about $3.5 billion" for Nike-Zeus and Nike-X work. Thus Western Electric was ready to proceed in September 1967 when Defense Secretary Robert S. McNamara announced the Johnson Administration's decision to proceed with construction of the ABM.

Normally, an American corporation devoted to the well-being of its shareholders and bankers could be expected to brag just a bit about bagging a project with a potential price tag of anywhere from $6 to 600 billion, the speculation range of the ABM. But Western Electric disposed of this mammoth project in an annual report with two low-keyed sentences which give no indication of the financial avalanche that was falling into its lap: "With Bell Laboratories we continued to do extensive research and development work on the Government's high-priority Nike-X Missile Defense System. This system is designed to counter intercontinental or submarine-launched missiles." Southern militarist senators and star-festooned generals may shout themselves hoarse praising ABM, but the phone company has yet to mention the project aloud.

AT&T's silence resulted from a decision to maintain a cautious policy: Better to permit more conspicuous members of the military-industrial complex to do the public lobbying for ABM, lest citizens begin asking "What business does the telephone monopoly have involving itself in major defense contracts?" AT&T's sole role in the debate was providing technical data supporting the claimed efficacy of the ABM. But it was comfortable with the knowledge that the public relations campaign for ABM was coordinated by an old and true friend: Lieutenant General Alfred D. Starbird, Pentagon manager of the Sentinel project. Starbird formerly commanded the Defense Communications Agency, with which AT&T was intimately involved through its longtime stewardship of Pentagon phone lines.

AT&T employees knew what was happening, however—and, as is true with many Americans concerned about dubious military spending projects, they didn't like it. One such was B. G. Wallace, an idealistic Virginian who in 1968 was working at the Kwajalein missile range in the Pacific as a carrier equipment expert for the Bell System. Wallace, then thirty-two years old, previously had worked for Chesapeake & Potomac Telephone Company of Virginia, for thirteen years, attaining the rank of plant manager in Richmond. This experience did not prepare him for what he saw at Kwajalein.

Kwajalein serves as the down-range target area for shots of simulated nuclear missiles from Vandenberg Air Force Base, California. Bell scientists used these bogus missiles to test the workings of Sentinel components. Wallace had been at Kwajalein about a month when he observed the reentry of a simulated nuclear warhead.

"The thought occurred to me that had the missile been armed, the warhead would have detonated, killing every living creature for miles around and rendering the earth a mass of black, charred radioactive rubble," Wallace said later. "I was very much moved by seeing the reentry. It was by far the most spectacular and awful sight I have ever witnessed." That evening he expressed his feelings in a brief, personal note to Colonel D. B. Millar, commanding officer of the highly classified test site:

> Have the selfish desires and ambitions of the individual caused this society, as a whole, to completely forget the horrors of Nagasaki and Hiroshima? If the individual conscience in a position of authority does not speak out for fear of humiliation or personal loss, the collective conscience of the civilization will continue to spiral downward toward total disintegration. Last night's mission made a profound impression—had to get this off my chest.

Colonel Millar and Bell officials had Wallace promptly on the carpet the next morning—acting, as he said, "like a bunch of nervous school boys about the whole thing." Wallace said Millar told him the ABM was "highly sensitive" and that the military "could not afford to have a man with his views in his position." With Bell's concurrence, the military ordered Wallace off Kwajalein immediately. "It all seemed like a fantasy. I kept thinking it couldn't really be happening," Wallace recounted. "I'm still stunned by the whole affair."

On December 18, 1957, a group of Western Electric officials met with Army procurement officers at the New York Ordnance District, which then had the responsibility for purchasing defensive missile systems. Some of the Army officers were beginning to have qualms about Western's high rate of profit on the work, and suggested reductions. Fred Lack, a Western Electric vice-president, didn't like the idea at all. Walter R. Bylund, a civilian employee of the Army, recorded his reaction in a memorandum written immediately after the meeting ended:

> Mr. Lack stated that Western is regulated by the [Federal Communications] Commission, who constantly looks over their shoulders. If the government profits were reduced, the commission might suggest that telephone profits be reduced. . . .

The government profits were not reduced.

8

I should like to ask the Senator from Utah whether the telephone company has offered him the kind of proposal that it has offered me.

Has the Senator had proposals made to him that he could own a telephone building in his state and that the telephone company would make the loan and endorse the loan to build a building in a big city in his state just on the assurance that the Senator would give sympathetic consideration to the company's problem, if he would go along with them, and that the company would then build the building and endorse the mortgage loan and engage the bank to make the loan with the probability that he would wind up eventually being worth $5 million or $25 million?

—*Senator Russell B. Long, of Louisiana, in the U.S. Senate, August 10, 1962*

THE American Telephone & Telegraph Company's lobbying and public relations program is intended to keep its telephone monopoly as protected, palatable and profitable as possible. This AT&T does by cultivation of favorable public opinion through its economic strength in the community, the commonality of interests it has with the remainder of U.S. business, and exploitation of every person, every business, every institution which have contacts with Bell and its employees.

An AT&T vice-president once told a company meeting that Bell wants such a good image that regulatory agencies reflexively approve anything it requests. If Bell does its public relations homework properly, this official said, the agencies' response will be: "That telephone bunch, they are all right. I know them. They know the job and they are doing it. I am ready to bank on them. If they say they need more rates, they need more rates. You don't need to take the time to prove it to me. I will take their word for it."

AT&T seeks the same aura of good feeling and omnipotence in a variety of areas. It wants the public to think that the Bell System's present organization is ideal and that Bell service is the most efficient in the world and as advanced as the progress of telephony will permit. It asserts that wide ownership of Bell stock makes it a "publicly owned institution" and that tampering with Bell profits would harm so many millions of persons that the government should keep its regulatory hands off the company. It justifies and defends Bell rates existing at any given time as reasonable and fair and seeks to reserve for itself the initiative to reduce them. It propagandizes the academic and legal communities on behalf of depreciation and accounting policies that are beneficial to AT&T in rate cases, so as to cultivate the men who will adjudicate and be expert witnesses in rate proceedings.

AT&T public relations effort is effective because the vast majority of it is soft sell. In this category are the *Bell Telephone Hour,* which brings Van Cliburn and Gian Carlo Menotti into the American living room, and the humorously self-disparaging ads in such journals as *Atlantic, Harper's,* and *Saturday Review.* Bell's intention here is to create a favorable impression of the company among the nation's present and future opinion and policy makers and to make the company intellectually attractive to prospective scientific employees.

Political scientist Jerome B. McKinney of the University of Nebraska, who spent several years studying utility lobbies in Missouri, gave high marks to Southwestern Bell's techniques. Bell's market analyses, according to McKinney, included "close and thorough examination . . . [or] cultural habits and orientations and civic leadership in the various towns and cities in the states. These aspects have significance far beyond telephone market analysis. An understanding of social and political syndrome provides Bell with additional leverage and knowledge from which she can determine the strategy and direction of public relations." One Southwestern Bell official told McKinney that company officers "spend as much as 40 to 50 percent of their time on public relations."

Bell's careful cultivation of politicians is worthwhile. When the company was asked, in the early 1960's, to reduce rates by $2,000,000 a year, the Missouri governor told the public utilities commission "to go easy" with Bell, according to McKinney. Through sponsorship of "faculty conferences" Bell executives form amicable relationships with academicians which make them political allies. "When expert witnesses are needed . . . to assist Southwestern Bell in vindicating her position," comments McKinney, "she can often look to this reservoir of academic talents."

By strictest definition, anyone who receives a cent of the $7 billion spent each year by AT&T and its subsidiaries for services and supplies is a potential lobbying or public relations contact. Thus, the fact that AT&T has an economic presence in virtually every hamlet in the United States is the single most important contributor to its political potency.

To many businesses, a bank deposit is simply a commercial transaction; to a local Bell company, a deposit of telephone funds is an opportunity to communicate with and influence that part of a town's power structure represented among bank directors. (Bell has some 4,600 bank accounts throughout the country.)

A stranger can readily ascertain the most qualified legal firm in a city by inquiring who represents the Bell company, and the lawyer is selected, not only for his court skills, but also for his political and social contacts. If a member of the firm is a legislator or city official, so much the better.

Although Western Electric nominally is the purchasing agent for the entire AT&T apparatus, operating companies are given permission to buy enough supplies locally to make Bell a desired customer—motor oil for the fleet of telephone service trucks (AT&T owns more vehicles than any other U.S. enterprise); stationery for the business office; the 40,000 quarts of ice cream consumed each month in cafeterias of New Jersey Bell plants.

The cultivation of these merchants, lawyers, and bankers as Friends of Bell is the responsibility of the local Bell managers. Their job is all the easier because in many respects Bell is astoundingly responsive to community feelings on such matters as putting telephone cables underground to keep unsightly blight from downtown areas or in furnishing a gratis public-address system to the local Little League or just by doing a good job of supplying phone service to business and homes. For these reasons Bell managers can in good conscience ask the community leaders to reciprocate when Bell needs help—and herein lies Bell's power.

Consider: A legislator is neutral or mildly hostile toward Bell, and a bill affecting telephone company interests is before him for a vote. Were this man to be contacted directly by a registered Bell lobbyist and asked for a favorable vote, the impact could be minimal. This is the situation in which the Friends of Bell are valuable. The Bell manager in the legislator's home district works obliquely. Within three days the legislator has letters, telephone calls, telegrams, or visits from his town's banker, law firm, four or five merchants, even a minister, all suggesting that his vote be favorable to Bell. At other times Bell will even bring its local managers into Washington by the planeload for personal contacts with Congressmen, as was done during the first stages of the Communications Satellite Act debate in 1961.

The danger in such a relationship is the ever-present temptation for AT&T to misuse its economic muscle. In 1963 Dan Struve, a member of the Texas Legislature who had sponsored bills that Bell didn't like, ran for reelection. A friend who operated a service station in Struve's south Texas district reported a disturbing experience: "A man from Bell was in to buy a tire for a truck, and as I was putting it on, he said, 'You know, if that guy Struve wins and goes back to Austin, I'm not sure how many more of these we'll be able to buy from you.' " The service station man said his right of free vote was more important than Bell's business, and that he would vote for whom he pleased. Struve lost anyway.

Bell constantly reminds legislators and Congressmen of the money it spends in their districts. H. Allen Carroll, long one of AT&T's most effective Washington lobbyists, in 1961 sent Senator Russell Long an itemization of Southern Bell's expenditures in Louisiana the previous year, a total of $3,331,039 from 309 merchants, ranging from $995,237 from 186 companies in New Orleans down to $8 from one store in Leesville. Carroll's motive: to dissuade Long from opposing creation of a communications satellite operating company under terms dictated by AT&T.

Bell's cultivation of local people and institutions increases Bell's expenses. But this causes Bell no discomfort, for the costs are passed on to the consumer as a public relations expenditure. An Illinois Bell official once noted in a speech that his treasurer "could save a little work" by having fewer bank accounts in Chicago, and thereby increase the company's interest income. However, we think that the advantage of our contacts with the various interests represented in these banks more than offsets any disadvantages." Again, the FCC investigation of AT&T in the 1930's turned up numerous instances in which Bell subsidiaries awarded directory printing contracts to the highest bidder "due to political reasons" (the words are Bell's).

Bell encourages its employees to be joiners and to involve themselves in community affairs. As AT&T pridefully notes in its 1965 annual report, Bell people occupied such diverse positions as chief of the Lawrence Road Fire Company in Lawrence Township, New Jersey; head of the Community Chests in Columbia, Wisconsin, and Wichita Falls, Texas; man of the year of the Savannah, Georgia, Junior Chamber of Commerce; president of the national Jaycees; organizer of a Civil Air Patrol chapter in Lawrence, Kansas; and senior vice-president of the National Urban League.

Undoubtedly many of these people would be active on their own initiative. But Bell unabashedly uses their myriad interests for public relations purposes, promoting the idea that AT&T and the community it serves are inseparable and that AT&T is "human" because it consists of the man next door and the woman across the street. In this way AT&T shunts into the background the fact that it is the world's largest corporation. New Jersey Bell points up this "humans in the community" view of Bell in a brochure entitled *Phonetown, New Jersey, the Third Largest City in the State.*

According to New Jersey Bell, "Phonetown" has 200,000 people, consisting of the 60,600 Bell employees and their families:

> 425 Smiths, 150 Jones, and 2 Zygalas. They live up the street or around the corner. . . . They're all spending—and saving—in New Jersey. Most of Phonetown's $475 million payroll goes right into the economy of our state—to buy everything from groceries to appliances to bubblegum. Part-time scoutmasters, volunteer firemen, councilmen—there are even

11 mayors in Phonetown. Telephone people are the kind who take an active part in community life.

Why promote all the community activity? For one thing, Bell says, such memberships "reflect credit on our organization." A public relations department bulletin is more to the point: "It is always within the realm of possibility in these organizations that telephone issues may be discussed. A timely statement of the real facts with a prompt clearing up of some misunderstanding by an employee member on the spot might often prevent ill-considered action and would always tend to check a further spread of misstatements and misunderstanding."

Unfortunately for the public, AT&T often builds this "good citizen image" at the expense of telephone users. During a 1964 rate hearing the California Public Utilities Commission discovered that the Pacific Telephone & Telegraph Company was charging subscribers $852,000 a year in dues, donations, and contributions by counting them as operating expenses. PT&T undoubtedly made Californians think highly of the company with announcements that it contributed to the United Fund, the Community Chest, assorted university fund drives, and cultural organizations, and PT&T increased the membership rolls of chamber of commerce and service clubs by paying the dues of employees "assigned" to join them for public relations purposes. In previous years, however, such costs had been borne by stockholders rather than by subscribers, and the PUC was irked that PT&T had changed the system.

"Dues, donations and contributions, if included as an expense for rate-making purposes, become an involuntary levy on rate payers who, because of the monopolistic nature of utility service, are unable to obtain service from another source and thereby avoid such a levy," the PUC said in an opinion. "Rate payers should be encouraged to contribute directly to worthy causes and not involuntarily through an allowance in utility rates. [PT&T] should not be permitted to be generous with rate payers' money. . . ."

Until the 1940's AT&T policy forbade employees to seek public office; if a worker became a candidate, he was expected to resign, rather than risk having his individual views confused with corporate positions. By doing so, Bell sought to avoid such controversies as that which arose in Boston in 1937 when a well-known former supervisor for the New England Telephone & Telegraph Company filed for mayor. An opponent attacked him in newspaper advertisements that said Bell was trying to "seize control of the city of Boston." Bell refuted the accusation by proving he had resigned before becoming a candidate.

Bell has since changed this policy, and its employees hold such positions as mayor of Portsmouth, New Hampshire; alderman of Columbus, Wisconsin; and president of the Board of Commissioners of Harford County, Maryland. Bell gave a manager a leave of absence to serve as administrative assistant to Representative Rogers C. B. Morton, a Republican from Maryland.

The political activities can be embarrassing. In February, 1967, Newton Miller, a traffic manager for New Jersey Bell in Wayne, New Jersey, and the vice-president of the school board there, urged voters to reject two candidates because they were Jewish. He gave the local newspaper a statement which said in part:

"Most Jewish people are liberals especially when it comes to spending for education. If [they] are elected it would only take two more votes for a majority, and Wayne could be in real financial trouble. Two more votes, and we could lose what is left of Christ in our Christmas celebrations in our schools. Think about it."

The American Jewish Committee jumped on Miller for "overt anti-Semitism and religious bigotry," a charge which he denied, while nonetheless refusing to retract or modify his original statement. The two Jewish candidates ran last in a nationally publicized election. (Another New Jersey Bell official got into a similar, but much quieter, incident the same month in West Orange. Frank P. Combs resigned from the school board and then complained that "unfortunately" his replacement "was a person of the Jewish faith.")

Frederick R. Kappel, while board chairman of AT&T, was dubious about businessmen "getting into politics" as a counterbalance to organized labor. He felt direct involvement would be harmful in the long run, because the public would turn against representatives maneuvered into office by a particular group, be it labor or the business sector. He advocated involvement of businessmen as *individuals* rather than as spokesmen for the business cause or for a specific corporation (such as AT&T). And Arthur W. Page, the architect of AT&T's present public relations setup, once wrote flatly: "No successful or un-successful candidate for any public office can truthfully say that he has had the support or opposition of the management of the company."

And indeed, neither AT&T nor any of its subsidiaries have even been caught red-handed in any act which confirmed the frequently voiced suspicions of political opponents that Bell dollars are used against them. The difficulty lies in drawing a line between what Bell officials do in politics as individual citizens and their participation in campaigns at company direc-tion. One clue is the fact that "individual" political activity of Bell officials is frequently directed against people who are un-friendly toward AT&T.

Ed Gossett, Dallas attorney and onetime Congressman, was a longtime counsel for the Southwestern Bell Telephone Com-pany. While working for Bell, he consistently opposed Ralph Yarborough, the Populist leader of Texas' liberal Democrats, in races for both the governorship and the U.S. Senate. After many tries Yarborough finally beat down the Texas conserva-tive establishment in 1958 and went to the Senate (where he promptly verified the direst of Gossett's predictions about his attitude toward AT&T).

What reason would Southwestern Bell have to wish that Ralph Yarborough was practicing law in Austin rather than serving as governor of Texas? During his campaign he urged creation of a public utilities commission to set telephone and other utility rates in Texas—the only state lacking such a reg-ulatory agency.

What reason would the American Telephone & Telegraph Company have to wish that Ralph Yarborough was not in the United States Senate? Well, in 1962 he fought the Communica-tions Satellite Bill as a "giveaway of a national resource," and in 1963 he badgered the Federal Communications Commission into red-faced embarrassment over its tolerance of short-dis-tance long-distance rates that are considerably higher on a per mile basis than those over 800 miles. Yarborough will be a hair shirt for AT&T as long as he is in office.

But Yarborough doesn't attribute Gossett's opposition to any Bell connivance. "Ed and I went to college together; he's an archconservative, and I think he would have fought me bitterly no matter who he worked for," the Senator says.

However, Yarborough did have a peculiar encounter with

Southwestern Bell in 1954, when he was running for governor. Members of the Communications Workers of America local who worked in Bell's Austin, Texas, exchange contacted Yarborough one night and asked that he meet them immediately and secretly.

According to Yarborough, the CWA people told him that Bell had put tape recorders onto lines to his Austin campaign headquarters, ostensibly for service monitoring purposes.

For the remainder of the campaign the Yarborough camp avoided discussing confidential matters over the telephone as best it could; sometimes aides would preface a talk by stating, "Everything I'm telling you is being monitored, so listen carefully, and be careful what you say in reply."

Yarborough talked about the monitoring from the stump that year but never revealed the source of his information. "I've kept it quiet because the CWA men who gave it to me were vulnerable in their jobs. But they're all out of Bell now and can't be bothered.

"Who ordered it? I have no idea, and I don't think this is something that the AT&T office in New York would tell Austin to do or condone. But the people who were involved in this monitoring told me what was happening and that it was happening in the Bell office."

The record isn't one-sided, for every Yarborough is offset by an AT&T story about its own mistreatment by politicians. Officials of St. Clair County, Illinois, once raised the Southwestern Bell Telephone Company's assessment from $591,000 to $864,945 overnight in what was later admitted to be a tax-graft scheme. A court came to Bell's rescue.

In 1960 the Philadelphia Democratic organization, one of the most muscular big-city machines in the country at the time, sent a letter to Pennsylvania Bell's public affairs department asking that tickets be purchased for a Kennedy-Johnson campaign fund-raising dinner. A supervisor collected $100 each from nine officials and contributed $100 himself. Bell's Philadelphia general manager then delivered the amount, in cash, to the politico arranging the dinner. The entire sum was listed in campaign records filed with the state government as coming from one man, Bell's public affairs supervisor, a stratagem that concealed the scope of the company's participation. When the contribution came to light during an investigation of Democratic Party financing, Bell justified it on the ground of "community participation," although some of its officials said privately "good politics" was a more accurate explanation.

Several Texas politicians other than Ralph Yarborough have encountered troubles directly attributable to their efforts to set up a state public utilities commission. Texas now is the only state where utility rates must be set by municipal governments. And this is one instance where grass-roots government is wholly inadequate.

The car dealer, the filling station operator, the insurance salesman, the real estate broker, and the postal clerk who make up the city council must overnight become conversant with the complexities of utility regulation. "Full-time utility commissioners are generally paid salaries of $20,000 or more per year, where the city commissioner serves free of charge," noted Garland S. Smith, city attorney of Weslaco and perhaps the state's leading municipal utility rate lawyer. "If a city commissioner attempts to understand the case, it is no less time-consuming than it is to a full-time utility commissioner. A city commissioner who does his full duty could neglect his personal business and go broke."

The Southwestern Bell Telephone Company, which operates more than 80 percent of Texas' telephones, earns one of the highest returns of any Bell subsidiary—9.8 percent of its average net plant. The figure is deceivingly low; application of the FCC's more realistic rate base valuation puts it nearer to 12.5 percent.

Because there is no state-wide regulation, Southwestern Bell refuses to tell Texas' cities how much it makes from long-distance service, either intrastate or interstate, and maintains that local rates must be based on local operations alone. The answer to who sets intrastate toll rates came in 1960 when Garland Smith was questioning the controller of the General Telephone Company of the Southwest, the state's largest independent company, in a case involving Weslaco rates:

Q. [By Smith] On what basis, then, does your company charge higher rates for intrastate calls than is permitted by the FCC for calls crossing state lines?
A. The toll rates in Texas are set by Southwestern Bell Telephone Company, and we use the same rate that they do between two Texas cities.

Q. Do you know whether or not that rate is fair to the subscriber?

A. As to the rate, I can't answer it.

Q. Have you made any study of that intrastate rate . . . to determine whether or not it is fair to the subscribers to have a higher rate intrastate than interstate?

A. No, we haven't. Since they are Bell rates, we couldn't gain, we couldn't lose, couldn't get anything by making such a study.

The General Telephone official went on to say that "when the Bell company has something like 70 to 80 percent, maybe 90 percent, of the total telephones in the United States, they of course have the predominant [sic] hand in this thing."

In 1961 freshman State Representative Dan Struve introduced a bill that would bring telephone companies under state regulation. Texas Populists have advocated similar measures regularly for half a century; Struve, however, received unexpected support from some city officials who were tired of trying to make sense of telephone rates. Hugh Myer, city attorney for Hondo, was typical: "No one in Hondo knew whether the telephone company was getting one-half of 1 percent or 50 percent rate of return on their investment. It's kinda like the old boy playing poker, pushing all the chips to the middle of the table and then pulling in the pot without letting us see his hole cards."

A Texas economist gave another example of Bell's freewheeling in rate setting. The federal government until the late 1950's taxed intrastate calls 25 percent, then cut the rate back to 10 percent. "On a $1 call, that would have meant the total charge would have been cut back from $1.25 to $1.10. But just before the reduction went into effect, Southwestern Bell announced a 10 percent increase in rates. That means the $1 call is now $1.10, plus 11 cents tax, bringing the old $1.25 call to $1.21. Of the 25-cent tax reduction, the company benefited by 10 cents. Only a 4-cent reduction was passed on to the Texas customer."

Dead cats began raining down on Representative Struve. The Texas Telephone Association, a trade group whose dominant member is Bell, sent out a mailer asking citizens to write their legislators opposing the bill. The mailer stated (falsely): "We understand the author of the bill has repeatedly stated that his

purpose and ultimate goal is Federal ownership of all utilities."
Southwestern Bell's lobbyist, Claude Gilmer, also got busy
against the bill. Not as a Bell lobbyist, however. Gilmer owns
the Rocksprings Telephone Company, and it was in that capacity that he testified in opposition to Struve's bill. A rumor campaign began in Austin that Struve "participated in sit-in and
stand-in civil rights demonstrations." If these charges sound
absurd, be it remembered that Struve represented a rural Texas
constituency.

The bill died a natural death. Struve died a political death.
During his next campaign, well-financed opponents gave voters
the impression he was Mao Tse-tung's brother-in-law or worse
(Struve, a former Army counterintelligence officer, is a member of the American Legion, among other groups), and he ran
third in a three-man field. The Southwestern Bell Telephone
Company remains immune from any state regulation in Texas.

"It is desirable that we enjoy the friendship and confidence
of the newspapers, for through them is mirrored or molded
the sentiment of their readers—our customers," the advertising
manager of the Ohio Bell Telephone Company told a Bell
System publicity seminar in the 1920's.

Bragged a Michigan Bell official during the same decade:
"Through the constant contact of our publicity people with the
press, and that maintained for us by our commercial managers,
we are enabled to more or less control items that go into the
newspapers." Another Ohio Bell publicity man said he made
life easier both for his company and the press corps in Columbus, the state capital: "In rate cases, Columbus newspapers and
the press associations do not send reporters to cover hearings
but accept our stories as written."

Another Ohio Bell man said, "A good editor will not sup-
press a news story, but the closer we are to the newspaper, the
better the chances he will edit the story and take out some of
the sting." This official had so tight a relationship with editors
in his territory that they frequently showed him letters to the
editor in advance of publication. "In many cases the letters
never are printed after our side of the story is told." A report
on a public relations seminar reveals another facet of AT&T's
modus operandi: "Mr. —— of the Southwestern [Bell] company stated that his company plans to try rate cases in newspaper offices, that is, by presenting facts to the editors of news-

papers before the case is presented to the commission for hearing." By swaying public opinion to the belief the phone company needs more money, the utility commissions do not face political dangers in increasing rates.

After four decades, Bell's press aims, methods, and accomplishments have not changed to any noticeable degree. Bell publicity men, former reporters in large part, are the most accommodating, the most informed, the most sincerely convinced believers in their own companies and its policies that a working newsman encounters—provided that newsman is working on a story that Bell agrees should be told and in the manner Bell thinks it should be told.

Bell's critics claim—and could not in a thousand years prove —that the company's good press relations are directly related to the amount of advertising dollars it spends ($19,318,262 for AT&T in 1968, a sum which does not include the considerably higher expenditures of the subsidiary companies). The press' sins, however, more often are those of ignorance and omission, rather than of deliberate distortion or commission. The subject of rate regulation is so complex that informed coverage of a rate hearing on a day-to-day basis would tax the comprehension of both reader and reporter. *The New York Times,* which has the most complete coverage of any U.S. newspaper, devoted considerable space to stories in 1965 saying the FCC was going to investigate AT&T. The *Times* had a reporter present for one or two days of testimony, then forgot the matter entirely for months until a decision was reached.

There is also the outright laziness of reporters and editors who accept unquestioned press releases from Bell which permit the company to tell its story the way it wants it told. When Southwestern Bell announced intrastate toll cuts for Texas in 1962, at least seventeen state newspapers ran unedited the same Bell press release, identical in each city except for the name of the local manager making the announcement. Included were the Houston *Press* (now defunct), the Dallas *Times Herald,* the Laredo *Times,* the Longview *News,* the Port Arthur *News,* the Mineral Wells *Index,* and the Cuero *Record,* a sampling of the big, the medium, and the small. Only the Waco *News-Tribune* went beyond the press release to point out that Senator Ralph Yarborough only a few months previously had criticized AT&T for not including Texas among states enjoying toll cuts and that the reductions were made in response to his pressures.

Through selective use of evidence, however, one can arrive at some generalizations about the past correlation between Bell advertising dollars and Bell's treatment in the news columns. During the one period in the company's history when its general files were open for inspection (the FCC investigation of the 1930's), instance after instance was uncovered in which Bell *did* use advertising dollars to reward its friends or reform its enemies.

In 1923 the Southern Bell Telephone Company, noting that the Jackson *Clarion-Ledger* in Mississippi had been "very unfriendly," decided to buy advertising in a special edition "to bring this paper into line." Commenting later on a favorable news item, the company publicity man noted that "the increased advertising has helped."

When residents of Mullins, South Carolina, griped about phone service, Southern Bell's press department promptly started an ad campaign in the local paper, saying, "If we can keep the newspaper editor in a good frame of mind, possibly we will come out all right." Editors received advertisements because of their political connections. ("Very friendly towards the company and for some time has been soliciting a part of our advertising," Southern Bell commented on a small-town Florida mayor who was also a publisher.)

The FCC concluded after its study of Bell's public relations in the 1930's, "By the practice of suppressing criticism at its source, the [Bell] System has kept from commission attention and from public prints evidence of discontent with its policies and practices and movements for reductions in rates."

Editors of small-town dailies regularly receive the "institutional" advertisements they well know could be discontinued without the slightest damage to Bell's revenues or prestige. Is it fair to describe as "bought" an editor who is accustomed to having a Bell System ad occupy the lower right-hand quarter of p. 2 every Thursday? The editor doesn't think so, and if he does, the thought is promptly shoved to the bottom of his conscience. Bell doesn't think so, for its advertising men say the ad makes people think better of Bell's work, a legitimate aim of private enterprise. And the average citizen doesn't think so, for the editor in all probability has never published a single news item that would give him reason to have an unfavorable impression of the American Telephone & Telegraph Company.*

Bell's reaction to newspaper criticism can be swift, frightening—potentially harsh. Company operating procedure calls for the public relations department to send copies of unfavorable items to division headquarters. The district manager for the territory in which the item was published must report "the general reasons for the appearance of the article, and outline his plans for seeing the editor of the paper, and the persons involved in the article, and [his plans for] meeting the general situation."

There is not necessarily any correlation between the size and influence of the offending paper and the intensity of the plan Bell adopts for "meeting the general situation."

Circle Pines, Minnesota, is a bedroom town of 2,789 persons about 15 miles northeast of Minneapolis, a pleasant little place founded in the 1940's as a cooperative community. The experiment failed because of financial troubles, but the sentiment lives on in the town name, derived from the co-op emblem of two pine trees within a circle. The founder published a newspaper, the *Co-op Way*, to acquaint residents with cooperative principles and methods, but it ceased when he died in 1950.

The idea of living in a town without a newspaper troubled many residents, including research chemist Andrew C. Gibas and his wife, Grace. "People were interested in what was going on in the town, and we felt that there should be a source of news which they could rely upon," Andy Gibas recollects. Together with neighbors they began putting out a mimeographed paper which they called the *Circulating Pines*. "It was strictly volunteer—no advertising, no business office, just an information service. We all pitched in and did the work in our homes." The *Circulating Pines* was popularly received and in 1958 became what Gibas calls a "legal publication," with advertising that was intended to make it at least self-supporting and hope-

---

* Media timidity about criticising AT&T extends beyond the press. Following publication of the hard-cover edition of this book in 1968 a publicity representative from G. P. Putnam's Sons, Inc., contacted numerous radio and television stations concerning promotional appearances on interview shows. Ronald D. Miziker, executive producer of the Bob Braun "Fifty/Fifty Club" show on WLW-TV in Cincinnati, wrote the publisher: "As I mentioned over the telephone, discussing this book *Monopoly* on our show would be very difficult. I have checked with our Sales Department and their policy strictly prohibits it."

fully profitable. Gibas continued working as a chemist during the day; Grace Gibas did much of the reporting and writing.

From its inception the *Circulating Pines* commented occasionally, but critically on the Northwestern Bell Telephone Company, the Bell subsidiary for the area. "We thought their rate structure was unfair because, as a small community, our charges were pretty high. We also had four and eight party service, which was bad, and we kept asking 'Why?' in our editorials," Gibas said.

Every time the *Circulating Pines* ran an editorial on Bell, a visitor appeared at the door soon thereafter: Joe Cervenka, a friendly tall chap who was Northwestern Bell's public relations chief for Minnesota. "Joe came out to see us the first time we ran an AT&T editorial, and he was back again frequently. Mrs. Gibas got to know Joe pretty well, he was around so often. He was right on the job . . . a public relations man, you know how they are, very smooth and active. He would politely argue that we were misinformed about rate structures and try to point out that Northwestern Bell was doing a good job and improving."

On one issue, however, the Gibases and Cervenka were irreconcilable, and ideologically so. The Gibases thought a telephone service run by the government would be cheaper because there would be no need for profits and costs of bond issues would be lower. Also, they pointed out editorially that many Bell System executives are paid a higher salary than the President of the United States—an expense they felt could be reduced considerably under public ownership. (Frederick R. Kappel was receiving $304,600 a year when he retired as AT&T board chairman in 1967, three times what Lyndon B. Johnson was paid.)

The Gibases' real troubles began on May 31, 1962, when they published an editorial on the Communications Satellites Act dispute in Congress under the title "The Biggest Give-Away Yet!" The editorial began:

"In the past seven years the American Telephone & Telegraph Company (the Bell System) has overcharged long distance phone users a billion dollars. But this is going to look like peanuts if AT&T succeeds in getting the government to hand over its communications satellites." The editorial recited many of the arguments against AT&T involvement in the Comsat company that were made by opposing Congressmen:

that because of the sizable public investment in the space program, the satellites should be publicly owned; that AT&T's domination of the communications field should not be increased further; that the foreign policy implications of the satellites made essential their retention by the government. The Gibases lamented there had been "little public information on the give-away and no discussion," and asked: "Is the Democratic Party changing its role as the protector of the ordinary taxpayer and becoming the champion of the super giant corporation?"

The editorial brought public relations man Cervenka to Circle Pines in a hurry and in a polite huff. First, he called to tell Gibas to forget about the Northwestern Bell advertisement scheduled for the next issue. Further, if Gibas were interested in his paper, they'd best have a little talk.

Once in Circle Pines, Cervenka told Gibas copies of the editorial had been sent via teletype to Bell executive offices in Omaha (Northwestern's headquarters) and New York. Bell lawyers there, Gibas heard, were showing "great interest" in two statements in the editorial: the $1 billion overcharge on long-distance calls and the fact that the government would pay for the rockets that took the satellites into orbit. "He was indicating that they were going to bring some kind of action," Gibas stated. "But I wasn't particularly scared of them. I had been a town officer before—clerk and a member of the utilities commission—and the mention of a court wasn't ominous because I knew what we said had a factual basis." *

Visits by irate press agents are a fact of life in the newspaper business (and also a barometer of an editor's willingness to speak out on controversial issues at the risk of making people mad). Cervenka, however, went several steps farther than registering a protest.

Through a neighboring editor, Cervenka found the name of a man thought to be the money behind the Gibases. Cervenka

---

* The $1 billion figure came from a speech in the House of Representatives by Representative Emanuel Celler (Democrat, New York) on May 2, 1962. Celler stated that the FCC, in 1953, had said AT&T was entitled to a 6.5 percent rate of return, but that it had exceeded this figure beginning in 1955. Celler computed that if AT&T's return had been held to 6.5 percent during the period 1955 to 1961, long-distance users would have saved approximately $985,000,000. "Thus, over the past seven years, AT&T has overcharged the American public by nearly a billion dollars," Celler said.

sounded this man out on whether he felt as the Gibases did on AT&T—only to learn that he had no interest in the *Circulating Pines,* that it was solely owned by Gibas. Gibas said, "What are we to conclude except that AT&T wanted to have someone with a financial interest put pressure on us?"

Next, Cervenka called on residents of Circle Pines—the mayor, some town councilmen, Andy Gibas' friends and neighbors. According to what these people reported back to Gibas, Cervenka was interested in their attitudes toward him and the *Circulating Pines* and also toward the telephone service they received. Cervenka also told them the "give-away" editorial was both untrue and unfair.

A Lutheran minister told Gibas that the press agent gave subtle implications that the couple was pro-Communist. The minister retorted this was "rot" that best should be forgotten.

Cervenka also talked with advertisers. The town's leading grocery store chose this time to drop its ads. The owner told Gibas that Cervenka had not suggested any economic boycott, but "we don't want to get involved." Cervenka did restore Bell's ad to the paper and said he had canceled it only to make changes in the copy.

When the Gibases learned of all these visits by Cervenka, "it made us very uneasy." So one night Mrs. Gibas sat down at her typewriter and wrote an editorial which appeared a few days later under the title "This Is for You, Joe."

This editorial is for Joe. Joe is a public relations man for Northwestern Bell Telephone Company. Probably no one reads our editorials with more interest or concern than does Joe. And whenever we have something to say about Northwestern Bell Telephone Company we get a personal visit from Joe. Joe is a nice guy, but we don't think he realizes quite what he is doing. That's why we're writing this for Joe.

Joe is a tall gentleman with a pleasant personality. Our criticisms of the telephone company wound him to the quick. With the greatest feeling and touching sincerity, Joe pleads the cause of the telephone company. When Joe talks you see the telephone company not as a heartless, powerful monopoly, out to get every cent the traffic will bear, but as a struggling organization with tremendous problems. You get to feeling positively hard-hearted because you can't feel more sympathetic about the tough time the telephone company has getting its hands on capital. . . .

Joe's loyalty to his company is a fine thing. But his company is asking him to do some very questionable things. He wants us to send our editorials to him before we print them so he can check them for facts. This suggestion we do not favor.

Just as no government should be without critics, so no corporation, especially one as big and powerful as AT&T, should deprive itself of the opportunity to hear how folks feel about it.

And yet this is exactly what AT&T is trying to do. They want us to keep quiet. They want no breath of criticism. They want the public to hear nothing except a selling job on the good qualities of the telephone company.

The editorial told of Cervenka's visits in Circle Pines, repeated the belief that the communications satellite should be a public enterprise, and gave the source for the $1 billion overcharge statement. Mrs. Gibas quoted Cervenka as replying that "Congressman Celler is not a friend of ours" and that the FCC now felt AT&T was entitled to a 7.5 percent return and thus had not overcharged the public. Mrs. Gibas continued:

. . . Here's what bothers us even more. Joe says Congressman Celler is not a friend. Does AT&T divide the world into friends and enemies? If folks who criticize AT&T aren't friends, then obviously the editors of this paper and AT&T are not friends. And, as we said before, who wants a powerful monopoly like AT&T for an enemy?

Joe, you're a nice guy, but don't you see what AT&T is trying to do to freedom of the press?

Well, the *Circulating Pines* survived. The grocer who didn't "want to get involved" eventually returned as an advertiser. About 100 persons who heard of the incident sent in money for subscriptions from as far away as Maine and Florida. "They [AT&T] have a very big foot and are apparently stepping on an annoying ant in your section of the country," wrote a citizen from Hollywood, Florida. "However, there may be too many ants to step on if publicity of this sort becomes widespread." "Wouldn't you know it would take a small town paper with guts to take a slap at the goliath AT&T?" said a person from Limestone, New York. "Wish we had more of your type of men operating local newspapers," said someone from Holly,

Colorado. "It is amazing to read of intimidating tactics being used instead of intelligent argument," said a person from Syracuse, New York. "Thank you for having the backbone to stand up to it."

After the "This Is for You, Joe," editorial, Gibas heard no more of the threatened lawsuit. "The higher-ups apparently decided to leave it alone." He thought briefly of doing something in court himself. "It hurt us," he said. "If I was in a suing mood, I might have done something. But the little man doesn't have much of a chance in a case like this; it costs too much money." Cervenka was transferred to Northwestern Bell's home office in Omaha, Nebraska, a bit later, and now another public relations man has the responsibility of calling on Andy and Grace Gibas.

And Grace is well acquainted with this chap, too, for the *Circulating Pines* retains its habit of questioning Bell's omnipotence in print. In 1967, Bell started permitting Circle Pines residents toll-free service to a town 15 miles away but continued charges to another hamlet only 5 miles distant which is in the same school district. "Please, let us call our neighbors," the *Circulating Pines* was pleading.

Benjamin Gordon, the chief staff economist for the Senate Small Business Committee, is an erudite man who likes chess and fine music. He also enjoys stories about spies and how to catch them, which was his job while an agent for the Army's Counter Intelligence Corps. He was talking about a woman who was a big name in one of the major spy cases of the late 1940's:

"She was in the Metropolitan Museum of Art in New York one afternoon and she stepped back so she could have a better view of the paintings. She stumbled into a man who was very apologetic, very charming—and a Soviet espionage agent, although she didn't know it when he took her to dinner that evening, and discussed the exhibition they had seen. The Soviets, knowing of her interest in art, baited her with a similarly inclined man and were able to recruit her into a spy network."

Gordon thought of this incident with amusement a few years back when a man came into his office, introduced himself as a lobbyist for the American Telephone & Telegraph Company, and eventually got around to talking about his interests in chess and music. "AT&T had made a careful study of me before 'assigning' the lobbyist, just as they do of anyone they think should be lobbied."

In Gordon's instance, AT&T lobbying consisted of several lunches with genial conversation, an occasional pair of symphony tickets, and candid presentations of the company's views on the communications satellite legislation which was before the Senate Small Business Committee at the time.

AT&T's man wasn't particularly effective, a reflection more of Benjamin Gordon's ideas on monopolies than of the lobbyist's prowess. But Washington is the most important lobbying beat that there is for AT&T, for there are centered the agencies with the power to touch almost every activity the company undertakes:

—The Federal Communications Commission, which oversees AT&T's long-distance rates and approves or disapproves new types of service the company wants to offer in interstate commerce.

—The Justice Department, whose antitrust division makes occasional worried sounds about AT&T's size and position of power in the communications industry and its control of telephony manufacturing through the subsidiary Western Electric Company.

—The Defense Department, from which Western Electric has obtained contracts worth scores of millions of dollars of profits, both on its own work and that which it "manages" at other companies on behalf of the Pentagon.

—The Congress, always unpredictable, always infiltrated by at least half a dozen mavericks who would like nothing better than to make AT&T a branch of the Post Office.

The majority of the time AT&T's approach to bureaucrats is genteel and restrained. AT&T lobbyists keep a file of birth dates of key Congressional staff members and surprise them with office parties. A new Senator who is appointed to a committee which has jurisdiction over fields affecting AT&T—the Commerce Committee, for example—can expect a jolly lunch, with an AT&T lobbyist as the host and perhaps an AT&T vice-president in attendance, along with an invitation to visit a Bell Laboratories installation. (One solon so treated came away talking about a "scientific Disneyland.") AT&T lobbyists are among the most active members in the various state associations through which transient Washingtonians maintain contact with home. Indeed, AT&T likes to make the Congressmen *themselves* feel at home. For that reason the lobbyist currently assigned to the Southern bloc comes from Southern Bell's office in Atlanta, Georgia, and has a hominy-dripping accent to prove it.

The Washington lobbyists are responsible for keeping AT&T's Congressional friends happy, and coming up with occasional little favors for special favorites. Senator John Pastore of Rhode Island, as chairman of the subcommittee on communications of the Senate Commerce Committee, has long held the power to force the Federal Communications Commission to do a more effective regulatory job vis. a vis. AT&T. Yet this Pastore has refused to do, choosing to put Bell's financial well-being above the interests of the individual citizen. Bell demonstrated its appreciation for his services in 1968 by constructing, in Rhode Island, the United States terminus of a transatlantic telephone cable. Its choice of the site puzzled telephone people who were unaware of Washington's political realities.

At hearings AT&T lobbyists have company witnesses coached so that the Bell position can be stated in a manner capable of penetrating the thickest of Congressional skulls. Testimony is reduced to chalk-talk simplicity, and key words and phrases are thrown at Congressmen in slides and posters until eventually the effect is subliminal. A favorite is a map of the United States which shows varying distances that could be called for $1 over the years. One Senator half-seriously swears he has seen the same map seventeen times in his seven years in Congress. At committee hearings friendly Representatives and Senators are given sheafs of questions AT&T would like to have asked, and they serve as little more than batting practice pitchers for company witnesses, tossing queries that can easily be knocked out of the park. Congressmen like this role because the skillfully phrased, often technical questions give them an aura of intelligence in the eyes of innocent onlookers.

There is a peripheral advantage in having a network of strong friends in official Washington. In lobbying, what the friends can do *directly* for you is important; yet an effective lobbyist wants friends who can help him *indirectly* by getting rid of people and agencies who are bothering him.

There once was a minute part of the Washington bureaucracy known as the Transportation and Public Utility Service of the General Services Administration. Probably no more than a couple of hundred people outside the government had ever heard of it. But this little office caused AT&T trouble, and what happened to it thereafter shows how tough those genial, smiling telephone company lobbyists can become when there is executioner's work to be done.

In 1956 Congress authorized the Air Force to establish a new communications system to shorten the time interval between the discovery of invading enemy aircraft and the deployment of defensive planes and missiles. The system was known as SAGE, the first-letter abbreviation for its full name of semiautomatic ground environment system. Insofar as possible, the Air Force was to use leased telephone lines.

The estimated costs of $222,000,000 annually disturbed Congress. The House Committee on Armed Services, in approving SAGE, said that in view of the magnitude of the program "the rate charged should be kept under strict surveillance by the appropriate government agencies." The committee pointed to GSA's statutory authority to represent the federal government in utility rate negotiations and also at hearings before federal and state regulatory bodies.

Congress' fears about rates proved justified in the first years of the SAGE program. The Air Force quite simply wouldn't be bothered. A general told the Senate during this period: "I have enough faith in the regulatory boards concerned and in our experience in doing business with the telephone companies of the country, Bell, independents, cooperatives, to think that we get our money's worth for the taxpayer."

No, sir, retorted the Comptroller General of the United States, whose office discovered in an audit that in one year alone AT&T overcharged the Air Force $1,226,996 for minimum service charges on SAGE lines. This audit stated the "Air Force depended too much on AT&T and did not provide adequate surveillance or sufficient cross checks of its own" to ensure that billings and rates were proper.

A House subcommittee found a "marked philosophy of *laissez-faire*" in the Air Force, which was "relying on the communications industry to initiate adjustments, and then trusting that the industry and the [regulatory] commissions will see that the government gets its fair share."

For years GSA's Transportation and Public Utility Service (TPUS hereafter) had used its rate-intervention authority sparingly and none too effectively. Bell System companies and other utilities didn't take TPUS seriously as an opponent. Says T. A.

Kennedy, GSA Assistant Commissioner: "For a number of years these utilities felt that we were highly ineffective and could be laughed off because we were just some group that was in from Washington, a little noisy maybe in some areas, but that our efforts would be discounted by the commissions in their evaluation later of the issues."

The attitude of AT&T and other utilities changed overnight when TPUS got into the SAGE rate cases. The SAGE work was done by a twelve-member team headed by Frederick W. Denniston, formerly a GSA staff lawyer.

Within two years Denniston's team won reductions on SAGE rates amounting to $10,000,000 a year—worth $100,000,000 when applied over the ten-year contract period. In other rate proceedings TPUS succeeded in cleaving government phone bills by another $6,000,000 a year, at AT&T's expense for the most part.

Even in cases where increases were authorized, the GSA saved the government money. In Maryland AT&T's subsidiary, the Chesapeake & Potomac Telephone Company, asked a rate increase of $13,500,000 for types of service that would have increased the federal government's $5,000,000 annual bill with them by $500,000. After GSA's intervention the Maryland Public Service Commission permitted total increases of only $400,000, the government's share of which was $40,000 rather than the threatened $500,000. "Avoided increases" from 1956–59 totaled $5,419,386, by Denniston's computations.

TPUS carefully defined its role in such appearances. As Denniston states, "Every statement made to the Maryland commission and every pleading filed with it spelled out with complete exactitude that we represented the government only as a consumer, and there was not even an inference that we were representing the general public."

GSA constantly turned up evidence that embarrassed Bell at rate hearings. In a California case GSA claimed that the Pacific Telephone & Telegraph Company increased its executives from 201 in 1956 to 334 in 1962 (an increment of 66 percent) and their total salaries by 131 percent, while its total employee force during the period declined from 71,926 to 67,522 (6 percent). GSA argued that this "excessive executive expense" should not be borne by California phone subscribers, in whose ranks the federal government was included. Although PT&T claimed GSA indulged in guess work and knew not of what it spoke, the Public Utilities Commission said it found no excuse for maintenance of such a high-paid executive corps and ordered $2,150,000 of the $7,200,000 expense for them cut from the California rate base.

TPUS' work in rate regulation became increasingly important as nonmilitary governmental phone bills rose. In 1956 the federal government spent $205,000,000 on communications; by 1961 this had almost doubled, to $386,000,000.

Despite its accomplishments, TPUS began drawing criticisms from the Senate in the late 1950's. The record is uncertain why certain Senators put TPUS on a lukewarm griddle simply because it was doing what Congress had ordered it to do; indeed, Senator Warren Magnuson, after a series of needling questions directed to GSA officials during an appropriations hearing, made the *Eureka!* exclamation: "This committee in effect practically directed you people to get into these things."

TPUS always managed to escape intact and with no more serious chastisement than an admonition "to act with good judgment and not enter into any harassing activities; to avoid trivialities and to protect the interest of the government."

A man who was high in the General Services Administration at the time recalls that AT&T lobbyists frequently protested TPUS' rate work. "Every time we had a change of command, a lobbyist came over promptly to try to persuade him to take GSA out of the rate business. The new boss would react indignantly, for AT&T made the work sound rather awful, and then would call for a report. After he saw the facts, however, the rate unit would be troubled no further."

On July 14, 1959, the SAGE team split a $10,000 government incentives award, highest ever in GSA, ranging from $3,000 for Denniston down to $200 each for a couple of secretaries who had typed legal briefs. The formal citation said their work "resulted in vast savings to the government and reflected credit on GSA."

The citation didn't set any amount of saving, but GSA records put it at $16,000,000 annually or $160,0000,000 over the ten-year life of the major SAGE contracts involved, *and this by a bureaucratic unit with a $300,000 annual budget.*

All this was ample provocation for AT&T to begin a cannonade at TPUS in general and the SAGE team in particular. The lanyard was pulled by Edward B. Crosland, who bore the title of AT&T vice-president for regulatory matters and the unofficial rank of chief lobbyist.

Crosland worked from offices both at AT&T headquarters at 195 Broadway in New York and at 1730 K Street, NW, in Washington, and he worked very well.

Ill-defined traces of Crosland's footprints are encountered in many areas where AT&T needed protection or a boost from the government. In 1956 Crosland was in intimate contact with members of the Federal Communications Commission while the FCC was trying to decide its position in the Western Electric antitrust case. There were many long-distance calls between Crosland and FCC members, some of which he made from his home. Again, in 1961, Crosland was in the background when the FCC attempted to put the communications satellite system in the hands of a carrier group dominated by AT&T.

This time Crosland used as a front for his activities no less prestigious an organization than the Chamber of Commerce of the United States. The way Crosland went about killing TPUS is worthy of exploration at length, for his campaign brings into focus the elements that make the AT&T lobby such a potent force: Congressmen who at times appear to be little more than puppets for the Bell System; other U.S. businesses, which aided AT&T in return for an implicit promise of reciprocal aid the next time they needed help; trade associations which AT&T was able to maneuver, both through its memberships and the contacts of its executives; and, finally, the state regulatory agencies, which were more interested in preserving their rights and powers than in achieving fair telephone rates. Crosland brought up all this artillery while keeping AT&T hidden in the background. Not until late in his campaign did Bell's interest become apparent, and by then he had almost succeeded.

Crosland's first overt move against TPUS came at a meeting of the Chamber of Commerce's transportation and communications committee on September 9 and 10, 1959. Crosland complained about the intervention of GSA into rate cases, saying this work was wasteful and duplicated that done by the FCC.

"We think its unfair for the government to appear in these cases as prosecutor," Crosland said. "Recently, at the FCC, the GSA filed a petition to reduce our private-line rates, and the FCC did reduce them. I haven't proposed any recommendations, but I think we [meaning the Chamber of Commerce committee] should spell out our opposition." The committee chairman appointed a subcommittee to "study" the question and named Crosland its chairman.

How was Crosland able to have his way within the Chamber of Commerce? Because AT&T historically has maintained enough members in the Chamber of Commerce to have an influential voice in the organization. (A Bell public relations guide advises that by "systematically cultivating" officers of trade associations the company "can have available a medium through which to effectively place before the membership educational facts that will permit better understanding of telephone problems and motives.") AT&T paid $15,000 in membership dues to the Chamber of Commerce of the United States in 1968. The Bell operating companies, in turn, maintained membership in local and states chambers which support the national chamber. Further, AT&T's Washington office helps the Chamber on special projects. All this, of course, at the expense of the telephone consumer.

Crosland next created and mobilized antagonism against TPUS among outside organizations and businesses. This project swiftly became so wide that AT&T gave Crosland reinforcements. A lawyer from Southern Bell wrote legal briefs, letters, and reports, all supporting the proposition that TPUS should be curbed. (The American telephone consumer, of course, financed all these activities.) Crosland and his Southern assistant relied on what politicians call cross-lobbying—a technique in which one party tells another, "I have a problem, and I need help. If you'll line up your friends for me this time, I'll do the same for you next time you have trouble."

AT&T's cross-lobbying touched an impressive array of corporations, financial institutions, trade associations, and law firms, whose sum would be enough to make even a Congressman blink. A partial list of the allies recruited by Crosland includes: the Eastern Railroad Presidents Conference, the Railway Express Agency, Connecticut Power and Light Company, Washington Gas Light Company, Western Union, the Baltimore & Ohio Railroad, the First National Bank of Chicago, the Commonwealth Edison Company, The American Waterways Operators, American Airlines, the American Gas Association, the Pacific Northwest Power Company, and the Continental Illinois National Bank & Trust Company of Chicago.

Just how much help any of these solicitees gave AT&T isn't in the record, for cross-lobbying requires nothing more than a long-distance phone call from a corporation president to his home state's Senator. And if in the same day the Senator also hears from the state's leading law firm, its most powerful utility, and a couple of railroad heads, it's human for him to listen. Crosland's assistant thought these groups significant enough to make a special trip to Chicago to deliver anti-TPUS material to the Continental Illinois Bank in person.

Concurrently, Crosland and AT&T lobbyists at the state level worked on the National Association of Railroad and Utilities Commissioners (NARUC), composed of members of the various state regulatory agencies. With increasing frequency Congressmen got complaints that TPUS was "infringing" on state prerogatives by appearing in rate cases and that its very presence insinuated the state agencies didn't know what they were doing. Here again the complaints were doubly beneficial to AT&T, for the state utility commissioners are generally men of political stature, and a Senator or Representative who hears from one of them isn't apt to question his motivation for calling.

The "complaints" in this category had a peculiar feature. Denniston notes that most came from states "where we had never appeared." T. A. Kennedy of GSA adds: "These same commissions that have 'complained' about our intervention have on other occasions requested our help, and we have provided them with witnesses, testimony and assistance, documentation to support their cases."

At NARUC's national convention in Las Vegas in November, 1960, AT&T's lobbyists moved to appropriate the prestige of the organization for its attack on GSA. A resolution was offered criticizing TPUS's activities and calling on Congress to limit severely its funds and freedom of activity.

Some of the commissioners immediately saw the resolution for what it was: "basically a fight between American Telephone & Telegraph Company and the federal government," in the words of Commissioner Richard J. McMahon of the Maine PUC. Commissioners from New Jersey and California (including Peter E. Mitchell, the NARUC president-elect) spoke against it. McMahon questioned the wisdom of excluding from hearings "the largest customer of most untilities" and said TPUS "has never abused their right to appear."

McMahon described the way the AT&T resolution was whisked through the convention on voice vote: "When the vote was taken, there were several individuals standing, asking for a call of the states by roll call and by commission. But the president announced the results before he would recognize anybody on the floor." A motion to reconsider was shouted down by voice vote.

McMahon added, "In the room at the time were possibly 100 commissioners representing most of the state and federal commissions. Also, another 200 guests of the convention representing the affected industries of all the resolutions passed at that session were present."

Senator E. L. Bartlett of Alaska says he was told by people who attended the convention that "by far the majority of these 200 guests were employees of the Bell System, and that many of these joined in shouting for the resolution at the time when the voice vote was taken."

Analyzing the vote, Denniston points out that states opposing the AT&T ploy "were the ones where we have done most of our appearing"—Maine, California, and New Jersey. Most stridently in favor of AT&T were Maryland (two GSA appearances in eleven years); Virginia (one, in 1952); and Connecticut (no appearances at all).

During the same period similar resolutions were passed by the Air Transport Association, the Movers Conference of America, the Association of American Railroads, the Independent Natural Gas Association, and the Transportation Association of America—*all of which had been contacted in advance by AT&T's Washington lobbyists.* Officers and lawyers of each of the groups were supplied with a lengthy anti-TPUS memorandum written by AT&T, copies of which in some instances were also given to individual members.

Crosland's next objective, the United States Senate, submitted as easily—if not as quietly—as did the Chamber of Commerce and NARUC. The chamber subcommittee which had been appointed to "study" the problem and which Crosland headed predictably produced a sixty-five-page report which suggested that TPUS be chopped into small pieces and thrown off the Washington Monument. The report bore the imprimatur of the Chamber of Commerce of the United States, not that of AT&T, and gave no hint that it was actually composed by AT&T's chief Washington lobbyist. A subcommittee of the Senate Appropriations Committee listened to the report and to a recitation of the "NARUC" resolution. In neither instance was mention made of AT&T's role in securing its passage.

Witnesses supporting AT&T received an unfailingly glad-hand treatment from the committee. One of these was Judge H. Lester Hooker, of the Virginia State Corporation Commission, which regulates utilities in that state. "Judge, you are appearing before a friendly forum," said Senator A. Willis Robertson, a Virginia Democrat. "I am mighty glad to see that," Hooker said, beaming, and then made a speech about states' rights as they apply to public utility regulation.

AT&T's friends came laden with restrictions they wanted put on TPUS. One would have limited TPUS appearances to instances when the rate charged the government was discriminatory compared with that paid by other phone subscribers.

"Senator, I think that would put us out of business," remarked the GSA witness testifying at the time. "It is a good deal like saying, 'It is all right to go swimming but stay out of the water.' This proposal would . . . eliminate us from making the contention that the rate is too high even though everyone is paying it."

The subcommittee ultimately produced an amendment banning TPUS from presenting testimony on utility earning levels or property valuations—akin to permitting someone to write about sex as long as he doesn't mention men or women. It also cut the $300,000 GSA had asked for regulatory agency appearances—in sum, a decisive victory for Crosland and the AT&T lobbying effort.

A handful of Senators found AT&T's activities too unpalatable to swallow and scornfully questioned the "economy" of denying TPUS $300,000 for work that saved the government $16,000,000 a year.

Senator Ernest Gruening of Alaska said the amendment would "gut this important service," leave it "helplessly crippled," and "redound to the benefit only of those interests that would, of course, prefer no regulation at all for the protection of the consumers. The struggle of the consumers for a fair break in these cases is one in which they are almost always unevenly matched with the great utilities. Because of their vastly greater financial resources with which to carry on the interminable litigation required to establish a rate determination, the utilities and the carriers have an undue advantage which is, in many cases, overcome by the consumers only with great difficulty."

"We all know what is behind this move," exclaimed Senator Paul Douglas. "The General Services Administration has obtained reductions of $145 to $150 million from the AT&T. The proposal of the committee is a reprisal against the good work of the GSA in recovering these millions from AT&T."

AT&T's restrictions had been put into the bill by Senator Gordon Allott of Colorado, and Senator Estes Kefauver, sarcastically speaking of the "so-called Allott Amendment," told the Senate: "With all due deference to my colleague from Colorado, this is substantially what Mr. Crosland's Chamber of Commerce committee recommended."

Despite these protests, AT&T won in the Senate. But its influence wasn't as great in the House of Representatives, which in a conference committee insisted on removing the restrictive amendment, restoring all but $75,000 of the $300,000 cut from the TPUS budget, and directing that the reduction be spread throughout the entire unit, rather than be applied solely to the people involved in the SAGE rate cases.

A loss for AT&T? Surprisingly, no, for a while a majority of Congress was reaffirming its desire for GSA to continue rate interventions, GSA decided on its own to stop doing so.

Why? Expediency is a harsh word, so let us say GSA's leadership decided to view "realistically" its deteriorating relationship with the Independent Offices Subcommittee of the Senate Appropriations Committee, which controls the agency's yearly allowance.

No federal agency can survive and do its work if its direct Congressional overseers are unhappy for year after dreary year. The House saved GSA on the TPUS issue in 1961, yet could GSA count on support the next year if the subcommittee decided to perform a thorough hatchet job on the entire agency? So GSA decided to take itself out of rate cases, save in instances where "the government is being penalized by rates or services," in the words of Bernard L. Boutin, head of GSA during the first part of the Kennedy Administration.

The capitulation satisfied AT&T. When Congress is in session, AT&T's Washington office sends the subsidiary companies periodic legislative reviews. The issue that told of the Congressional conference committee's revival of the TPUS funds and authority also informed the Bell System that everything would be fine nonetheless because there had been a "realignment" of functions and personnel in the Transportation and Public Utility Service.

The "realignment" was in actuality a purge. Despite twenty years' experience in rate regulation, Denniston was removed from rate work and shoved sidewise into the office of assistant general counsel. He remained there six months, then retired. "I didn't want a sinecure, or a job in charge of doing nothing," he told friends.

The team that worked on the SAGE cases was formally disbanded and soon scattered, with the other rate specialists who had worked under Denniston leaving GSA as quietly and quickly as they could. Even the two secretaries who had done nothing more harmful to AT&T than type legal briefs were marked. After Denniston left, GSA brass assigned them to duties in no way related to rate work.

Were Crosland and AT&T satisfied with the outcome?

In the 1961 appropriations hearings, Crosland's captive Chamber of Commerce committee had yelled "economy" in urging that $1,000,000 be cut from a TPUS request for $2,500,000.

In the 1962 appropriations hearings, after Denniston's team had vanished, not a complaint was heard from the chamber when GSA asked $4,400,000 for TPUS' successor division— promising, as it did so, to do nothing to disturb the peace of mind of the state regulatory agencies and AT&T and noting with pride that nobody seemed to be complaining about TPUS aggressiveness anymore.

Crosland's destruction of the GSA unit, despite its complexity and subtlety of execution, nonetheless stayed within the ethical code of American politics. His marshaling of lobbying forces is nothing more than what other industries do annually in every state capital of the nation (though on a lesser scale) to protect their interests.* Yet occasionally Washington has a

---

* The counsel for the New York Public Service Commission accused the New York Telephone Company of spending $500,000 in three months during 1957 on a "propaganda campaign" to kill legislation that would have affected its rates. The counsel, Kent H. Brown, said New York Telephone lobbyists persuaded chambers of commerce that service would suffer and labor unions that wages would be hurt if the bills passed. When New York Telephone won, Averell Harriman, then governor, criticized a "small coterie" of state senators who "appear more interested in doing the bidding of the telephone company than in protecting the people they are elected to serve."

fleeting glimpse of a more crass form of pressuring legislators
that is deserving of another name than lobbying.

On August 10, 1962, the U.S. Senate was caught up in the
debate over the Communications Satellite Act. Washington was
an ugly place that summer, with Senate friend pitted against
Senate friend. The Kennedy Administration was keeping itself
delicately aloof from legislation which it formerly backed but
unofficially doubted, and the defense manufacturing establishment was seething as AT&T inexorably moved toward domination of the Comsat program. Nothing stood in AT&T's path but
the ten Senators who hoped, by filibustering, to delay action on
the legislation until after the fall elections. Of these ten men,
the most powerful in the Senate Establishment was Russell B.
Long of Louisiana.

Someone had a talk with Russell Long on August 10, and
what this person said made Russell Long mad—so mad that
when he swept through the cloakroom toward the Senate floor
a few moments later, his face was flushed and his voice was
strained. He paused in the cloakroom just long enough to tell
a few Senatorial friends that they might want to hear what he
had to say.

Senator Frank E. Moss of Utah, a part-time ally of the filibusters, had the floor, and Long broke into his colloquy. "Mr.
President, will the Senator yield for a question?" Moss looked
curiously at the grim Long and yielded.

Long's first sentence brought every head in the Senate snap-
ping around to stare at him:

> When this bill first started out I thought it was as crooked
> as a dog's hind leg. I am now convinced that that would be
> a compliment. This bill is as crooked as a barrel of snakes.
> I ask the Senator whether he does not agree with me that
> this is the most corrupt and the most crooked and most dis-
> honest piece of legislation that he has experienced while he
> has been in the Senate.

Whereupon Russell Long launched into a half-hour string of
rhetorical questions, whose content speaks for itself. Under the
Senate's parliamentary ritual, had Long made positive statements rather than pose his thoughts in interrogatives, Moss
would have had to yield the floor. For tactical reasons the fili-
busterers sought to keep him in command as long as possible.

So each of Long's questions was preceded by the formalistic "Mr. President, will the Senator yield for a further question?" The bystander Moss would agree and then listen with growing astonishment to what Long said:

> I should like to ask the Senator from Utah whether the telephone company has offered him the kind of proposal that it has offered me?

> Has the Senator had proposals made to him that he could own a telephone building in his state and that the telephone company would make the loan and endorse the loan to build a building in a big city in his state just on the assurance that the Senator would give sympathetic consideration to the company's problem, if he would go along with them, and that the company would then build the building and endorse the mortgage loan and engage the bank to make the loan with the probability that he would wind up eventually being worth $5 million or $25 million?

> Has my good friend ever heard the old saying, "Keep the price as high as the traffic will bear?"

> Did it occur to the Senator that what the American Telephone & Telegraph Company is worried about is cheap rates, and the fear that if the bill should not become law, AT&T might not be able to control the satellite, and, therefore, rates might be cut by 100 percent? [sic] Did it ever occur to the Senator from Utah that the whole object of the bill might be to enable AT&T to control this operation and thus prevent telephone rates from coming down?

> Did it ever occur to the Senator that he might be one of the few Members of Congress who has never had the opportunity to own a telephone building?

> Does it not appear to be unfair that some Members of Congress are permitted to own telephone buildings, while others are not, and that this is a matter of discrimination among Representatives and Senators?

> I ask my good friend, who is a moral, conscientious man, would it not occur to him that if some Senators and Representatives are to own telephone buildings, others are also entitled to own telephone buildings?

Did it ever occur to the Senator from Utah that if a Representative from one district in Louisiana should be permitted to own a telephone building in his hometown, Representatives from the other districts should be permitted to own the telephone buildings in their respective hometowns?

If one is to become rich from this bill, why should not we all become rich?

If this bill passes, it may be that some people will own telephone buildings, have their loans for such endorsed, and will get great advantages. Does the Senator feel he should be excluded from some of the beneficial advantages simply because he votes against the bill?

Senator Long finally halted the questions when Moss said he wanted to finish his speech in time to keep an important engagement; the Comsat debate was to go on for several more days, but the subject of ownership of telephone buildings never came up again.

Since the speech Russell Long has made his peace with AT&T. One factor, according to a man who worked on his staff during the Comsat debate, was Western Electric's construction of a vast manufacturing facility at Shreveport, Louisiana, to the delight of thousands of his constituents. Long now declines to discuss the obvious implications of his August 10, 1962 speech. Thus the statements, unmodified and unamplified, must speak for themselves.

9

(d) Changes in Telephone Numbers.

The assignment of a number to a subscriber's telephone will be made at the discretion of the company. The subscriber has no proprietary right in the number, and the company may make such reasonable changes in telephone number or central office designation as the requirements of the service may demand.

> —*Operating rules and regulations of the Pacific Telephone & Telegraph Company, AT&T subsidiary in California*

Phones are for people.

> —*Motto of California's Anti Digit Dialing League*

ON March 23, 1961, Los Angeles lawyer Arthur Garrett, a candidate for the office of city attorney, issued a press release declaring that telephone service would be his chief campaign issue. He complained about high rates, about coin boxes that take citizens' dimes without completing their calls, about the difficulties in dealing with rude information operators of the Pacific Telephone & Telegraph Company.

"If I am elected I intend to see that utility rates go down and not up," Garrett avowed, "and that the public utility regulatory setup is reformed from top to bottom."

Arthur Garrett had reason to be irked with PT&T. For the previous four years his service had been at best sporadic. Two of the three trunk lines to his office were cut off. When he would try to use the remaining phone, "sometimes there would be other conversations going on the line, sometimes there would be no response on the line." Garrett's clients told him they would dial his office for hour after hour and receive no answer, even though he had been there at the time.

The California Public Utilities Commission heard some of Garrett's complaints during the 1950's. He called pay phones "public petty larceny machines" and argued that PT&T should itemize message unit charges so citizens could verify the accuracy of their phone bills. The dispute frequently reached the ultimatum stage: Garrett threatening not to pay his phone bills until his service problems ended; PT&T threatening to cut off his service if he didn't pay.

PT&T won all the cases aired before the PUC, but it did occasionally make refunds to Garrett for the times his phone was out of order. However, these rebates covered only trouble periods of twenty-four hours or more; the odd fifteen-minute or two-hour intervals during the middle of what could be a busy afternoon for a lawyer didn't count.

Garrett's phone service became even worse right after his campaign press release. One particularly frustrating afternoon he called the PT&T service office for the Madison 2 exchange and told his problem to a supervisor. She replied: "Your telephone is out of order. It is going to stay that way. I will see that it stays that way. We have our instructions concerning you."

A day or so later Garrett called another service office to complain about trouble on his residence line. Another PT&T supervisor made substantially the same statement, concluding with the words: "We have our instructions concerning you."

Arthur Garrett sued, charging that PT&T "in retaliation" for his campaign statements interrupted his service "to discourage his candidacy."

It wasn't much of a trial; indeed, more time was spent in picking a jury than in actual testimony. Garrett had only one witness: himself. PT&T had but two. Garrett simply recited his troubles and said the statements of the supervisors indicated malice on the part of PT&T.

PT&T's evidence was as concise. One company official recapped Garrett's billing troubles, stating that at one time the lawyer ran up a bill for $245.97 and that he was frequently threatened with discontinuance of service for nonpayment. Another official said no supervisors could be found who remembered making the statements reported by Garrett.

In his closing argument Garrett said the company's attitude was easy to fathom: "Let's take care of this individual . . . let's quiet his protests." But proving that this was the case was not so easy, Garrett conceded:

> It is like a conspiracy to harm or any conspiracy to injure. It isn't formed in public. It isn't announced in public. It isn't made in Bullock's show window at 7th and Broadway [referring to a Los Angeles department store]. . . .
>
> It is a little inadvertent slip that will occur in any large corporation—and did in this case occur—which reveals the true situation. . . .
>
> [D]ifferent instructions necessarily must be given to different people. One [person] will be circumspect. A second will have been forewarned. A third, who has those instructions, will not even have any contact with the subscriber. . . . It is the slip . . . which will appear like a periscope hoisted by a submarine, and while it is small, it indicates the great mass that is attached to it at the bottom.
>
> That is the condition—that is the signpost that tells us what the policy of the company is!

PT&T's lawyer called Garrett's case a "fantasy" and a "delusion"; he scoffed at insinuations that PT&T was a "great evil boogie-man."

Judge Delbert E. Wong told the jury that Garrett was entitled to damages only if it found a "wilful intent to injure" on the part of PT&T, that mere negligence would not warrant compensation. Damages other than Garrett's actual monetary loss could be given only if the "intent [to injure] was to oppress and was malicious," the judge said. If this was found to exist, the sum given "will justly deter [PT&T] from similar acts against him and other telephone subscribers and will serve as a punishment and a warning."

The jury found that Arthur Garrett's sparse evidence didn't prove his law business suffered because of the telephone troubles. For actual damages it awarded him only the token $1 minimum allowed by the law. The Pacific Telephone & Telegraph Company's malice was another story. The jury gave

Garrett exactly what he asked: $1,500,000 in punitive damages.

That Judge Wong later set aside the jury's award as excessive and "given under the influence of passion or prejudice" is really immaterial.* The moral of the Arthur Garrett case is that a cross section of the Los Angeles citizenry—people who receive telephone service from the Bell System—shared his frustration at the futility of trying to argue with the phone company. The severity of the punishment meted PT&T serves as a gauge of the depth of their feelings—a depth that should be disturbing to the men responsible for managing the Bell System. Yet AT&T writes off such imbroglios as a regrettable but unavoidable accompaniment of big business. In a memorandum to Judge Wong asking that the $1,500,000 verdict be set aside, PT&T stated:

> As a public utility, defendant necessarily has day to day relations with almost every individual in each of its service areas. Inevitably it has become and must be a large corporation. To provide communication services to millions of telephones it must rely upon the capability of thousands of employees, many of whom are involved in the constant interaction between the company and the public. It is too much to expect that this interaction would please everyone. It is natural that a small percentage of its millions of subscribers would, justifiably or not, be unhappy.

AT&T *can* go out of its way to be nice to people. The men who install Bell telephones carry little whisk brooms so they can brush up the sawdust that spills onto the floor when they drill holes for wiring. They won't block the driveway with their truck or tramp mud onto the carpet. Move into a new house in the morning, and chances are that Bell will have your phone installed before dark (although a four-day wait isn't abnormal in such fast-turnover areas as Washington and its suburbs). The installer may look unhappy if asked to put the phone in an out-of-the-way place that requires him to crawl into a tight

---

* Judge Wong ultimately ordered a new trial. However, PT&T and Garrett as of this writing were negotiating toward an out-of-court settlement, with neither party willing to discuss publicly the status of the case.

corner of the basement; but he won't say anything, and if pressed, he'll do as requested.

AT&T conducts a continuous random sampling of customers to find out what they like or don't like about telephone procedures. And the company reacts to many of the complaints. People didn't appreciate the reprimanding words, "I'll look it up for you," when they called information to ask a number in the next county. Most Bell System companies banished the phrase from their operators' lips upon learning how much it irritated customers. The surveys made it possible for a citizen to call a Bell business office without being subjected to a hotbox sales talk on whether he wants a Princess phone for the laundry room or a ninety-seven-foot extension cord that reaches the backyard barbecue pit.

But, oh, those annoyances!

Columnist Robert Sylvester tells of the man who deposited his next-to-last dime in a nonworking pay station. He went to the next booth and reported his loss to the operator, who wanted his name and address, so the New York Telephone Company could mail him a dime.

"No, I don't want a dime," said the man. "I have several calls to make; I have only one dime in my pocket, so just dial one of the parties for me. That way you'll save postage and the trouble of sending the dime to me, and I'll finish my calls."

"Sorry," she replied, "but it's against the policy of the phone company to let you make a call you would have made if you had not used a broken phone."

The Los Angeles metropolitan area is so vast that five hefty phone books are required to cover it; each covers a portion of the city proper and adjacent suburbs. If you call Los Angeles information and do not know the person's address, the operator will look in a maximum of three of the five books. If she can't find it by then, that's tough, call information again, for she won't search any further, and she can cite a rule of the Pacific Telephone & Telegraph Company as her authority.

A suburban Philadelphia couple moved into a new home and were assigned a phone number that formerly belonged to a tax consultant. When income tax time arrived, they discovered—after dozens of calls to their house—that according to the phone book, the number was *still* listed for the tax man. Pennsylvania Bell gave them another number, and for the next several weeks they got dozens of middle-of-the-night orders for hamburgers. Their "new number," it seemed, appeared in the phone book as that of a popular all-night restaurant.

In Old Bethpage, a Long Island community, the New York Telephone Company extended the area in which subscribers could make toll-free calls and increased their phone bills by 75 cents a month. The change cut Bell's billing cost for toll calls, but residents discovered that the new "free" area was almost all in Suffolk County, whereas Old Bethpage is in Nassau County and few people had occasion to make out-of-county calls. Citizens protested to the phone company that they would prefer to be put in the so-called metropolitan exchange, along with other Nassau County residents, so that their calls into New York City would be toll-free. The phone company replied that it uses "natural boundaries," rather than county lines, in determining its rate schedules and that putting Old Bethpage into the metropolitan exchange would necessitate $1,000,000 worth of equipment changes.

Attorney Marvin Wagner took the case as an unreimbursed volunteer and made some interesting discoveries. Many Nassau residents living farther from New York than Old Bethpage were in the metropolitan exchange and enjoyed cheaper tolls. And an informant in the New York Telephone Company told him the equipment change would cost $100,000—not the claimed $1,000,000. Bell wouldn't flinch.

So the Old Bethpage citizens formed a committee, circulated petitions, and began withholding 75 cents a month from their bills, the amount of the rate increase when NYT expanded toll-free service into what Wagner called the "almost completely useless" new area. Some 2,000 persons—including civic officials, school board members, and assorted community leaders—signed the petitions.

The New York Public Service Commission wouldn't help Old Bethpage. It went through a ritual public hearing and ruled that services offered Old Bethpage "are not unjust or inadequate" and that rates are "not unduly or unreasonably prejudicial or discriminatory."

Why was Bell so adamant in refusing to change a decision that was clearly unpopular with the majority of Old Bethpage? Wagner deduces, "They were afraid that if this precedent were permitted, communities all over the country might also ask for such changes." Nonetheless, he is still curious why NYT didn't come to the Old Bethpage people quietly, after the fuss had died down, and comply with their request.

AT&T executives seem cognizant of the public discontent. H. I. Romnes, now board chairman, said in a 1965 speech, "Recently, I've had the feeling that the telephone company . . . has fallen somewhat short of the high esteem it once enjoyed as a pleasant and responsive outfit to do business with." Romnes said he found something curious about "customer irritants" mentioned in press articles and in letters to the company.

"Interestingly enough," he said, "there was hardly an item on the list that pertained to actual use of the telephone. Complaints centered on such things as deposit requirements based on residence location or occupation, treatment of customers in arrears by some arbitrary formula rather than individual consideration, inability or unwillingness to plan installations to meet the customer's schedule, a lack of responsiveness to pleas for help in dealing with telephone harassment, etc."

Romnes said each gripe had a common element: "that somehow we had failed to take adequate account of the customer's individuality and to match or respond to his particular needs." He concluded: "The customer is the one who shouldn't be folded, spindled or mutilated."

Yet although Romnes now heads the entire Bell System, he has not succeeded in imbuing his subordinates—even those at responsible executive levels—with his stated feelings on customer treatment. There is a border to Bell's amenability, and beyond it lies a land where company plans, not customer preference, are paramount.

Democracy flourishes in the United States because the dictum of majority rule is balanced by guarantees of respect of the minority's viewpoint. This is not necessarily so within the Bell System, which over the years frequently has treated with disdain the minority of its customers. Assuredly, Bell statisticians, engineers, and managers can usually state logical business or operational justifications for everything the company does and prove that the majority of subscribers either benefit from the innovation or are indifferent to it. The question thus becomes: Is operational efficiency the sole objective of American communications, and is there a way in which the minority among Bell's customers who object to a company action can give meaningful voice to their dissent?

A good case history of AT&T mendacity and bullheadedness
in its customer relations and the relative potency of a large
corporation and the small consumer is afforded in the way
the company went about changing the nation's telephone
numbers to all digits.

For a few years after the beginning of commercial telephony
neither letters nor numbers were required to place a call. Because of the limited number of customers, the operator knew
by memory which hole on her switchboard matched the
Jones residence or the feedstore. When subscribers became
so numerous an operator couldn't remember them all, the
switchboard holes were numbered—in Washington the White
House was No. 1 and the phone outside the Senate chamber
was No. 2.

So long as a town had only one central phone office, no
complications arose, for there would be only one "2345" in
Dubuque, Iowa. But when telephone demand forced establishment of branch offices, some way had to be found to distinguish their numbers from those of the centrals. Around
1880 the phone companies began assigning names to the
branches—"Central 2345" and "Branch 2345." The names
continued when dial service began, with letters imposed on the
face of the telephone as follows:

Hole Number	Letters
1	Blank
2	ABC
3	DEF
4	GHI
5	JKL
6	MNO
7	PRS
8	TUV
9	WXY
0	Operator

Bell's selection of word names for exchanges is interesting
in light of its insistence later on the virtues of an all-numeral

system. Stanley G. Ericson, an AT&T engineer, discussing the evolution of digit dialing in a 1954 Bell internal publication, says exchange names were chosen over digits because they were "considered to be simpler." He added, "If all the future involvements both technical and emotional could have been foreseen, the less colorful but more anonymous all-numeral method might have been selected instead."

Words selected for exchange names had to be easy to read, say, hear, and remember. Pitt F. Carl, Jr., telephone pioneer at the New York Telephone Company, wrote in a semanticists' journal in 1940: "Persistent siftings showed that the total of names most suitable in every way for calling central offices by voice was about 240." AT&T maintained a central registry of "suitable" names but allowed its branch managers considerable leeway in choosing names. Some managers displayed imagination and an appreciation of local history. As attorney Melvin Belli states with San Franciscan pride, what names would be more appropriate for his city than Klondike, Yukon, and Sutter. Manhattan's first exchange name was Spring (now Spring 7), initially listed in 1881, less than five years after phones were offered to the public. The designation came from the proximity of Spring Street (which in turn was named for a spring-fed well nearby). The Butterfield exchange to which John O'Hara gave a semblance of immortality in his novel *Butterfield 8* was named for the Civil War hero Major General Daniel Butterfield.

Some New York exchanges matched existing geographical designations, such as Murray Hill, the area now occupied by Grand Central Station, where a man named Robert Murray once grew lush stands of corn. In other instances arbitrary names were adopted by residents of previously anonymous areas, as when the Pennsylvania Bell Telephone Company assigned the prefix "Mayfair" to a Philadelphia neighborhood. The phone companies indulged in an occasional subtlety. An exclusive Dallas neighborhood is in the Fleetwood exchange, because that variety of Cadillac is popular with millionaires living there.

Customers weren't always happy with their exchange names. One city council said emphatically that "Gypsy" did nothing to enhance its citizens' reputations. Another city which its boosters proudly called the Garden Town suffered hurt feelings when the Garden exchange went to a nearby rival community. A stock insurance company protested when put into a Mutual exchange, for it felt customers would think it was a professionally inferior mutual insurance company.

Bell says technical strictures kept the 1 and 0 holes free of letters when its present dial was designed. Bell reserved the 1 for the first dial pull of service calls (information, repairs, and the like). Also, because of a quirk of the dialing equipment, 1 could not be distinguished from an accidental jiggle of the switch hook. The 0 on the first dial pull was saved for operator calls. Therefore, with a two-letter four-number system, there were sixty-four (8 times 8) two-letter central office code combinations possible. Bell, however, considered only sixty of these usable, saying there were no intelligible words beginning with the letters matched to 55, 57, 95, and 97. (This claim notwithstanding, San Francisco got along well with a Klondike exchange, which uses the 55 hole.)

Bell had a second chance to abandon letters and switch to an all-numeral system in 1930. Again, it declined. This opportunity arose when the growth of metropolitan areas threatened to exhaust the supply of letter combinations that could be used for exchange names within a single city. Bell apparently considered all-numerals. But Pitt Carl of New York Telephone said that the companies thought it best to make innovations involving "only the slightest possible change from the method with which the public is familiar . . ." and that any numbering change "as far as possible . . . must retain existing central office names, with which the public has become familiar and which have acquired locality significance." So each central office branch got a distinguishing numeral—Central 2, Central 3, Central 4, etc. The two-letter five-numeral system (2L-5N) became standard in larger cities.

As long as only local calls could be dialed directly by customers and operators handled all long-distance messages, the fact that there might be 50 Locust 3 exchanges in the nation wasn't important. But in 1947 Bell's long-distance business became so heavy that the company began an intensive automation program. Equipment changes enabled operators to dial long distance without having to page a sister operator for assistance in the destination city. The second phase would be for customers to dial directly, but here some changes in telephone numbers were necessary.

The 2L-5N system gave Bell only 540 central office combinations (allowing for reservation of 1 and 0 as first-pull numbers, the unworkable letter combinations, and discarding of the numeral 0 as a third-pull digit to avoid confusing it with the letter *O*). But there were already 14,000 central offices in the United States, meaning a considerable overlap. Fifty years previously Bell had been forced to find a way to distinguish one telephone exchange from another within a city; now it had to make the Locust 3 exchange in Seattle, Washington, distinct from the Locust 3 exchange in Daytona Beach, Florida.

The answer was an area numbering plan, or ANP, and assignment of a three-digit area code to each region of the United States and Canada. ANP boundaries were drawn to coincide with state and provincial borders wherever possible, so as to facilitate identification of codes with existing political units.

Every U.S. phone company—both independents and the Bell subsidiaries—joined the long-distance automation program. AT&T set the membership rules. Companies had to maintain AT&T-decreed standards of switching, signaling, transmission, and maintenance. They had to convert to the 2L-5N system for "uniformity." Some smaller companies went overnight from three digits to 2L-5N, and any telephone dial plate equipped with only numerals had to be replaced.

This was the third opportunity AT&T had to switch to all digits. Yet it chose to introduce a mixture of letters and numerals even into exchanges where no letters were used previously. (My family's home phone in Marshall, Texas, was 2469 at the time; we mysteriously acquired a Webster 5 prefix from the Southwestern Bell Telephone Company. The prefix is meaningless for local use; residents can still dial the last four digits of a number and be connected to whomever they want in the city.) Bell's insistence on 2L-5N at this time diminishes considerably the validity of its later arguments that a mixture of letters and numbers was totally unsuitable for efficient telephony.

Bell's area code system had a built-in restriction which later was to cause the company trouble. Engineers decided to make the 1 or 0 the second-pull digit of all area codes, so that the switching equipment would be alerted that a long-distance call was being placed. (No central office designations have 1 or 0 or their letter equivalents as a second-pull; thus, when the switching equipment feels the impulse from one of these pulls, it knows the caller wants long distance.) And, as is the case with local exchanges, Bell excluded 1 and 0 as first-pull digits in area codes—the first to prevent accidental signals because of switch-hook jiggling; the second because it is reserved for operator calls. Therefore, there were 160 potential area codes (8 times 2 times 10), of which 152 were reserved for number plan area (NPA) use and 8 (those with 1 in the second- and third-pull positions) reserved for information, repair, and other special service calls. The number proved grossly inadequate.

The average phone user knew naught of this area code magic which Bell concocted on his behalf. So long as he didn't call outside his own area, he didn't need it. If he placed a long-distance call, the operator used the code to dial into the target area. Occasionally the citizen might hear her chanting strange codes in the background as she placed his call ("Two One Four Tandem Seven Digits"), but that was telephone company business and none of his concern. AT&T agreed, and no general public announcement was made of the code system or what was planned for subscribers.

To recapitulate, to this point AT&T had willingly retained letters as an intricate part of its dialing system on each occasion when it had a chance to abandon them. It was not the telephone *subscriber* who inaugurated the letters; it was the telephone *company*, beginning in 1880. In planning the area code system, however, AT&T made a grievous error and forced customers to rescue it by accepting digit dialing at the expense of the letter-number system which AT&T had taught to four generations of American telephone users.

The error was a misestimate by AT&T of the number of area codes it thought adequate for the United States and Canada. When the area codes were first assigned, one was considered sufficient for each of the states and Canadian provinces except for sixteen, where two or more were assigned, for a total of eighty-six. This left AT&T a storehouse of sixty-six area codes (it started with 152), which AT&T said later "was thought to provide adequate safety in the capacity of the numbering plan to meet all unforeseen developments *beyond 1947.*" Yet in the next twelve years alone, expanding telephone demand ate up 31 of the "extra" area codes, which were assigned to fast-growing metropolitan areas, and the states and provinces requiring two or more codes jumped from

16 to 26. AT&T hastily revised its estimates and concluded that by the mid-1970's the area code supply would be exhausted if the 2L-5N numbering system were continued. The problem became one of increasing the number of exchanges within each area code, and Bell considerad a host of possibilities:

—Adding an extra pull of the dial (either by using three letters plus five numbers or two letters plus six numbers, or by adding a letter to the end of existing numbers). Bell rejected this idea because it felt the customer would not like the extra pull on every call.

—Changing the dial to put letters in all ten holes. This would have meant physically changing some 77,000,000 phone dials simultaneously, an "economically prohibitive" scheme.

—Leaving present numbers unchanged and using all digits for new customers only when necessary. Bell claimed a permanently mixed system would be confusing.

—Leaving present numbers the same and adding more area codes. This would have forced customers to use ten dial pulls on many of their calls, which would have caused errors and confusion, in Bell's view.

Therefore, Bell chose to junk the 2L-5N system used by the majority of its customers and convert to an all-digit system. By doing so and using 1 and 0 as second pulls, it increased the number of central office codes in a single numbering area from 540 to 792. Here is how the mathematics works:

All-Digit System

First number:	8 possible dial turns (1 and 0 reserved for special prefixes)
Second number:	10 possible dial turns
Third number:	10 possible dial turns
8 X 10 X 10 =	800 potential codes for exchange names

Minus those reserved for service codes ending in 11	−8
Central office codes	792

Two-Letter Five-Number System

First number:	8 possible dial turns
Second number:	8 possible dial turns
8 X 8 =	64 potential letter combinations
	—4 combinations that do not form usable names
	60 usable combinations

Possible combinations of letters	60
Number possibilities in third pull:	X9
Central office codes	540

The changeover began quietly enough. Bell's first experiment was to use letters in directory listings rather than the full exchange name (CR-1-2345 for CRestview 1-2345). The *Bell Telephone Magazine* reported in 1954 that tests in several cities indicated "no adverse effect to date on customer dialing accuracy nor on the handling of toll calls." The abbreviated listings also cut AT&T directory printing costs. AT&T conceded: "Still unsolved, however, are the problems as to application in the larger areas and the ultimate effects of using two letters in placing toll calls." *

AT&T next used employee groups as guinea pigs; predictably they did well with all digits. Many found that all digits posed a memory problem when there was a time lapse between hearing and dialing a number. Of one batch of seventy-three workers in New York City and New Jersey suburbs who were given all-digit directories and phones, thirty-one liked the new

---

* Bell press agents argued later that digit dialing was necessary because customers confused sound-alike letters such as *C, T, E,* and *P.* If so, AT&T had no one to blame but AT&T, for it was AT&T who taught its customers to say "PE," rather than "Pennypacker," and if there is another telephone exchange in the English-speaking world that one could mistake for that word, the fact has gone unrecorded by the historians. AT&T's stratagem has Machiavellian ancestry. If you wish to dispose of something that is popular, change it slightly so that it becomes inconvenient and then cite the inconvenience as a pretext for doing away with the entire system.

system, twenty-four the old one (eight "strongly so"), and seventeen found them equal.

The *Bell Laboratories Record,* in reporting the tests, said:

> On the basis of laboratory results alone, no one can say definitely that telephone users would surely accept or reject all digit numbers. The most one would want to say at this point is that with [all digits], dialing speed should increase and the error rate should be about the same or slightly lower. There should be little strong feeling against [all digits] and there is a good chance that it would be widely accepted.

The first city to receive digit dialing was Wichita Falls, Texas, in January, 1958. Bell claimed that customers liked it, and the switch was ordered throughout the AT&T empire. The digits got to the West Coast in 1960, when the Pacific Telephone & Telegraph Company began conversions in rural areas —an odd choice considering that the stated purpose of digit dialing was to relieve telephone congestion in cities where letter prefixes were in danger of depletion. The San Francisco and Los Angeles areas are covered by codes 415 and 213 respectively; yet AT&T's first changes were in the six other California numbering areas.

The switch went rapidly. By midsummer, 1962, 48 percent of PT&T's phones were changed, and PT&T began plans to move into San Francisco and the adjacent Bay area in the fall.

And then something awful happened to the Pacific Telephone & Telegraph Company. A man named Carl V. May became bored at a peace meeting and walked out with a friend for a cup of coffee.

By profession Carl May was a free-lance public relations man. By avocation he was a free-lance do-gooder, and not in a derogatory sense. A person who believed that a man who is truly civilized deliberately involves himself in issues of public import, regardless of their popularity, he was a Quaker, and thus many of his "causes" were in the fields of civil rights and pacifism. In the early 1960's he helped organize the *Everyman I* protest in which a small vessel he owned was sailed into a test area in the Pacific in an effort to halt nuclear weapons experiments.

As do many Americans, May felt there must be resistance

to what he called the "cult of technology," the concentration of power which he said makes it "increasingly difficult for the individual to assert his rights, preferences, and personality." May said, "At times I have a wild fantasy that one day all the people will rise up against technology, that they will walk instead of drive, grow their own food, refuse to communicate except by writing or face to face, that they will entertain themselves instead of being entertained, refuse to buy any advertised products, form vast consumer cooperatives, and elect representatives on the basis of candidates' ethical and moral convictions." In the shorthand of modern politics one would have called Carl V. May a left-of-center liberal.

The peace meeting that was indirectly responsible for PT&T's woes was run by the American Friends Service Committee in San Francisco, where May lived in 1962, and it was incredibly banal and desultory. May beckoned to a friend, and they went across the street for a cup of coffee.

"I was in one of my moments of frustration," May said, "and when we sat down, I said to Paul, 'You know, our *real* enemy is apathy—sheer apathy. People gripe about things but never want to do anything about them.' "

As an example he cited PT&T's new digit-dialing system, which was causing subdued grumbling in the areas where it had been inaugurated. The friend politely disagreed, whereupon May conducted an impromptu public opinion poll of the other patrons in the shop. Not a single one of them was in favor of the digit-dialing system. The unanimity surprised even Carl May. And activist that he was, he decided on the spot that so many dissidents deserved a leader.

The next morning he inserted a classified advertisement in the San Francisco *Chronicle:* "Got the digit fidgets? Join the Anti Digit Dialing League." He listed his office address and phone number. Within ten days more than 3,500 letters—overwhelmingly opposed to digit dialing—cascaded onto May's desk. The two phones jingled so busily that he had to recruit two volunteers to help answer them.

The complaints were varied: The digits were hard to remember; people could no longer tell when they were dialing a toll call; and Bell was "impersonalizing" San Franciscans by taking away vintage exchange names and replacing them with numbers. There were even a few scattered letters from telephone operators who maintained the digits were so confusing they were jittery after a day's work.

Almost without exception the callers were upset because Pacific Tel & Tel was making a decision affecting hundreds of thousands of people without displaying the courtesy of asking what they thought of the change.

The volume and vehemence of the response brought May face to face with a big decision: Was the Anti Digit Dialing League to be a spoofing organization via which people could have some fun and charge off the expense to the phone company's dignity, or should a serious effort be made to halt the digit conversion?

From the initial callers May winnowed out a group of people who (1) were willing to devote time and effort to fighting digit dialing; (2) had a skill that could be used in the battle; and (3) were level-headed enough to prevent the ADDL from becoming dominated by Bay Area oddballs.

When a ruckus such as the digit-dialing fight develops, AT&T likes to give the public the impression that its foes are bomb-throwing anarchists who are dedicated to the overthrow of capitalism or else sandal-wearing kooks who live out under the viaduct and drink 69-cent-a-gallon wine.

Admittedly, one would be hard pressed to find the prototype of the "average" American among the inner group which ultimately ran the ADDL. But their diversity was proof enough that no particular segment of society—least of all, a band of like-minded eccentrics—was ganging up on the phone company.

There was Dr. S. I. Hayakawa, internationally famed semanticist and author, who taught at San Francisco State College. There was Dr. Jack Block, a professor of psychology at the University of California in Berkeley, and his wife, Jeanne, also a Ph.D., a research physiologist at the Children's Hospital of the East Bay. There was John D. Schick, an investment counselor and self-described Goldwater Republican, whose San Francisco firm manages a number of small businesses. A young woman named Bonnie Burgon, who worked as an editor in suburban Mill Valley, helped the ADDL people put their ideas on paper. And, finally, there was Hiram W. Johnson III, heir to the most respected political name in California history and a lawyer skilled enough to strip the blather and emotion-

alism from the ADDL case and put it into the rigid, factual
format required for a legal proceeding.

Just how two men as diverse as Carl May and Hiram Johnson managed to work together on any project is one of those
questions one occasionally encounters in life to which there are
no answers. Fifteen minutes after meeting Hiram Johnson, I
wrote him off as some sort of eccentric. He told me in apparent
seriousness that the world had never recovered from the "dangerously liberal innovations" introduced into society by Louis
XIV and asked what I thought of a plan he had to "tax babies"
as a means of controlling the population (Johnson is a
bachelor).

Conservative Republican Johnson practices law in Belvedere,
an exclusive Bay Area residential town. Although I didn't ask,
I suspect his annual income matched that of liberal Democrat
and do-gooder Carl May fivefold. And it is customers such as
Hiram Johnson who must occasionally cause AT&T to wish it
did have competition, so that they would trade elsewhere.
PT&T, for instance, has never been able to convince Johnson
that its message-unit system for billing local toll calls is anything other than bald, outrageous piracy; consequently, he insists that the phone company send him an itemized listing of
every message-unit call he makes during a month. And there
are many of them, for Johnson's law practice covers a wide
swath of the San Francisco area. One of his friends who has
seen a Hiram Johnson phone bill insists that it would stretch
halfway across San Francisco.

Johnson's bombast, I ultimately concluded, is akin to the
deliberate caricaturism of H. L. Mencken. State a proposition
strongly, exaggerate it past the point of credulity, and 5 percent
of it (the amount of new knowledge the average adult is
capable of absorbing at one sitting) will remain with your
listener.

Johnson's grandfather and namesake, who was the progressive Republican governor and U.S. Senator from California, initiated the Public Utilities Commission in the state
as an agency through which the "power of the state is always
at hand ready to be invoked for the aid of the most humble
of its citizens, whose cause, be it ever so small, is just." Two
generations later the PUC became the forum for the digit-
dialing controversy, with a Johnson right in the middle of it.

Not too many people like to spend their own money on a

lark, regardless of how funny the joke. The more people involved in the ADDL, the more money available for legal expenses and also the more the pressure on PT&T to listen to public sentiment. So ADDL sold buttons and memberships and put out a ten-page booklet outlining its case against digit dialing. (The cover showed a faceless man saying into a telephone, "Hello, 274-435-4946? This is 483-235-5896.") ADDL held benefits at places like the No-Name Bar in bohemian Sausalito and in night spots on San Francisco's North Beach. Comedian Allan Sherman, in town for a nightclub appearance, joined the fun and composed a marching song urging citizens to call up Frederick R. Kappel, the AT&T president, and raise hell about digit dialing.

All this the San Francisco press loved. May had a knack for creating situations that, if not actually earthshaking, did provide what reporters call good copy. PT&T was an ideal straight man, and its unyielding intransigence made the company an ever-plump butt for ADDL's jokes. May issued frequent invitations for PT&T to debate digit dialing publicly, and San Francisco radio stations offered time. PT&T wouldn't respond— for either formal debates or the radio talk shows. Okay, said May, send a spokesman to one of the bar-party benefits; if your case is as good as you claim, you shouldn't be afraid to defend it before an audience.

PT&T wouldn't respond. Finally, an ADDL delegation led by May marched on the PT&T office, only to be turned aside at the door as TV cameras whirred and flashbulbs exploded.

Based on its actions, PT&T's policy was to stifle, rather than participate in, debate. Art Hoppe, whose humor column in the San Francisco *Chronicle* is nationally syndicated, encountered a PT&T press agent—a former newspaperman—one day at lunch and jokingly said he intended to do a column on ADDL. Shortly after Hoppe returned to his office, the phone rang. The next morning Hoppe's column began:

A public relations gentleman for The Telephone Company just called up to say his superiors preferred I didn't write a column about The Company's campaign to eradicate MOntrose, EXbrook and such from the English language.

Well, there's nothing that tugs at my heartstrings more than a powerful corporation telling a minor member of the free press what he shouldn't write about. In gratitude, I shall back The

Company all the way in this battle. All the way to the hilt. It's the least I can do.

And then Hoppe proceeded to roast PT&T over a bonfire of 400 words of ridicule. The issue, he said, was evenly drawn: "The Company is for ANC [all-number calling, AT&T's term for digit dialing]; the people are against it."

He agreed with PT&T that the digits would be more efficient:

> Of course, asphalt is more efficient than grass, barracks more efficient than homes, survival wafers more efficient than ham and eggs, artificial insemination more efficient than fatherhood, and totalitarianism more efficient than democracy.
>
> But this simply shows that the people must get over their unreasoning preference for grass, homes, ham and eggs, fatherhood, democracy and HYacinth 7-2987. It's a question of efficiency. I'm sure The Company will agree.

Hoppe says the press agent sounded embarrassed when he called and apparently did so "on instruction from his superiors in the public relations department. That evening he called me at home in a somewhat wavering voice to offer me two free tickets to, if I remember, The Ice Follies."

Hoppe's attack had scant effect on PT&T.* A bit later Carl May suggested that the *Chronicle* do a poll of its subscribers on digit dialing and said Dr. Hayakawa would be happy to supply a list of scientifically sound questions. The *Chronicle* liked the idea and called PT&T for comment and suggestions on questions the company might want to have included. Whereupon a platoon of PT&T executives marched into the *Chronicle* offices to "discuss" the poll with Scott Newhall, the executive editor. Newhall listened—and went ahead with the poll.

The *Chronicle*, in its editorials, threw frequent harpoons at digit dialing and other phone company practices. On one occa-

---

* AT&T was extremely touchy about newspaper discussion of digit dialing at this time. After reading of the West Coast ruckus and noting the introduction of all-digit numbers in Philadelphia suburbs, I began gathering information on the subject for an article. A press agent for the Pennsylvania Bell Telephone Company argued against the idea, stating that conversion was not planned for Philadelphia "on any foreseeable date," and thus the subject could not possibly be of interest. The same day he sent some material to the office with a memo that concluded, "I'll give you a call on 563-1600," which I finally recognized as my newspaper's digitized phone number.

sion the *Chronicle* said it would not oppose a requested rate increase "because we have been conditioned over the years to accept the squeeze without groaning out loud." Then it talked about digit dialing:

> But we feel bound to offer a mild protest when the short-sighted management of this misguided company sets out arrogantly, if not maliciously, to discommode, confuse and oppress the rate-paying public by high-handedly foisting upon it an unwanted, awkward, senseless and intolerably difficult system of dialing.
>
> We refer, of course, to the execrable all-digit dialing system, whereunder mournful numbers are substituted for the traditional, friendly, readily recallable words that make exchange prefixes pleasant to the ear and endow them with happy geographical, historical and personal associations.
>
> Though the company's most eloquent masters of public relations have worked hard at it, they have never made us understand what the company can possibly gain by this wrong-headed change one-half so precious as the good will and public acceptance it throws away. . . .
>
> It is natural under the circumstances to believe that the little tyrants responsible for this brutish imposition upon the public are victims of a violent arithmomania, a wild obsession with numbers, with neither knowledge of nor feeling for poetry, singing praise or the beauty and magic of simple language. We suspect that they must always be uncomfortable and confused by words—including these.

The *Chronicle*'s polls bore out the editorial's contentions that digit dialing was unpopular. In the first sampling the paper asked that readers mail in printed ballots, and about two-thirds of those who responded opposed the digits. The editors suspected phone company "tampering," however, because some envelopes arrived containing fifty to seventy-five "pro digit dialing" ballots.

So the *Chronicle* conducted another survey, this time by telephone, and found 80 to 90 percent of the telephone users favoring the old 2L-5N system. Yet professional samplers felt this poll to be subject to criticism on methodological grounds. Because San Francisco residents had not fully experienced digit dialing, their answers were based on an emotional reaction rather than actual experience. To answer criticisms, the

Anti Digit Dialing League arranged for a scientifically valid poll in suburban Marin County, where digit dialing had been in use for some months.

In late December, 1962, and early January, 1963, volunteer pollsters, using a systematic sampling plan, called 510 telephone users in Marin County and asked the following question:

"This is the Bay Area Polling Associates and we are conducting a survey on how people in Marin County feel about the telephone company's new procedure for dialing, all-number calling. Now that you have had some experience with the new system which uses all numbers, would you tell us what your preference is. Here is our question: Do you prefer the new system using only numbers? Do you prefer the old system, using names combined with numbers? Or, do you have no preference between the two dialing systems?"

When the person had a preference, he was further asked the strength of and reason for his opinion. ADDL members were involved in the poll, so a record was kept of all answers on the assumption that PT&T's public relations department would challenge the results as biased and incorrect. The survey found that excluding the people who had no preference, for every telephone user who preferred digit dialing, there were more than five who wanted to return to the old name-number system (16.2 percent versus 83.2 percent). When the no-preference responses (19.2 percent) were included, the number of users preferring digit dialing became 13.1 percent, and 2L-5N, 67.2 percent. Persons opposing digit dialing seemed to have stronger feelings than its supporters, many of whom would not state their reasons for preferring it.

The publicity brought the Anti Digit Dialing League numerous offers of free legal help. Hiram Johnson, because of his long interest in utility matters, his grandfather's background in the field, and his ability to devote time to the fight, did the brunt of the initial legal work when ADDL decided to file a formal complaint with the Public Utilities Commission. But he told May he thought someone more experienced in court work should present the case.

When someone in San Francisco hears the words "trial lawyer," his mind immediately clicks out two other words: "Melvin Belli." John Schick says, "I went to his office and asked him to take the case. He said, 'How much money do you have?' None, I told him. 'Good,' he said, 'I'm your lawyer.' "

In addition to his status as a plantiff's attorney (there *are* trial lawyers who have won bigger verdicts than Mel Belli, but no one else is so consistently effective with a jury), Belli had other qualities consistent with the general character of ADDL: a congenital inability to view PT&T with awe or respect; an appreciation of the humor that kept bobbing to the surface, regardless of how seriously ADDL tried to act on the occasions when propriety demanded sobriety; and a genuine dislike for his foe. Many lawyers righteously declare they never have ill will for a courtroom adversary. Belli considers this attitude so much humbug, especially when he is fighting a large corporation or insurance company that he thinks is taking advantage of people.

Immediately after joining ADDL, Melvin Belli firmly planted his tongue in his cheek and announced plans to write a book "How to Murder the Telephone Company." The general tone of what he had in mind (he never wrote it) is shown through one of the operational plans he announced for his guerrilla war:

"People all over the country, millions of us, will pick up the phone and dial the operator and demand that she connect them with Mr. George Funkernickle, Jr., of Dayton, Ohio. If he is not at home, find out where he is and reach him there. No, we do not want to be connected with information. No, we do not want area codes. We are through doing the telephone company's work. We want to speak to our party in Dayton, Ohio, and if he isn't there, find out where he is and reach him."

Someone else had the idea of inundating Pacific Tel & Tel with numbers, and the true ADDL adherent would place his long-distance calls: "Operator, give me Mr. Smith at four billion one hundred fifty-five million eight hundred forty-two thousand three hundred and one."

To many Californians digit dialing was irksome because they had been doing more and more of the "phone company's work" while paying higher rates. The digit-dialing opponents felt it was time PT&T returned some of its automation savings to customers.

During 1948–58 PT&T asked seven rate increases totaling $234,600,000 annually, of which the Public Utilities Commission granted $114,800,000. While the digit-dialing case was in progress, PT&T requested a further increase of $43,900,000. (Its revenues on California operations at the time were running just over $1 billion a year.)

Yet PT&T customers demonstrably were placing many calls formerly handled by operators, as this five-year breakdown shows:

Toll Messages in California

Year	Operator-Handled	Customer-Dialed	Total
1957	184,266,000	25,811,000	210,077,000
1958	176,671,000	48,984,000	225,655,000
1959	182,537,000	73,582,000	256,119,000
1960	186,803,000	94,076,000	280,879,000
1961	186,231,000	109,332,000	295,563,000

Between 1957 and 1961 PT&T's wage expense per telephone dropped from $55.62 to $49.48, while revenues per phone increased from $132.10 to $149.08—an overall gain of $23.12.

Johnson and Belli filed their formal petition on December 4, 1962, asking that digit dialing should be halted for these reasons:

—PT&T "misled the public by false claims that the number of dialing combinations available under the present system is insufficient to allow the inevitable expansion occasioned by growth. In truth, engineering, scientific and mathematical computations prove that our present system of letters and prefixes provides more than enough combinations."

—PT&T "has admitted that the change will not save money, and refuses a lowering of rates after said change."

—PT&T "has repeatedly refused to discuss this new scheme responsibly, and to present valid reasons for it to the complainant and other interested parties."

—Digit dialing "fetters the public to a permanent, ever present and significant inconvenience," because strings of numbers are harder to remember and cause dialing errors.

—"To force this change upon the public is to make us do the work of machines and calculators; it is to make us suffer a loss of personal and geographic identity; it is one more snatching away of the human element in our lives which needs so much protection in this age of the machine."

Presentation of the ADDL case and the PT&T rebuttal required five days, with the testimony of eighteen witnesses filling 904 pages of transcript. Belli went about proving his point in two ways: First, he showed that the system was inconvenient; second, he pointed out some alternative plans that would be better for the public.

On the issue of inconvenience, Belli made plain there were objections to digit dialing not readily detectable in AT&T laboratory trials. The presentation was vintage Belli. A bartender, called to tell his customers' experiences with digit dialing, said his patrons got "real cute" when they tried to remember all digit numbers after a couple of drinks. Belli brought in a masked man who, he said, had "some professionalship with horses. "Now, I think we can all appreciate that the telephone company's users, like the subject upon which the rain falls, are of all sorts of people, needy people, the doctors, and some people whose endeavors go more into the field of the song of *Guys and Dolls*."

The PT&T lawyer didn't think this at all humorous and wouldn't accept Belli's request that the man be permitted to testify unsworn and unnamed for his "protection." "I am going to demand—pardon me, request—that the commission pursue its regular practice," the lawyer huffed. Belli eventually let the masked man go. For a while he talked about putting a call girl on the stand to testify to her loss of trade because "Johns" couldn't reach her on the phone with digits but let the idea slide.

These were Belli's "fun" witnesses. In a more sober vein, scientific witnesses attacked PT&T's premise that digit dialing would be no trouble for telephone users. Dr. Jack Block, one of the ADDL founders, said his tests at the University of California showed that "the possibilities of accommodating to the use solely of numbers are very, very limited. Indeed, this is what caused me as a professional psychologist to become concerned about the whole matter."

Dr. Block said his tests showed telephone number errors tend to be less repetitive when letters are involved. "If one spells 'CYpress' 'CI' incorrectly, one is quickly informed that it should be spelled 'CY' and at a subsequent time doesn't make this kind of error. However, with only numbers, you have the phenomenon of interferences, which continue to exist and which the individual cannot accommodate to, and the error continues since the source of the error continues. Consequently, an error made early may well continue to be made." The 2L-5N combination, Dr. Block argued, is ideal for memory because it provides two distinct blocks, enabling a person to break a telephone number into two easy-to-remember segments. Other witnesses told of the difficulties children and the elderly would find with all-digit numbers and troubles even adults encounter in trying to learn "nonsense" items such as a string of numbers. Stripping away the exchange name, said Dr. Harvey Peskin, a clinical psychologist who also taught at San Francisco State College, is akin to removing a street name from an address.

In rebuttal Bell put on the stand a man who took the position that AT&T provided ample directories so that people could check numbers before dialing and that telephone usage "is not, and never was intended to be a memory exercise." Besides, he argued, people could learn digits very easily by doing so in groups—the first three digits; dial; then look again to see the remaining four.

In testimony on alternative conversion systems and the validity of AT&T's claim that conversion was really necessary, Belli elicited several interesting admissions from telephone company witnesses. For instance, he got Neil M. Calderwood, PT&T traffic engineer, to admit there was no technical consideration that made mandatory the conversion of the 70,000,-000-odd U.S. telephones containing the 2L-5N number. Belli specifically asked Calderwood why PT&T wasn't willing to let him retain YUkon 8-1849 for his office, a number Belli chose for its gold rush and forty-niner connotation.

CALDERWOOD: There is no reason for the moment and for many years in the future why if you choose to use YU you cannot do so.

BELLI: Well, why don't you let me use what I want for the many years in the future?

CALDERWOOD: Well, we have not said that you could not retain YU for your own use. What we have done is to translate your YU into the corresponding dial numerals, and the number, when San Francisco is cut to ANC [all-number calling], will so appear in the information operator's record.

BELLI: Well, if I can use it for many years in the future, why can't YOU use it for many years in the future in the phone book . . . rather than changing for all-number calling?

CALDERWOOD: Well, for the reason that we need more central office codes.

BELLI: I don't follow you. If I can use it, you can use it, can't you?

Calderwood went into a tedious oration about the history of area codes and the shortage of exchange designations, but Belli kept banging away. Sure enough, Calderwood admitted it was "mechanically possible" to leave Belli's YU 8-1849 in the phone book. However, Calderwood said customers would charge "discrimination" if some people had 2L-5N numbers and others had all digits, and vice versa.*

Belli heard this claim with ill-disguised disbelief. "Well, no one wanted any numerals until someone in your company came up with the idea, did they? Did you have a clamor for all-number calling?"

This brings us to what was really the most important point in the entire digit-dialing affair—the fact that it wasn't necessary and that AT&T could have obtained just as many exchange designations by continuing with the 2L-5N system. Here a digression into arithmetic is once again necessary. Belli and Johnson gave a lucid explanation in their summary brief filed with the PUC.

—Of the ten numbers on the telephone dial, only eight have three letters on them. Thus, there can be eight letters for the first pull, eight letters for the second pull, and ten numbers for the third pull. This totals $8 \times 8 \times 10$, or 640 central office codes in each area code. The telephone company insists that some of these do not make usable words (100 of them, leaving 540 usable codes), *but all could be used if nonword-forming two-letter combinations were used, or all 640.*

—If all digits were used, since the 1 and the 0 in the first

---

* Calderwood's testimony on the nondesirability of mixing 2L-5N with all digits is baffling to this date. Of seventeen Bell directories I examined at random in 1967, fourteen contained mixtures of 2L-5N and all digits. Of the twenty-eight central offices included in Pennsylvania Bell's Delaware County-Main Line directory, ten are all digits, the remainder 2L-5N. And people who live in the 565 dialing area (Media) seem to get along well with the KI 3 (Springfield Township) neighbors. Melvin Belli's phone number, I read in the San Francisco telephone book, is now 988–1849.

pull and the 1 and the 0 in the second pull are reserved for other purposes and cannot be used in these central office codes, they likewise total 8 × 8 × 10, or 640, *exactly the same as the letters and numbers.* Thus, no actual increase for telephone expansion is achieved by digit dialing alone.

—However, if office equipment changes are made [as AT&T said would be necessary to utilize fully digit dialing] and a change to digit dialing is persisted in, then the 1 and the 0 can be used in this system for the second pull, raising the number of central office codes from 640 to 800 (8 × 10 × 10).

—A similar number of choices can be effected using letters and numbers if the same changes are made in the office equipment as for digit dialing and a Q is added to the now vacant 1 hole and a Z to the now vacant 0 hole. There would then be 800 codes here also.*

Bell didn't like the idea of putting new letters on its dial and said such an operation would be so expensive and drawn out as to be unworkable. And perhaps it might. Yet in all the days of testimony, Bell was unable to give Belli any convincing evidence that warranted *changing existing numbers.* One AT&T argument was that some nations use different alphabets and that digit dialing would facilitate international long-distance telephony. "Remember that the next time you call Iraq," one ADDL man suggested.

Periodically during the testimony Belli challenged PT&T to run public opinion polls and tests on digit dialing. He suggested that Stanford, Harvard, or some "pseudo-government" bureau answer the question: Would all digit dialing give any more combinations, and if so, why? He promised to drop the PUC complaint if the answer was in PT&T's favor. He made the

---

* In order of practicality ADDL's alternatives to digit dialing may be listed as follows: (1) retain existing 2L-5N numerals where possible, which would have permitted perhaps 80 percent of all Americans to keep their old phone numbers, and assign all digits only where necessary; (2) modify the dial with Q and Z; (3) add another numeral prefix to existing numbers. ADDL's occasional forays into absurdity weakened its case: Belli put on the witness stand one man who advocated renumbering every telephone in the United States under an elaborate grid system of digits and letters. The advocate of the plan was the only person who could understand it. Other ADDL people tried to prove that Bell had 820,000,000 possible dialing combinations—540 letter combinations in an area code × 10,000 possible phones per combination × 152 area codes. In actuality, the average phone exchange in the United States has about 1,500 numbers, because AT&T policy is to assign a separate identity to every town, regardless of how small.

same offer if a public opinion poll in "any community in the country" showed the residents favored digit dialing.

"Mr. Examiner," replied PT&T attorney Francis N. Marshall, "the telephone company does not submit its operational needs and operational decisions of management to popularity polls. The offer is entirely out of order.

> BELLI: Is the reason for that, as the old expression which has been said formerly goes, "The public be damned"?
>
> MARSHALL: Mr. Examiner, such remarks are out of order.

ADDL won the first round with the PUC. During the hearings Johnson and Belli discovered that PT&T was proceeding with the conversions as if the PUC were not involved. So they asked for and received a temporary restraining order against further conversions. The order delighted ADDL. Johnson called it "the first time PT&T has had any restraint in its headlong conversion to all number dialing which it so arrogantly insists is necessary."

But the euphoria was short-lived. On March 17, 1964, the PUC ruled for Pacific Tel & Tel, stating that while no numbering system was perfect, digit dialing provided the most feasible solution to the problem. Although public opinion must be considered, the PUC said, it does not "provide an answer to the question of which system out of all alternatives provides the best, least expensive and most practical solution to the anticipated shortage of central office codes." Any "dehumanization" resulting from the change, it said, "is not so significant as to require the retention of central office name prefixes without any other justification."

The commission, while unanimous, was not necessarily happy. Commissioner William M. Bennett, in a concurring opinion, wrote:

> It is no easy task to cast this vote upon the twilight years of such faithful servants as UNderhill, MIssion, LOmbard, MAdison and others. These and other letter prefixes have served us long and well, but it is inevitable that we must recognize the cold hand of technology and the obsolescence it creates. Faithful friends must be dispatched to some other better place since they are no match for the ruthless competition and efficiency of digits. . . . Digit dialing is in a large measure al-

ready a fact, and it is not consistent with maximum communication efficiency to cling to the letter prefixes. Sentiment cannot change this fact.

The next morning a strange little rite was carried out in the courtyard of Melvin Belli's baroque Montgomery Street law office. While secretaries and lawyers milled around, their black armbands somehow not giving the impression of total sobriety, Belli heaped Pacific Telephone & Telegraph Company directories into a pile, doused them with kerosene, and struck a match.

He also threatened to thrash the first girl in his office he heard placing a long-distance call with digits, and as of mid-1967 no one there had been convicted of cooperation with the telephone company.

10

Remember: No Classified Conversations!

*—Sign above telephones in the Bell Telephone
Laboratories, research adjunct of the American
Telephone & Telegraph Company*

In May, 1966, a woman who works for the Pacific Telephone & Telegraph Company in Ukiah, California, was assigned to monitor what Bell calls nonticketed calls—those made to the operator rather than to the designated numbers for time, information, and the like. The monitor's job is to evaluate how well the answering operator handles customer inquiries. A light goes on before the monitor when 0 is dialed, and often she is silently on the line, listening before the operator answers.

There is nothing to warn the calling party that his call is being monitored, and as far as he knows, the telephone is dead until the operator answers. It isn't—anything he says can be heard by the monitor. And the woman monitoring Ukiah calls heard a ten-second fragment of conversation while waiting for the operator to respond:

"There were two male voices. The calling party male voice was discussing some relations he had had with a young girl the night before, illicit relations. He named the girl to the other male in the background. We (me and my husband) were acquainted with this girl he mentioned. This is very upsetting to say the least . . . and he never knew I heard him relate this experience he had had with her supposedly. He had no idea that anyone could hear what he was saying."

Bell would have people believe that all phone conversations are completely private. It sprinkles promises of this privacy throughout its advertising. A phone book frontispiece advertisement shows a woman sitting on the side of her bed, Princess phone in hand, above the caption: "A bedroom telephone helps you . . . have privacy when you want it." An intimate setting— and one that could be shared with:

—A blackmailer who purchased information on how to tap her telephone from a corrupt AT&T employee for as little as $25 or who cracked AT&T's eggshell security system without the need of inside guidance.

—Bell monitors who hear every word the woman speaks while on her line for any number of "quality control" checks: the strength of the transmission on the telephone; the amount of time required for the dial equipment to complete her call; her exchanges with any operator involved in the call; whether her conversation faded after connection with the other party. Possibly the woman's voice was amplified so that it could be heard by a dozen Bell supervisors or operators at a time, some of them 500 miles away in a higher-echelon Bell System office.

—FBI agents or police for whom AT&T installed special lines so that the snooping could be carried out in the comfort of their office. A court order isn't always necessary if the Bell security agent—often a retired cop himself—decides that the police have sufficient reason to tap.

—Any neighborhood teen-ager with a rudimentary knowledge of electronics and the nerve to open the unlocked boxes containing Bell terminal points.

—A private detective who drives to "work" in a distinctively painted secondhand Bell truck and installs a sophisticated tap which the Bell Telephone Laboratories, despite all its scientific prowess, maintains it cannot detect or neutralize.

The frightening quality about eavesdropping in and around the Bell System is its random pattern. Aside from purchasing hundreds of dollars of antitapping equipment (not from Bell, which doesn't offer it for public sale), the citizen has absolutely no way of guaranteeing that any one single phone call he makes is private.

Further, the Bell Telephone System, which has the responsibility for providing telephone privacy, is the worst offender. During a three-month period in 1966 alone the Pacific Telephone & Telegraph Company *admitted* to listening in on 320,000 telephone calls from customers—a sampling that is statistically ominous when projected throughout the Bell System.

telling which numbers match what house. Once the tapper learns these numbers, his task is simple.*

According to Newman, when he needed any pair of numbers, he went to Brewster.

SENATOR LONG: What kind of arrangement did you make with him [Brewster] about giving that information?
MR. NEWMAN: I ask him and he supplies it.

Brewster readily said this arrangement did exist "in certain cases that are of certain importance." Senator Long, in straight-faced amazement, asked: "He just calls you and tells you he wants you to give the information about the pair number for this individual and you give it to him?"

"Yes, sir, I rely on his integrity," Brewster said.

"Is that the company's policy?" asked Long.

"That's what we do here, Senator," the Southwestern Bell security man replied. He added that there was no written order authorizing such a practice.

Brewster and Southwestern Bell also helped the FBI tap subscribers' telephones. (Brewster's relationship with the FBI was a close one; when the Long committee subpoenaed him to testify, he notified the FBI's Kansas City office.) Said Brewster: "We furnish them [the FBI] a line from a terminal that happens to be in their office to a terminal pole close to the place they have under surveillance. That's all we do. I assume they hook it up to something."

SENATOR LONG: Do your employees ever go with the FBI men when they were disguised as telephone employees?
MR. BREWSTER: I will put it this way. I think there were some bureau men who went with the telephone company people. They had on old clothes and those things. . . .

Brewster professed to see nothing out of the ordinary. "This is just a leased private line," he told Senator Long.

SENATOR LONG: Do you do this for private detectives?
MR. BREWSTER: No, sir.

* At first I had a short how-to-do-it section on wiretapping as part [of] this chapter and then decided against it. Tapping is a damnably dirty business, and enough goes on already. If you *really* must try it, in-formal lessons are scattered through the Long committee hearing reports.

And Bell continues to defend its snooping even when gross violations of customer privacy are proved. R. U. Skibinkski, PT&T assistant vice-president, says of the Ukiah case related earlier: The monitor's "admission that she overheard and repeated conversations is a violation of company practices on secrecy of conversations, and is one of many reasons why regular supervisory observations are necessary." That PT&T would put an employee in a position to overhear and repeat private conversations is also a violation of the code by which decent people live.*

That many billions of Bell calls are unimpeded is not the issue; what is important is that eavesdropping and tapping are so prevalent that an AT&T subscriber must assume that anything he says into a telephone is being heard by unintended ears. So long as this uncertainty exists, there is no telephone privacy in the United States.

Senator Edward V. Long, of Missouri, who found tapped phones just about every place he looked during invasion-of-privacy hearings in 1965 and 1966, says a Bell System official once told him that if the snooping weren't controlled, "in a very short time there would be no such thing as a private conversation in this country." Long fears personally that unless the tapping is curbed, it "will adversely affect the entire telephone industry."

Human sensitivities laid aside for the moment, the commercial necessity for controlling tapping increases daily. Business firms which use Bell lines to transmit data between computers are exposing confidential sales, marketing, and manufacturing information formerly guarded in double-sealed envelopes. Industrial spies know this, and people who are active in the telephone security field are confident that the United States will witness its first computer-tapping case ere the decade ends.

* The pitfalls of promiscuous monitoring are shown by two 1966 cases. Two monitors for Southern Bell would break into conversations between Negro subscribers and begin talking in exaggerated Negro accents. One of the people harassed, a Negro civil rights worker, complained to the FBI, which found the employees responsible. Bell fired them. A man who worked as a monitor for Southwestern Bell discovered the phone number of the town prostitute and spent much of his midnight shift eavesdropping on her talks with prospective customers. This continued for three months; his game was discovered when he attempted to bring her into the phone company building for what Bell tactfully said were "immoral purposes."

(One Manhattan specialist says it's probably already being done. "Historically speaking, taps are discovered through accident or negligence. Anyone with the knowledge to plug into a data-transmittal setup is going to be sophisticated enough in his operation to make it hard to detect.")

That the wiretapping is done with the knowledge of certain telephone company officials interjects a frightening element into American society, for if Bell isn't to protect its lines, who is? Samuel Dash, Chicago and Philadelphia attorney who did a national wiretap study under auspices of the Pennsylvania Bar Association, said, "In cities where police wiretapping was known to exist, there was generally a sense of insecurity among professional people and people engaged in political life. Prominent persons were constantly afraid to use their telephones despite the fact that they were not engaged in any wrongdoing. It was clear that the freedom of communication and the atmosphere of living in a free society without fear were handicapped by the presence of spying ears."

Dash said these people—both public officials and prominent private citizens—told him they would send a letter or arrange a personal meeting rather than risk sending confidential communications over the telephone wires. His statement was based on interviews his investigators had had with persons in Boston, New York, Philadelphia, Chicago, New Orleans, Baton Rouge, Las Vegas, San Francisco, and Los Angeles.

When people begin playing with wiretap equipment, ridiculous situations result. John W. Leon, a highly respectable private investigator in Washington, D.C., taped telephoned reports of his operatives by plugging a recording into phone cables in his building. His office is next door to an adjunct of the French Embassy. Through accident, Leon said, "I know that once or twice we got on the wrong pair [of cables] in our office and it was from the French atomic energy attaché." This happened even though the telephone company had labeled the cables with numbers to make the sets going to a particular number easier to find. Bernard J. Fensterwald, Jr., counsel for Senator Long's committee, called this incident "illustrative of the dangers in the present telephone system, and the fact that these pairs and cables are not only accessible, but frequently marked so that any amateur can do it."

AT&T officials are correct when they say it is difficult to police the 80,000,000-odd telephones under their jurisdiction

from the James Bondish devices of the professional tappers. The Long committee ran across any number of t gadgets; one instrument which slips into the mouthpiece o standard telephone set can pick up anything said in the roo and surreptitiously transmit it to any point which can reached by the direct-dial system—New York to Honolulu, fo instance.

Nonetheless, Bell must take the blame for a good portion of the telephone snooping that goes on in the country—through acts of omission or commission. Bell *says* it tries to stop wiretapping, but there is much evidence available to make the citizen wary of its proficiency in doing so, if not its sincerity.

The AT&T policy on wiretapping was stated to a Senate committee in 1960 by Wellington Powell, then a vice-president of the New York Telephone Company:

> Our company and other companies in the Bell System believe
> that privacy of communications should be carefully protected.
> We believe that people have an inherent right to feel that they
> can use the telephone freely and informally, just as they talk
> face to face, and that any undermining of this personal right
> may seriously impair the usefulness and value of telephone
> communications, a fact which could adversely affect our busi-
> ness. We do not like any invasion of the privacy of communica-
> tions by wiretapping and we welcome Federal and state law
> which strengthen this privacy and reduce the opportunities a
> temptations to invade the privacy of telephone users.

Arthur S. Brewster is division security supervisor fo Southwestern Bell Telephone Company, assigned to the K City office. He is a lawyer and since 1950 has had the res bility, among other things, of assuring privacy of the hu of thousands of subscribers to the company's service.

One of Brewster's friends in Kansas City is James R man, chief of detectives for the police department. As a man, Newman finds wiretapping a handy tool, and B makes it easy for him. An essential element of informa a wiretapper is the location of the particular telephone is seeking. To the lay eye a terminal box is a maze colored plastic-coated spaghetti. Each pair of wires bered, however, and the telephone company has a

SENATOR LONG: Why not? It is a public service.
MR. BREWSTER: I would have to have a lot of explanation. . . .

Brewster agreed with Long that Bell's aid in placing of taps "raises a great question of apprehension" about whether subscribers' phones are being tapped. He also admitted that he kept no records of what phones were tapped with his aid, saying he didn't think this information important enough to retain.

SENATOR LONG: It does make it rather handy if there is an investigation made as to the activities of the telephone company in furnishing a customer's private numbers and wire information, doesn't it?
MR. BREWSTER: It could.

Services given the FBI by Southwestern Bell are varied. Paul J. Schmitt, a supervisor in the Kansas City telephone office, says that in the early 1960's he was assigned to install a phone booth on the outside wall of a manufacturing company. The FBI, he said, intended to plant a mike between the booth and the wall so that it could overhear conversations inside the building, which would be relayed to headquarters via a special leased wire.

SENATOR LONG: And then that way the FBI agents could sit in their office . . . and bug the premises of this gambler out at whatever address you were connecting?
MR. SCHMITT: That's what I understood, sir.
SENATOR LONG: They were using the facilities of the Southwestern Bell Telephone Co. to do it?
MR. SCHMITT: That is correct, sir.

This particular operation fell through when the building owner came out and said, in Schmitt's words, "He would like to know what we were doing there, and if we didn't have any authority to do it, he would just as soon we get our wire and pay station and get out of there."

The Long committee at no time questioned the necessity or purpose of Detective Newman's use of the taps, nor did it imply that he had ever obtained tapping information from Bell's Brewster for other than official and necessary reasons. Nonetheless, the arrangement raises a moral question which the AT&T hierarchy well might ponder: Is the Bell System treating its subscribers fairly when it permits a police officer to be the judge of when a telephone line is to be tapped? And, second, should not subscribers be informed that Bell is giving the police blank-check authority to determine which conversations are to be intercepted?

AT&T affiliates offer similar cooperation elsewhere. Rhode Island has a statute prohibiting law enforcement wiretapping but makes an exception to permit service monitoring by the telephone company. The attorney general's office in the past used this exception as a loophole through which it wiretapped. Joseph J. Nugent, who was attorney general in 1960, told a regional conference of attorneys general that the New England Telephone and Telegraph Company (69.3 percent owned by Bell) placed on its staff a former FBI agent who decided when the company would use its wiretapping powers to aid law enforcement officers. Nugent's staff members, when they had a problem, would contact the former agent and present their grounds for wanting New England Telephone to tap for them. If the ex-G-man felt it proper, he ordered the line monitored (with New England Telephone equipment).

One of the attorneys general who heard Nugent's speech asked whether such a procedure didn't substitute the judgment of a private citizen—and a former policeman at that—for the law. Nugent was quoted as replying that since the request was made orally and informally and since the wiretap recordings were used only to obtain leads for other evidence and were not offered as court evidence, he thought the system justified. A Bell spokesman, later queried about the supposed Nugent speech, denied knowledge of any such use of New England Telephone tapping facilities. A former FBI man did work for the company as security officer, he said, but "as far as being a tribunal as to who was to decide whether wiretapping should be done or not, that is absolutely not so."

Bell connivance with law enforcement officers, at the expense of customer privacy, is also reported in Louisiana, where officers are permitted to wiretap without a court order. According to Samuel Dash, New Orleans and Baton Rouge policemen said the Southern Bell Telephone Company cooperated in placing of taps.

Secondhand Bell Telephone trucks—sold by the company without any attempt to disguise or conceal their original innocent appearance—are frequently used by law enforcement officers in snooping. The Richmond Bell Telephone Company lends trucks to the Internal Revenue Service (IRS) for use in gambling investigations. The Miami police department has its personal pseudo-Bell truck. And the Philadelphia and Pittsburgh IRS offices have old Bell trucks in stock for use whenever needed.

William O. Marsh, IRS intelligence agent in Pittsburgh, says it is simple to find trucks. He told the Long committee of a 1961 shopping trip. "This used car dealer had five trucks—five used Bell Telephone Company trucks—on his lot. Four of these trucks were small . . . and the fifth was a one-ton size." To complement the trucks, the IRS men donned telephone linemen's uniforms and climbed poles in peace to place their wiretaps.

"Where did you learn where to buy a used telephone company truck?" Fensterwald asked Marsh. "From the telephone company," replied the IRS agent. Later testimony showed that the Pittsburgh security director for Pennsylvania Bell was the contact.

Marsh wouldn't admit whether the Bell Telephone Company of Pennsylvania gave him any additional help. This colloquy tells the story:

Q. [FENSTERWALD] And could you tell me where you got the cable and pair information so that you could install this tap?
A. [MARSH] I received this information from a confidential informant.
Q. Did he work for the telephone company?
A. I am not able to directly or indirectly disclose the identity of a confidential informant.

This leaves the observer with two possibilities: Either AT&T is so careless with cable and pair information that it can fall into the hands of unscrupulous outsiders, or AT&T is willing to give the police the information necessary for invasion of a cash-paying customer's privacy. But Marsh did admit to other cooperation from the Pennsylvania Bell Telephone Company:

Q. [FENSTERWALD] Can you get pen register tape?
A. [MARSH] Yes.
Q. Who did you give the pen register to have it hooked up on the phone company office?
A. To a confidential informant.

The pen register records the numbers dialed from a particular telephone without physically intercepting or recording the message. Bell developed the pen register supposedly for checking and training purposes, in order to determine how to teach both its personnel and customers to dial correctly. Pen registers also detect plant troubles by determining if the dialed digits are translated faithfully by the central office equipment; to trace nuisance calls; and to ferret out customers who frequently—and fraudulently—claim they didn't make long-distance calls for which they were billed. (When a phone is dialed, each number appears on a piece of paper tape in the pen register in the form of dots.)

Bell also uses the pen register to determine the identity of people to whom its subscribers make local calls—although it isn't any of Bell's business. As justification Bell cites the lack of any FCC prohibition on pen registers. Nonetheless, the fact that Citizen A called Citizen B on a certain day is no one's concern but that of A and B; further, disclosure that Industrialist C called Financier D could be the tip-off that a confidential business transaction was under way.*

During the 1950's a security officer of the New York Telephone Company set up a wiretapping school for police. "We were having a lot of problems with your police officers who did not know the first thing about pairs of cables or how to trace a line to find the culprits," William J. Hussey, who formerly was chief investigator of security for New York Telephone Company, told the Long committee. The New York security man for Long Island, Andrew J. Burke, a retired Army colonel, was friendly with Stephen P. Kennedy, the police commissioner. So, in Hussey's words, "Mr. Burke opened up a wiretapping school to teach the young police officers how to tap lines. It was in the telephone company building. . . . He showed them what a terminal box looked like, how you count the pairs. When you call for a certain number, it

---

* The federal judiciary doesn't share the Bell view that pen register snooping can be done on a whim. On July 5, 1966, U.S. District Judge Wade H. McCree, Jr., of Detroit, said the Michigan Bell Telephone Company violated federal law by using pen registers on telephones of men under investigation by the Internal Revenue Service for gambling activities. IRS got the phone numbers from the obliging Michigan Bell and used them as the basis for warrants in raids on sixteen houses and offices. Judge McCree quashed the warrants and threw out all evidence obtained through their use.

takes a certain countdown in a cable box. He told them how to find these things without calling us to go out and find them."

Hussey testified this school didn't last long. "When somebody in the New York legal department found out about it, they broke the thing right up, just as quick as this." He also insisted that the "company" didn't run the school. But Long disagreed. "I don't know how much further it would be necessary to go to tie up the company as an agent. He gets caught and the company says, 'It is not our fault, he was doing it.'"

Hussey said phone officials live in "mortal fear of any law enforcement or government agencies. If you tell them to throw four or five vice-presidents out the window, out they go. You have to believe this. This is slightly exaggerated, but they really are scared."

Hussey also said that New York police regularly tap all the public booths at the Long Island Railroad Station—in the concourse and stores alike—four or five days before racing seasons open. Every call made from those phones until the tracks close is recorded in an attempt to find bookies. Hussey said even though there are court orders for the taps, "the possibility does exist" for blackmail.

Bernard B. Spindel, of Holmes, New York, who describes himself as "an electronic technician specializing in the detection and prevention of eavesdropping in all its forms," said bugging increased threefold between 1964 and 1965—and in each succeeding year. "You can walk into a dozen stores in New York City and purchase any of this equipment without any difficulty whatsoever. The use of it by laymen . . . makes it almost an everyday occurrence to anyone who needs to use it."

Spindel said that when an FBI agent is asked in court, " 'To your knowledge, was there any wiretapping in this case?' he can say, 'No,' and speak the truth. But when he is working on this case, he may have had what they call in the bureau information sheets, and this information sheet says 'Informant Tiger.'"

"Now Informant Tiger, in the cross-confidential file, indicates that the *T* stands for telephone tap. The information that he is taking from that information sheet and using for part of his investigation is in violation of what our Supreme Court has said, yet they have then developed an entire case from that point on. But it is the fruit from the poisoned tree. It was the wiretap that started this."

Private detectives get just about as much help from the Bell companies—but on a *sub rosa* basis and through the medium of bribed employees. The net result, however, is the same. A. U.S. citizen loses his right to telephone privacy.

Richard E. Gerstein, district attorney of Dade County, Florida, said, "There is a considerable improper activity by some employees of the telephone company in our area and I think in many areas throughout the United States. These employees are retained by private detectives or by other persons who desire to listen in or tap telephone conversations without authority to do so, and illegally in my state." Gerstein avowed that the phone company, "in our state at least," does what it can to squelch this activity and that the overwhelming majority of phone workers are honest citizens. Yet those who *are* crooked give the same efficient service for which Bell likes to be known (even if in a somewhat different context). "Our information," Gerstein said, "indicates they go so far as to actually help in the installation of illegal equipment or otherwise provide means to tap phones and listen in on conversations."

Owen D. Young, who is a wiretap specialist for the Internal Revenue Service, also boasted that "dedicated employees of the telephone company" supply his agents with tapping information. And George W. Robinson, a director and owner of the International Bureau of Investigation, a private agency in Kansas City, candidly said he bought cable-pair information from phone workers. The price, he said, was "in the vicinity of between $50 and $100; it all depends on the man's attitude when you make the contact."

Once a law enforcement agency receives a court order permitting a tap, Bell System policy (officially) is to give all the help possible without making the actual interception itself. Edward Silver, former Brooklyn district attorney, said that under the supposedly tightly supervised New York State system a copy of the court order authorizing the tap automatically went to the New York Telephone Company. Subsequently tappers would go to the company, which would point out the telephone wire pairs where a tap would be placed. This would be off phone company premises. Yet, he said, such cooperation is risky. "When we show a copy of the court order to the telephone company to get their aid, it is a common thing for the underworld to reach in and learn of our operation," Silver said. In another forum, however, Silver has praised the phone companies' "substantial safeguards" against taps by their own employees and by outsiders.

As a matter of policy AT&T downplays and belittles reports of wiretapping. An official of the Mountain States Telephone Company claimed not enough complaints are received from customers who suspect taps to "warrant the keeping of statistics on them." Many of the customer suspicions that do arise, he said, stem from domestic relations cases, from "persons who tend to be neurotic, or who are involved in heated disputes of some sort."

Irwin Block, Miami attorney and former prosecutor, testified Southern Bell is very cooperative "on the surface" in efforts against wiretappers. "But I may make the observation that they desire to wash their own dirty linen." He continued:

"If they find someone within their company who is involved in this, it is my personal opinion that they will take measures to see that he doesn't do it again, but they will not bring it to the attention of the law enforcement officials if it is a member of their own company. I think that the adverse publicity that such a disclosure would bring to them limits them. When they participated with me in an investigation, I just got the impression that although on the surface they were trying to assist me . . . that if they found anything they wanted to take care of it themselves, they did not want the information to be known."

Block said stories are rife—and unprovable—that in Miami it is possible to hire phone company employees to do wiretap jobs that negate the use of specialized equipment. The snoop has a phone installed in the same exchange as the one in which the target party is located. Once this is done, according to Block, "somebody from that exchange in the telephone company can strap in the line you want to listen to to your line, so long as it is on the same exchange, and by the use of earphones you can listen to this." *

---

* The Bell companies have several methods to make it difficult for one crooked employee, acting alone, to obtain pair and cable numbers. For obvious reasons, most of these methods are kept secret. A typical practice is to require the field workman who needs a cable number to call a test deskman, who in turn connects with the cable assignment

According to Alan F. Westin, professor of government at Columbia University, and an expert in wiretap law, the first prohibitive statutes were aimed at telephone company employees. "At the time the telephone was first used," he said, "you didn't have an automatic switchboard, and every call would have to be, to some extent, for some time period, listened in on by the operator who would plug you in after you gave her the number. There were sufficient instances of divulging by telephone company employees that a lot of states had that kind of problem in mind when they talked about [in the statutes] people listening to and divulging telephone conversation."

Telephone industry legend has it that eavesdropping led to invention of the dial telephone. Almon B. Strowger, an undertaker, suspected that an operator was diverting his calls to a competitor and in self-defense devised the dial system. The company which he founded is now the Automatic Electric Company, a manufacturing subsidiary of the General Telephone & Electronics Company, which runs the largest non-Bell group of phone companies in the country.

Federal prosecutions for wiretap violations are infrequent in comparison with the activity. From 1952 through May, 1961, the U.S. Justice Department initiated only fourteen cases, all involving private citizens or private detectives, but no law enforcement officers. Although the Federal Communications Commission is charged in the Federal Communications Act with enforcement of wiretapping prohibitions, the function is in the hands of the FBI. Citing its lack of a field staff to make criminal investigations, the FCC in 1953 turned the chore over to the FBI, agreeing, however, to lend whatever technical know-how that Hoover's people might not possess. FCC policy is for its staff to relay immediately any wiretap complaints to the nearest FBI office.

While district attorney of Kings County (Brooklyn), Edward S. Silver cited recurrent reports that the phone companies, if they found a tap on a customer's line as the result of a complaint, "will take it off and tell the subscriber that 'your wire is clear' because they don't want to give the im-

---

desk to establish a three-way conversation. Both the field workman and the test deskman must identify themselves and give the reason they need the number. Another method requires the person receiving the request for the information to hang up and call back the man in the field.

pression that perhaps the telephone isn't quite as private as it
should be." For that reason he advocated enforcement of
statutes that compel telephone companies to advise district
attorneys when taps were discovered. The nonreporting he
blamed for the lack of wiretap prosecutions. "The lack of
prosecutions does not come about because of any lack of desire on the part of the prosecutor to do so," Silver said.

District Attorney Gerstein termed it "virtually impossible"
to nab wiretappers and prosecute them. "The discovery of
taps, usually by accident, is insufficient evidence unless the
party is caught in the act of installing or using," he says.
According to Gerstein, a Miami husband or wife who is
cheating on his or her mate is a prime target, and the activity
is widespread regardless of what the phone company says. "I
cannot claim to provide statistics," he said, "but from the
number of complaints presented to my office, I would estimate
that one of every three contested divorce cases involves the
use of tapped telephones and intercepted conversations."

Gerstein had no illusions about privacy on his own telephones. "The use of devices for interception of conversations
for personal gain, as well as criminal intent, has reached such
proportions that I advise my assistants to conduct every telephone conversation with certain knowledge that the information they are discussing is being monitored by an unknown
third party."

Congress first expressed concern over AT&T's lack of wiretapping safeguards in 1950 after investigating the use of phone-
connected listening devices to snoop on financier-airman Howard Hughes and his lawyers in a Washington hotel during a
controversial hearing on his wartime government contracts.
A Washington police lieutenant hired by Hughes' opponents
told of the ease with which he convinced people on the repair
desk of the Chesapeake & Potomac Telephone Company, an
AT&T subsidiary, that he was a lineman and entitled to pair
and cable numbers of Hughes' phones. The disclosures alarmed
Senator Claude Pepper, and his committee urged strongly that
Chesapeake & Potomac Telephone "address itself to the technical problems of protecting the secrecy of telephone conversations; for example, the relatively simple device of placing
locks on such terminal boxes would materially assist in preventing unauthorized access to them."

Pepper also threw down the gauntlet to Bell to bestir itself in defense of the American citizen's privacy. "Unquestionably, technically qualified persons could develop additional safeguards to hamper the practice of wiretapping and more adequate methods for detecting it when it occurs."

The evidence is, however, that AT&T is running a poor second to the wiretappers. The Bell Telephone Laboratories has demonstrated such remarkable skill in developing equipment in other areas of telephony that one easily could conclude AT&T just isn't interested in making the all-out effort required to protect the privacy of its subscribers. Conversely, the tappers have access to equipment that makes conversing on a Bell System telephone about as private as skywriting.

Mosler Research Products, Inc., of Danbury, Connecticut (a subsidiary of Mosler Safe), advertises a "telephone line transmitter" ($200) which makes it possible for the snoop to "eliminate the most tedious and difficult task of phone monitoring, the running of wires from telephone line to the location of the recording equipment." The gadget, contained in a little box, can be placed on the telephone line at any point and transmit what is said over it for a distance of three blocks. Boasts a Mosler brochure: "The transmitter does not load the line in any way and cannot be detected except by physical search. It is automatically actuated only when the phone is put into use." For less sophisticated snoops, Mosler offers an induction coil ($29) which "is simply placed close to the telephone wire and plugged into the amplifier." Any call over the line can be overheard or recorded. The coil may be put into place or removed "without audible indication that the line is being monitored." (Japanese-made induction coils which do essentially the same quality of tapping can be bought at any number of stores in New York for $3.)

AT&T's direct-dialing system, biggest boon ever to long-distance calling, also opened new vistas for the buggers. Emanuel Mittleman of Brooklyn, operator of a one-man electronics outfit, in the early 1960's developed a transmitter which fits into a phone receiver and is able to pick up everything said in its vicinity. The transmitter can be "activated" by calling the phone from as far distant as 3,000 miles.

"The only limitation," said Mittleman, "is that it must be a direct-dialing system. There must be no live operators in the circuit." The snoop doesn't even have to let the phone ring if the transmitter is adjusted so that it will activate at the sound of a specially pitched harmonic or tuning fork. Mittle-man sells his device for $400.

A related piece of equipment—sold by Mosler—is the "three-wire tap," which converts the telephone into a transmitter even when the receiver is in the cradle. Said Ralph V. Ward, Mosler vice-president: "It hears both sides of the telephone conversation, and after you hang it up, it continues to monitor that. It is particularly important to get the comments after a phone is hung up. An agent that is really trained and doing a first-class job won't be satisfied with anything less than a three-wire tap."

Push-button telephones with multiple lines make the snoop's job easier. Each push button has at least three sets of wires: a holding circuit, a trunk circuit, and the light circuit. Any one of these can be adapted for use as a surreptitious microphone.

From Bell's statements about "plant security" and "line protection," a naive citizen would get the impression that tapping would be impossible unless the snoop were able to ascertain, from the telephone company, just which wires ran to his home or office. "But this isn't true," said the Mosler Company's Ward. "The way to find your pair of wires is simply to know you are in your office and go to any junction box where your telephone circuit appears." The Bell companies' methodical way of doing business helps, Ward said. "On every floor or every corridor there is going to be a terminal box, and that reappears on every floor, and it appears in the master terminal box in the basement and then goes out in an underground cable."

To pick out the right wires, Ward said, the bugger takes an induction coil and "goes over" the terminals, not actually connecting them, but coming close enough to hear what is being said. "We just keep going until we hear your familiar voice and wait until you hang up and then connect right across the terminals, and we have a direct tap. We don't know what pair number it is or what cable number it is, but that isn't important. We have got the wires we want." *

* I offer personal testimony to Ward's statement about the accessibility of Bell's terminal boxes in office buildings. One afternoon I was waiting for the elevator in a center city Philadelphia office building with another reporter and wondered out loud whether Bell had any security on its terminal boxes. We walked around the corner and opened the first box we found. We had the same success in two other buildings. At the

The most effective way of squashing phone bugs is use of a phone line jammer, a gadget that puts out a sound like a crisply frying egg. The noise overrides any listening devices that may be present. Most security men, however, would prefer to remove all telephones from any room or office where confidential conversations may take place. For this reason, many industrial firms have plug-in phones in conference rooms that can be easily removed when the boss is ready to talk serious business.

Ward was skeptical of the ability of security people to find telephone bugs. Visual searches are the best way, he said, but even a trained agent can be fooled. "If he can't find the tap when he is finished, that is all it means. It doesn't mean there is not a tap there." A more scientific method is the line analyzer, which produces a chart of the current in a telephone circuit that resembles a cardiograph. To detect a tap, security men review the ups and downs of the chart periodically to determine if there is any significant change. Extremely sensitive line analyzers can even determine whether an induction coil is being employed. However, said Ward: "Basically, you have to accept that you can't find a two-wire tap." A three-wire tap on a phone, though, can be found in a hurry with an induction coil, which picks up the sounds being transmitted over the supposedly dead telephone receiver.

All this tapping, however, involves only secondary participation by the Bell companies, and the activist villain is the person who relies on Bell's lack of defensive measures or acquiescence to spy on other citizens.

There is another type of snooping, in which the Bell companies are the activists.

The Right Reverend James A. Pike, onetime bishop of the Episcopal diocese of California, was in New York in 1964 when a sudden emergency situation required him to make ten or twelve long-distance phone calls within the space of an hour or so. "I was in considerable personal distress, I was disturbed, and because I was calling out of the hotel, I seemed to hit almost every time the same long-distance operator, a young

---

fourth building a superintendent asked what we were looking for—and lent me a screwdriver so I could "test contact points" in the terminal box we had opened. Telefonos de Mexico, the Mexican phone company, is even more slovenly: Painted above each cable pair is the number of the phone it services.

lady that I never met in person," Bishop Pike recollects. "By about the third call she sensed the personal distress factor. And although I am a professional counselor and pastor, before this series of calls was over, she had been a pastoral help to me, kind of calmed me down in the matter, and indicated she knew and understood that something was bothering me very much."

What Bishop Pike didn't know at the time—and what caused him considerable upset when he learned it—was the fact that as many as ten New York Telephone Company employees could have been listening in on his extremely personal conversations.

This variety of snooping goes under the name of service monitoring. And Bell would have us believe that the employees assigned to service monitoring are emotional eunuchs who can listen to a conversation and determine the "quality of transmission" and not pay any attention to what is said.

On September 14, 1966, Hubert L. Kertz, a vice-president of AT&T, told Senator Edward Long's committee that monitoring had been a standard company practice for half a century. "In all these years we know of no instance where a service observer has violated the company rules designed to protect the privacy of our customers' conversations."

On August 25, 1966, an operator for the Pacific Telephone & Telegraph Company told the California Public Utilities Commission during privacy hearings: "Once a week we are asked to leave our office and monitor our coworkers [while they handle routine customer calls]. *Of course, we run right back downstairs and tell them what we overheard.* (Apprised of this testimony, vice-president Kertz harumphed: "It is certainly not the Bell System policy."

Bishop Pike reflected the feelings of millions of Americans when he said his realization that the most personal of calls were subject to monitoring brought a "sense of self-consciousness, an inhibition, [that] will change my relationship with the telephone."

AT&T would prefer that the public remain ignorant of its monitoring and that done by commercial firms that conduct considerable business by telephone and want to see how their employees deal with the public. During a 1964 hearing on commercial monitoring, Miss Elinor Charles, a staff counsel for the California Public Utilities Commission, asked if the

Pacific Telephone & Telegraph Company would object to putting decals on its instruments stating calls on them could be monitored.

"Oh, yes, we would object to that," replied Clifford F. Goode, PT&T's general commercial manager. "It is another item that has really nothing to do with the basic obligation of the company to provide a good, reliable telephone service. It is a policing type of thing. It is a matter, to a degree, of cost and keeping these things in good legible condition. There are all kinds of things that people constantly want to stick on a telephone."

That surreptitious telephone monitoring is common at business firms became known to the general public in 1964 during a staff dispute at a California hospital. One of the physicians claimed that his calls were being monitored. The PUC got into the fuss and ultimately discovered the surveillance gear was all over the West Coast, with 307 subscribers obtaining it from PT&T alone. Department stores, airlines, newspaper circulation and advertising departments, and transportation company information desks used the monitors to check the efficiency of workers.

Californians became rousingly mad about the practice, and the PUC members talked among themselves about ordering a formal hearing. They ultimately did so, but only over the protests of Commissioner William M. Bennett, who said PT&T's rental of the equipment was so grossly unlawful and disrespectful of human rights that no further discussion was necessary—that the stuff should be junked forthwith. He said that firms that monitor are "oblivious to the constitutional rights of others" and could be dealt with under the penal codes.

What really rumpled Bennett was the increasingly limited rights of privacy as society urbanizes (a sensation one feels more acutely on the West Coast perhaps than anywhere else in America). "The areas [of privacy] that remain—and the use of the telephone is among them—should be protected, not destroyed. Like Shakespeare's rose, third party listening which Pacific makes possible is *still eavesdropping no matter how called*. Telephone efficiency pertaining to business and commercial transactions is not a higher right to which we should sacrifice our privacy. What sins are committed in the name of efficiency! The telephone instrument itself is designed for the use of a single person and no more, except for the party at the opposite end. It does not have attached to it a loud-speaker and for good reason."

Selective hiring, he said, is a better means of obtaining good employees than posthiring snooping. "If employees who utilize business phones are that inefficient," Bennett reasoned, "I suspect that the public will make its dissatisfaction known to the employer." Bennett also feared the "gravity of exposing people of whatever political belief to the possible criticism, censor and discipline of employers or others of opposite belief."

The majority of the commissioners overrode Bennett's objections and listened to what Pacific Telephone and monitoring subscribers had to say in defense of the equipment. PT&T argued that moral questions shouldn't bar monitoring. Why? Well, conversations on a business phone typically are between employees and customers, and such phones are not intended for personal calls. Business subscribers "generally" inform employees of the existence and use of monitoring equipment, and its operation is the responsibility of the subscriber. No employees had complained during the twenty years the equipment had been marketed.

The commission bemusedly heard PT&T's explanations, cited the section of the Public Utilities Code that requires phone companies to take "adequate steps to insure the privacy of communications over such corporation's telephone communication system," and ordered that (1) the monitors be equipped with beeper signals forthwith and (2) any phone subject to monitoring be "clearly, prominently and permanently" marked.

Somehow no one at the PUC ever asked the obvious next question. If PT&T so assiduously peddles monitoring apparatus to other business houses, what does PT&T do in the way of internal eavesdropping itself?

A frightening quantity. During 1965 the American Telephone & Telegraph Company and its subsidiaries "observed" conversations in no fewer than 39,500,000 instances. AT&T says that 2,500 employees were assigned to monitoring full time; thousands of others became involved in monitoring as a peripheral part of other duties. The monitoring costs AT&T and its affiliates $19,000,000. It is true, as AT&T points out, that the number of monitored calls is a small percentage of the 120 billion handled, something like three one-hundredths of 1 percent. It is also true that the law of averages makes it certain that some of the 79,000,000 persons who had calls monitored (assuming the minimum two parties for each call) would have been damnably unhappy had they known some-one else was on the line. (Think back over the past week, and recollect how many calls *you* would not wish to share with a Bell operator or a Bell supervisor.)

The extent of Bell's aural voyeurism is illustrated in the case of a citizen who wishes to call long distance and doesn't know the number. He calls information, and what he says to the operator can be overheard by four sets of ears: the super-vising operator, who sits in open view in the main operators' room and systematically samples what the girls under her are doing; the assistant traffic operating manager (ATOM, in phone company jargon), whose private office is equipped with a jack that cuts into any conversation carried on in his ex-change; the district supervising operator, miles away in a downtown office; and the company-wide observing department, equipped so that a supervisor in the home office of the South-western Bell Telephone Company in St. Louis can monitor what an operator is doing in Houston.

Once the citizen receives the number, he dials the long-distance operator and places his call. Again he could be moni-tored by the four persons who overheard his information call. Two other sources can join the eavesdropping: the plant de-partment, which wants to check on how well the transmission is going, and the dial people, who want to see if their part of the phone mechanism is working well.

There is the chance that the telephone the man calls in the other city is also being monitored, thus multiplying the num-ber of Bell snoops with access to his conversation, but let's not get into that.

The monitoring isn't necessarily over now. Several weeks later the citizen receives his phone bill and thinks the long-distance charge is high. He calls the business office and is monitored as he tells the switchboard girl his complaint. She transfers the call to the service representative for his exchange, and what they say is monitored. If the billing error seems seri-ous enough, the service representative may put his call through to the investigation office, where there is a further monitoring.

Some citizens get mad enough to complain in person to the phone company. They're monitored if they do. When the citi-zen sits down before the friendly phone company employee to talk, he may notice a desk set with a calendar between the pen and pencil. The calendar contains a microphone, and a wire runs from it through a hole cut in the desk to a conduit in the floor and then to a back room, where what the citizen says is either magnified over a loudspeaker as supervisors listen or tape-recorded for later study. (Bell's eavesdropping on people who come into its buildings is nondiscriminatory. Even employment offices desks are equipped with the big-eared desk sets.)

AT&T defends the monitoring as essential to efficient phone service. Said Vice-President Kertz: "You can't take a girl and put her at a switchboard and say, 'Handle calls,' any more than you can take a service representative and put her at a a service representative desk and say, 'Handle the calls from the public on new installations.' It is necessary to train them, and we do this through weeks of training, in classrooms, and then when we put them on the switchboards or in the service representatives' positions, it is necessary to get them familiar with the procedures when they are actually dealing with live customers, and that is what this is for."

The same philosophy supposedly guides service observing, the monitoring of a random sampling of forty phones weekly on a continuous basis, from each of the 13,000-odd exchanges Bell has throughout the country. Kertz insisted that the object here is to determine the quality of service being given by the entire plant. "We are not after what a particular line does or what a particular operator does or what a particular service representative does."

The phones are selected for monitoring to make up a statistically valid cross section of the traffic of the entire telephone network. Even the private telephone line of a governor, a Congressman, an archbishop, or a corporation president would be subject to monitoring because, as Kertz said, "if you start to exclude lines for one reason or another, you have destroyed the statistic sample that you are trying to make, and you just don't get the right picture."

Kertz didn't see any security problems in the monitoring of official conversations because Defense Department rules prohibit the transmission of classified information over any telephone lines.

Long disagreed. "There is a difference between classified

and highly confidential," he said. "The governor of the state of Massachusetts might have a highly confidential conversation with me or with his Senator. That would not be classified but he certainly would not want some individual, telephone operator or otherwise, listening in on it."

According to Robert B. Conrad, of the General Services Administration's Transportation and Communications Service, AT&T also monitors 500,000 telephones in federal offices throughout the country—including some leased by the CIA, the FBI, the State Department, the Treasury Department, the Justice Department, and the Federal Communications Commission.

Prior to June 1, 1966, AT&T policy permitted monitors to stay on the line "surveying" private conservations for as long as ten minutes. Then there was a peculiar juxtaposition between public exposure of monitoring and AT&T's decision that monitoring really wasn't necessary anymore for efficient telephone service.

For several decades the Communications Workers of America, which represents more Bell employees than any other union, had complained about service monitoring because the company used the information gained through it to discipline employees. The CWA's concern over the invasion of customer privacy initially was of secondary importance, but the complaints raised by the union did bring the practice to public view.

Joseph A. Beirne, the CWA president, fought for contract clauses barring the use of information gathered through monitoring for disciplinary purposes. Such a clause was obtained from Michigan Bell Telephone in 1950. Yet Beirne stated before the Long committee that in 1965, "We were forced to go to arbitration over a case in which one of our members, a woman suffering from terminal cancer, was fired for poor performance on the basis of just such information."

Beirne simply did not believe Bell management when it says monitoring is done for "training and correction purposes only." For fourteen months, he said, supervisors built up a case of poor performance against the woman, using a multiple-outlet listening device known as the Octopus. This is a two-foot-square box with ten cords coming from it, each with an earphone, enabling as many as ten people to listen to what is being picked up on the monitoring board.

"Such machinery is bound to corrupt people," said Beirne. "Can you imagine a decent, honest guy spending fourteen months bugging a woman who has terminal cancer?" Over a period of time the man in charge of monitoring "got so used to this thing being around . . . that his own morality slipped, his own sense of values got corrupted by it."

In Louisiana the Southern Bell Telephone Company was found to have put a listening post in the bedroom at the home of the chief operator which enabled management to listen in on any of ten operators as they worked at a switchboard in the main office blocks away. Some of the "observations" lasted as long as thirty minutes, with everything exchanged between the operator and the subscriber recorded. The information gained enabled Southern Bell to fire ten employees and suspend nine more for supposed violations of regulations.

Defending the bedroom monitoring, Southern Bell said attempts to do the work secretly from an in-plant location had failed. The company also said the monitoring device enabled supervisors to hear not only what the operator said while on the line, but also any remarks she might make to other operators in moments when they were not busy.

"In other words, the company was able to eavesdrop on operators' casual conversations with a fellow worker," says Joe Beirne. "Surely intelligent, modern management does not have to rely on such practices to perform proper supervisory duties."

Dina Beaumont, a CWA official in Los Angeles, testified before the California PUC that the Pacific Telephone & Telegraph Company frequently uses monitoring as a means of harassing operators into blunders—and consequently out of their jobs. She cited an instance where management wanted an airtight case against a girl and monitored every call she handled for a two-week period, with as many as four persons at a time sitting around a conference table and listening. The girl received no training as a result of what the supervisor heard, the monitoring being used "simply to gather evidence," said Mrs. Beaumont. An Anaheim operator who won a grievance proceeding was told by her manager: "You are going to be monitored continually. We think your work is slipping."

A conceivable outcome of monitoring pressures could be worse, rather than improved, service. An information operator in Hawthorne, California, told Mrs. Beaumont during a grievance proceeding: "Every time I see my supervisor or ATOM [assistant traffic operating manager] at one of the monitoring boards or desks, I nearly always panic for a few moments. I sweat and forget what my customer is saying. I think I have made more errors due to this than for any other reason. I went through hell for the better part of a year due to this, and I surely would like to see [monitoring] abolished." The woman who spoke these words had worked for the Pacific Telephone & Telegraph Company for seventeen years.

In Santa Ana, California, an operator who had been unable to get a transfer remarked to the girl sitting next to her: "I am going to have to go to the union." She was immediately admonished for complaining about her supervisor, and a notice of the warning went into her personnel file.

In Santa Monica, a toll operator joshed, "I have taken forty-one calls now, I guess I don't have to work any more." A supervisor came to her board and said, "You are malingering when you say you will take no more calls," and suspended her on the spot. (The CWA intervened and had the girl reinstated with pay for the time she lost.)

"The tensions and the pressures are such that it is heartbreaking," states Mrs. Beaumont.

Beirne complained to Senator Long's committee about these abuses during invasion-of-privacy hearings in May, 1965. Long, however, at the time was in full bay after the Internal Revenue Service for its own wiretapping and bugging and could not stop to chase AT&T. But his investigators kept tripping over AT&T wherever they turned, discovering that Bell security personnel regularly helped law enforcement officers in wiretapping. Indeed, at times Bell appeared to be the essential element of the wiretapping. Thus, Long's men gradually built up a dossier on AT&T, although they weren't exactly sure what would ever be done with it.

"AT&T was completely cooperative with us during this entire period," says Long's chief counsel, Bernard J. Fensterwald, Jr. "The company assigned a man from its Washington office to work with us, and it made available to us any witnesses we requested. The cooperation was all that we could ask for."

Simultaneously, investigative reporter Ronald Kessler, then

of the *Boston Herald,* learned of a secret room at New England Telephone Company's main Boston office from which calls could be monitored. When Kessler published the story New England Telephone first denied, then admitted, the existence of the room. Massachusetts State Senator Mario Umana took up the chase, and demanded on-the-record answers from the phone company. He learned that from 2,400 to 2,500 long-distance and local calls a month were monitored in Boston, and some 150,000 in all of New England Telephone's territory. Although there was nothing to prevent an operator from listening as long as she wished, Bell claimed that the girls stayed on the lines only until contact was made between the two parties. Nor did Bell call this practice monitoring. "Tagging" was the term the company preferred, although Umana said, "It is rather difficult for me to see any difference in the result . . . a conversation is being overheard, . . . the existence of a conversation can and probably is being divulged to a superior."

All this was duly noted by Long, who then decided it was time for exploration of what AT&T does to protect the privacy of its subscribers' communications. Until this point AT&T had received gingerly treatment from Long. Admissions of Internal Revenue Service agents that they received wiretapping assistance from Bell employees gave Long many opportunities to demand that responsible AT&T officials be brought in to define company policies. Yet he did not do so, restricting his inquiries (in public) to a handful of second-level employees.

In late spring of 1966 Long and Fensterwald talked with AT&T's Washington office and received promises they would be given anything they wanted in Boston. H. G. Homme, Jr., an assistant committee counsel, was dispatched to Boston to look at the monitoring operation. Homme, naturally, wanted most of all to talk with the girls who actually did the service monitoring, for they are the ones best qualified to tell how the system works in practice, as opposed to theory. It was his understanding—and that of Long and Fensterwald—that the girls would be made available to him.

But William Hogan, vice-president of New England Telephone, balked. Sure, he said, Homme could talk with all the service monitors he wished—but Bell intended to have a lawyer present when he did so. Homme's arguments were futile, and he went back to Washington. Whereupon Long let AT&T

know it could expect public hearings.* Long and Fensterwald also began treating AT&T to publicity on monitoring. "AT&T is the snoopiest company in the whole United States," Fensterwald told a syndicated columnist. Long suggested it would be equally logical for electric company employees to burst into private homes at night to see if bedroom lights gave proper illumination or for the gas company to come in at dinnertime to check the height of the flame on the kitchen range.

And then occurred a remarkable coincidence. On May 10, 1966, the general traffic manager of every Bell subsidiary in the United States received notification that operator monitoring of customer-to-customer calls was to be halted as of June 1. The notification bore the notation "Emergency Handling Required." The companies were told that after June 1 they should use mechanical devices to measure the transmission quality of telephone transmissions and keep human operators' ears off the lines.

AT&T says there was absolutely no connection between the exposure of monitoring, the imminent Long hearings, and the abandonment of monitoring. "There was no emergency about it at all," stated Kertz. "We had been planning this for some time."

Why, then, demanded Senator Long, the "Emergency Handling Required" order on the notice to discontinue personal monitoring.

KERTZ: We all have to do it together. We cannot have the Southwestern Bell do it on June 1, the New England company on July 15 and someone else on August 1.
SENATOR LONG: What would be the immediate rush about it? You had been doing this for years?
KERTZ: That is right, sir, but we want to make them do it all together on the same day. . . . If we are going to make a change that involves the whole Bell System . . . you have to

* Long later jumped on AT&T for refusing to permit the private interviews. "It smacks of inference that there is something you are covering up," he told AT&T Vice-President Kertz, saying that to have a company lawyer present during the interviews was akin to expecting an Army private "to testify in front of the general." Edward B. Hanify, lawyer for New England Telephone, in a warm exchange with Long, argued that the girls had a right to counsel because the interviews would be done "under company auspices with company sanctions."

do it in a way like this or they will never get it done altogether.
SENATOR LONG: Very well. We are still curious about the
emergency . . . why there was an emergency to do it at that
time when this committee was starting to look at it.

Bell now *says* it does not eavesdrop on customers when they
make local and long-distance calls, that it has devised electronic
surveying devices to check on transmission and dial quality.
But this statement of corporate policy should not be interpreted
as a guarantee that phone calls are not heard by unauthorized
Bell ears. Two examples:

—In August 1968 lovelornist Ann Landers ran a letter from
a thirty-four-year-old widow who had been a phone company
supervisor for nine years. The woman said she had needed to
tell a supposedly faithful boy friend of a change in plans. "I
tried his line for nearly twenty-five minutes and got a busy signal. I know it is against company rules, and I plead guilty,
but my curiosity got the better of me and I cut in to find out to
whom Van was speaking. I heard him say, 'Good-bye, sweet,
I'll call you tomorrow—same time.' A woman replied, 'So long,
darling.' " (Miss Landers' advice: "Get back into circulation
and give Van the busy signal for a few weeks.")

—In October 1968 a Florida college student learned to
whistle the tones that enabled him to cut into the Bell System's
long distance circuits and call anywhere in the country free of
charge. He performed this service for other students for $1. He
was apprehended when an eavesdropping operator overheard
one of his "clients" describing the scheme during a long-distance call.

Bell encourages commercial firms to use the telephone for
huckstering. Each Bell operating company has a special division which consults with peddlers who can get into a citizen's
home via the telephone when they couldn't do so by the front
door. For a price many Bell companies supply these pests with
what the telephone industry calls trick books—listings of telephone numbers by street addresses. With a trick book a salesman can go house-to-house in a chosen neighborhood without
leaving the comfort of his office.

Because of customer complaints against invasions of privacy,
several Bell operating companies—the Chesapeake & Potomac
trio in Maryland, Virginia and the District of Columbia, for

instance—stopped selling listings of new numbers. The rule is no handicap to the hucksters, who obtain the new numbers anyway. Mrs. Susan Klein, wife of a Justice Department lawyer, and operator of Phone Power, a "telephone interviewing firm" in suburban Virginia, states, "There's no question in my mind that there is collusion between phone company officials and various vested interests. Such lists are exchanged either sub-rosa or above board. . . . It's definitely a black market situation. The list sells here for about ten cents a name."

The Chesapeake & Potomac companies supposedly keep a tight watch on their "Daily Addendum"—a list of new and changed numbers. But nonetheless the numbers circulate in a hurry. During the April 1968 riots a Washington newspaper editor installed a private hot line between his desk and that of other top editors, with a number supposedly known only to them and the phone company. The first call the next day was from a cheerful woman who wanted to sell him a subscription to his own newspaper.

A naive legislator occasionally tries to push through a law requiring the phone company to denote with an asterisk or other distinctive mark in the directory the names of people who don't want to be bothered by salesmen. Bell's answer is the familiar alibi that this would interfere with "operational efficiency." If a person seeks privacy by taking his name out of the phone book—a so-called "unpublished" number—Bell charges him an extra 50 cents per month, on the grounds that information operators spend $6 worth of time each year giving his number to callers. The charge is based upon highly unempirical statistics. Another alternative is the unlisted number, which is theoretically available to no one. But neither category of private listing offers the citizen a defense against hucksters. The Haines Criss Cross Company of Ohio, which sells phone numbers by name and address (870,000 listings in the Washington area cost $95), also offers trusted patrons a list of unlisted and unpublished numbers for an extra fee (30,000 are on its Washington list).

Nor is taking the phone off the hook a solution. Do so, and the instrument howls like the hounds of hell until replaced.

Hanging up on pests is no longer a defense, for the phone salesmen are equipped with a device known as the Monster. No human huckster is necessary. The Monster automatically dials every listing in an exchange, one after the other, and emits a recorded spiel for a politician, a soap, a movie, a storm door company. The Monster is persistent; hang up on him, and he'll call back and repeat his message from the beginning —and he'll keep calling until he finishes it.

One can't escape the phone hucksters, but one can harass them and thus perhaps drive them into decent lines of work. "You are selling life insurance. I am so glad you called. You see, I'm going into the hospital tomorrow, and the doctor says he must take out one lung and maybe two . . . Cancer, you know, and since I already have this heart condition, I think maybe I had better increase my coverage . . . Hello?" A politician friend of mine in Dallas found a device that parallels in tone and intensity the blast of an air horn, and magazine salesmen beware. You get much the same effect with a police whistle. If of a gentler nature, chuckle gently, and leave the phone off the hook; the huckster will be surprised and stay on the line a couple of minutes, expecting you to return. Free dancing lessons? "I'm a paraplegic, and this is the second time that *you* have called me this week, and I'm complaining to the American Legion." Newspaper subscriptions? Find out the editor's name, and the next time you come in at three o'clock on a Sunday morning, give the chap a ring and let him know how much you appreciate having your dinner interrupted. On sales calls of lesser importance let your two-year-old son improvise; kids need practice on the telephone anyway.

A striking instance of what AT&T permits its phone users to do under the guise of "unrestricted nondiscriminatory service" involves a Florida-based organization called Let Freedom Ring. The founder was one Dr. William C. Douglass, onetime Navy flight surgeon who settled in Sarasota and became an active and proudly professed member of the John Birch Society. Dr. Douglass pictures himself as a sort of latter-day Paul Revere, whose role in life is to Alert America to the Communist Menace Around Us—in the schools; the churches; the Army; the courts; yes, indeed, even the White House itself, for four occupants in a row.

To put his message before the public, Dr. Douglass hit upon a method wreathed with the conspiratorial haze so beloved by the far right: a telephone message service, through which an anonymous militant voice produces the Warning of the Week. Dr. Douglass wrote the messages and peddled them (forty a year for $24) to Birch colleagues all over the country. The local Birchers were responsible for putting the messages on tape and arranging for the message service through their phone company. The automatic phone-tape service is available to anyone, is easily installed, and is cheap enough to be an economical medium for propaganda. The apparatus incorporates recorder, playback and telephone connections in a single unit and can be rented from Bell companies for $20 to $25 per month, depending on the area.

Dr. Douglass promoted his idea vigorously through Birch publications. The head Bircher, Dr. Robert Welch, gave his blessing, calling the project a "worthwhile interest." Dr. Douglass described Let Freedom Ring as "anti-communist, anti-socialist, pro-American. Your 'customer' dials a number (just like time and weather) and hears two minutes of anti-communist dynamite. Let Freedom Ring brings to your area a hard-hitting, often shocking program that is 'on the air' 24 hours a day. . . . You will be amazed at the frantic reaction that you will get from your enemies . . . they will hate it."

Almost without exception the Birchers used phone numbers which they had the phone company keep out of the book, thus making it impossible for the public to know the identity of the person or organization responsible. The numbers were circulated by word of mouth, in classified newspaper advertisements, and through surreptitiously distributed cards and handbills.

Let Freedom Ring created a tizzy among eager Birchers, and "outlets" appeared throughout the country beginning in 1962. Detroit alone supported ten tape machines with ten numbers. The messages followed the fantasy format of the far-far right:

> America will be in a position of hopeless military inferiority to the beasts of Russia because of deliberate disarmament by traitors in the Johnson Administration.

> How long will the American people put up with treason right in the White House itself? How long before the American people demand the impeachment of John F. Kennedy?

> At the University of Michigan a plan is being developed for the systematic house-to-house search of the United States for arms of any kind. The search is to be made by the U.S. Army

by blocking off five states at a time, beginning in the western part of the country. The entire civilian population is to be disarmed by the end of 1965. [The Defense Department retorted, "This charge is absurd, completely false, and reflects the hallucinations of an aberrated mind."]

In the United States, there is no law against printed or spoken absurdity, and idiocy is a regrettable but unavoidable companion of free speech. But Dr. Douglass' grove of Birchers left themselves vulnerable in a key area—their anonymity. With scant exception the "telephonocasts" did not identify the source of the scare messages. Citizens familiar with the structure of the far right picked out a clue from some messages that suggested listeners buy publications from the local American Opinion Book Store, which are outlets for Birch and radical-right literature.

Dr. Douglass' visions of a vast Communist conspiracy became increasingly lurid, and by the summer of 1964, during the Presidential campaign, luridity was his keynote. One attack was against the National Council of Churches, which represents thirty Protestant, Anglican, and Orthodox denominations with 40,000,000 members. Let Freedom Ring proclaimed: "Another fact ignored by the press is that the Communist-lining National Council of Churches is openly promoting bloodshed through armed revolution by Negroes. There is documented proof that Negroes are being armed for open revolution this summer."

The editor of a newspaper or magazine, when he discovers that his publication is being used for transmission of libelous material—by either his own staff or other people—quickly halts further publications and makes amends, even if it means halting the presses while printers chisel out the erroneous material. But Bell didn't unplug Let Freedom Ring or force the Birchers to reveal who was tolling the bell.

Gordon N. Thayer, an AT&T vice-president, admitted that Bell knew of the nature of Let Freedom Ring as early as August, 1964. Bell "hoped it was an isolated case" but began thinking of "possible action we could take."

"Our hope, of course, was that this problem would go away," Thayer explained in defense of AT&T's nonaction. "You will recognize, I think, that the Bell System is a big operation, and we have to check with a lot of people to find out what kind of procedures they thought they could live with from an administrative standpoint."

The National Council of Churches, while Bell worried about its "administrative procedures," was living with daily Douglass slanders. B'nai B'rith, the Jewish service organization, also became a target, and Arnold Forster, its general counsel, complained to AT&T.

B'nai B'rith's adjunct, the Anti-Defamation League (ADL), said that although it had no objection to political comment, it thought authors of such attacks should be identified, as are publishers of periodicals and owners of broadcast stations. As was stated by Forster: "We believe it to be essential that, among other protections, some means be made available to persons and groups defamed by these reckless accusers to ascertain the identity of the persons responsible for the message and to obtain the full text of the message so that they can be in a position to seek legal redress if they are so disposed."

But AT&T wouldn't act to halt the libels, taking what New York lawyer Marvin Berger, an ADL counsel, calls a "too restricted view of the civil liberties question." The flavor of AT&T's position was given in a letter which the Pennsylvania Bell Telephone Company sent the Philadelphia Commission on Human Relations.

Bell asserted it has the duty to furnish services and facilities to anyone who intends to use them in a lawful manner and quoted a Pennsylvania Supreme Court ruling that public utilities are not censors. (ADL did not want to censor anything; it only wanted the source identified.) Automatic announcement service, Bell said, is available to any customer, and the customer determines the content of the message used. (ADL said it is fortunate that reputable gun stores do not permit juveniles to determine for themselves what use they make of shotguns.) And, finally, Bell maintained that it is prohibited from interfering with the lawful exercise of a customer's right of "free speech." (Again, ADL's concern was the source, not the content, of the messages.)

AT&T's position, thus, was that it was powerless to force Let Freedom Ring sponsors to identify themselves. The phoniness of this position was revealed in short order.

On August 29, 1965, ADL filed a complaint with the FCC asking that the anonymity be stripped from Let Freedom Ring and any other message service which dealt in political messages. Bell's role in the service was well publicized.

In September, 1965, AT&T suddenly discovered it did have the power to do what ADL had asked more than a year previously. The Bell operating companies received orders from New York to require in recorded announcements "the name of the organization or individual responsible for the service and the address at which the service is provided."

Let Freedom Ring vanished immediately—thirteen months after the American Telephone & Telegraph Company had been advised that its facilities were being employed for systematic, anonymous libel.

11

Reductions in rates for interstate long-distance telephone calls will be submitted shortly by the Bell System telephone companies to the Federal Communications Commission. It is expected that the reduced rates will save users of telephone service about $150 million per year. . . .

—*FCC press release, November 5, 1969*

The commission today offers for public view the result of its recent informal negotiations with the Bell System on the appropriate level of interstate rates. . . . The commission here issues a press release designed to show that significant decreases have "voluntarily" been agreed to by Bell. The implication is that some wonderful victory has been achieved for the consumer through the activities of the commission and the benevolence of AT&T. Unanswered is the question of whether *enough* has been achieved or whether the commission's representation is a true reflection of the facts.

—*Commissioner Nicholas Johnson in*
separate statement, same date

THIS chapter concerns regulation of the American Telephone & Telegraph Company, and to leave the next forty or so pages blank would be a flippant, but not overly inaccurate, way to dispose of the subject.

The regulatory system is supposed to work as follows: The Federal Communications Commission has jurisdiction over AT&T's interstate and foreign long-distance operations and sets rates sufficient to give the company what it considers to be a "fair return" on the amount of money it has invested in this portion of its business. Each state (save Texas) has a public utilities commission with the same responsibility for the phone companies' local and intrastate long-distance service.

But the regulatory system *does not* work that way. To use a military analogy, AT&T is a modern, well-equipped army with trained troops and fortified garrisons, supported actively or through acquiescence by local governments which it has won over by power or by propaganda. Its opposition consists of ill-armed, undermanned, demoralized, and uncoordinated local militia, many of whom are collaborationists; the motivation of the remainder is weakened by the acknowledged hopelessness of their task.

Nicholas Johnson, a member of the FCC who has no illusions about the effectiveness of his agency, once opined, "There is substantial question in my mind whether the David-FCC is capable of 'regulating' the Goliath-Bell in anything other than the most superficial terms. I believe the states and the municipalities have similar difficulties, and that our problems are further complicated by dividing the regulatory responsibility among 52 or more jurisdictions." The FCC has a staff of some 60 persons, professional and clerical, with which to attempt regulation of a long-distance business which in 1968 brought AT&T slightly more than $1.3 billion in revenues. The FCC's budget for telephone activities in 1967—the year the commission was completing the only formal telephone rate case in its history—was $627,936, or less than was spent by the President's Commission on Post Office Organization.

On the staff level the FCC is afflicted with the malaise of hopelessness. Never in its history has the Commission had even a near majority of members who were interested in serious rate inquiry. "It does something to your morale," said one career upper-echelon official, "when you see an AT&T vice-president go into the chairman's office and close the door, and you pick up the phone later in the afternoon and receive an order to 'be reasonable' on a point AT&T is trying to make with you."

The state regulatory system, with few exceptions, is even

worse. A New York legislative committee on consumer protection, after a year-long study of that state's Public Service Commission, concluded that its control over power and telephone utilities was a "fiasco" that cost citizens millions of dollars a year in excessive charges. The Florida Public Service Commission, in astoundingly candid criticism of its own abilities, has declared, "The public provides public utilities, through rates, with such experts as the public utilities may require to protect the utilities' rights, but the public, through taxes, does not provide adequate funds for its own protection." In other words: utilities have the good business sense to hire rate experts to protect their interests; state governments do not. Chairman James A. Washington, Jr., of the District of Columbia Public Service Commission, believes that budgetary restrictions and "significant" understaffing "affect our ability to operate as effectively as the companies do in the fields of advancing technology."

Such admissions do not impress the National Association of Regulatory Utility Commissioners (NARUC), which critics call—tartly, and without discernible overstatement—"The Bell System's Division for Rate Gouging." George I. Bloom, a portly Republican politician who is chairman of the Pennsylvania Public Utility Commission (through the grace of his good friend Governor Raymond Shafer) and also President of NARUC, has piously proclaimed, "In my opinion, the American people now receive the finest and most reliable utility service in the world, and they receive this service at rates which have been markedly stable in the present spiraling inflationary trend which continues to grow stronger."

Four public service commissions have no attorney on their staff; seventeen, only one; another nine, only two. Six commissions have no rate analyst; sixteen, only one; another seven, only two. Twenty commissions have only one or two accountants, despite the fact, as Senator Lee Metcalf has noted, "that effective regulation relies almost entirely on accurate analysis of the accounts of hundreds of companies subject to regulation." Twenty-six of the commissions do not have a security analyst, even though most utility security issues are subject to state rather than federal regulation. Twenty-seven commissions pay their staff attorneys less than $12,000 a year. Forty-five commissions pay their accountants less than $12,000. Only three state commissions employ economists.*

These staffing problems meant the regulatory agencies encounter a somewhat basic problem when they deal with Bell System companies: that of sorting out the information needed for an intelligent appraisal of their operations.

Consider the process known to professionals in the field of public utilities as "separations." Most of the Bell System's physical plant is used in common in intrastate long-distance, interstate long-distance, and local service. That is, you use the same telephone and switching equipment when you call the corner grocer, your aunt in the next town, a vacationing friend six states away.

The state agencies, the phone companies, and the FCC must determine what percentage of this equipment is used in the various categories of service. Telephone rates are set to permit a percentage return on the value of the phone companies' investments. The higher the value, the higher the rates. Thus, the state agencies want as little of the total Bell plant assigned to intrastate service as possible, and the FCC wants as little of the total Bell plant assigned to interstate service as possible. The less plant, the lower the rates, and the more popular the regulatory body.

The problem is resolved annually at a meeting of the FCC; a committee of the National Association of Regulatory Utility Commissioners, consisting of the state regulators; and representatives of the United States Independent Telephone Association (USITA), the non-Bell companies. Each agency has its own manual on how it thinks separations should be made, and each differs in substantial detail. Bell, however, owns most of the telephones, and Bell has a striking community of voice with the FCC on the separations issue, which prompted the plaintive remark of a USITA official: "Ma Bell really shows her maternal instincts when it comes to those meetings. The Bell people simply get together with the FCC and decide what will be done; then they shove it down our throats."

The lack of expertise is keenly felt when a state agency

* These statistics are derived from the statistical study, "State Utility Commissions," U.S. Congress, Senate Document # 56, prepared by the Subcommittee on Intergovernmental Relations of the Senate Government Operations Committee, November 2, 1967. This document is the best existing guide to the inadequacies of the state commissions. It was prepared by Vic Reinemer, executive secretary to Senator Metcalf.

attempts to explore Western Electric's pricing structure—a hall of mirrors that can keep a commission busy for years. Even the California Public Utilities Commission, once the best in the land,* when it entered the Western Electric maze in the 1960's came out sounding confused about what it found there (so much so that its final report hysterically quoted something which Commissioner Paul Walker of the FCC had said in the 1930's). This gives one an idea of the abundance of information available on Western Electric pricing, and of the ease with which it can be pried from AT&T's hands.

Commissions find it impossible to rely upon outside experts. As political scientist Jerome B. McKinney discovered during a study of the Missouri Public Service Commission, "the high retainer fees demanded by experts create a real obstacle. Also, many such individuals are affiliated in some manner with utility companies. The telephone industry is one in which this is particularly true." McKinney quoted one PSC member as telling him: "There are also experts who have set views, and for reasons of objectivity, cannot be employed."

In only sixteen states are public utility commissioners elected by popular vote. The remainder, who are gubernatorial appointees (save for two states where they are elected by the legislature) are inherently political, and prior loyalty and service to a regulated utility is no barrier to office. Soon after taking office Governor Ronald Reagan moved to hamstring the PUC there by installing as a commissioner Frank Morrissy, who had been a rate consultant for the Pacific Telephone & Telegraph Company. Columnist Pete Hamill has tartly (and accurately) described the New York State Public Service Commission as the "Republican Party's Fealty Retirement Foundation." Chairman James A. Lundy, former Republican borough president of Queens, was in the paint business before he ran for comptroller on the same ticket with Governor Nelson Rockefeller—and lost. Whereupon Rockefeller put him on the PSC. Edward Larkin, another commissioner, was Republican state senator from Nassau County until 1961, when he was refused renomination. Again, Rocky to the rescue with a PSC appointment. Ralph Lehr of Buffalo was appointed because of friendship with Republican leader Walter Mahoney; Frank J.

---

* The California PUC staff includes 4 attorneys, 59 rate analysts, 168 engineers, 87 inspectors/investigators, 46 accountants, 11 economists, and 384 clerical, research and secretarial workers.

McMullen of Brooklyn because of friendship with Brooklyn GOP leader John Crews. The sole member with professional expertise is John T. Ryan, onetime PSC staff professional. Each of these men is paid $31,660 a year plus expenses.

The Florida Public Service Commission, which is elected, is equally drab. Alan Boyd, who was chairman of the Commission before joining the Johnson Administration as Secretary of Transportation, has stated, "There is little interest in the commission political campaigns and little knowledge on the part of the public for whom or for what they may be voting. The cost of a statewide political campaign is very expensive and the ability of candidates to raise money is severely restricted. Because of the lack of interest and knowledge in the office, the net result is that companies regulated by the commission are in a position to exercise tremendous power in selecting candidates, even though this power has never apparently been exercised." The current* Florida PSC consists of the following:

—Jerry W. Carter, eighty-one years old, a former sewing machine salesman with a grade school education who has been on the PSC for thirty-five years. Carter once described himself as "just a cheap politician because that's all Florida can afford." Carter attends few meetings, and has the disconcerting habit of dozing during complex testimony. During his 1966 campaign Carter accepted $5,610 in contributions from utilities regulated by the PSC.

—Jess Yarborough, sixty-two, a onetime state legislator who once told an interviewer there "ain't nothin' highfalutin' about utility regulation," and said he ran for the post for three reasons: (1) "I like politics." (2) "It's an important office." (3) "I thought I could win." Yarborough was a Miami football coach before entering politics; his campaign literature boasts he "lost only one game for Florida schools during ten years." About one-fourth of his 1968 campaign funds ($24,307) came from donors linked with utilities. ("They're old friends," he said.)

—William T. Mayo, fifty-one, who had two years of college, but avows his most valuable experience was as a car dealer. Floridians consider him the strongest "consumer man" on the PSC because he had argued that quality of service should be a factor in rate setting. Nonetheless utility-linked sources gave $9,075 to his first campaign.

* December, 1969.

The dominant figure on the Florida PSC staff is general counsel and Executive Director Lewis Petteway, whose philosophy was summarized in a talk to the Public Utility Securities Club of Chicago: "We are convinced that nit-picking regulation can never make a worthwhile contribution to the economic growth and development of our state. On the contrary, we recognize that regulation must merit the respect and confidence of the sophisticated investors."

AT&T-linked money has gone to the Florida utility commissioners during their campaigns. Dade County attorney Miller Walton, whose firm represents both AT&T and the subsidiary Southern Bell, gave $500 to candidate Yarborough in 1968 and $100 to candidate Carter two years earlier. Walton's firm lists as a speciality "practice before the Florida [Public] Service Commission." The wives of Tallahassee lawyers D. Fred McMullen and Charles Ausley, whose firm is local counsel for Southern Bell, gave $200 to Yarborough in 1968; in a previous election, McMullen and Ausley personally gave $750 and $250 respectively to Edwin Mason, a former PSC chairman. (Mason once told a Senate committee: "The best regulation is little or no regulation.") Harold B. Wall, of the Jacksonville firm of Loftin and Wall, gave $100 to Carter during his 1966 campaign; the firm represents AT&T and Southern Bell.

Commissioners from a number of states relate that a Bell System public relations man—he might bear the title of legislative representative—is among their first callers when they take office. "He left enough printed material in my office to fill a bookcase," related a commissioner who formerly served in an Eastern state. "He asked me to pick a date so they could fly me up to Murray Hill, New Jersey, to inspect the Bell Telephone Laboratories. He gave me a list of telephone numbers—home and office—of his company's top executives and told me to call them any time, night or day, when I had a question about Bell, and to call collect.

"I felt overwhelmed my first couple of years on the commission. The Bell men had a good sense of timing. About every three weeks or so they'd run in with a proposal for rate reduction in some little out-of-the-way corner of the state, affecting maybe 150 people, and ask us to approve it. I'd ask questions of our own engineering and finance experts, and they'd come back with answers. After a while it dawned on me that they were just going down to the Bell lobbyist's office and asking him to come up with the information.

"I got rather sore about all this—after all, I had practiced law for more than twenty-five years, and although I'm no genius, I wanted to do a serious job, for that's why the governor put me on the commission.

"So I asked at one of our meetings, 'Why can't we make our own studies of Bell? We're not regulating—we're just sitting up here in a nice boardroom and giving their decisions our blessing, and putting the sanctity of the state upon them.'

"The other commissioners just laughed at me. 'Go over to ——,' one of them said, mentioning the man who was Democratic majority leader in the legislature, 'and ask him to give us the money we'd need to hire a competent staff.'

"I did just that, and —— told me I was out of my mind—that he had more important things to do that session than to get into a hopeless fight with the Bell lobby. So I let it drop.

"A year or so later we did have a young firebrand of a lawyer come onto our staff. He knew economics, and he had taken quite a few courses in public utilities. He lasted seven months. Bell hired him at a salary 69 percent over what he made for us, and the last I heard he's in one of their offices way out West.

"I gave up trying to do anything in the telephone area and concentrated on bus fares. You can yell at the transportation companies without having the roof of the capital fall on your head. But Bell—well, my term was six years, and I'm too pragmatic a man to try to climb a mountain barefooted."

AT&T prefers to resolve rate issues without becoming enmeshed in a formal hearing before a regulatory agency—either state or the FCC. It generally succeeds, for there are few instances in which a Bell company has been required to put into the public record the data which it uses as the basis for rate changes. Under the Bell policy, the company presents privately and informally—often at the staff level—the reasons it thinks rate reductions or increases are necessary. This method tends to give an exaggerated picture of the agencies' activities, for even when the companies originate a rate reduction, it appears as a "commission order."

AT&T says it relies on this method because there is a minimum of expense, both to itself and to the commissions, and also a minimum of diversion of managerial talent to the rate-making process. Too, rate cases can be semiperpetuating in character if they are conducted properly. A New York Telephone Company case that began in 1920 was not resolved until 1930; an Ohio Bell case dragged from 1924 to 1937; a case in Michigan from 1919 to 1936. Another New York case in the 1950's had been before the utilities commission and the courts for six years when the Bell-dominated legislature abruptly intervened in the rate-making process and changed the state utility laws to give the phone company what it desired.

The danger of "negotiated" rate making, even when it results in periodical reductions of charges, is that the commission becomes dependent on the Bell companies for cost and profit data and seldom verifies it through outside examination.

AT&T is not an eleemosynary institution; it is a business, and businesses do not haphazardly surrender profits. When a Bell company voluntarily cuts a rate by 5 percent, objective review could reveal that the reduction should be two to three times that amount. The regulatory agencies, however, lack the zest for vigorous, independent inquiry that any man (or institution) must have to do the job properly.

The weakness of the states' rate making is well revealed in the disparities of charges for interstate and intrastate long-distance calls. About the only similarity in these rates is that they are stated in United States currency. Anyone who has even a minor encounter with AT&T discovers that it costs more to call a short distance than it does to call a greater distance.

The Bell statisticians have all sorts of figures to prove that the Southwestern Bell Telephone Company, for instance, spends more money in transmitting a citizen's call from Austin, Texas, to Texarkana, Texas, than it does from Austin to Texarkana, Arkansas. The Arkansas half of the twin city is divided from the Texas half by the width of a city street. Here are the comparable rates on calls from Austin:

	Station-day 3 minutes	Station-day 6 minutes	Person-day 3 minutes	Person-day 6 minutes
Texarkana, Tex.	$1.05	$2.10	$1.80	$3.60
Texarkana, Ark.	1.00	1.75	1.50	2.25

That these calls travel over the same long-distance facilities is irrelevant to Bell statisticians. They have the figures, and they say it costs less to call Arkansas than it does to Texas—not less per mile, mind you, but less, period.*

Because of the feebleness of the state agencies, AT&T keeps as much of its investment as possible under their jurisdictions. A dollar of investment that yields only 8.5 cents a year under Federal supervision brings from 10 to 12 cents if charged to Bell operations in Texas or Alabama. Also, although Bell's laboratory work has been directed toward maximum economies for telephone service as a whole, it has "produced the greatest toll lines economies on heavy routes and longer circuits which are predominantly interstate," in the words of the National Association of Regulatory Utility Commissioners.

Until the early 1920's intrastate and interstate rates generally were at the same level, based solely on mileage. Reductions in both categories between 1926 to 1946 generally left the per mile interstate rates lower than those for intrastate calls. Since the Second World War, interstate reductions have continued. Intrastate charges, however, are on the rise. The NARUC tabulates them as follows, based on the call that could have been made for $1 in 1940:

1940	$1.00	1961	$1.46
1945	.98	1962	1.46
1950	1.21	1963	1.45
1955	1.38	1964	1.45
1960	1.46	1965	1.43

There is no discernible pattern in the setting of intrastate long-distance rates. One reason is that only two states—California and Wisconsin—require the telephone company to distinguish its operating costs for intrastate toll service and local exchange service. The procedure is for the Bell company to give lump figures to the regulatory agency and to propose rates that put its *overall* return at the permissible level. There is no attempt to ascertain whether any particular part of the service is self-supporting—that is, whether intrastate long-

---

* A college friend of mine who knew something about mathematics once computed that if this were so and costs continued to drop at the same rate as the call went farther and farther from Austin, AT&T should pay *him* $1.71 when he called Chicago. He explained this in great detail to a long-distance operator one night. She hung up.

distance callers pay more than is necessary for their calls so as to keep residential rates low. In most states long-distance callers do pay more than their calls actually cost, the state commissions operating on the assumption that long-distance calling should be considered a "luxury" when compared to home service. Table I shows the wide range of prices citizens pay for the same intrastate toll service in the different states as compared with FCC pricing for interstate long-distance calls.

Table I

Disparities in
Long Distance Message Telephone Rates
of the Bell System in Effect June 1, 1968

Tolls for 6-Minute Person-to-Person Day Messages
under the Interstate and State Schedules
Between 7:00 A.M. and 5:00 P.M. Monday through Friday

	25 Miles	Per cent Excess of State	100 Miles	Per cent Excess of State	300 Miles	Per cent Excess of State
	Toll	Toll	Toll	Toll	Toll	Toll
Interstate	$ .80	–	$1.30	–	$2.25	–
Alabama	1.20	50%	2.45	88%	3.60	60%
Arizona	1.09	36	2.29	76	3.41	52
Arkansas	1.01	26	2.10	62	3.19	42
Calif.-Sch. A	1.10	37	2.05	58	3.10	38
Colorado	1.09	36	2.10	62	3.30	47
Connecticut	.85	6	1.45	12	–	–
Delaware	.80	0	1.30	0	–	–
Florida	.95	19	1.80	38	3.05	36
Georgia	.90	12	1.54	18	2.51	12
Idaho	1.09	36	2.21	70	3.41	52
Illinois	.90	12	1.85	42	3.70	64
Indiana	.90	12	1.64	26	2.99	33
Iowa	1.20	50	2.59	99	3.98	77
Kansas	1.01	26	2.21	70	3.60	60
Kentucky-So.	1.10	37	1.90	46	2.60	16
Kentucky- C. & S.	.95	19	–	–	–	–

| | 25 Miles | | 100 Miles | | 300 Miles | |
| | | Per cent Excess of State | | Per cent Excess of State | | Per cent Excess of State |
	Toll	Toll	Toll	Toll	Toll	Toll
Louisiana	$1.28	60%	$2.78	114%	$3.19	42%
Maine	.90	12	1.90	46	2.90	29
Maryland	.90	12	1.64	26	–	–
Massachusetts	.85	6	1.40	8	–	–
Michigan	.80	0	1.60	23	2.60	16
Minnesota	1.20	50	2.59	99	3.98	77
Mississippi	1.35	69	2.45	88	3.80	69
Missouri	1.01	26	2.21	70	3.60	60
Montana	1.20	50	2.81	116	4.10	78
Nebraska	.98	22	2.29	76	3.79	68
Nevada	1.00	25	2.75	112	4.20	87
New Hampshire	.80	0	1.30	0	–	–
New Jersey	.55	(31)	1.30	0	–	–
New Mexico	1.01	26	1.99	53	3.49	55
New York	.80	0	1.55	19	2.60	16
North Carolina	1.28	60	1.99	53	3.30	47
North Dakota	1.50	87	3.30	154	4.50	100
Ohio-Ohio Bell	1.00	25	1.55	19	2.75	22
Ohio-C. & S.	.65	(19)	–	–	–	–
Oklahoma	1.01	26	2.21	70	3.60	60
Oregon	.70	(12)	1.75	35	3.50	56
Pennsylvania	.80	0	1.30	0	2.25	0
Rhode Island	.70	(12)	–	–	–	–
South Carolina	1.35	69	2.40	85	–	–
South Dakota	1.39	74	2.78	114	4.20	87
Tennessee	1.10	37	1.93	48	2.92	30
Texas-Mtn.	.70	(12)	–	–	–	–
Texas-Sw.	1.01	26	2.10	62	3.41	52
Utah	1.00	25	2.10	62	3.35	49
Vermont	.90	12	1.45	12	–	–

( ) Indicates that intrastate bill is less than interstate bill.
SOURCE: National Association of Regulatory Utility Commissioners, "Message Toll Telephone Rate Disparities," July, 1968.

| | 25 Miles | | 100 Miles | | 300 Miles | |
| | | Per cent Excess of State | | Per cent Excess of State | | Per cent Excess of State |
	Toll	Toll	Toll	Toll	Toll	Toll
Virginia	$ .90	12%	$1.80	38%	$2.86	27%
Washington	1.00	25	2.80	115	4.60	104
West Virginia	1.35	69	2.25	73	–	–
Wisconsin	.90	12	1.65	27	2.68	19
Wyoming	.90	12	2.10	62	3.19	42
Between U.S. and Canada	.80	0	1.35	4	2.70	20

Each of the state regulatory agencies, at one time or another, has set a figure which it considers a fair return for phone companies operating within its jurisdiction. The Bell companies, however, consistently exceed these limits, and there is not much the states can—or will—do about the violations. The California PUC in 1964 ordered the Pacific Telephone & Telegraph Company to refund $80,000,000 in excess charges it had collected from citizens the preceding two years. But the California Supreme Court overturned the ruling as confiscatory, and PT&T kept the $80,000,000. (Moral: When a utility gouges the public through overcharges, it's accepted business practice; when a state regulatory commission demands that the utility return the loot, it's confiscation, and not to be tolerated.)

Figures on Bell earnings in individual states are extraordinarily untrustworthy. Many of the Bell companies operate in two or more states. New England Telephone & Telegraph Company, for example, runs the phone systems in Rhode Island, Massachusetts and Connecticut. And as Representative John O. Tiernan has said of the regulatory commissions in these states: "It is extremely difficult for them to be able to decipher the facts and figures that are presented. . . . They don't have the manpower. They don't have the money or the ability to hire these people that are necessary to determine whether or not this is all related to the operation in Rhode Island, for example." The only existing figures on state earnings come from Bell, which can charitably be called a prejudiced source. But even these figures reveal the extent to which the

Bell System violates the "limits" set on their returns by the state commissions. Senator Ralph Yarborough challenged the figures from AT&T during the early 1960's during one of his periodic campaigns against inequitable phone rates. In several states the rate of profit has increased in intervening years.

Table II

Bell System Earnings Ratios from Interstate, Intrastate and Total Operations, and Permissible Limits

Company	State	Inter-state	Intra-state	Over-all	Permissible
Illinois Bell	Ill.	7.7	8.2	8.1	4.04*
Southern New England Telephone & Telegraph	Conn.	7.7	6.8	7.0	6.00
New York Telephone	N.Y.	7.7	7.5	7.5	6.20
New Jersey Bell	N.J.	7.7	7.8	7.8	6.37
Pennsylvania Bell	Pa.	7.7	7.1	7.2	6.17
Diamond State Telephone	Del.	7.7	7.4	7.4	6.19
Chesapeake & Potomac of Dist. of Columbia	D.C.	7.7	7.5	7.5	6.25
Chesapeake & Potomac of Maryland	Md.	7.7	6.9	7.0	6.30
Chesapeake & Potomac of Virginia	Va.	7.7	7.2	7.2	6.38
Chesapeake & Potomac of West Virginia	W. Va.	7.7	6.3	6.5	6.45
Ohio Bell	Ohio	7.7	7.8	7.8	6.35
Michigan Bell	Mich.	7.7	7.1	7.2	6.80
Indiana Bell	Ind.	7.8	7.7	7.7	6.00
Wisconsin Telephone Company	Wis.	7.7	6.7	6.8	5.94
Bell of Nevada	Nev.	7.7	6.1	7.0	6.03
	Me.	--	--	6.7	6.00
	Mass.	--	--	8.2	6.35

* The Illinois rate base appears low because it is based on reproduction value of the telephone plant. Breakdown between interstate and intrastate returns is given only when company reports it to the Federal Communications Commission.

SOURCE: FCC submission to the Subcommittee on Communications of the Committee on Commerce of the United States Senate during hearings on FCC effectiveness

Company	State	Inter-state	Intra-state	Over-all	Permissible
New England Telephone & Telegraph	N.H.	– –	– –	6.8	6.20
	R.I.	– –	– –	7.0	6.25
	Vt.	– –	– –	6.9	6.00
	Ala.			7.0	6.20
	Ga.			7.4	6.20
	Ky.			7.1	6.10
Southern Bell Telephone	La.			6.9	6.00
	Miss.			7.0	4.96 to 5.08
	N.C.			7.3	5.14
	S.C.			6.7	5.50
	Tenn.			7.2	6.10
	Ia.			7.8	No state regulation at time of computation
Northwestern Bell Telephone	Minn.			7.7	4.75
	Nebr.			7.6	6.75
	N.D.			7.1	6.38
	S.D.			7.1	6.25
	Ark.			7.8	6.20
Southwestern Bell Telephone	Kan.			7.1	7.243
	Mo.			7.4	6.45
	Okla.			7.7	6.00
	Tex.			8.3	No state regulation
	Ariz.			6.5	6.25
	Colo.			7.8	6.69
	Ida.			7.7	6.35
Mountain States Telephone	Mont.			7.2	5.79
	N.M.			6.7	5.91
	Tex.			7.5	No state regulation
	Utah			7.5	6.25
	Wyo.			7.5	6.75
	Calif.			6.9	6.25

Company	State	Inter-state	Intra-state	Over-all	Permissible
Pacific Telephone &	Ida.			5.7	6.35
Telegraph	Ore.			6.9	6.35
	Wash.			7.3	6.25 to 6.50

A striking anomaly in AT&T's image of national uniformity is the widely varying rates for residential service. The telephone is as much a staple of life in modern America as is bread, yet it is a staple whose price varies more than 100 percent between Boston and Los Angeles. The NARUC gives this breakdown of the cost of one-party residential rates in the 25 largest U.S. cities as of June 30, 1969:

Los Angeles	$4.65	Atlanta	$6.50
San Francisco	4.65	Memphis	6.05
San Diego	4.90	Pittsburgh	6.15
San Antonio	5.50	Denver	6.30
Dallas	5.80	Seattle	6.45
New Orleans	5.60	Detroit	6.50
Chicago	5.60	Milwaukee	6.60
New York	6.00	Philadelphia	6.65
Cincinnati	5.65	Buffalo	6.75
Minneapolis	5.70	Cleveland	6.90
Washington, D.C.	5.95	St. Louis	6.65
Houston	7.75	Baltimore	7.70
		Boston	6.95

Exceeding the earning limitations set by the regulatory agencies is what we might call the visible overcharging of the Bell System. Concurrently, AT&T indulges in a less obvious overpricing that is every bit as costly to the American public. This overpricing isn't blatant corporate skulduggery, with AT&T keeping two sets of books to deceive regulatory agencies or illegally inflating the value of its plants with nonexistent buildings and machinery. The system works in a much more sophisticated manner, and it has several components.

One is AT&T's innate overconservatism, the tendency of system-produced, inbred executives to continue unquestioned the financial policies inaugurated during the heyday of Theodore N. Vail. There is no disturber of the peace whose job it is to sit at a desk and ask, "Why do we do this, and what changes could we make that would enable us to give the same service at lower costs?" Although Bell's expertise in technological innovation and exploration is unmatched elsewhere in American business, its financial rigidity would be better matched to the management of a nineteenth-century butcher shop. Another component is the lack of competitive and regulatory stimuli. And, finally, the public utility rate procedures are so incredibly complex that the lay citizen, even when he suspects his phone bill is unreasonable, does not have the mental equipment to dig out confirming evidence, and men don't start mass movements with slogans about the unfairness of corporate depreciation policies.

Telephone overpricing involves business and accounting policies over which honest men can differ—and with equal sincerity. Even purity of motive wouldn't detract from the fact that these policies force Americans to pay higher phone bills than is necessary. Here are some of the reasons why:

Accelerated Depreciation

Congress in 1954 amended the Internal Revenue Code to permit businessmen and industrialists to depreciate their equipment purchases for tax purposes at about double the actual physical depreciation rate. That is, if the Acme Company bought a whiffin-lathe for $100, and its actual value decreased by $10 per year, Acme could write it off at $20 a year, applying the extra $10 as an income tax reduction. The tax saving was supposed to encourage Acme to buy more whiffin-lathes; the economy, set rolling by the increased capital expenditures, was to maintain momentum and grow faster than it would were the more conventional depreciation schedules followed.

The American Telephone & Telegraph Company, unlike the majority of U.S. businesses, has failed to avail itself of the tax benefits possible under the amendment (Section 167 of the code). As a result, the American public has paid an unnecessary $4,209,479,000 for phone service. (That's right, $4.2 *billion.*)

AT&T's attitude toward accelerated depreciation seems peculiar to many persons in the public utilities field. Nor are the accelerated depreciation advocates "funny money" faddists

or nuts who think AT&T should be broken up and turned over
to the Peace Corps. Section 167 was adopted during a Republican Administration at the request of the American business
community, and American business is satisfied with the way
it has worked.

Donald C. Cook is president of the American Electric
Power Service Company. In 1967 he was one of the men Wall
Street considered for the presidency of the New York Stock
Exchange. He began an article on accelerated depreciation in
the prestigious *Public Utilities Fortnightly* in 1966 with these
words:

> If there were one thing to which we might expect business-
> men to be uniformly opposed, it would seem to be taxes. We
> are commonly supposed to devote much effort to reducing
> them, and it must come as a surprise to many that the manage-
> ment of some public utilities would rather pay taxes than not,
> and that others, while welcoming any accretion to cash re-
> sources, prefer to see their expenses undiminished.

Why so? There are two schools of thought. The stated
grounds on which AT&T refuses to consider accelerated depreciation and the suspicions of Bell watchers (notably the California PUC) that AT&T's conservatism in this area is intended
to keep its cash flow as high as possible.

AT&T offers several reasons: fear of impairment of its
financial integrity; fear that the tax laws might be amended
at some unspecified future date to drop accelerated depreciation; fear that the regulatory commissions would treat the tax
depreciation deductions as tax savings and flow them through
to customers in the form of rate reductions, rather than permit
their reinvestment in capital plant; fear of its inability to
convince the Internal Revenue Service of the correctness of
the deductions it claims; fear that the techniques could not
be applied to an operation so massive and far-flung as the Bell
System.

AT&T notes that the state regulatory agencies have differing
policies on depreciation. Some insist on the straight line
method, where a fixed percentage is deducted annually, and
would not recognize an accelerated write-off in their rate-
making process. Further, AT&T claims that taxes saved today
carry over as an obligation for tomorrow's phone users, and

AT&T has no way of knowing that telephone growth will continue unabated.

All but one of these problems might be surmountable, AT&T concedes. Its overriding concern is that any tax reductions gained would have to be passed on to customers as rate reductions. This risk, AT&T asserted to the FCC, "is aimed right at the heart of our financial integrity. This is a risk that we are not justified in taking."

Bell's argument is sorely flawed. As the company and the American economy continue to grow, the new depreciations available each year will more than amply cover both new expenditures and those of the past. Forty-three major electrical utility companies, including the giant Consolidated Edison of New York, as well as sixteen gas companies, apparently think so, for they use accelerated depreciation.

Melwood W. Van Scoyoc, of the California PUC, is one of the many economists who display more faith in the future of AT&T than does AT&T in disputing claims that Bell's growth cannot continue forever: "To assume that the Bell System will die or fade away at some indefinite time in the distant future and that its subscribers should pay rates at the present time to provide for the anticipated demise seems to me to be indulging in fantasy unparalleled in the history of utility regulation."

Donald C. Cook agreed that the issue of future tax liability is a bogus one. "The increase in taxes in later years in the case of liberalized depreciation . . . is only theoretical," he wrote in the *Public Utilities Fortnightly*. "It has been pointed out by many that, assuming a constant tax rate, taxes will never become greater as long as plant investment continues to expand or even remains stable because of replacements." Cook uses the adjectives "narrow, rigid, pessimistic and defeatist" in referring to utilities that reject accelerated depreciation.

The $4 billion overcharge (to round off the figure) is based on: (1) the taxes that AT&T would not have had to pay had it used accelerated depreciation; (2) the revenues necessary to produce the extra tax dollars; and (3) the use-of-money loss to consumers who paid the unnecessary dollars. William J. Powell, a financial expert on the staff of the Federal Power Commission, did the computations which produced this figure at the behest of the FCC in 1966. The data on capital expenditures on which Powell's study was based, it might be noted, came from AT&T.

One thought to ponder: If AT&T continues to ignore accelerated depreciation, and if AT&T's expansion follows the course predicted by AT&T, *the American public will pay another unnecessary $31 billion in telephone bills by 1995.*

Exaggerated Rate Base

It is to AT&T's advantage to include in its rate base every dollar it can and to put the highest possible value on every piece of equipment used to provide service. AT&T gives the broadest interpretation possible to the words "operating expense," for items in this category are charged to the consumer, not to the shareholder. Thus, AT&T for decades has insisted on a double return on certain of its monies. Here a prime part of the mechanism is its working-capital accounts—literally, the funds with which it does its day-to-day business.

The regulatory agencies agree that a utility is entitled to keep a reasonable amount of cash in the till for this purpose and to collect profits on the portion of it supplied by investors. Bell, however, constantly attempts to blur the distinction between capital provided by investors and capital provided by customers. Consider the month-in-advance revenues collected from telephone users. The amounts are substantial. In 1965 advance revenues from interstate and foreign ratepayers alone were an average of $133,600,000 on any given day.* These funds came from phone *users,* not phone *investors,* yet Bell nonetheless maintained they should be put into its rate base and return a profit. The FCC's authorized rate of return at this time was 7.25 percent, which means Bell "earns" $9,680,000 on its customers' money—said "earnings" to come from customers' pockets.

Bell also wants a profit (in the form of interest) on the tax funds it collects from customers and holds in special accounts until the time comes to pass them on to the government. The Bell System's total tax bill in 1966 was $2.7 billion. The tax dollars spend an average of forty-seven days in Bell's coffers en route to the tax collectors.

These dollars could be used to maintain required minimum

---

* Long-distance users do not, of course, pay for their calls in advance. However, under the separations system, a portion of AT&T's physical plant is assigned for long-distance use, and a portion of the monthly bill paid by subscribers—in advance—is counted as long-distance revenue.

Table III

Analysis of Possible Savings Lost to Bell System and to Its Consumers Because Liberalized Depreciation for Taxes Was Not Taken for Period 1954 Through 1965. (Thousands of Dollars)

Year (A)	Tax Effect (B)	Possible Revenue Reductions (C) Annual @	(D) Cumulative	Imputed Value of Money Lost to Consumers # (E) Annual	(F) Cumulative	Possible Savings Lost to Consumers Column D Plus Column F
1954	10,823	22,548	22,548	676	676	23,224
1955	34,185	71,219	93,767	3,530	4,206	97,973
1956	61,867	128,889	227,656	9,745	13,951	236,607
1957	88,440	184,250	406,906	19,724	33,675	440,581
1958	112,790	234,979	641,885	33,484	67,159	709,044
1959	131,615	274,197	916,082	50,769	117,928	1,034,010
1960	148,730	309,854	1,225,936	71,337	189,265	1,415,201
1961	166,914	347,737	1,573,673	95,344	284,609	1,858,282
1962	185,329	386,101	1,959,774	123,080	407,689	2,367,463

1963	202,224	421,299	2,381,073	154,687	562,376	2,943,449
1964	211,192	422,384	2,803,457	189,279	751,655	3,555,112
1965	222,671	428,214	3,231,671	226,153	977,808	4,209,479
	1,576,780			977,808		

@ Column C reflects the amount of revenue which AT&T had to collect to meet tax obligation of Column B. Based on varying income tax rates in effect during period, AT&T had to collect 208.333 percent of Column B in 1954–63, 200 percent in 1964, and 208 percent in 1965.

Computed by taking 3 percent of Column C plus 6 percent of Column D one year prior—3 percent represents one-half year interest.

SOURCE: FCC Staff Exhibit No. 29 in FCC Docket No. 16258: *In the Matter of American Telephone & Telegraph Company and the Associated Bell System Companies; Charges for Interstate and Foreign Communications Service*

bank balances and thus lessen the amount of working capital that must be obtained from investor sources, thereby reducing the amount of revenue required to support AT&T's rate base (and, in turn, cutting phone bills). Such a procedure would be legal, for as AT&T admits, "The government doesn't care what you do with them [the tax funds] as long as you pay them over to the government on the day they are due."

Bell, however, puts the tax funds into special accounts and collects interest on them. The California PUC stopped this practice in a 1964 rate case by stating that "as a tax collection agency of the United States government . . . [a] utility should not be seeking a return on funds that it has already collected." *

California disposed of the advance payments anomaly by deducting all consumer-supplied funds from the working cash requirement. The result left PT&T with a negative working cash requirement of $18,640,000, rather than the $8,957,000 requested—a difference of $27,597,000. Considering the California rate of return of 6.75 percent, this bookkeeping change alone meant a saving to customers of $1,860,000 a year.

Is the owner of an apartment house under construction entitled to receive rents while the foundations are still being poured? AT&T puts itself into an analogous situation by trying to include plant-under-construction in its rate base, even though the practice is forbidden by several state regulatory agencies. Here again the California PUC was pungent in halting the practice: "Such opportunities do not exist in the pragmatic everyday life of modern competitive American capitalism."

Bell's argument is that investors expect a return on all dollars they supply to an enterprise, regardless of whether the funds have actually been committed to productive activity. "Only in the warm climate in which regulated utilities bask is such a contention possible," California maintains. "[I]n the chilly climate of vigorous competitive enterprise, return comes from revenues, and revenues are impossible until plant is completed and operations begin." Allowing a full return on these "riskless and nonproductive cash assets" would permit cash balances to

---

* The PUC could not order the Pacific Telephone & Telegraph Company to take the tax funds out of the interest-drawing bank account and deposit them elsewhere. What it could (and did) do was to reduce PT&T's working capital requirement by the daily average of the tax funds on deposit.

rise to higher and higher levels. "Management would, no doubt, sincerely convince itself that such massive accumulations of cash were in the interest of the ratepayer. California contends, however, that the banking business is best left to the banks, who [sic] can obtain deposits at little or no cost and who are able to lend funds at an interest rate that is considerably lower than a full utility reasonable rate of return and the associated taxes on income."

Western Electric Charges to Bell

We explored earlier the intimacy and profitability of Western Electric's Siamese twin relationship with the Bell System and the difficulty encountered by regulatory agencies in attempting to determine whether Western's pricing is fair.

The California PUC found a route around this problem in 1964 by deciding that Western Electric's rate of return on its equipment sales should be no more than that allowed the Pacific Telephone & Telegraph Company on its California operations. Had Western Electric been held to this limit during the forty-six-year period 1916–61, chosen by the PUC for study, its earnings from sales to PT&T would have been reduced by $340,746,000 (the difference between its composite earnings of 9.1 percent and the composite 6.1 percent authorized by the PUC). Not only did this $340,000,000 come from phone subscribers' pockets, but they also had to pay PT&T an annual return on it averaging 6.1 percent.

The standard AT&T defense to accusations that Western Electric overcharges is to wave a comparative price list showing that non-Bell equipment manufacturers are higher. The technique is somewhat misleading.

[T]he massive and unique market enjoyed by the non-operating segments of [AT&T] in the purchases by operating segments provides an advantage so great in volume alone in each of the fields of manufacturing, installation, purchasing and distribution that competition is effectively eliminated [the California PUC stated]. Were [AT&T's] manufacturing, supply and installation unit not more efficient than outside suppliers who do not possess the manifold advantages enjoyed by Western, the very existence of Western under [AT&T's] control would be subject to great question. We find that little, if any, weight can be accorded such price comparisons in judging the reasonableness of Western's prices. It is the cost to Western that is significant.

And it is the cost to Western that regulatory agencies have never been able to ascertain. The expedient of limiting Western's return to that authorized for the parent AT&T is flawed in that it provides no way of establishing Western's true profits.

In addition to its suspect pricing of Western Electric equipment, AT&T takes another profit on the Western Electric profit. Items purchased from Western by the Bell operating companies are entered in their accounts at cost to them, "which includes the return realized by Western on its investment devoted to this business," (to use the language of the 1965 AT&T annual report). Once this equipment goes into the rate base of the Bell operating company, of course, the Bell company earns a second profit on it. "The Bell System, by recording its investment on its books in excess of its cost, makes a profit by taking in its own washing," asserted the California PUC.

Conservative Borrowing Practices

AT&T's board ownership fetish costs telephone subscribers some $250,000,000 a year in excess rates. As a matter of policy, AT&T shies away from debt in its capital spending plans, preferring to obtain new money through issues of stock and holding its debt ratio to one-third of its capital structure (that is, two-thirds of the funds invested in AT&T are in the form of stock, or equity, one-third in the form of bonds, or debt).

The cost of raising money with equity financing is considerably more expensive than through debt. People who buy stocks expect (and receive) a higher return than that which would be paid bondholders, for their money is risk capital. (The interest due bondholders must be paid before a company can declare dividends.) More important to telephone consumers, however, is the fact that a business can deduct interest charges from its income before it starts calculating its tax bill. Such cannot be done when the cost of capital takes the form of dividend payments. A dividend dollar, because of taxes, requires $1.92 of revenue (at 1967 tax rates). The difference comes from the consumer.

AT&T justifies equity financing with the stolid words "fiscal responsibility." Its officers maintain that it would be unsafe to increase the debt ratio, for interest charges continue even when the economy collapses. AT&T, if strapped for cash, could stop paying dividends (although it has never been forced to do so); it could not declare a moratorium on interest, and the Bell people feel their company could be ruined. They point backward in history to the experience of the railroads and electrical utilities, which collapsed resoundingly during the 1930's because their high debt ratios made it impossible for them to meet interest payments.

Much of American business disagrees with AT&T. One critic states, "An armored car would be good insurance against the risks of Broadway traffic, but you don't really need that kind of insurance." The telephone industry has been little affected by the three postwar recessions, for as the USITA stated, "Telephones are a basic utility with built-in recession resistance." Not only has the number of phones increased during the recessions, but the monthly revenues per telephone also went up: from $8.83 in 1953 to $9.14 in 1954; from $10 in 1957 to $10.25 in 1958; and from $10.80 in 1960 to $11.03 in 1961. Over the period 1950–65 Bell System sales increased faster than the gross national product—9.5 percent versus 6.2 percent.

AT&T doesn't think its debt ratio should be a matter of regulatory concern, ignoring the fact that the cost of capital has a direct bearing on what U.S. citizens are charged for their telephone service.

Although these AT&T policies have long been known to utility rate experts and although they are common to the entire Bell System, the Federal Communications Commission, despite its statutory obligation, did not begin to consider them within the structure of a formal rate case until October, 1965, thirty-three years after its establishment.

The blame must be shared by the appointive members of the commission, who for decades ignored pleas of its professional staff that AT&T be regulated, not watched from a distance, and the Congress, which annually succumbed to pressures of the AT&T lobbyists and refused to give the FCC enough competent personnel to do more than review the information supplied by AT&T.

The period beginning in 1953 deserves detailed examination, for it illustrates both the regulatory laxness of the FCC and the willingness of AT&T to take advantage of an ineffective agency at the expense of the American public.

In June of that year AT&T representatives called on Rosel H. Hyde, then the FCC chairman and who over the years was exceedingly sympathetic to the Bell System. The AT&T visitors complained of the company's "dangerously low" rate of return. No formal petitions were filed, nor did anything go into the public record to show that AT&T wanted higher rates. The AT&T people said that notwithstanding a continued rise in interstate long-distance traffic and revenues, the ratio of earnings to investments of the Bell System had shown a steady decline since late 1951. As reasons they cited plant expansion during a period of inflation, wage and income tax increases, and a separations procedural change which resulted in assignment of more Bell System facilities to interstate long-distance use.

FCC calculations put the return then being earned at 5.1 percent. AT&T, which uses a higher plant valuation in its bookkeeping system, set the return at 4.8 percent. No matter which figure was accepted, FCC chairman Hyde said, the FCC thought that the "interstate earnings were deficient" and that an increase "to about 6.5 percent . . . would be within the bounds of reasonableness."

The FCC's Common Carrier Bureau (of which the telephone division is a part), while agreeing that the reported rate of return was insufficient, tried to alert the commissioners about the source of the data from which it was derived:

> It should be kept in mind that such figures are constructed from operating results data as reported to the commission by the company. In other words, the operating expense items included by the Bell System and the base to which its earnings are related have not been subjected to any detailed examination by the commission to determine the propriety of all amounts reported as plant investment and operating expense.
>
> To the extent that any such amounts should be found to be improper for rate-making purposes, the above return figures would be increased and thereby reduce the amount of revenue required to produce whatever return the commission will decide is fair and reasonable.

As the commission knows, questions have been raised from time to time by its staff as well as by other telephone regulatory bodies concerning various matters which have an important bearing upon Bell System revenue requirements, but which have never been the subject of a formal determination by this commission for rate-making purposes.

To boost AT&T earnings to the 6.5 percent level deemed reasonable by the FCC required $65,000,000 annually in new revenues (apart from taxes), which in turn meant an 8 percent increase in interstate phone rates. The company in September, 1953, filed a new rate schedule asking for such increases.

In considering rate increase requests the FCC can do one of three things: (1) suspend the increases for three months pending a decision, after a hearing, on their lawfulness; (2) let the rates take effect, but begin an investigation in which the phone company would have the burden of proving at a formal hearing that the increases were necessary, and then prescribe the "just and reasonable rates" to be charged by the carrier in the future; or (3) take no action whatsoever and permit the rates to become effective. The last alternative implies no determination on the justness and reasonableness of the rates, although they remain legal until such time as the commission decides otherwise at a formal hearing or through its own administrative action.

The staff warned that if AT&T were forced into a public hearing "the amount of increased revenues for which Bell would undertake to show justification would likely be considerably greater than the 66 million [dollars] involved herein." For example, the staff said, AT&T "would probably contend for a rate base reflecting reproduction or replacement cost of plant," rather than the considerably lower real-cost valuation then employed by the FCC. If this were to be allowed by the FCC or by courts on appeal, the staff said, the amount of revenue required to produce a fair rate would "greatly increase."

The staff's warning is a revealing commentary on FCC rate-making policies. It demonstrates the strong bargaining power that AT&T wields in a negotiation type of regulation: "Give me this amount, and I'll be satisfied; make me work for an increase, and I'll work for more." It shows that both sides are prone to compromise rather than risk total defeat in a formal hearing. And it shows the lack of an objective base for determining what is a justifiable rate of return and that reasonableness in actuality is no more than a mixture of educated guess, corporate aspiration, and regulatory permissiveness.*

The increases were the first general ones for interstate service the FCC had ever considered in its history—and it let them become effective by sitting silently and taking no action whatsoever. Only one commissioner dissented. Mrs. Frieda B. Hennock charged that by "passing on the reasonableness of such a sizable rate increase without sworn testimony and evidence subject to cross-examination . . . the commission is abdicating its responsibilities" under the Communications Act of 1934.

(A year later the White House, through Presidential assistant Sherman Adams, inquired of the FCC whether AT&T "dictated" terms of the increase, as a citizen had complained in a letter to President Eisenhower. Hyde responded with a letter denouncing the "falsity and unfairness" of the citizen's charge—and said nothing to dispute the fact that AT&T received exactly what it requested from the FCC.)

The increase became effective on October 1, 1953, and despite a continued dip in long-distance traffic (the nation still felt the economic effects of the end of the Korean War), the higher rates sent AT&T's interstate return to 6.5 percent almost immediately. In the last quarter of 1954, long-distance traffic began turning upward, soaring a full 10 percent over the preceding year, and the rate of return went to 7.7 percent.

The FCC staff, noting these figures, began what was to become its most frustrating pastime of the next three years: reminding the commission that AT&T was doing far better than the 6.5 percent return that had been anticipated with the 1953 increases. In constrained language the Common Carrier Bureau said the earnings were "liberally adequate to insure the financial integrity and safety of the capital invested in the plant devoted to the furnishings of these services."

This memo went to the FCC at its June 29, 1955, meeting. Bernard Strassburg, chief of the bureau's telephone division,

---

* Senator Russell Long says his late father, Huey, used the same strategy in reverse while a member of the Louisiana Public Service Commission. If Southern Bell or another utility reacted coolly to a suggested rate reduction, Huey Long would threaten to double the amount of the cut he wanted and tell the company, "I'll see you in court." Because of this leverage, Huey Long's version of negotiation proved very effective.

says, "There was discussion, as there is on all of these memoranda, and the commission decided to take no action at that time."

With the FCC's acquiescence, AT&T's long-distance profits soon far surpassed the "justifiable and reasonable" rate of 6.5 percent set in 1953. By July, 1956, the return reached 8.4 percent—almost a third more than authorized. The Common Carrier Bureau kept writing memoranda on the excess returns, six times in all between June, 1955, and October, 1957. Twice the memoranda recommended reductions, but the FCC wouldn't even give the staff permission to open informal negotiations to see if AT&T would be willing to reduce rates voluntarily. As a result, the American people paid grossly higher telephone bills than the FCC had authorized.

Strassburg estimates that had the commission held AT&T to the authorized 6.5 percent, telephone users would have saved "roughly $52 million" in 1955, $62,000,000 in 1956, and $45,-000,000 in 1957, a total of $159,000,000 during the period of the staff's most vocal protests.

When the House Antitrust Subcommittee headed by Representative Emanuel Celler made growling sounds about the excess profits in the spring of 1958, the FCC busied itself finally with a negotiated reduction of $45,300,000 a year. There was scant effect on Bell. Long-distance returns were 7.9 percent in 1959; 7.8 percent the next year; 7.7 percent in 1961. Again, the FCC declined its staff's recommendation that a serious study be made of AT&T's return. (By this time, according to Celler's computations, AT&T's returns for 1955–61 were $985,000,000 above the authorized 6.5 percent—*nearly a billion dollars in excess telephone payments by the U.S. public.*)

The FCC finally agreed with its critics in 1961 that the difference between AT&T earnings and the permissible limit made an unsightly gap, so it moved to narrow it—by increasing its definition of an "acceptable" return from 6.5 percent to 7.5 percent.

Celler's ire gradually rose. He said the FCC had "a most curious generosity in granting rate increases to AT&T" and flogged its "negotiations rather than hearings" policy. "Negotiate? Why negotiate rates? It's dead wrong . . . the time must come when that must change."

The highly respected management firm of Booz, Hamilton

and Allen made a study of the FCC for the Bureau of the
Budget in 1961–62 and found little worthy of commendation.
The study team said the Common Carrier Bureau was ill-
equipped physically and financially to oversee "the largest
corporate enterprise in the world"—the Bell System. Booz,
Hamilton and Allen wrote:

> Further, there is evidence that much of the bureau staff be-
> lieves that the commission has far less interest in the bureau's
> activities than is warranted. Under these circumstances, bureau
> management has been adequate but uninspired.
>
> . . . It is clear that the important functions of surveillance
> and regulation of common carrier rates and rate base have not
> been adequately undertaken. These functions do not seem to
> have been accorded an appropriately high priority by the
> commission in the allocation of resources and direction of
> attention.
>
> While the staff has sought to establish essential criteria for
> judging rates of return, the commission, in fact, has established
> no firm criteria governing such rates . . . and does not dem-
> onstrate that the reductions negotiated actually bring the
> overall rate of return down to reasonable limits. This actuality
> merits far greater emphasis if the public interest is to be
> properly served.

Noting that the Bell System has a physical plant valued at
twenty-five times that of all other common communications
carriers combined and that it "constitutes the largest corporate
enterprise in the world," Booz, Hamilton and Allen stated:
"The existence of this huge strategic enterprise places a particular burden on the Federal government to look to the public
interest."

An agency slapped with such a damning appraisal can either
refute it or accept it as true and make the recommended re-
forms. The FCC did neither. Instead, it collaborated with
AT&T in a rate-making mockery which one cynic on the FCC
staff offers as proof that "phone rates can go up and down
simultaneously, right before the eyes of the unaware public."

The mockery was AT&T's so-called after 9 long-distance
rates, which the FCC pridefully called "one of the major
accomplishments of the year" in its 1963 annual report.

The charade was announced in February, 1963, by the FCC
in a press release with the boldface, mouthful caption: "FCC

ANNOUNCES PLAN FOR REDUCED NIGHTTIME TELEPHONE RATES
OF $1 OR LESS TO ANY POINT WITHIN CONTINENTAL UNITED
STATES."

What the rates did was to permit phone users to call station
to station between 9 P.M. and 4:30 A.M. for $1 or less. Pre-
viously, the charge for a call from Washington to the West
Coast had been $1.75. The release continued: "The 'after 9'
reduced rates are designed to encourage telephone users to
take advantage of the technological improvements in telephone
plant introduced by the Bell System in recent years, much of
which is engineered for peak daytime usage."

The press release rambled on for some 200 words and then
began talking about "small increases of 5 to 10 cents in person-
to-person calls up to 800 miles." The FCC stated that these
calls "have not borne their proportionate share of the cost of
furnishing such services, and these minor increases will help
to correct this inequity. . . ."

What the press release *did not say* is that some 82 percent of
the person-to-person long-distance calls handled by AT&T are
for distances of less than 800 miles. The mileage limitation
proposed by AT&T (and accepted by the FCC) encompassed
comfortably the most populated areas of the United States:
Washington to Chicago is 693 miles; swing the arc southward,
and it brushes the Gulf of Mexico; swing it northward, and it
goes far beyond Boston, top of the megalopolis of the Eastern
Seaboard.

Further, the "minor" increases in the person-to-person rates
weren't exactly minor when you consider that adding 10 cents
to the 50-cent toll between Washington and Baltimore means
a 20 percent rise in price.

Senator Ralph Yarborough immediately saw what AT&T
and the FCC were doing and the reasons AT&T put the decreases into the after-9 time period. "That is because people
weren't using that 2,300 miles after 9 o'clock," he told Rosel
Hyde of the FCC at 1963 hearings on FCC's effectiveness.
"You had space open there when lines weren't being used.
Didn't the telephone company really do this like an airline will
put in a tourist rate, hoping to lure more traffic in? Don't they
hope to make more money out of that dollar rate? They didn't
put that in just to give something away.

"Don't you think that . . . there are many, many more times

the number of people calling within an 800-mile limit than the after-9 callers at 2,300, or 1,200 or 1,000 miles?

"Aren't you making the masses pay for the calls of a few, when you cut the long rate after 9 and raise evedybody else 5, 10, 15 or 20 percent?"

Hyde resisted. "No, sir. As a matter of fact, our findings would indicate that telephone users generally were contributing more than they should to the cost of this person-to-person, under 800-mile business. In other words, this business was not paying its proportionate share of the cost of running the plant. We did not increase these rates for the purpose of making up to the telephone company any costs incident to the adoption of the after-9 plan."

Then Senator Yarborough proceeded to ask Hyde six consecutive times whether the FCC had done any analyses of the costs of the different categories of long-distance calls that would justify his statement that the short-mileage person-to-person calls were not self-supporting. Five times Hyde resisted. "We had information submitted," he said once. "We get our information from them [the phone company]," he said at another juncture. Finally, Yarborough got him to the mat: "We did not send out any engineers or investigators. . . ." Hyde conceded.

Yarborough couldn't conceal his suspicions that the after-9 plan was nothing more than a token gesture to divert attention away from the increases in the other categories. He had grounds for suspicions. In the same hearings, after solemn denials by Hyde that any "deal" had been made, Newton Minow (then the FCC chairman) let drop a most significant remark.

While still arguing that the after-9 rate was a "very good idea," Minnow continued: "But if you asked me if the telephone company came in and said they wanted to raise short-haul person-to-person rates, period . . . I would say I would have been opposed to that."

If there is any fairness to regulation, AT&T either deserved the person-to-person increase or didn't deserve it, and the public was entitled to the after-9 cut or was not entitled to it. The moral is that when the FCC and AT&T start making a commotion about what they are giving away, the discerning citizen should immediately ask, "Okay, what's it going to cost me?"

Perhaps people are more long-winded on the telephone than they were a decade ago, but AT&T's revenue per interstate message has risen steadily since 1956—in spite of the "reduction" gimmicks such as the after-9 rate:

1956	$1.54
1957	1.58
1958	1.60
1959	1.65
1960	1.65
1961	1.70
1962	1.74
1963	1.75
1964	1.79
1965	1.76
1966	1.83

The series of events which ultimately goaded the FCC into its first full-fledged, on-the-record study of the American Telephone & Telegraph Company's rate structure began at the other end of the United States, in the California State Building in San Francisco, the starkly modern headquarters of the California Public Utilities Commission.

The Pacific Telephone & Telegraph Company, the Bell subsidiary which owns most California telephones, since the Second World War has followed the same pattern as other Bell operations around the country. It has slowly but inexorably increased the price for local telephone service, especially for intrastate calls, while devoting cost-cutting efforts to the interstate field. During the period 1948–58 PT&T seven times asked rate increases in California totaling, on an annual basis, $234,692,000. The PUC approved $114,887,000 of these requests. PT&T's authorized rate of return rose along with phone prices: 5.6 percent from 1948–54; 6.25 to 1958; then 6.75 percent.

But PT&T's appetite was insatiable. In 1962 its representatives told the PUC that soon the company would be asking for more money—and considerably more money. This request came almost simultaneously with a shift in the ideological balance of the PUC. (No more shall be said, for rate regulation is complex enough without wandering off into California politics.)

Previously, the commission had followed the FCC's "negotiation" system of regulation, permitting the PT&T to present its case in private, then to increase its rates.

This time, however, the PUC refused to approve the hikes automatically. Instead, the commission heeded staff studies which questioned the necessity of an increase and of the propriety of various PT&T bookkeeping techniques.

The PUC ordered formal hearings, and PT&T couldn't prove its case. The PUC found that PT&T had overcharged California subscribers $40,722,000 for their service in a single year (on billings of $1.4 billion). The PUC ordered sharp cuts in phone bills: 45 cents a month in individual line residential service; 70 cents a month in business service; from 10 to 15 percent on intrastate toll calls—in sum, decreases in every category of service.

The savings to Californians didn't come easily. The commission began its inquiry on July 26, 1962, and held forty-nine days of public hearings over fifteen months. The record of the case runs more than 7,000 pages, with additional thousands of pages of exhibits. The commission's order, issued on June 11, 1964, was appealed to the California Supreme Court by PT&T and was upheld on April 28, 1965. Several more months were required to put the lower rates into effect.

All in all, a whopping expenditure of time, manpower and money. "For several years all we thought about around here was 7409," a PUC staff member says, referring to the rate case by its docket number.

All through the hearings certain of the PUC staff members held another thought in their minds. AT&T and the associated Bell companies share common operating practices. Southern Bell, Northwestern Bell, PT&T, New England Telephone & Telegraph follow the same depreciation formulas, use the same income tax procedures, buy their gear through Western Electric at the same prices, divide their revenues between interstate and intrastate phone use in the same manner. From an operational and financial point of view, therefore, the nineteen associated companies are carbon copies one of the other and, in turn, of the parent AT&T.

Thus, it could be said that what a state regulatory agency finds in one Bell company could be discovered elsewhere in another. Further, if PT&T could be treed, so could the other Bell companies and also AT&T.

California had no particular interest in intrastate rates in other states, for such matters fall outside its jurisdiction. However, the PUC was concerned over the interstate rates paid by Californians, a concern heightened by the FCC's then unwillingness to regulate AT&T. As soon as the California Supreme Court upheld the rate reduction finding, the PUC filed a federal court suit asking that the FCC be required to reopen a recently announced "negotiated" cut in interstate rates and that it be compelled to investigate to determine whether AT&T's rates indeed were "justifiable and reasonable."

The suit put the FCC in a tenuous position. California could cite its own rate case findings as evidence that something was frightfully wrong with U.S. telephone rates. California could cite the FCC's own intraoffice memoranda from the Common Carrier Bureau as evidence that the commission's staff felt that a proper job was not being done. And California could cite AT&T's own profit figures on interstate long-distance service as evidence that the company had exceeded the 7.5 percent return limit set by the FCC in 1961 and in earlier years had violated other, lower limits. Finally, certain of the FCC members were wearying of having Congressmen chide them in appropriations hearings each year about why they had never conducted a formal rate investigation.

But the FCC did not want to reopen the rate increase case which had prompted the California PUC's suit, for to do so would cloud the propriety of its "continuing negotiation" technique of regulation.

The FCC worriedly searched for a way out and found it in another AT&T rate case that was then pending. Bell and Western Union were feuding over charges for private leased wires, with Western Union claiming that AT&T was doing some old-fashioned price cutting to drive it from the market. The FCC asked AT&T for cost data on its various categories of interstate service that fall within the federal regulatory jurisdiction.

This study was submitted by AT&T on September 10, 1965, soon after the filing of the California suit. The FCC professional staff, long anxious for a chance to conduct an in-depth study, saw what was in the report and recognized it as the desired opening. The full commission agreed (although Rosel Hyde, AT&T's friend, argued against an investigation in private before announcement of the publicly unanimous decision). On October 27 the commission issued a five-page memorandum and order stating that the AT&T report "disclosed wide variations in earnings" among the various interstate services:

> At one extreme, message toll telephone and WATS [wide area telephone service] were earning at the rate of 10 percent and 10.2 percent, respectively, while Telpak, at the other extreme, was earning at the rate of .3 percent. . . .
>
> It is significant that message toll telephone and WATS services, with the highest level of earnings, account for 85 percent of total interstate revenues.
>
> Although certain message toll telephone rates were reduced, effective February 1 and April 1, 1965, subsequent to the study period, the current level of earnings on total interstate operations is above the total level of interstate earnings which obtained during the study period. These levels of earnings, as well as the wide variations in such levels for the different classes of service, indicate the desirability for a thorough examination by the commission of the interstate rate structure of the Bell System to determine the lawfulness of the rate levels and rate relationships within the structure.
>
> The importance of such a determination is underscored by the fact that certain of the services involved are furnished in direct competition with services offered by other carriers [i.e., Telpak and Teletypewriter services]. To the extent that these services may be underpriced by the Bell System, this may have a competitive impact on such other carriers.

The FCC posed five broad questions to be answered in the study:

—The revenue requirements of the Bell System companies applicable to interstate and foreign communication services and the basis on which they should be determined;

—Whether the overall charges of the Bell companies are "just and reasonable" within the meaning of the Federal Communications Act of 1934;

—Whether the charges for individual categories of interstate services (ordinary toll, private line, WATS, etc.) are reasonable;

—Whether the charges for these services would subject any persons to "unjust or unreasonable discrimination" or give anyone preference or advantage;

—Whether the commission should prescribe "just and reasonable charges" for interstate services and, if so, what they should be.

For a company that says it "welcomes" regulation, AT&T's reaction was furious. Frederick R. Kappel, then the AT&T board chairman and chief executive officer, called the investigation "totally unwarranted and unnecessary," and added: "The telephone-using public will be the loser." He urged continuation of the old "continuing surveillance-negotiation" system of rate making. Although the FCC's order was perhaps the most significant phone action in its history, Kappel insisted the company had "absolutely no inkling" that the commission intended to start the probe. (FCC staff members tell another story. They assert that Edward B. Crosland, AT&T's chief Washington lobbyist, was still arguing against the investigation with FCC members up until the morning of the day the decision was announced.)

AT&T stock had been caught in a general market decline for eighteen months, sliding from a peak of $75 to $66.875 on October 27, the day of the AT&T announcement. Investors interpreted the investigation as an indication that AT&T rates —and profits—were to be cut, a belief heightened by what one FCC member calls the "stuck pig" reaction of AT&T management. Certain FCC members felt then—and still think—that had AT&T simply stated that it disagreed with the decision and withheld the pained histrionics and forecasts of telephone disaster, there would have been little change in the stock prices.

Wall Street's reaction was equally visceral. Merrill Lynch, Pierce, Fenner and Smith, whose 7,000,000-plus shares of AT&T stock made it one of the largest single investors in Bell, then as now, sent out a "flash" wire to its offices downgrading AT&T stock and recommending against additional purchases. John H. Moller, a Merrill Lynch officer, later admitted that his firm sent the wire without having read the FCC's order. Despite the flash (which Merrill Lynch never bothered to rescind), the holdings of its customers increased markedly during the months after the order.*

AT&T stock prices reflected the Cassandra attitudes of AT&T

---

* From early 1966 through early 1967, according to a study by the New York Stock Exchange, AT&T gained 249,000 shareholders—slightly below its 1965–66 rise of 325,000, but "easily the largest gain registered by any company. The percentage gain was 8.8 percent—highest among the five companies with the largest number of shareholders.

and the brokerage houses. They dipped quickly below $60, and in three months investors suffered a "paper loss" of $3.7 billion. FCC statements which sought to reassure investors that it did not intend to ruin the company sent it back above $60 briefly in February; later, however, the slide began anew, to a 1966 low of $49.75.

Each day FCC members blearily read through denunciatory letters from stockholders and listened to angry telephone calls from Congressmen who demanded that the hearings be canceled.

An AT&T Shareowners Committee, headed by Manhattan lawyer Benjamin Javits, brother of Senator Jacob Javits, bought newspaper advertisements: "AT&T Holders! Worried? Read! Act!" Javits' committee urged that shareholders "speak up" against the commission. It suggested that the hearing order "may have started a chain reaction that depressed AT&T stock and contributed to a general market decline." More than 3,000 persons joined within ten days, and added their typewriters to a Letters to Washington campaign with the theme "A large segment of our population is being damaged by an ill-conceived and unfair act on the part of its government." Javits' people became so vociferous he ultimately begged them to desist lest they irritate the commission and damage the phone company's position.

The FCC ignored this noise as best it could and went about collecting evidence and preparing for its hearings. It decided to split them into three phases: determination of a fair return; an exploration of the mechanics and philosophy of rate making; and AT&T's relationship with Western Electric. Some 103 parties were given permission to appear—35 state utility commissions, other communications carriers, broadcast and television networks, press agencies, private businesses and trade associations dependent on communications, federal agencies that are big Bell customers.

All these parties churned out impressive quantities of statistics and paper: 66 witnesses testified during 71 days of hearings, their words filling 10,094 pages of transcript. The 119 exhibits put into evidence added another 3,485 pages to the case file. AT&T detached more than 100 employees to devote their full time to the case, and hired numerous outside consultants. AT&T's prepared testimony, submitted in advance of appearances by its witnesses, formed a stack of paper some 4.2 feet high and weighing 23.7 pounds.

Yet one class of individuals went unrepresented: The American consumer.

Soon after instituting the rate case the FCC emasculated small consumer protection by issuing a procedural order crippling its staff's advocacy of citizen interests. "The function of the Common Carrier Bureau is *not* to be the advocate of a preconceived position or to take a conventional adversary position," the commission ordered. "Rather it is to ensure the development of a full and complete record which presents the facts and other rate-making considerations relevant to a fair and meaningful legislative determination by the commission of the complex issues involved."

Utility rate cases are trial-type hearings in which effective advocacy maximizes the strength and minimizes the weakness of each position so that the regulatory authority will be helped to understand the weakness of each position fully. The commission order in effect made the rate proceeding a one-sided fight. On the one hand, Bell was permitted to be an advocate for a preconceived position and to take a conventional adversary position. On the other hand, the staff was left in the position of referee. David C. Fullarton, Executive Secretary of the National Telephone Cooperative Association, comments tartly of this situation: "Bell can aim haymakers at the staff as and when it chooses, but the consumer protector cannot take the offensive or attempt to trade blow for blow. It may on occasion return a blow but whenever it has referee duties to perform it must avoid swinging. Throughout the case, Bell's advocates are free to do anything that suits their strategy but the staff must play referee even when effective consumer advocacy would require them to be fiercely partisan."

The bankers and financiers who profit from AT&T stock issues and bond sales presented the backbone of the AT&T case, which was that the company needed earnings high enough to make its stock attractive to investors when compared with alternative purchases. The witnesses said U.S. economic conditions demanded a return that would permit investors to earn 10 percent on their equity—which translates into an AT&T earning of 7.5 to 8.5 percent of its plant value, "preferably in the upper end of the bracket," as one economist stated. The financial witnesses sounded gloomy indeed about Bell's investment value.

John Moller of Merrill Lynch, Pierce, Fenner and Smith computed that a man who invested $1,000 in AT&T on January 1, 1950, would have stock with a market value of $2,488 on December 31, 1965. In the same sixteen-year period, $1,000 invested in International Business Machines would have swelled to $27,250, and $1,000 in what is now Xerox to $606,000. Moller said, "If a portfolio were submitted to us for review, we would suggest to the client that he hold American Telephone. But we would not include it as a purchase recommendation."

Charles W. Buek, of the U.S. Trust Company, asserted that his company had sold more AT&T stock than it had purchased since 1964. Investors were no longer impressed with AT&T's regular dividends. "Growth is weighed now more heavily than ever before and dividend return less heavily," he said.

In other words, these financiers expected the phone consumer to pay rates enabling the telephone monopoly to match the growth rate of two of the fastest growing speculative stocks in Wall Street history. IBM and Xerox were stock market aberrations whose fantastic growth is attributable to the new products they marketed (computers and copying equipment). To expect AT&T to match their performance is either greed or wishful thinking. But none of the financial experts arguing for high phone returns could be termed impartial. They included, among others:

—Moller, whose firm, Merrill Lynch, regularly acts as underwriter for AT&T securities issues and is one of the largest holders of AT&T stock.

—Buek, whose company, U.S. Trust, is trustee for half of the New York Telephone Company pension trust fund, is the New York registrar for the securities issues for five Bell System companies, and maintains special accounts for the paying of interest of two Bell System bond issues. H. P. Moulton, vice-president and general counsel of AT&T, is a member of the U.S. Trust board.

—Adrian M. Massie of Chemical Bank of New York and Trust Company, which administers the AT&T and Western Electric pension trust funds, holds bank accounts of AT&T and New York Telephone, and has established a line of credit for AT&T, Western Electric, and New York Telephone totaling $150,000,000. H. I. Romnes, AT&T board chairman; Irwin

Miller, AT&T director; and Harold Helm, Western Electric president and an AT&T director, all serve as board members of the Chemical Bank.

—F. J. McDiarmid, associated with a life insurance company which holds Bell System securities.

—Gustave L. Levy, associated with Goldman, Sachs & Company, which has been underwriter for many Bell System security issues. He is a director of New York Telephone.

These men, of course, have a keen interest in keeping Bell earnings as high as possible, and they testified that the primary objective of the stock portfolios they represent is to seek growth in value, as well as regular dividends. One of them said outright that the ability of his firm to retain clients depends on how well it does in comparison with portfolios managed elsewhere. And another, asked how he would characterize AT&T earnings during a particular period, replied, "Woefully low." During this period AT&T had raised almost $5 billion in new capital—hardly the mark of a company in the doldrums.

The pessimism of this testimony was calculated. AT&T has to provide justification for its earnings level, which continued to rise even as the hearings progressed. During the nineteen months between January, 1966, and July, 1967, the monthly rate of return was at, or above, 8.5 percent for nine months. In five of those months it exceeded 8.9 percent—in March, 1966, hitting 9.17 and in August, 1966, 9.33 percent. The FCC, it must be noted, had not changed its 1961 ruling that 7.5 percent was an equitable return—and here was AT&T almost one-third in excess of the permissible limit. Thus, the dire portrayals of AT&T's standing in the investment community.

Testimony presented by the California Public Utilities Commission did much to dash the insinuations of AT&T witnesses that Bell stock is slow-growing, poor-paying, and thus unattractive as an investment. One Bell expert produced data showing that the average price of the twenty-four stocks in the Moody's Utilities group rose from $34.05 per share in 1946 to $117.08 in 1965, an increase of 243.8 percent. By comparison, the market price of AT&T rose from $30.95 to $66.83, an increase of 115.9 percent (adjusted to allow for stock splits).

"From the foregoing data we are led to infer that AT&T shareholders have fared very poorly indeed," the California PUC noted tartly. Then it used the same stocks and charted comparative growth since 1929, rather than 1946. The twenty-four utilities began the period with an average price of $133.20, and in 1965 were at $117.08—a *decrease* of 12.4 percent. By comparison AT&T stock rose from $39.50 in 1929 to $66.93 in 1965, or an *increase* of 69.44 percent.

"In other words," said California, "how poorly or how well AT&T stock has performed in comparison with . . . utilities depends primarily on the base year that is selected for the comparison."

The Federal Communications Commission's decision in the rate phase of the case was issued July 5, 1967. It is notable both for what it said and what it avoided saying.

The FCC refused to rule on the merits of requiring the Bell companies to adopt accelerated depreciation as a means of cutting their federal tax requirements, thereby reducing costs to phone users and increasing returns to shareholders. The commission did promise to "evaluate" this question at a later date; as of December 1969, it had not done so. While it ponders, the public pays half a billion a year extra in telephone bills because of AT&T's failure to use an accounting technique employed by other utilities.

When the commission decided early in the inquiry that the debt-ratio question was a valid subject for investigation, AT&T moved to vent the issue. It announced it had decided to start raising more of its money through bond issues, rather than stock sales, and to pass on the savings to phone subscribers. AT&T's debt-ratio at the time was about 35 percent; by 1969, it was 40 percent. By declining to set any specific equity-debt ratio in Bell's capital structure, the FCC left AT&T free to revert to its fiscal arch-conservatism at any time it desires—and there are professional staff at the FCC who remain dubious of Bell's long-range intentions.

For two short months the FCC appeared to have dealt a serious blow to Bell's "double-profit" system of earning on funds that are not its own and that are not in productive use. It ordered AT&T to exclude from its rate base $296,300,000 of working capital that consisted of precollected taxes and payments which customers had made in advance and $544,-044,000 of plant-under-construction. The net effect of these exclusions would be to lower AT&T's revenue requirement by $63,000,000 a year—a saving that could have been passed directly to consumers. This AT&T would not tolerate. After a brief flurry of appealing petitions the commission relented and permitted Bell to keep the $544,044,000 in its rate base, thereby wiping out $40,800,000 of the possible rate cut.

On the subject of rates, the FCC's decision was dangerously ambiguous.

The FCC ruled that a "fair rate of return to [AT&T] on their interstate operations is in the range of 7 to 7.5 percent." It ordered AT&T to reduce interstate rates sufficiently to cut its revenues by $120,000,000 annually, so as to drop its earnings —then at 8.25 percent—into the prescribed range. (AT&T was permitted to defer $20,000,000 of this cut until late 1968 out of the professed fear that earnings might fall below the 7 percent level.)

But the FCC made clear that the 7 to 7.5 percent bracket was by no means a firm ceiling. The order, it stated, "is not to be construed to mean that any future level of earnings which exceeds 7.5 percent or falls below 7 percent will warrant immediate action toward rate adjustments. Whether or not remedial action will be required will depend upon all relevant circumstances obtaining at the time."

These last two sentences, as we shall discover in a moment, constituted a loophole that, in effect, made a mockery of the entire proceeding.

Despite the fact that the first-phase decision had no significant effect upon its business, AT&T greeted it as a veritable declaration of war. AT&T called the 7 to 7.5 percent earnings bracket a "bare bones rate of return contrary to the law and the evidence," and its executives spoke grimly of the company's future prospects. Predictably, AT&T stock skidded again, this time to near $50. An investment advisory service accused the FCC of causing a $6.8 billion loss of stock value by Bell shareholders, "some of whom have their life's savings invested in what they always thought was the soundest investment of all in a country founded on the free enterprise system but which, disgracefully, is fast becoming a damn football." This service said the reductions came to $1.50 per year per telephone—"a couple of packages of cigarettes or a few beers courtesy of the FCC."

Most of the abusive mail went to Nicholas Johnson, a thirty-three-year old Texas lawyer who was the FCC's junior member. Johnson had concurred in the original decision with "serious reservations about both the procedures and substantive principles" used by the commission. Two months later, when the FCC modified the original order, Johnson appended a dissent in which he attacked the justice of the 7 to 7.5 percent earnings range. During the past fifteen years, he wrote, the median return allowed by the state regulatory agencies had been from 5.5 to 6.5 percent, varying from the 6.89 percent permitted by Wyoming in 1953 to the low of 4.53 percent allowed by Indiana in 1956. He continued:

Thus, whatever, may be said about the onerous limitations of a 7 to 7.5 percent rate of return for a national monopoly regulated by law as a public utility, it must at least be conceded to be generous by comparison with the rates of returns authorized by the states.

How much money are we talking about? Bell's total net plant represents about $30 billion. Thus, a 1/10th of one percent change in rate of return represents $30 million in revenue needs. That is, it would but for federal taxes, the result of which is that roughly $60 million must be earned to produce a $30 million return.* As a result, a 1/10th of one percent increase in rate of return means subscribers must pay an additional $60 million in annual telephone bills—roughly $1.30 per subscriber per year.

The difference between the roughly 6 percent allowed by the states on intrastate rate base, and the 8½ percent average rate of return earned by AT&T on its interstate operations during 1967, if applied to total rate base, would be $1½ billion—or roughly $33 per subscriber per year. The difference between the 7 percent edge of the FCC's range and AT&T's 1967 8½ percent rate of earnings would be $900 million. In short, however the amounts are calculated they are not inconsequential—even when spread over 45 million subscribers.

Johnson concluded by saying he had no idea of what constituted a fair return—indeed, that it might even be higher than 7.5 percent, even though he had seen no evidence from AT&T to convince him this was so. "Given its past history at the hands of the FCC," Johnson said, "I think there is little likelihood that AT&T is headed for the Biblical valley of bones, and

---

* Because of federal income tax requirements Bell must collect $1.92 in revenues for each $1 available for application to earnings.

I regret the efforts to conjure up such ghosts before the eyes of millions of innocent shareholders."

Johnson's words were prophetic.

In 1968, the first full year in which the 7-7.5 range was effective, Bell exceeded the *higher* limit, earning 7.6 percent. As if this were not enough, only the Vietnam War and its attendant surtax saved the FCC from further embarrassment. By Johnson's computations, without the surtax Bell would have earned in the range of 8.2 percent—a full 0.7 to 1.2 percent above the range supposedly established by the 1967 decision. "The record suggests that commission decisions systematically err in Bell's favor on rate of return matters," Johnson says.

In 1969 AT&T earnings continued to rise, and in midsummer company representatives began meeting with FCC staff and members to discuss rate adjustments. There were several alternative courses of action.

—The FCC could have cut rates sufficiently to reduce AT&T earnings to the 7–7.5 percent return authorized in the 1967 public hearings.

—The FCC could have ignored AT&T's excessive earnings and permitted the company to continue making more profits than those to which it was entitled. AT&T's earnings were moving rapidly towards 8.5 percent. On an annual basis this amounts to $360,000,000 *more* in profits than permitted by a 7 percent return; $240,000,000 *more* than permitted by a 7.5 percent return. This is a lot of money, even by AT&T standards.

—The FCC could have increased the permitted rate of return, giving *ex post facto* approval to AT&T's excessive earnings subsequent to 1967, and allowing the company to continue increasing its profits.

The FCC chose the latter, and the proceedings which resulted in its decision had several remarkable features.

First, and foremost, they were conducted behind closed doors—even though the objective was modification of an FCC order that had resulted from a formal public hearing. Second, the FCC denied consumer and other groups the right to appear, rejecting appeals by such organizations as the New York City Consumer Affairs Department, one of the few agencies in the country with the funds and the expertise to talk intelligently about utility regulatory matters. After months of staff work, the final details of the package were worked out personally between Dean Burch, who was confirmed as FCC chairman only two weeks before the decision was announced, and H. I. Romnes, the AT&T board chairman. And, finally, the decision was announced in the form of a press release, rather than by formal order.

The press release—which AT&T officials helped write—is a remarkable document in its own right. It is headed, "Rates for Interstate Long Distance Calls to Be Reduced," and its first paragraph talks only about reductions in long-distance rates that will "save users of telephone service about $150 million per year." Further reductions of $87,000,000 for Telpak and teletypewriter users are also discussed.

Several hundred words later the press release, in most oblique language, says that the FCC expected that ". . . growth trends in traffic, revenues and earnings will continue . . ." and that "AT&T's own forecast of interstate operating revenues . . . ranges . . . to levels above 8.5 percent, depending on economic conditions." The FCC continued:

> Consistent with experience following prior rate reductions, we also anticipate that the interstate revenues and earnings will be stimulated to some extent by the reductions in rates the company is now proposing. Thus, it is anticipated that the rate adjustments announced today will not, in themselves, prevent the company from achieving earnings in the aforementioned range. The commission will maintain a continuing surveillance and take such action as is appropriate in the light of future conditions.

Restated in everyday English, the FCC is saying that (1) the lower long-distance rates will boost AT&T's business; (2) the reductions are not enough to keep AT&T profits to the legal 7-7.5 percent level, nor to keep them from rising to 8.5 percent; and (3) the FCC will watch these events from afar, but does not promise to do anything about them.

Despite the $150,000,000 in "reductions," therefore, the net result of the order is to permit the telephone monopoly to *increase* its cash-in-pocket profits by $240,000,000 to $360,000,000 per year. These are minimum figures, for the FCC's order ignored the fact that the 10 percent income tax surcharge was due to expire by June 1970. The FCC has permitted Bell to pass the entire tax on to its consumers. When it expires, AT&T

will retain revenues amounting to about $140,000,000 per year that now go to the Federal treasury.

The total bill for the American citizen who is dependent upon the AT&T monopoly for his phone service: half a billion dollars a year in excessive charges.

12

And I would like to say
To Hell!
With Alexander Graham Bell.

—New York Post columnist Earl Wilson, after
several hours of waiting for a phone repairman
who never got there

As has been demonstrated in the preceding eleven chapters, there are ample grounds for Americans to be howling mad at the telephone company. But let us not heap calumny upon the late revered Mr. Bell, for a live and deserving villain is at hand more deserving of a clubbing. Nor, for that matter, should we waste any further time and energy *cursing* the phone company. This citizens have done—mostly as individuals, sporadically through such short-lived groups as the Anti Digit Dialing League—for years. No one has listened, and Ma Bell's ear has been especially deaf to her customers' caterwauls of rage.

Curbing the phone company should be the next order of business. And, despite AT&T's considerable economic and political power, several achievable means exist for bringing the phone company to heel and forcing it to behave.

First, and foremost, is a total reformation of the Federal Communications Commission. For rate-making purposes, the FCC has authority over about 25 percent of the Bell System's plant and equipment, the portion devoted to interstate long-distance service. State commissions regulate the remaining 75 percent. Although the FCC is a "junior partner" in rate-fixing, for practical purposes it dominates telephone pricing. The state agencies follow—sometimes slavishly, sometimes reluctantly—

the FCC's example in rate-making. If the interstate return is boosted, state returns increase.

Yet the FCC, as presently constituted, is a grossly inadequate pace-setter. Each of its seven commissioners is required to be conversant with, if not expert in, such highly diverse fields as utility pricing, television and broadcasting, and international satellite communications. Television and telephony alone are important enough activities in the United States to demand the full-time attention of competent watchdogs. The technological explosion in communications means FCC members are having to work harder and harder to remain knowledgeable about the subjects they are supposed to regulate. Commissioner Kenneth Cox has stated of phone regulation, "The function is so complicated, the proceedings are so intricate, our staff is so small, that any assistance we could get in this area . . . would be of advantage to us and the public."

Recommendation: Split the FCC into separate agencies, one to regulate broadcast and TV activities; the other to deal with common-carrier telephone, telegraph and related companies.

The public must be assured a voice in rate proceedings. Under the "continuous surveillance" system of regulation, in which FCC and Bell officials meet privately to haggle over rate changes, no outside voices are heard. Commissioner Nicholas Johnson has described one such continuous surveillance proceeding: "Virtually all of the information was selected, packaged and presented by Bell—there was no direct case from our staff or outside representatives. . . . The negotiating process depends on the skill and dedication of the negotiators—and a company with a single position faces a multi-member commission with a variety of problems." Parallel one-sided proceedings are found in the various state commissions.

Recommendation: Create an independent office of utility consumers' counsel, charged with representing consumers before federal and state agencies. Senator Lee Metcalf of Utah and Representative Bob Eckhardt of Texas, joined by numerous cosponsors, have struggled to interest Congress in legislation creating this office. Their bill also provides for federal funding of research, at universities and other nonprofit institutions, into utility matters.

The Metcalf-Eckhardt bill would give the American consumer a tolerably fair chance against the telephone and other utility monopolies.

As AT&T has come to maturity it has spawned numerous subsidiary activities which by now are strong enough to become separate entities. Foremost among these is the Western Electric Company. Because of the captive-supplier relationship and Bell's refusal to purchase non-Western telephone equipment, other United States communications manufacturers are effectively excluded from most of the American telephone market.

This situation is unfair—a daily perversion of the free enterprise system. An inventor who produces the telephone equivalent of a better mouse trap has no place to market it. Companies which do develop equipment which Bell decides would be useful find it easier to sell their patents to Bell, or to be merged into Western. The telephone market will continue to grow indefinitely; as it does, Western's dominance will become even greater.

Historically, competition has tended to lower prices. Whether Western pricing to Bell companies is fair is a question which even AT&T cannot answer with accuracy. But Bell has no recourse when Western lags with deliveries (as she did in 1968–1969 with the new electronic switching system, or ESS, a failing which contributed materially to the concurrent service collapse). Were Western an independent supplier, Bell could demand better treatment upon pain of taking its business elsewhere.

Recommendation: Require AT&T to divest itself of Western Electric, and open the AT&T telephone market to competitive bidding by any manufacturer who has equipment to offer.

As we noted earlier, in 1954 the Justice Department refused to bring the divestiture question to trial before an impartial judge, choosing to permit AT&T to settle the Truman Administration's antitrust suit under terms dictated by AT&T. Perhaps it is naive to expect the Nixon Administration to reopen a suit settled almost two decades ago under another Republican Administration (and one in which Nixon was Vice President). Failing a reopening of the case two other avenues are open for bringing meaningful regulation to Western Electric, which is, after all, a major component of the Bell System:

—The FCC and the state regulatory agencies could refuse to recognize, for rate-making purposes, any Western profits in excess of the legal limit in their jurisdiction. The California Public Utility Commission, in the rate case discussed in Chapter Eleven, demonstrated that it is possible to relate Western profits to the amount of money earned by individual Bell companies, and to make balancing reductions in the relevant company's recognized rate base. The FCC and the agencies could simply inform AT&T that henceforth Western must hold its income to the level authorized for AT&T and the operating companies.

—Western Electric should be required to resign from the military-industrial complex, and cease accepting defense contracts. AT&T was given a telephone monopoly for the very good reason that she was expected to provide adequate telephone service for the areas in which she held franchises. AT&T is no longer fulfilling her basic mission, and one of her excuses for failure is a shortage of equipment. Yet her sole supplier, Western Electric, devotes 15 percent of its time to government work, including the demanding role of prime contractor for the ABM. Western should be required to spin off her military contracts as a separate, non-Bell company.

Because AT&T is concentrating its technology on long-distance telephony, rates for this service are fast becoming negligible, compared to the levels of a decade ago. Reduced rates prompt more traffic and higher traffic, and Bell is moving towards a basic monthly charge for unrestricted long-distance calling. Simultaneously, rates are increasing for basic home and business service. The time has come for a basic public policy decision: Since home and business phones are an integral part of the Bell *System* (the emphasis is mine), should not a portion of the long-distance savings be filtered through to the consumer?

The FCC, because it is a pliable agency which does Bell's bidding, refuses to give any of these savings to the states. The state regulatory agencies, which are equally docile, do not have the courage to refuse Bell the high profit rates granted by the FCC on interstate traffic. And the states are unable to change the portion of Bell's physical plant that is "assigned" to intrastate and local service under separation formulas dictated by AT&T and the FCC.

Recommendation: Create a joint committee of state regulatory commissioners and FCC members (each group having equal representation) with the specific assignment of drafting a new separations formula that would divide savings from future long-distance technology between long-distance and home service. AT&T's division of the Bell System into a host of operating companies plus the long-lines department for long-distance service is a bookkeeping device and should be so treated.

William D. Hickman, who writes on communications matters from Washington for McGraw-Hill publications, frequently defends the value of competition as a regulatory tool. The revocation of a Bell franchise in one of the states now suffering abysmal phone service would put AT&T on notice that its monopoly, while long established, is no longer to be taken for granted. Does any state regulatory agency have the fortitude to take such a drastic step to bring the telephone monopoly into line?

I doubt it—and so does Ma Bell; otherwise, she wouldn't have behaved so irresponsibly during her three-quarters of a century of monopoly.

Appendix A

Board of Directors of American Telephone & Telegraph Co.

H. I. Romnes, chairman, member executive committee and director, American Telephone & Telegraph Co.:
  United States Steel Corp.
  Cities Service Co.
  Mutual Life Insurance Co. of New York
  Seamen's Bank for Savings
  Chemical Bank New York Trust Co.
  Colgate-Palmolive Co.
John D. deButts, vice chairman and director, American Telephone & Telegraph Co.:
  Sears, Roebuck & Co.
  First National City Bank
  Southwestern Bell Telephone Co.
  New York Telephone Co.
Frederick R. Kappel, chairman executive committee and director, American Telephone & Telegraph Co.:
  Chase Manhattan Bank
  Presbyterian Hospital, New York City
  Standard Oil Co. of New Jersey
  Boys Clubs of America
  Columbia University
  University of Minnesota Foundation
  Metropolitan Life Insurance Co.
  General Foods Corp.
  Whirlpool Corp.
  Aerospace Corp.
  International Paper Co.

Ben S. Gilmer, president and director, American Telephone & Telegraph Co.:
  First National Bank, Atlanta
  Rich's, Inc.
  U.S. Pipe & Foundry
  Manufacturers Hanover Trust Co.
  Merck & Co.
  New Jersey Bell Telephone Co.
  Southern Bell Telephone & Telegraph Co.
Lloyd D. Brace:
  Bank of Boston International
  Gillette Co.
  USM Corp.
  John Hancock Mutual Life Insurance Co.
  Mitre Corp.
  General Motors Corp.
  Rockefeller Foundation
  Stone & Webster, Inc.
  First National Bank of Boston
Edward W. Carter:
  Southern California Edison Co.
  Western Bancorporation
  United-California Bank
  Del Monte Corp.
  Pacific Mutual Life Insurance Co.
C. Douglas Dillon:
  Chase Manhattan Bank
  U.S. & Foreign Securities Corp.

331

Edward B. Hanify:
- Ropes & Gray
- Provident Institution for Savings
- John Hancock Mutual Life Insurance Co.
- State Street Bank & Trust Co.
- Boston Edison Co.
- Tufts University
- John Fitzgerald Kennedy Library

Henry T. Heald:
- Heald, Hobson & Associates
- Equitable Life Assurance Society of the United States
- Teachers Insurance & Annuity Association
- United States Steel Corp.
- Lever Brothers Co.

J. Victor Herd:
- Continental Insurance Co.
- Beekman-Downtown Hospital
- Brooklyn Hospital
- Brooklyn Institute of Arts & Sciences
- Dominick Fund
- Firemen's Insurance Co. of Newark, N.J.
- Diners Club, Inc.
- Franklin Life Insurance Co.
- IBM World Trade Corp.
- Boston Old Colony Insurance Co.
- National Ben Franklin Insurance Co.
- Brooklyn Union Gas Co.
- Niagara Fire Insurance Co.
- Fidelity & Casualty Insurance Co. of New York
- Manufacturers Hanover Trust Co.
- Adelphi University

- Seaboard Fire & Marine Insurance Co.
- Union Carbide Corp.
- Commercial Insurance Co. of Newark, N.J.
- Packer Collegiate Institute
- New York University
- American Arbitration Association
- American Title Insurance Co.
- Economic Development Council of New York City, Inc.
- Continental Corp.
- American National Red Cross
- Export-Import Bank of the United States
- Salvation Army

William A. Hewitt:
- Deere & Co.
- Continental Illinois National Bank & Trust Co.
- IPL, Inc.
- Continental Oil Co.

James R. Killian, Jr.:
- Massachusetts Institute of Technology
- General Motors Corp.
- Polaroid Corp.
- Cabot Corp.

Joseph Irwin Miller:
- Cummins Engine Co.
- Irwin-Union Bank & Trust Co.
- Chemical Bank New York Trust Co.
- Purity Stores, Inc.
- Equitable Life Assurance Society of the United States

William B. Murphy:
- Campbell Soup Co.
- Campbell Soup Co., Ltd.
- Merck & Co.